Fashion Innovation and Marketing

Fashion Innovation AND Marketing

Kathryn Moore Greenwood
Professor, Fashion Merchandising
Oklahoma State University

Mary Fox Murphy
Director, Fashion Associates
President, PTL Designs, Inc.

MACMILLAN PUBLISHING CO., INC.

New York

COLLIER MACMILLAN PUBLISHERS

London

Dedicated to

Our Lord and Savior, Jesus Christ

Praise His Holy Name Forever

Macmillan Publishing Co., Inc.
866 Third Avenue, New York, New York 10022

Collier Macmillan Canada, Ltd.

Library of Congress Cataloging in Publication Data

Greenwood, Kathryn Moore.
   Fashion innovation and marketing.

   Includes bibliographical references and index.
   1. Clothing trade.   I. Murphy, Mary Fox, joint
author.   II. Title.
HD9940.A2G73   1978   338.4'7'687   77-532
ISBN 0-02-346950-1

Printing: 3 4 5 6 7 8   Year: 9 0 1 2 3 4

Acknowledgment

We have not labored alone in developing the materials included in this book. We both have had the encouragement and the tremendous support that can only come from one's family. To each of our families we owe a special debt of gratitude.

It has also been our good fortune to work for a number of years with college students who found a real joy in learning about the exciting world of fashion. Many of these students are now pursuing successful careers in retailing and in other areas of the fashion industries. These we acknowledge for motivating us to put our teachings into print.

It would be difficult to give recognition to the many people who have contributed to the concepts we have presented in the text. Guest lecturers, participants in field studies and seminars, and store representatives in conferences and interviews are examples of the knowledgeable professionals from whom materials for this book were gleaned.

Not the least among the persons who have influenced the development of this book are our co-workers and educators in the textile and clothing field. Some of these we have studied under, others we have studied with, and others we have taught.

Several people have played a very special role in the preparation of this book. Our sincere appreciation is extended to Martha Cherry, Anne Scott, Paula Fonfara, Holly Murphy, Muriel Cutter, Joyce Tatchio, and Mildred Lee.

To all these and to any others who may see their influence in this book, we wish to extend our heartfelt thanks.

K. M. G.
M. F. M.

Contents

Introduction

Fashion Innovation and Marketing is a book dealing with an extremely competitive business made up of an intricate network of small firms as well as giant conglomerates, all working together to produce, distribute, and sell fashion. The opportunities are many and the risks are high. The fashion business is big business—in fact, so big that the "rag trade" in a recent year grossed $69.8 billion. The textile industry (which of course serves not only the apparel industry but many others, such as home furnishing and automotive) is the third largest industry in the world.

Fashion is sometimes dismissed as a synonym for frivolity, but this book demonstrates that it is something else. Our clothing, like our music, our art and our literature, is a reflection of our life styles, our images of who we are and, sometimes, of who we hope to be. The successful person in the fashion industry must not only understand the existing society, but use that understanding to predict the fashions of the future.

In Part One, "Fashion Interpretation," the nature and creation of fashion are discussed relative to the impact of the fashion world on our environment. In "The Fashion Makers," Part Two, the production of fashion is explored, from raw materials to the manufacturers' and retailers' markets. This in-depth study helps the reader understand the importance of textile resources, the role of the mass producer, the process of fashion marketing, and the excitement of the fashion

markets. Part Three, "Fashion Retailers," is focused on the concept of fashion merchandising. In conclusion, various aspects of buying and selling are considered in relation to the nature of fashion.

The beginning student needs an overview of the fashion business to be able to grasp the basic facets of this large and complex industry. There is a dire need today for competent employees on every level, and there are thousands of career opportunities. There must be someone to provide the zippers and buttons, the thread and trim, the interfacings; someone to work the machines in the factories that sprawl across our country; someone to supervise the production room and to ship the finished product; someone to "pick up the pins." There must be buyers to procure the merchandise for the store, merchandise managers to oversee the buyers, artists to sketch the merchandise for the advertisements, display designers to dress windows, fashion coordinators to present fashion shows, loading dockhands to receive stock, bookkeepers to work in credit departments, saints to take the complaints, and the indispensable salespeople to come face to face with the customer.

This brings us to the question, "Could the fashion business be your business?" Perhaps, but not unless you like hard work, long hours, and believe in the fashion world. A positive attitude, initiative, flexibility, enthusiasm, excellent health, and an overwhelming love for the

1

business—all these are necessary ingredients for one on the brink of a fashion career. If you possess these qualities, then you have the potential of becoming a partner in the fashion world.

If you really do have the physical and emotional characteristics that it takes to function in the fashion world, if you have a firm understanding of fashion facts, if you can truly love it enough to endure the hard work, you will begin to feel the vibrations of the fashion world, the excitement, the challenge, and the power that it possesses. If the vibrations are strong enough, then you will know that the fashion business is for you. The most important thing that you must learn is that it is an industry suffering from a form of schizophrenia because it manufactures clothing, but it sells fashion,[1] and that is what the fashion business is all about.

PART **One**

Fashion Interpretation

PART ONE of this book is dedicated to the interpretation of fashion.

Chapter 1, "Fashion Retrospect," leads you into an exciting study of how our changing twentieth-century life styles relate to fashion change.

Chapter 2, "Fashion Concepts," defines the vocabulary of fashion. Fashion is then dissected to expose its exact nature—what it is, how it changes, and what influences it.

Chapter 3, "Fashion Analysis," explores the fashion variables—the tools of fashion analysis—identifying them by what they are, how they relate to the fashion industry, and how they are used in the prediction of fashion trends.

Chapter 4, "Fashion Creators," begins with the couture designer of fashion, who by definition is above the level of mass production. The role of the designer is currently being altered. This change will be discussed, as well as the history of prestigious fashion creators.

Part One deals with many fashion philosophies and ideas. However, most fashion experts will agree that a thorough knowledge and understanding of theories of fashion are essential to the success of an individual in the fashion business.

4

1

Fashion Retrospect

Fashion, like a clear, still pond, reflects. It reflects a way of life. A fashion does not just happen, without cause or purpose. It is a response to many things: a feeling, an event, an era, a crisis, an action, an enthusiasm. Fashion reflects the current, the now. This is what makes it an ever-changing, captivating facet of our lives—a facet that needs exploration because it enhances and enriches life.

Chapter 1 looks at fashion in retrospect: the life styles that determined the fashions of the first three quarters of the twentieth century. During the last seventy-five years, fashions have changed drastically in silhouettes, design, color, and fabrics. The pendulum has swung from the completely covered body to the see-through blouse. Changes in fashion are a direct reflection of life styles.

This phenomenon of fashion as reflection is a mirror of social change, economic success or failure, political strife or its absence, technologic advancement, psychological implications, and current events. The reflection, of course, is called fashion.

A very important factor in the realm of fashion is the essence of fashion. Defined by the dictionary, essence is "the basic, real, and unvariable nature of a thing or its significant individual feature."[2] The essence of fashion is not so much the particular style that is fashionable at a given time but, more specifically, the why of it and the feel of it. What happened to produce the Gibson Girl or the miniskirt or the flapper? What were the specific causes behind each innovation? Fashion essence is the emotion, the event, the vibration that is cast on the waters of the pond and is reflected back as fashion.

Similar reflections will be found in a nation's music, literature, art, architecture, and home furnishings. These forms of human expression reflect man's way of life. Each will be comparable in feeling during a particular period of time. For example, in the late 1960s, youth power was paramount; the miniskirt and the kooky "Do your own thing" were acceptable modes of dress; music was expressed in the wild sensations of hard rock; literature was entering a new era of brashness; art was entering a new phase called the "psychedelic experience"; and youths' public vocabulary included four-letter words. The essence of each form of expression was consistent with the others. All were reflecting the same feelings: confusion, discontent, unrest; only the form differed.

Chapter 1 will be used as a reference throughout this book. These references will not only relate to fashion trends and changes, they will correlate fashions to economic, social, technological, and political happenings throughout the twentieth century. Specific events and times will be linked with the evolution, and sometimes revolution, of the total fashion industry—the development of manufacturing and the growth and innovation of retail outlets, the changes in merchandising techniques, and of course the changes in fashion itself. This chapter is the foundation for understanding the remainder of the book. As you read the developments of each decade, be aware of the underlying theme of the book: *fashion is a reflection of a way of life*.

1900–1910

America greeted the twentieth century with bursts of fireworks and self-congratulation. The bustling republic of 76 million souls boasted forty-five stars in its flag; in the continental United States only Oklahoma, Arizona, and New Mexico were still territories. The country was linked with 200,000 miles of railroad, more than in all of Europe. During the preceding century American invention had given the world the harvester and the sewing machine, the safety pin, the phonograph, the electric light, the typewriter, the telegraph, the telephone, the elevator, the rotary press, the paper dress pattern, the camera, the motion picture. The then-recent introduction of the American-invented electric streetcar and interurban line was permitting explosive horizontal growth of the cities at the same time that American engineers were beginning to raise office towers to astonishing heights. The economic hardships of the depression of 1893 had passed, and in 1898 American arms had ended Spanish rule of Cuba, Puerto Rico, and the Philippines with electrifying ease. By 1900 the economy was booming, the don't-rock-the-boat William McKinley was about to start his second term in the White House, the budget was balanced, the dollar was sound, and America viewed the future with boundless optimism. Liberty with her torch in New York harbor would greet nearly half a million immigrants in 1900— nearly half a million voters for the proposition that our forefathers had indeed brought forth on this continent a nation that was better.

The arrival of a new century in itself was one cause of America's exuberance in 1900, just as the 1976 bicentennial celebration produced its own distinct national mood. But more basic was the recovery from the depression that had started in 1893, a depression perhaps the worst in all of America's history. The crash began with a more-or-less routine financial panic that grew with appalling speed into an avalanche of bank failures, international runs on the dollar, bankruptcies, violent strikes by hundreds of thousands of workers, hordes of unemployed roaming hopelessly from city to city. Many states mobilized their militias to control disorders, and federal troops were needed as well. During 1894 and 1895 it seemed possible that the country was in danger of collapse.

But the election of William McKinley as president in 1896 began to restore confidence and in the early summer of 1897 the picture changed with miraculous abruptness. Crops overseas were going to be poor; the expected American surplus, which would otherwise have been a disaster, became immensely valuable. On August 21, wheat hit $1 per bushel and it kept on rising. The agricultural boom produced a transportation boom, and soon the boom had spread to retailing, manufacturing, mining, and the largest American industry of all, construction. Meanwhile, American financiers and industrialists, fed up with chaos, were putting together a revolutionary new system of corporate organization. Most of the nation's railroads were being merged into seven enormous systems, and undercapitalized manufacturing firms were being consolidated into the giants that are with us today: International Harvester, National Biscuit, U.S. Rubber, Republic Steel, U.S. Steel, General Electric, American Tobacco, American Can, United Fruit, American Smelting and Refining. A new science, business management, was being created to rationalize the day-by day operation of the firms, and their preferred and common stocks were being publicly sold and traded on the exchanges for the first time. Discovery of gold in Australia, South Africa, and the Alaskan Klondike, together with the new cyanide process for extracting gold from low-grade ore, ended the gold shortage that had imperiled the dollar. Rapid electrification of manufacturing was resulting in unheard-of increases in efficiency. In the autumn of 1899, President McKinley was able to announce that American exports had exceeded imports for the first time in history.

We can argue that this flood of economic, po-

FIGURE 1.1 *A fashionably ornate interior, 1899. (Photographed by Byron. The Byron Collection, Museum of the City of New York.)*

litical, and technological news was not necessarily good news, but at the time it seemed *very* good news, and the end of the 1890s was quite as gay as legend records. Nowhere was the gaiety of turn-of-the-century America more evident than in the cities. The cities had become the new frontier; more than 30 million of the 76 million Americans already lived there, and the rest had no doubt that the cities were where the action was. If we could see them as they were then, we would find the central cities fantastic places, whether we were in central-city Chicago or New York or Kansas City or Minneapolis or St. Louis or San Francisco or Birmingham or Denver. There were some sections that fully deserved to be called slums, but the problem was one of maintenance rather than of age, for even in the older cities great fires and a passion for demolition had left scarcely a building older than fifty or sixty years. The rest was spanking new and over-

whelmingly ornate, block after block of temples and palazzos and chateaux and gothic fantasy, a swirl of arches and columns and pinnacles, a dazzle of marble and bronze and gilt. Much of this ebullient glitter housed department stores and shops and banks and theaters and restaurants and universities and museums and offices, but startling portions of it were streets of parade for the mansions of the magnates, and these were the most ebullient and glittering streets of all, a stupendous spectacle of wealth unabashed.

All of those center-city residential streets of parade are gone now, and even if one had been preserved as a monument it could not faintly suggest the dash and splash and triumphant surge of 1900. The arrival of a carriage might mean the arrival of the president of the United States, the ambassador of an Imperial Majesty, an emissary from the financier J. P. Morgan, who was more powerful than them all and who knew it. Other

FIGURE 1.2 *Financier J. Pierpont Morgan, one of the most powerful men in turn-of-the-century America, photographed by Edward Steichen. (The Metropolitan Museum of Art, the Alfred Stieglitz Collection, 1949.)*

carriages might bring great ladies to an afternoon reception, ladies hatted with plumes and gowned in lace, with liveried footmen helping them to descend and to depart. In the evening the carriages might bring guests to a ball, an affair for 1,200, the female half blazing with diamonds.

American fashion and the life style it reflected in 1900 were a great deal more than this, but American high society was the group that epitomized American high fashion, and for a moment we need to pause to see who made up American high society, what their life style was, and how that life style affected the rest of the country.

American high society in 1900 was principally composed of families who had been in America for generations. Roughly 80 per cent were of English descent, although Dutch names were common in New York–Newport–Saratoga society and German names in the societies of St. Louis and Milwaukee; in Wilmington, Delaware, it was usual to be of French ancestry and almost as usual to be named DuPont. Most of high society had also been wealthy for generations, although in the East and particularly in the South a historic name was not only more important than money but often a means of acquiring it. High society in the West, based as it was on ranching, mining, shipping, and railroading fortunes, was decidedly a newer society, but it, too, was generally restricted to the people who had reached the West first and who had made their money first; Jim Brown might use his Leadville mining riches to buy his beloved Molly a brownstone mansion in the very best part of Denver, but when she paid calls on her neighbors they were "out" and when she invited them to parties they were "previously engaged."

In short, high society was very much a closed society, something you usually had to have been born into, preferably around 1620. However, it appeared to most Americans to be very much larger and more open than in fact it was, for most Americans neither knew nor cared that high society excluded many of the wealthy and almost all of the successful, the "*nouveau riche.*" What most Americans saw was a pageant of flamboyance that appeared to be everywhere: those miles of mansions in every city, carriages flashing by to offices and shops, great ladies sweeping into their jewelers and great gentlemen into their clubs, "horseless carriages" chugging expensively and unreliably about on Sundays, passenger trains with private cars hitched to the rear, fleets of steam yachts on the coasts, the Great Lakes, and the rivers, pleasure palaces (unaccountably called cottages) for Eastern society at Newport and Palm Beach, and more for Chicago society at Wisconsin's Lake Geneva, and more for Minneapolis society on Lake Minnetonka, and so on to the Pacific and the Gulf. The business affairs of the group dominated not only the financial pages but the front pages of the newspapers, their parties the society pages, and their other amusements the sports pages. When Mrs.

Astor held her annual ball, *Harper's Illustrated Weekly* edified the country with a sketch of that lady graciously greeting her guests. When the marvelously turned out Vanderbilts strolled in the Easter Parade, newspaper photographers recorded the event for posterity. When William C. Whitney raced his stable at Saratoga, all sporting America read about it. Streets and hotels and subdivisions and cities were named after them, as well as libraries, hospitals, and universities.

American high fashion in 1900 was of course quite as flamboyant as the mansions, carriages, yachts, private railroad cars, and "cottages." But with their male strut and female decorum, the fashions also conveyed a rigid separation of the roles of the sexes, men who ruled and women whose obedience was lavishly rewarded. American law reflected this separation—all but four Western states denied the woman the vote, most denied her an equal share in the guardianship of her children, a full third allowed her no claim to her earnings, a quarter denied her the right to own property. American social custom was even more restrictive—a lady might sip champagne but never drink whiskey or gin, a lady did not enter a saloon, a lady did not smoke, a lady did not use cosmetics, a lady did not go to the evening theater unescorted, an unmarried young lady went nowhere without a chaperone, a married lady did not get a divorce. In America in 1900 the least hint of female waywardness was no joke. Once questioned, a lady's reputation was never quite the same. If they cared to exercise it, men had the moral and often the legal authority either to compel restraint or to turn wife and daughters out of the house.

This insistence on propriety had the effect of making fashionable dress not only a delight but a

FIGURE 1.3 *Tea-gowns, 1900. Women were expected to be modest and obedient; the fashions of the time reflected this expectation. (The Metropolitan Museum of Art.)*

FIGURE 1.4 *Butch Cassidy and the Wild Bunch. Cassidy is on the extreme right. (Courtesy of Pinkerton's, Inc.)*

duty: to go to church you wore Sunday best, and that was that. Of course, most Americans could not afford the high fashions, but the ready-made clothing industry was established by 1900, and adaptations of the high fashions were available in all price ranges. Americans wore these as often as the occasion even remotely permitted; they dressed up to travel, to shop at the grocery store, to take the children on a picnic, to visit their best friends, who lived next door. Not to be left out were those classes that many Americans considered disreputable: actors, actresses, saloon keepers, swindlers, politicians, prostitutes, gamblers, cardsharps, burglars, and pickpockets were in the business of *looking* all right, and look all right they did. When Butch Cassidy and the Sundance Kid arrived in Forth Worth, Texas, with three other members of the Wild Bunch and the proceeds of the robbery of the First National Bank of Nevada at Winnemucca, they bought new clothes and had their picture taken, wearing the same wool vests, wool suits, white shirts, silk ties, gold watch chains, and derbies that proper gentlemen were wearing from sea to shining sea.

Approximately two thirds of the 29-million-member "working population" was already employed in nonagricultural occupations, and American wages and salaries were and always had

been one-and-a-half times higher than those in Europe. One happy result was to make brute physical strength so expensive that employers were forced to substitute machinery as rapidly as possible; Carnegie Steel not only replaced all equipment every three years, but *new* equipment as soon as anything better was available. Another benefit was to push wages and salaries constantly higher. Yet another was the rapid creation of new kinds of jobs and of opportunities for employment in old ones; when individual workers grew more skilled and therefore more expensive, it was economically imperative to move them up.

The rise in American incomes was accompanied by a fall in consumer prices. The average worker's pay had risen from 14 cents an hour in 1893 to 22 cents an hour in 1900, and purchasing power had more than doubled. One young Jewish immigrant from Poland who worked in a New York sweatshop making undershirts earned $4.50 a week, but she and her roommate lived on $2 a week each. "Of course we could have lived cheaper," she said, "but we are both fond of good things and felt we could afford them." The secretary's $10 a week meant independence, the public school teacher's average salary of $325 per year middle-class affluence in a time when a tailor-made suit was $10 and a shawl 50 cents.

FIGURE 1.5 *Eating breakfast by candlelight. A real-life Gibson Girl, 1897. (Photograph by Byron. The Byron Collection, Museum of the City of New York.)*

Wallpaper was 5 cents a roll, a sewing machine $12, a wood-burning stove $17.48, a piano $98.50. You could build a house for as little as $300, and the "streetcar suburbs" of the cities were filled with comfortable homes owned not only by the middle classes but by skilled laborers and even factory workers.

But while most Americans could and did wear the fashions, very few Americans wore them all of the time. Of course, gentlemen's daytime fashions were suitable for managerial, professional, sales, and white-collar wear, and any photograph of a city business street on a weekday in 1900 will show you hundreds of sprucely tailored men in derbies. But you will find other men dressed for the requirements of other occupations, and comparatively little evidence of the feminine fashions as we have described them. Instead of plumes

and laces and furbelows, you will find the long, cool, chic elegance of the Gibson Girl.

The Gibson Girl was created in 1890 by the popular illustrator Charles Dana Gibson. The women's magazines of the day were full of romantic fiction, of the kind we now call "gothic," concerning the unexpected good fortune of attractive, intelligent, plucky young women in reduced and often perilous circumstances. Mr. Gibson felt it was out of the question to depict these put-upon but deserving creatures in the smothering profusion of fashion. His breathtakingly simple solution was to retain the silhouette of fashion while discarding the ornament. The effect of this solution on American women of all classes was even more breathtaking; in probably the most startling example of life imitating art since the Emperor Napoleon Bonaparte commanded the painter Jacques David to redesign France, within months the blouse and skirt of the shirtwaist were everywhere. By 1905 the Sears catalog alone was offering 150 different versions.

The success of the Gibson Girl was no accident. The American labor force in 1900 included more than 5.3 million woman at all levels of the social scale, and they could hardly go about their business in a cloud of ostrich plumes. Among the working women was no less a personage than Mrs. Potter Palmer, social arbiter of Chicago but also a businesswoman who ran the famed Palmer House herself while using the time left over to double the $100 million real-estate fortune left her by her husband. There was a substantial professional class: women college presidents, college professors, public school teachers, physicians, lawyers, scientists, business proprietors, nurses, sculptors, social workers, painters, editors, journalists, poets, novelists. The reorganization of American business had produced an explosion in office workers; by 1900 there were 100,000 secretaries alone. Other white-

collar occupations included retail saleswomen and telephone operators, although in 1900 there were only 19,000 of the latter. Non-factory dressmakers totaled 413,000, milliners 17,000. Many factory workers were women, and of course so were many domestic workers. The domestic workers generally wore uniforms provided by their employers, but the rest (as well as most of America's housewives) blessed the name of the Gibson Girl. She was the first ideal American woman, enchanting in the sheer efficiency of her loveliness—but the greatest of her contributions was the suitability of her costume to the working woman: neat, practical, feminine; attractive enough to go without apology onto the street or into a smart shop, and simple enough to be appropriate to the store, office, factory, or home kitchen.

The attitude of America toward its working women was ambivalent, and so was the attitude of the working woman toward herself. There was not much question about a respectable woman who fell victim to undeserved misfortunes. Whatever else might be said about the chattel mentality, it did demand that men meet their obligations; if a father or husband failed to provide, it was incumbent on relatives, friends, and honorable strangers to make the failure good. But working women in the middle range, and especially the upper-middle range, left themselves and many Americans perplexed.

With the ambivalent position of the working woman in American society in 1900, we can contrast the unequivocal position of the immigrant. The newly arrived immigrant was beneath the bottom of the social scale, viewed as a scarcely human creature to be herded into the coal mines and the slaughterhouses and the textile mills and the sweatshops where clothing was made, or perhaps rented, with a lump of his fellows, to a railroad in need of a section gang. This view may seem shocking, but perhaps it will be more shocking to hear that the average immigrant expected nothing else. Between 60 and 70 per cent of the immigrants were single, able-bodied young men, by 1900 mostly from eastern and southern Europe, and they knew what they had come for. They would be offered the menial, backbreaking jobs that Americans would not accept, at wages that Americans would refuse, and

FIGURE 1.6 *Newly landed immigrants. Photographer Lewis Hine called his photograph "The Madonna of Ellis Island."* (*The Metropolitan Museum of Art, Gift of Clarence Mck. Lewis, 1954.*)

crowded into slums that Americans pretended did not exist. The immigrants, however, were accustomed to much more menial jobs at home, when there were jobs at all, and the wages that by American standards were trivial would nevertheless accumulate to a degree that would establish them as persons of substance when they returned to Europe. They did not consider themselves immigrants. Fully two thirds had as little intention of staying in America as had the workers on the Alaska pipeline in the 1970s of staying in Alaska. Many more immigrants did stay than had planned to, in part because American invention and the persistent American labor shortage created a staggering proliferation of opportunities to achieve the good life. But a third did go back, and in the meantime the migrant mentality (which was not confined to immigrants by any means) perpetuated wretched working and living conditions that permanent residents would have done something about.

In addition to exciting, unsettling, overwhelming big-city America, there were three other Americas in 1900: small-town America, rural America, and wild America, and it was in those Americas that contentment often lived. The East, the Midwest, and the Pacific Coast had been settled long enough to have developed substantial small-town and farming populations that were happy to stay where they were, living in the homes that their ancestors had built, farming the same land, running the same businesses, going to the same schools and churches. They were not opposed to progress; when the townspeople felt they could afford them, they put in an electric works, a telephone exchange, a sewer system, an addition to the high school, just as the farmers bought machinery from time to time to make their work easier, and both town and country wives picked out treasures from the new "wish books," the Sears, Roebuck and Montgomery Ward catalogs. But there was no rush, and no need to give up the old, mellow pleasures of picking wild asparagus in the spring, berrying in the summer, putting up jellies and jams, quilting, knitting, fishing, going to weddings and teas and musicales, singing carols at Christmas. In the South, too, the pleasures of tradition were greatly prized, although both small-town and farm life were much more primitive.

Wild America stretched from the Badlands of the Dakotas to the Rocky Mountains and from Canada to Mexico; it included the states of Idaho, Montana, Wyoming, Nevada, Utah, Colorado, and much of Texas, plus the territories of Arizona, New Mexico, and Oklahoma. It was the land of the lumberjack, the miner, the rancher, the cowboy, the trapper, the prospector, the outlaw, the Indian, of roaring saloons and bleak villages and lone ranches. The life it offered was hard and dangerous and yet so compellingly romantic and challenging that even today hundreds of thousands of Americans choose to live it and hundreds of millions of people across the earth watch dreams of it at the movies and on television.

An America that barely existed in 1900 was college-educated America. There were only 238,000 college students in 1900, as opposed to today's 10.5 million, plus two million more students in advanced vocational schools. The explanation seems to be that though many more Americans could have afforded to go to college in 1900, so few occupations required a degree that getting one seemed hardly worth the trouble. You did not need a degree to go into business, of course. You did not need a degree even to become a lawyer; you simply read up on the law and took an examination. Anyone with a gift for oratory could set up as an evangelist. The great inventor Edison was self-taught. And the quality of a college education was not high. When the DuPont company established the first systematic industrial research program in America in 1902, all of the required scientists had to be imported from Europe. The Carnegie Foundation released a report on the nation's medical schools in 1910 that created a scandal; *only* Johns Hopkins was giving sound medical training.

Which brings us to another point that must be made about the flamboyant, the mellow, and the wild Americas of 1900—the opposite sides of all three coins were complacency.

The events of the decade on their surface did little to alter this state of affairs. New Yorkers were merely amused in 1900 when a little woman from Kansas, Carrie Nation, suddenly began assaulting their saloons with a hatchet. She was arrested, of course, and it seemed a passing oddity that an increasing number of towns, cities, and states were forbidding the manufacture, sale, and consumption of alcohol. The assassination in 1901 of President McKinley by an anarchist, like the agitations of some steelworkers demanding less than a 12-hour, seven-day work week and of some married women demanding equal rights, was likewise regarded an aberration rather than an indication of the future. The immediate result of the assassination of President McKinley was merely the inauguration of Theodore Roosevelt, a man after the decade's heart, millionaire socialite and cowboy and cavalry hero and former governor of New York. He instantly recognized the independence of Panama when Colombia balked at the construction of the isthmian canal through its Panamanian province, began enforcing the antitrust laws, added 48 million acres to national forests and parks, settled the Russo-Japanese War, sent the Great White Fleet around the world, and startled some of his countrymen by appointing blacks to office and entertaining Booker T. Washington at the White House. After his "retirement," in favor of his hand-picked successor President Taft, he thundered off to hunt big game in Africa and to explore the jungles of Brazil.

The first airplane flight by the Wright brothers in 1903 was hardly noticed by the press. The decision of Henry Ford in 1908 to mass produce the automobile was regarded as ridiculous. It was such universal knowledge that the automobile would never be more than a plaything of the rich that Mr. Ford was forced to resort for financing to friends and neighbors rather than the banks. As all more sophisticated investors pointed out, the trick was not to mass produce at a low unit price, but to sell automobiles as necessities to people who could not use them. Would anyone fail to notice that there were no paved roads to drive the things on, no mechanics to fix them, no service stations to fuel them?

Nevertheless, America was changing during the decade. For one thing, opulence was getting to be a bit dull. President Taft, weighing in at 300-odd pounds, was something of a culmination of that style, and it was time for new direction. The first sign that one was coming, oddly enough, was a rage among the ladies of high society for interior decoration. The rage was launched by three brilliant American women of impeccable social credentials, the novelist Edith Wharton and the legendarily beautiful Jerome sisters. Writing with Ogden Codman, in 1897 Mrs. Wharton had published *The Decoration of Houses*, apparently the first book on the subject in over fifty years. At about the same time, the Jerome sisters, then living in London as Lady Randolph Churchill and Mrs. Morton Frewen, also developed an interest in interior decoration. Three such formidable names conferred instant respectability on a subject that had for decades been considered rather bad form. Society took a new look at its surroundings. Mrs. Wharton, Lady Churchill, and Mrs. Frewen counseled against the overwhelming profusion of the day. As the decade advanced, interiors began to be simplified, and so did clothes, and so did social customs—and these events, duly publicized by the press, reinforced the preference for simplicity that many Americans had shown all along.

Fashion Emphasis, 1900: Swirls of Curves!

In 1900 the lady's hat crowned her with glory—large, sweeping, lavished with ribbons, bouquets, feathers, plumes, birds, fluff and froth. Dresses were usually one-piece with a fitted and pinched waist, S-shaped with skirts to the floor. The arms were always covered and full-length leg-of-mutton sleeves were often used. The bodice was fitted and cut high with collars to the chin. White was very popular, as were pastels, with pale lavender ("wisteria") the favorite. The Gibson Girl, created by the illustrator Charles Dana Gibson in 1890, was also very much in fashion in the America of 1900. The first ideal American woman—graceful, long, chic, cool, and lovely—she wore the blouse and skirt of the shirtwaist.

The gentleman often carried an ornamental

cane. His jacket, featuring the extravagantly wide "concave" collar, was cut long and full. The trousers were wide at the hips, narrow at the ankles. His tie was silk, his vest might be also, and his pocket watch was attached to an imposing, vest-crossing gold chain. His shirt was white, the rest of his costume dark. In the winter he might wear a fur coat. He wore a derby on weekdays and a silk top hat during the evening and on special daytime occasions.

Clothes specifically and fancifully designed for children were well established, but when the young reached adolescence they became little men and little women.

Sportswear had not yet been invented; there were only clothes suitable to particular sports: baseball uniforms, football uniforms, riding habits, "bathing dress" for both sexes so comprehensively modest that anyone attempting to swim, rather than "bathe," would probably have sunk like a stone. For the young gentleman who boated or played tennis, there were white flannel trousers worn with a striped blazer, tie, and straw hat; both boating and tennis must have been gentlemanly pastimes indeed, in those days. Women who boated or played tennis wore formal daytime outfits, including hats. Though seersucker and "Palm Beach cloth" were developed during the decade, they did not catch on; Americans seemed content to swelter during the summer.

There were also clothes intended to be worn exclusively by workingmen. These seem to have been a nineteenth-century American innovation, for European custom was simply to wear "old clothes." However, in America the farmer had his bibbed overalls, the factory worker his blue-collar shirt, the lumberjack a bright plaid flannel shirt and a bright plaid jacket made of blanketing, the sheepherder a lambskin coat with the fleece on the inside, the cowboy his leather boots, chaps, and broad-brimmed Stetson hat, and the miner his Levis, created in 1850 when Levi Straus accepted a San Francisco prospector's challenge to make a pair of pants that would wear longer than a few days. The working woman adopted the costume of the Gibson Girl.

Fabrics were made mostly of natural fibers—linen, wool, cotton, and silk—although rayon had been introduced in the 1890s as a substitute for silk. The industrial revolution had begun in eighteenth-century England as a textile revolution, and by 1900 ready-made clothing had drastically reduced prices to bring simplifications of the latest fashions within the reach of most Americans. Custom tailors, dressmakers, and milliners survived to serve the rich, however, and the Paris couturiers and London tailors produced the fashion ideas that were sifted to determine the high fashion.

The idea for the sewing machine had been around as far back as 1790, but not until the 1840s was a machine, patented by the American Elias Howe, actually on the market. The machine did not work very well, and it was left to a thirty-nine-year-old unemployed actor named Isaac Singer to make a casual inspection and propose the crucial improvements. A pooling of patents eventually made Singer a household word around the world. Butterick and McCall paper patterns allowed almost any woman to make her own clothes. With a sewing machine priced at $12 in 1900, its purchase could vastly stretch a woman's clothing budget.

The great retail merchandising innovations of the nineteenth century were also made in America. The department store seems to have been the creation of Alexander Turney Stewart, a young Irishman who arrived in New York in 1820 and shortly thereafter opened a linen shop. By 1846 he had prospered to such a degree that he was able to build the Marble Dry Goods Palace, offering under one roof not only linens but mattresses, corsets, Oriental rugs, and practically everything else a shopper might want. He pioneered such amenities as fixed prices and free toilets and pleased his lady customers still more by hiring handsome young men as clerks. Eben Jordan and Edward A. Filene soon opened similar stores in Boston, John Wanamaker in Philadelphia, Joseph L. Hudson in Detroit, Morris Rich in Atlanta, and R. H. Macy, Nathan Straus, and Bernard Gimbel in New York. In Chicago, Potter Palmer had a great success; his gracious habit of urging ladies to take their purchases home, try them on for their husbands, and bring them back if the husbands weren't pleased added goods-on-approval to the shopping amenities. Potter Palmer's successor, Marshall Field, not only contributed the in-store restaurant but, when he admonished a clerk who was arguing with a customer, a slogan that became immortal: "Give the lady what she wants!"

The chain store was pioneered by the Hartfords of the Great Atlantic and Pacific Tea Company. The first A&P opened in New York in 1859; by 1875 there were sixty-seven stores. The Woolworth stores applied the principles of the chain to a vast miscellany of merchandise, including some clothing items. J. C. Penney was the first to concentrate on clothing, but it was not until 1902 that he opened the original Golden Rule store in Kemmerer, Wyoming, and not until the 1920s that the idea took off.

Mail order seems to have been the creation of E. C. Allen of Augusta, Maine, who in 1870 was using the mails to sell washing powder, engravings, and novelties. Montgomery Ward entered the field in 1872 and Sears, Roebuck in 1886. Starting in Minnesota as mail-order dealers in watches and jewelry, by 1900 the imaginative Sears and the hard-headed Roebuck were distributing catalogs by the carload, offering a fantastic profusion of items—talking machines, cherry stoners, stoves, pompadour combs, organs, ostrich feathers, irons, and both fashionable and practical clothing. More than anything else, mail order enabled rural and small-town America to join the city dwellers as up-to-date consumers.

The trend of the decade was away from the overwhelming flamboyance of the turn of the century.

1910–1920

The sunny serenity with which fashionable America entered the next decade is almost beyond our ability to imagine. In 1910 politicians were convinced that the civilized world would never again see a general war or a plague or a famine and that the less-civilized world, with the wise guidance of the great powers, would soon be as peaceable and prosperous as the rest. The great liner *Titanic*, then under construction in Britain, seemed a perfect symbol of the time, not only a marvel of convenience and luxury but by grace of modern scientific advances quite unsinkable.

The male asserted his continuing dominance in 1910 with one of the rare true revolutions in fashion, the introduction of the natural shoulder suit. The jacket was single-breasted, tight fitting, narrow of lapel, high-buttoned, and worn with straight, slim trousers: an English innovation, but the "Brooks Brothers suit" which the firm continues to sell today. The ladies hastened to adopt a similar narrow, tailored silhouette, necessarily discarding their corsets in the process to reduce the number of suddenly unstylish curves. The new fashion may have permitted the ladies to breathe a bit easier, but the requirement that the narrow silhouette be continued modestly to the feet had the unfortunate result of forcing the ladies into the impossibly tapered hobble skirt, slashed a very few inches at the ankles to permit a degree of locomotion. The lines of fashion had been simplified, however, and its essence, too, was changed: women remained restricted, but both sexes had abandoned ornamental exuberance for a lean, taut look that implied readiness for action.

The need for action was at hand. By 1910, America's population had soared to almost 92 million. The cities were vastly exceeding the countryside in growth, and the inadequacy of the services being provided city dwellers was painfully apparent. The schools were overwhelmed with the task of giving free public education, America's pride and the immigrant's dream, to millions of children and adults speaking no English. With the rapid expansion of factories, industrial workers were in such short supply that militance could no longer be discouraged. Women were becoming increasingly restive after a decade of quiet organization that suddenly began to bear fruit; in 1910 Washington became the fifth state to grant them the vote, California followed in 1911, Arizona, Kansas, and Oregon in 1912. The prohibitionists were pressing for a

FIGURE 1.7 *Professional women marching in a women's suffrage parade. New York, May 3, 1913. (Courtesy of the New York Historical Society.)*

constitutional amendment. A million-member Socialist party had appeared, advocating destruction of the capitalist system.

But it was the sudden dawn of the automotive age that brought home to the splendid and smug America of the previous decade the fact that change was overtaking it. In 1910, two years after Henry Ford's gamble on mass production, there were half a million cars on the road, and more were added at such a pace that just five years later there were two and a half million; by 1920 there would be eight million cars and a million trucks and tractors. Henry Ford had outguessed the objectors to the automobile as a necessity. His Model T, the "Tin Lizzie," was tough enough and high enough and light enough to negotiate the atrocious country roads. It was mechanically simple enough for almost anyone to fix. The country's blacksmiths were adept at more elaborate repairs, and livery stables were as happy to sell gasoline as hay and oats. A few paved roads began to spread across the countryside, streams were bridged, little towns abruptly within convenient travel time of the cities began to turn into suburbs. In 1914 Mr. Ford astounded the country by increasing wages from $2.90 per nine-hour day to $5 per eight-hour day. The friends and neighbors who had risked their modest savings to launch the Ford Motor Company became millionaires many times over.

Meanwhile, in April 1912, the proud, unsinkable *Titanic* steamed out of Southampton, England, on her maiden voyage to New York, struck an iceberg, and sank, with a loss of 1,500 lives.

That same year the Republicans' Grand Old Party shattered into a conservative faction led by President Taft and a reform faction led by Theodore Roosevelt. Both men ran for president. The Democrats nominated Woodrow Wilson, also a reformer, and won the election. Wilson received only 42 per cent of the popular vote; but when Roosevelt's 27 per cent was added, the vote against things as they were became an overwhelming 69 per cent. Taking office in 1913, President Wilson launched an extensive program of antitrust actions, labor legislation, tariff reform, bank reorganization, road building.

Preoccupied as it was with domestic affairs, America scarcely noticed that Europe in the summer of 1914 was plunging into a general war. Even after it started, America assumed that something would soon be worked out; America fully approved President Wilson's offers to act as mediator but had no intention of abandoning the policy of neutrality that had been recommended by George Washington a century and a quarter before. President Wilson's peacemaking efforts were unsuccessful, and by 1915 equipment and food were running short in Europe. America found itself in the midst of a colossal economic boom. The only limitations on growth seemed to be the speed with which offices and factories could be built and workers found to run them. Huge numbers of farmers and women were drawn into the industrial and office labor forces, and their numbers increased still more as inflation drove up prices and wages. Blacks began leaving the South to enter the factories of the North. Strikes became common, and many were successful. To replace the farmers and women entering industry, the farm and the home began to be mechanized.

President Wilson narrowly won the 1916 election with the slogan the Democratic convention chose by acclamation, "He kept us out of war." But as President Wilson himself had said, "I can't keep the country out of war. Any little German lieutenant can put us into war at any time by some calculated outrage."

In the event, it was the Kaiser and the German general staff who calculated the outrage. In February 1917, Germany began unrestricted submarine warfare. The sinking in March of several American ships without warning and the abdication of the Tsar in favor of a constitutional Russian government, which would continue to fight on the side of the Allies, made up America's mind. President Wilson called Congress into special session on April 2, and on the morning of April 6, 1917, Congress approved the declaration of war.

America's response was magnificent: By May 1917 the first American destroyers had reached British waters, and the rest of the fleet soon followed. An enormous bond issue was subscribed. A conscription act was passed and registration began in June. The nation's industry was mobilized under the direction of Bernard Baruch. Samuel Gompers, president of the AFL, gave the war his total support, preventing most strikes. The continuing mechanization of the farm freed millions of men to fight and to work in factories. The Tin Lizzie made it possible for the country population to get to the towns and cities where the factories were. Anxious to do their part, women replaced men in hundreds of formerly unsuitable occupations: women delivered ice, conducted streetcars, became mechanics.

By March 1918 nearly 300,000 American troops had reached France. By July 1 there were a million. Germany believed it would not matter. Having sent Lenin to Russia in a sealed train, "like a bacillus" (the words are those of Lady Randolph Churchill's redoubtable son, Winston), Germany had contrived the overthrow of the democratic Russian government and signed a peace treaty with the Bolshevik regime that fol-

FIGURE 1.8 A fleet of four 1916–17 Ford Model T salesmen's cars. (Photographed by Byron. The Byron Collection, Museum of the City of New York.)

lowed. The German armies from the east streamed across Europe to assault the Allies in France. During the summer of 1918, five huge German offensives were launched. On September 26, the Allied counterassault began. Within a few weeks the mighty Hindenberg line was crushed. The war ended on November 11, 1918.

The role that American women had played in the victory was recognized. The House voted to submit to the states a constitutional amendment granting women the vote in January 1918, and the Senate concurred in June 1919. The thirty-sixth state ratified the amendment on August 20, and it became law eight days later. The prohibitionists, long allied with the women's suffrage movement, won their battle also. Although there was so much dissatisfaction with the peace treaty President Wilson brought home that the Senate refused to ratify it and although the labor disturbances of 1919 were so alarming that the governor of Massachusetts, Calvin Coolidge, became an instant national hero because of his vigorous suppression of the Boston police strike, America expected to enter the next decade purified in politics by the ennobling influence of womanhood and purified in soul by the defeat of Demon Rum.

But what had happened to the American life style during the decade? Very early, under the pressure of the passion of reform, high society had gone out of fashion. Out with it went the gracious fiction that women are essentially ornamental. The hemline rose and the skirt was widened to permit women freedom of movement; decorative details were discarded in a visual assertion that females are quite as useful as males. The war accelerated the trend toward so-

---

Fashion Emphasis, 1910: The Angular Look

In 1910, clothes abruptly caught up with the interiors simplified under the influence of Edith Wharton, Lady Randolph Churchill, and Mrs. Morton Frewen. The man wore the revolutionary natural shoulder suit, with a tight, single-breasted jacket, narrow lapels, high buttons, and straight, slim trousers. His collar was high and stiff, often made of celluloid. The lady also adopted the narrow silhouette, shedding corset and petticoats to achieve it. Her hat became narrower and rather high, with greatly reduced decoration. The tailored walking suit became popular among women for daytime wear in 1910, and the lady might emphasize its masculine effect by carrying a cane and wearing a bow tie. In the evening, it was a matter of the hobble skirt; reported the New York Times *in 1912: "If you think the skirts of the last two seasons have been narrow, wait till you see the new ones. Some evening gowns are less than a yard wide and slashed in front for at least six inches so that one may move along somehow."*

Brilliant, exotic colors and bold patterns replaced the white and the pastels of the previous decade: the ladies were beginning to assert themselves. The slash in the hobble skirt, which made the female foot and ankle visible for the first time in years, turned the shoe and the stocking into fashion items, though the masculine look of the day kept both on the simple side.

Children's dress remained fanciful, and adolescents continued to be dressed as small, suitably modest copies of their parents. There was still no sign of sportswear, and fabrics, manufacturing, and merchandising techniques remained much as they had been at the turn of the century.

The trend of the decade was toward the masculinization of the female appearance. Decorative details were progressively discarded, the bust and the hips were suppressed, and the hair was worn shorter. The hemline rose and the skirt was widened to permit freedom of movement. Colors grew darker. Women were asserting their equality with men.

FIGURE 1.9 *The soaring, graceful tower of the Woolworth Building, completed in 1913, symbolizes the wealth and optimism of the decade. (Museum of the City of New York.)*

cial equality—many women had no choice but to learn to drive and to change their own tires, to buy bread at the store rather than spend time baking their own, and to live where there was available space rather than wait for a vacancy at an all-female residence for the unmarried.

The passing of the wealthy as arbiters of fashion also created a revolution in the national attitude toward the theater, the movies, professional sports. It was no longer considered disreputable to appear in a public performance for money. What, after all, was *wrong* with being so beautiful, accomplished, and charming that thousands of people would travel for miles and gladly *pay* for the delight of gazing on you?

During the teens, Broadway became the un-disputed entertainment capital of the world. From 34th to 50th Street, the marquees glittered nightly with the titles of comedies, revues, musicals, an occasional serious drama. Florenz Ziegfeld was king, filling the stages of his Follies with dazzling women dazzlingly turned out. On the West Coast, Hollywood was born. "More stars there than there are in heaven" were created to fill the silent screens springing up across America. Mary Pickford became America's sweetheart, Charlie Chaplin its hilarious and touching tramp, Wallace Beery its romantic ideal, Theda Bara the essence of unimaginable wickedness ("And do you know," whispered the young, with delicious shudders, "that if you rearrange the letters in her name, it spells *Arab*

Death?"). Meanwhile, a new music created by Blacks in New Orleans came up the Mississippi to Chicago and overland to Harlem. As the decade ended, jazz swept the nation.

1920–1930

The *Roaring Twenties* . . . the thrill of prosperity, the enticements of challenge, the glorious era of extravagance—these were the *excitements* of the 'twenties. The freedoms of a new morality . . . the speakeasy . . . the emancipation of women . . . flaming youth—these were the realities of the twenties. F. Scott Fitzgerald wrote, "America was going on the greatest, gaudiest spree in history and America's young people loved it."[3]

America's participation in the war had been short and crowned with overwhelming victory, the election of Warren Harding as president in 1920 assured an end to the daily interference of Washington and Europe in the citizens' private affairs, the passing of high society as fashion leaders had brought the passing of many of those pesky rules about what a lady could and could not do—and the pent-up demand created by wartime shortages and prosperity meant that it was preposterously easy for a great many people to make pots of money. The promoter, the broker, the moonshooter were the men of the age. Skyscrapers by the hundreds leapt up in the cities, subdivisions burst into being almost overnight, country clubs were laid out from coast to coast, Florida became a giant carnival of real-estate salesmen and their customers. Cars multiplied by the millions, buses made it possible to start closing one-room country schools and to provide high school educations to the rural population. Not only new but most existing urban homes were wired for electricity to operate the vacuum cleaners, washing machines, refrigerators, and stoves that were at last freeing the housewife from endless drudgery. The radio blossomed in the home to beguile the remaining hours of work—and when the work was done, off many a housewife drove to join the party.

It was a party truly wonderful, like nothing that had ever been seen before, a revel of millions who suddenly had the time and the money and the freedom and the inclination to play. Play was something new to America; during the reign of the wealthy and the restraints imposed by the following domestic and foreign crises, there had been no nonsense about anyone doing anything primarily for fun. But now, fashion leadership had passed to the successful, men and women who had made all that money all by themselves, who were confident of their ability to do it again if need be, and who saw money as something to be enjoyed, not hoarded to deprive their children and grandchildren of the satisfactions of making their own successes.

Many of the successful were indeed people who played for a living: Babe Ruth, sultan of swat; Bill Tilden, king of the tennis courts; Bobby Jones, master of the golf links. The Hollywood players included Clara Bow, possessed of that mysterious power called "It," and Douglas Fairbanks, Greta Garbo, Rudolph Valentino, the

FIGURE 1.10 *Duke Ellington, composer and jazz pianist, was an important participant in the party that was America in the 20s. (The Bettmann Archive.)*

shamelessly alluring Gloria Swanson, whose salary was $900,000 a year and who spent $6,000 of it on perfume alone! The great Louis Armstrong and Duke Ellington played jazz for their livings, and Mildred Bailey sang for hers.

Most of the successful, whether professional players or not, were young, and the life style they created was as mobile as the life style of the wealthy had been encumbered. Many chose to live in apartments, and the center-city mansions were rapidly torn down to make space for them. Those of the successful who did want houses disapproved of enormous structures devoted mainly to accommodations for the servants. The new houses were designed for minimal servant-dependence. Some were still European in style, but provincial European rather than palatial; more were American colonial, and not a few were the startling creations of Frank Lloyd Wright and other moderns. Whatever the architecture, the effect was light, airy, romantically insubstantial—dream houses that tomorrow might be something or somewhere else. The same impermanent quality was characteristic of jazz, a music of improvisation meant to be endlessly varied rather than repeated. And what could be more evanescent than the silent, flickering shadows of the silver screen?

America's party, in short, had an electric air of youthful surprise—which, as everyone knows, makes any party more fun. The young, emancipated woman had cut her hair short and flattened her bosom and hips as a grim declaration of equality with the man. The deeds done, she found herself looking irresistibly absurd. So she added circles of rouge to her cheeks and a cupid's bow of lipstick to her mouth and mascara to her eyelashes to complete the carnival picture. The Parisian designers of the early twenties ordered her to lengthen her short skirts. She ordered the Parisian designers to shorten them still more, and the skirt kept rising till it zipped above the knees. Whereupon the silk stockings were rolled down to the tops of the calves and two more spots of rouge impudently blossomed, on the kneecaps. The cloche hat framed her gaily painted face, and Chanel had that marvelous party idea, junk jewelry; with this and a few other accessories, today one could be a sultry señorita, tomorrow a

FIGURE 1.11 *A young couple dance to the sound of early radio in this photo from the 20s. (The Bettmann Archive.)*

haughty Parisienne, the day after a saucy Tyrolean peasant, the next day a mysterious Egyptian.

"Age cannot wither her, nor custom stale her infinite variety" had been written of an earlier Egyptian, and the American man was as entranced as Antony had been. He taught his new playmate golf and tennis, swimming, sailing, poker. He joined her at bridge, and when a craze for Mah Jongg swept the country, they learned it together. They smoked cigarettes together. They danced the fox-trot and Charleston and black bottom together. The more advanced even discussed the theories of Dr. Freud together, using not only the long words but that three-letter word still considered licentious enough to cause the fuddy-duddy police to close Mae West's play, *Sex*. Above all, they drank together, for Prohibition had turned out to be the most brazenly flouted law in history; the possibility that one might be caught seemed but to add the thrill that earlier generations had enjoyed while raiding Mother's cookie jar or the neighbor's watermelon patch.

A party as lighthearted as this was too much

fun to be a very wild party, sensational novelists with titles like *Flaming Youth* notwithstanding. Yes, chaperones for the unmarried had been left behind, but though this assuredly made it more possible for the young to hold hands, hug, and kiss, the birth rate confounded the fall-of-Rome group by declining. And though divorce had become respectable and was on the rise, it was considered as regrettable then as it is today that those two nice people, whom we had gathered together to wish so well, had found disillusion rather than happiness.

The nation's colleges were enjoying a greatly expanded enrollment, and though academic standards were much higher, this fact was concealed by the musical-comedy appurtenances of raccoon coats, flivvers with rumble seats, pennants, football heroes, prom queens, and the festivities of the fraternities and sororities.

There were signs as early as 1926 that the party would not go on forever. A hurricane flattened the Florida land boom. The country's farmers were struggling with immense debts and wretched prices, and though Congress had tried plan after plan, none of them worked; the machine had displaced more farmers than were willing or able to leave the land. The coal industry, on the other hand, had not mechanized enough; it could not meet the competition of oil, natural gas, and electric power. The cotton industry was in desperate straits, because women not only demanded the light shimmer of silk for their dresses but were wearing a third of the yardage that fashion had deemed necessary for a proper dress in 1900. Even the great Henry Ford was in danger, for his Model T had come to look decidedly ungainly when compared with the sleek new designs of General Motors and Chrysler. Businessmen in the towns were noticing the adverse effect of "roadtown"—the tourist courts, drive-ins, and shopping centers that were beginning to line the highways. The arrival of more and more chain stores was hurting the independent merchants, and the new speciality stores in the cities—Bergdorf Goodman and Saks Fifth Avenue in New York, Nieman-Marcus in Dallas, Bullocks Wilshire in Los Angeles—were alarming the department stores. The railroads were suffering from competition by trucks and buses. The

Piggly Wiggly stores, which pioneered self-service, made some salespeople wonder about the future of their jobs.

But these symptoms of dislocation were largely discounted by the successful, who were, of course, the people making the innovations. At the request of President Coolidge, the government, the banks, and the nation's economists took a hard look at the country's credit situation in 1926 and concluded that borrowing was not excessive. The response of the stock market to the lone forecaster predicting an immediate crash was to go up and up and up. President Coolidge felt he could safely resume his afternoon naps.

And of course, the general prosperity did make it possible for individuals who were not doing well to try something else. The work week had been shortened, wages were up, prices down, and competition for jobs drastically reduced by restrictions on immigration. Labor and management working together had arrived at a kind of "corporate socialism" (though both would have shuddered at the term), providing job security,

FIGURE 1.12 *When shy, young Charles Lindbergh made the first solo airplane flight across the Atlantic in 1927, he found himself perhaps the most famous man on earth. (The Bettmann Archive.)*

pensions, and a host of other benefits. Even those people who objected to America's party on moral grounds had more leisure and money to spend on their quieter pleasures.

Meanwhile the party went on. When a shy young aviator named Charles Lindbergh made the first solo airplane flight across the Atlantic in 1927, he found himself perhaps the most famous man on earth. Al Jolson electrified audiences of the film *The Jazz Singer* in 1927 by opening his mouth—and talking. A galaxy of new stars appeared within months as Hollywood converted to sound. Henry Ford restored America's faith in one of its folk heroes by bringing out the handsome new Model A in 1928. And if money had seemed easy to make before, just look at what stocks were doing! Ten per cent of the price was all you had to put up, and within weeks, some-

---

Fashion Emphasis, 1920: Surprise Party!

Once the vote was achieved, feminine austerity vanished before a gust of frivolity. As early as 1920, the skirt was at the calf, the sleeve had been discarded, stockings were silk, shoes were elaborate and their heels were rising; ruffles and flounces were definitely in. As the decade advanced, the shortening skirt flapped, the shortening hair flapped, and the women who sported both came to be called flappers. The flapper look had a flat-chested, long torso with a round-necked, often sleeveless bodice; a flounce of a skirt, pleated or draped, stopped at the knee. Long chains of pearls around the neck might swing to the hip. Stockings were rolled to just below the knee. The cloche arrived, as did junk jewelry and beading that swirled and glittered when women walked or danced. Silk was the favored fabric. Furs were used with flair: the long wraparound coat for evening and the wool coat with fur trim for day.

Women's clothes retained the straight silhouette of the teens, but men's moved in a new direction: trousers were widened and flared or bell-bottomed, the waistline was tucked in, and the jacket flared at the shoulders and hips. The soft collar replaced the stiff, high one.

Sportswear for both sexes was introduced. The knit polo shirt for men was the first innovation, followed by the knickers popularized by golf's Bobby Jones and the woolen cap by baseball's Babe Ruth. Some women tried knickers and culotte-type skirts, and many wore the new tennis dresses and riding breeches. Swimwear was pared down enough to permit swimming, but tops for men were everywhere required. Only the man's polo shirt and woolen cap were accepted for general leisure wear, however; sportswear remained very much tied to particular activities.

"Sanforizing," to control shrinkage of cotton fabrics, was a major innovation of 1928.

The automobile produced a revolution in retailing. Now that everybody could get to town, the chain stores expanded rapidly. The Country Club Plaza, established in 1922 in Kansas City, Missouri, was the nation's first outdoor shopping center. Sears, finding that mail order was dropping off, went into retail—and not within the cities but on the highways where the stores could provide plenty of free parking. Specialty stores like Saks Fifth Avenue concentrated on fashion, to the exclusion of all the other services provided by the department stores, and had a great success. Piggly Wiggly, introducing self-service, made the greatest innovation of all.

The youthful excitement of the decade concealed the trend that overtakes us all: however much fun we're having, we'll be ten years older at the end of a decade than we were at its beginning. The young, who had so easily succeeded in 1920, by 1930 were beginning to feel like the old and established, and noticed that their heels didn't kick quite as high as they used to.

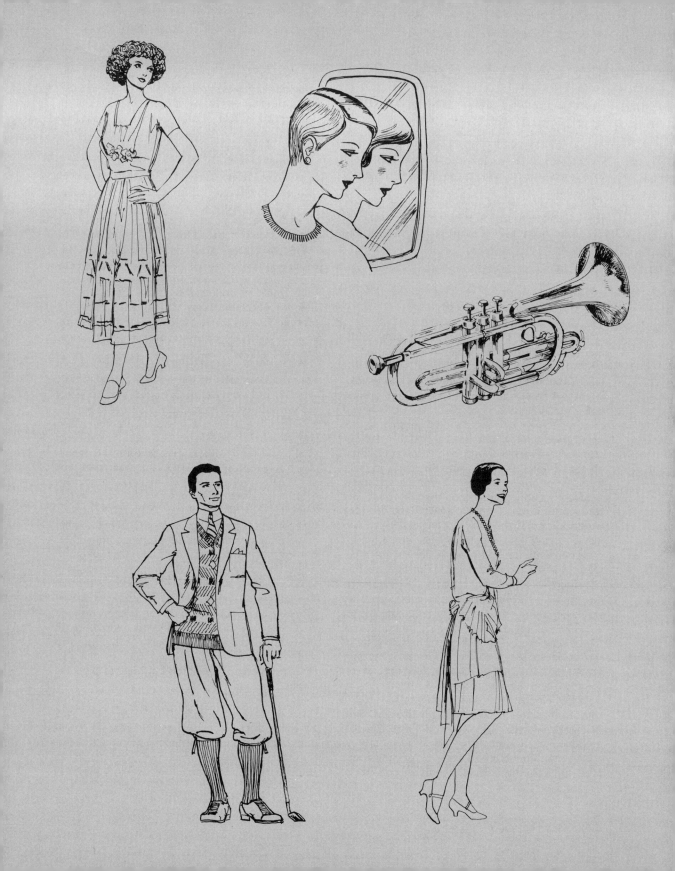

times hours, you would double or triple your money!

And so it went, until, on September 3, 1929, the stock market reached an unbelievable peak. Then it started to flutter, and then, jerkily, to go down. On October 23, it dropped 18 points. On October 24 there was a panic, hastily stabilizied by a $240 million bankers' pool. On October 29 came a dizzying 40-point plunge. By November 13, just 71 days after September 3, General Electric had fallen from 396 ¼ to 168 ⅛, Montgomery Ward from 137 ⅞ to 49 ¼, RCA from 101 to 28. The party was over.

1930–1940

There is often a strong element of wish fulfillment in fashion. The ladies who gathered in 1900 at a small-town tea given by the First Methodist Church for the benefit of the Asian missions knew that they were not Vanderbilts and Astors, but it was delightful to be costumed almost as if they were, and to vie with one another in the regal grace with which they accepted their cucumber sandwiches. Many of the flower children of the 1960s, padding barefoot and in rags through the summer in San Francisco's Haight-Ashbury section, knew, too, that their beggary was a midsummer's dream, that in the fall they would inexorably be back in their expensive colleges, driving their expensive cars, preparing for their conventional and expensively rewarded careers. And so, too, to a degree seen never before nor since, were the fashions of the 1930s an exercise in wish fulfillment. The Great Depression was everywhere, the system of corporate socialism had collapsed, millions were unemployed. There seemed no end to the accumulating disasters—and the architects, the couturiers, the musicians, the auto designers of the decade responded by decreeing a marvelously suave, understated elegance, a vision of wealth so vast and unshakable that it need not trouble to assert itself. Rockefeller Center in New York, the principal architectural monument of the decade, flatly rejected monumentality in favor of purling fountains and a skating rink and a centerpiece tower of superb slenderness. The Golden Gate Bridge, the principal engineering monument of the decade, was a miracle of visual economy. Under the influence of Greta Garbo women's hair was dropped gracefully to the shoulders, and clothes became feminine again, bias cut, softly draped and clinging to the body with hemlines dropping to midcalf. Men wore the "English drape," a straight-shouldered, full-chested, double-breasted suit with a pinched waist and full, pleated trousers popularized by the heir to the British throne, the Duke of Windsor. The "Windsor blazer" and summerweight suits became popular, a further move toward casual elegance. Jazz was smoothed into swing, a sweet, silky music introduced by the "big bands" of Benny Goodman, Glen Miller, Artie Shaw, the brothers Dorsey. And the cars were the classics, perhaps the most beautiful ever designed, long, low, unimaginably sleek.

As we have noted, there were serious economic dislocations in the United States as early as 1926. But even the stock market crash in 1929 did not immediately produce what could be universally recognized as a universal disaster. Many people saw no reason why they should be affected at all, and many others expected a quick recovery. It was not until late 1932 that the magnitude of the catastrophe could no longer be denied. Industrial production then was half what it had been in 1929, profits of the 550 largest corporations were off by 68 per cent and many smaller corporations were out of business altogether, home and commercial construction was one fifth of the 1929 level, at least 10 million workers were jobless and the number would reach 14 million the following spring. Many of those still employed had suffered substantial wage cuts and were working short days. Drastic reductions in prices failed to attract customers. As the humorist Will Rogers observed, things were so bad that even the people who didn't intend to pay had stopped buying.

But in November 1932, Franklin Delano Roosevelt was elected president. A former New York governor distantly related to the intrepid Theodore, he radiated the patrician assurance that was the style of the decade. Taking office in 1933, he immediately ended the most ominous threat of

FIGURE 1.13 *The 1930s had their darker side: the Depression. (Photograph by Berenice Abbott. Federal Arts Project "Changing New York." Museum of the City of New York.)*

all, the impending collapse of the nation's banking system, by proclaiming a bank holiday and delivering, via the radio, the first of his fireside chats to the American people. The people responded by redepositing billions of dollars that had been hoarded for fear of bank failures—thus preventing the bank failures. Congress rapidly enacted bills concerning repeal of Prohibition, employment for the jobless, support for crop prices, insurance for bank deposits, development of the Tennessee Valley, social security. These measures, collectively called the New Deal, did not end the Depression—until the outbreak of World War II there were never fewer than eight million unemployed, and the average was ten million—but they did reverse the mood of the country. The worst was over, things could only get better, and it was time to take a few chances and perhaps even to have fun again.

Costs had fallen along with prices, and manu-facturers discovered that they could profitably sell as many electric irons as they could make at a price of $2, cloth coats at $6.95, men's suits at $9.85, washing machines at $27.50. When a drought turned the Great Plains into the Dust Bowl, the pioneer spirit reasserted itself; many of the victims, like their ancestors coping with earlier hard times, piled into the cars that had replaced covered wagons and started west to the Golden State, California. National labor unions were formed to improve the lot of the working population. The nation's college population continued to grow, with a new emphasis on the sciences that by the end of the decade began to produce an explosion of new products. The introduction of plastics created a new industry, the development of nylon a textile revolution that still has not ended.

Meanwhile, the price of fun had gone down as much as the prices of everything else. A child

FIGURE 1.14 *The Duke of Windsor, seen here with the Duchess, had a great influence on men's fashions in the 30s. (The Bettmann Archive.)*

McGee and Mollie, Jack Benny, Burns and Allen, Bob Hope, Fred Allen: "*Land* has been discovered! It's on my property in Florida!" Movies were better than ever. There were the wildly funny comedies of Mae West and W. C. Fields, the harrowing crime dramas of Jean Harlow and James Cagney, romances featuring Joan Crawford, Bette Davis, Spencer Tracy, Erroll Flynn, Clark Gable, Claudette Colbert, Cary Grant, Myrna Loy. Judy Garland danced down the yellow brick road, Nelson Eddy and Jeanette McDonald sang love duets, Shirley Temple singing and dancing in *Stand Up and Cheer* at the age of five bewitched the country, putting millions of little girls into curls and tap-dancing classes. Fred Astaire and Ginger Rogers danced so very miraculously that, unlike Shirley, they failed to create a style; we could not hope to imitate, only admire. Walt Disney produced first his

with a nickel entering a candy store entered a garden of delights—a licorice stick was a penny, a box of peppermint cigarettes was a penny, a jaw-breaker was a penny, a paper strip with colored sugar dots was a penny, a set of hilariously grotesqne and deliciously flavored waxy red lips was a penny. The movies cost a dime—nominally to age 12, but no one dreamed of charging you the adult's quarter until you were unmistakably long in the tooth. And there was, of course, that hushed-up but self-evident bright side to unemployment: if you couldn't put in the day at the coal mine or the factory, why not put it in at the beach? Even more then than now, many of the best things in life were free: museums were free, concerts were free, dances were free, parks and pools and woods were closer by, much less crowded, much less littered, much more safe, and *they* were free; even a college education in New York City was free. The idle poor had the good sense to keep quiet about it, but, especially among the young who could leave the worrying to their parents, their lives were often quite as delightful as those of the legendary idle rich.

Entertainment in fact flowered in America during the 1930s as never before. Radio was in its golden age, offering a dazzling array of swing bands, mysteries and westerns and dramas, above all comedians—Edgar Bergen and the irrepressible Charlie McCarthy, Amos and Andy, Fibber

FIGURE 1.15 *Classic 1930s suit. This version, in green wool, was designed by Sophie Gimbel. (The Metropolitan Museum of Art, Gift of Saks Fifth Avenue, 1943.)*

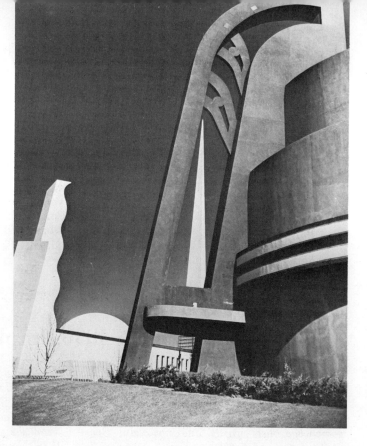

FIGURE 1.16 *The architecture of the New York World's Fair—"The World of Tomorrow"—exemplifies the optimistic and innovative mood of 1939. (Museum of the City of New York.)*

charming Silly Symphonies and then the first and perhaps the best full-length cartoon ever made, *Snow White and the Seven Dwarfs.* Margaret Mitchell's *Gone with the Wind,* a runaway best-selling novel chronicling the reverses and triumphant revival of the fortunes of Scarlett O'Hara in the South during and after the Civil War, became the greatest box-office smash in movie history. A whole new crop of amusing and instructive national magazines appeared. In New York, Times Square blazed with enormous neon signs proclaiming the latest attractions, and the plush supper clubs—El Morocco, the Stork Club, 21—opened to provide a showcase for Cafe Society, featuring stars and columnists and those among the affluent who wished to be seen in their company. There was even a media-created boom in debutantes. The most beautiful of them all, Brenda Duff Frazier, became famous, much to her own bewilderment and the distress of her mother. Miss Frazier's most irresistible attraction was that she saw nothing whatever remarkable in being a young and flawlessly photogenic seventeen-year-old heiress whose sole occupation was preparing for and attending an endless round of lavish parties and unbelievable dates. "After all," she remarked, protesting the fuss, when she was profiled by *The New Yorker,* "I'm only a debutante."

Yes, the wealthy, who had gone out of fashion during the prosperity of the teens, during the depression of the thirties had come back in. Not, of course, the *real* wealthy, whose great houses were closed while their owners struggled to retrieve their fortunes. The wealthy that America preferred were the wealthy as imagined in the movies and confirmed by the ingenuous Miss Frazier, impossibly glamorous.

The influence of movies about the wealthy on the American life style and the fashions that reflected it during the thirties was staggering. Clark Gable appeared, while courting an heiress in *It Happened One Night,* without an undershirt, and millions of men stopped wearing undershirts. In another film Clark Gable introduced the sport shirt, and when we contemplate the consequence from our distance of forty-odd years, we can only feel awe. Stars of both sexes pioneered slacks. Marlene Dietrich, as early as 1933, introduced the lady's trouser suit. In mid-decade, the smartly tailored skirt suit was revived as daytime wear suitable to the socialites and business executives played with such crisp, efficient charm by the likes of Rosalind Russell and Joan Crawford and Katherine Hepburn. Crisp, efficient charm being precisely the effect that every secretary, teacher, and businesswoman in the country wanted to convey, padded broad shoulders, longish skirts, and short jackets—

adorned as the occasion permitted by real or artificial flowers or jewelry and the inevitable smart, smallish hat—were presently being worn by every secretary, teacher, and businesswoman in the country.

The decade ended with the springtime 1939 opening of the New York World's Fair, "The World of Tomorrow," and the September 1939 outbreak of World War II in Europe. Tomorrow would surely be different, but the indomitable America of the depression had demonstrated that whatever it brought, tomorrow would be taken in stride.

Fashion Emphasis, 1930: Implausible Elegance

Casual, worldly elegance was the keynote in 1930. The hemline dropped to midcalf during the day, to the floor for evening. Dresses were cut on the bias, clinging sensuously to the body, and women had busts, waists, and hips again. Spaghetti straps and backless gowns were presently introduced, and later in the decade the famed debutante Brenda Duff Frazier created a sensation with the strapless evening dress. For daytime, the suit was revived, with padded shoulders, longish skirts, and short, tailored jackets. It was worn with real or artificial flowers and jewelry and a smart, smallish hat. The platform ankle-strapped shoe arrived in 1938, along with broad-shouldered fur chubbies.

In 1930 men wore the English drape, which had a square, military shoulderline, a full-chested, double-breasted jacket with a sharply nipped waist, and pleated trousers. The Duke of Windsor's widely spread collar points called for the triangular Windsor knot to bulk the tie. Princeton University students created a boom in the seersucker summer suit in 1934, launching a trend to the lightweight that has grown ever since.

But the major fashion innovation of the thirties was leisure wear. To the man's polo shirt of the twenties was added the sport shirt, adapted in

California from an Argentine "gaucho" shirt and first translated into flannel and then into cotton and silk. Shorts were introduced for both sexes, Helen Jacobs gaining national attention when she wore them in tennis tournaments in 1933. Slacks also became popular for both men and women. The lumberjack shirt of plaid wool was adopted for casual winter wear and the revived blazer foreshadowed the sportcoat.

The California influence was very strong in this fashion revolution, which emphasized bright colors and bold patterns. Another Hollywood influence was the revival of Western dress: Stetson hats, string ties, and embroidered shirts started to come back in the formerly wild West and in the South.

Nylon made its appearance at the end of the decade. Retailing methods were relatively stable, but mail order continued to decline and Sears disregarded the depression to open hundreds of new stores. The Fashion Group, formed in New York City in 1921 to promote fashion, in 1935 held the first of its fashion shows, "Fashion Futures," attended by 1,200 representatives of the press and the fashion industries.

The trend of the decade was toward the casual and the youthful.

1940–1950

The forties began with a surge of prosperity. Orders were pouring in from Britain and France, President Roosevelt's preparedness and lend-lease programs pushed the boom along still more, and newly affluent consumers added yet another boost by rushing to buy the things they had gone without for so many years. The languid elegance of the thirties vanished in a blast of exhilaration. Women's fashions were youthful again, with rather tight, short skirts, shoulders even broader than before, sharply pointed lapels, and suitably playful hats. Dancing was also geared to youth, for the coronary generations dared not attempt the new rage, the jitterbug. Music started to jump rather than swing; jive came in, and boogie woogie, Betty Hutton and the Andrews sisters. Hollywood's Betty Grable was perhaps the essence of the new style, young, blond, wholesome, snappily pretty rather than beautiful, warm, natural, full of life—the antithesis of that sophisticated creature in her clinging black dress and string of pearls who had fascinated the thirties. Miss Grable of the justly famous legs did not dance or sing or act all that well, but she did what little she could do with entrancing vivacity.

America felt its young deserved their good time, for the war news was so bad that many people stopped going to the movies rather than suffer through the newsreels. President Roosevelt had assured America that it would not be drawn into the fighting, and he was elected to an unprecedented third term in 1940 in part on the basis of that assurance. But France had surrendered in June 1940, Italy and Japan had joined Germany as belligerents, Britain was being bombed without mercy, and who knew when America's turn would come?

The commander of the lead Japanese formation recalled that Hawaii's Pearl Harbor was "still asleep in the morning mist"[4] when the surprise attack started on the American Pacific Fleet at 7:55 on Sunday, December 7, 1941. Congress declared war on Japan the next day, on Germany and Italy December 11. The awesome energies of America were mobilized. Great new technologies were created to build ships and planes and factories and defense housing and tanks and guns and bullets and bombs in quantities and at speeds never before dreamed possible. "Rosie the Riveter" put on overalls and joined the men on the assembly lines. Hundreds of thousands of women served in uniform with the Women's Army Auxiliary Corps (later, WACS), the Navy WAVES, the Coast Guard SPARS, the Women Marines. Sacrifices were called for on the home front: civilian goods were rationed, civilian housing construction and manufacture of civilian cars and appliances were halted, there were collections of scrap metal and bacon grease and paper and nylon stockings and everything else reusable, millions of Americans planted Victory Gardens, bond drives were continuous.

But by the end of 1942, America and its allies were everywhere starting to win; and though the young, who had dominated the American life style in 1940, were now in uniform or on the assembly line, their place had been taken by the still younger: the teenager had been born.

Before the war, there had been no such thing as the teenager, only the adolescent, an anomalous person between the ages of thirteen and seventeen. But now, for no apparent reasons beyond the facts that the labor shortage made it possible

FIGURE 1.17 *Bobby-soxers at Coney Island. (Museum of the City of New York.)*

for adolescents to earn money at odd jobs like babysitting and that their parents had decided to permit the young workers to spend their earnings as they pleased, there was a mysterious, distinctively costumed group with a language and customs of its own. Observe them: boys and girls usually dressed so alike that only hair length and make-up made it possible to distinguish the sexes. Both boys and girls wore bulky jeans, rolled up to show the socks. The socks were ribbed white ankle socks, though the girls called them bobby sox and were themselves called bobby-soxers. Shoes were either inexpensive copies of Loafers or saddle oxfords. Shirts were copies of men's shirts, and it was essential that they appear a size or two too large and never be tucked in. Sweaters, called Sloppy Joes, also must look a size or two too large. Thus clad, teenagers spent Saturday nights at places called teen towns, youth centers, or soda fountains. There they danced the jitterbug or the lindy hop. All of them collected records and played jukeboxes. All of them united to make a star out of a painfully thin young crooner, indistinguishable from a thousand others so far as the adult eye could see, who happened to be named Frank Sinatra. A frighteningly large number of teenagers shrieked and fainted in apparent ecstasy when Mr. Sinatra sang. This activity they called swooning.

America, land of marvels, had clearly created another. The older generation wondered even more than usual what the world was coming to, but aside from their excesses over Mr. Sinatra the teenagers seemed a well-behaved group, and a number of their elders perceived that here were the makings of a new market. Cosmetics companies wondered if they might not do well by introducing a line specifically for teenagers after the war. An astute publisher began making plans for a new magazine to be called *Seventeen*. Clothing manufacturers suspected the potential for junior fashions.

Meanwhile, however, the teenagers did their very substantial part in helping to win America's war. Many of them, of course, reached eighteen (at which age one ceased to be a teenager) and entered the services. President Roosevelt, elected to a fourth term in 1944, died in office a few months before total victory. Germany surren-

FIGURE 1.18 *The end of the war in Europe was a moment of wild rejoicing. (The Bettmann Archive.)*

dered on May 7, 1945. President Roosevelt's successor, President Truman, ordered the first atomic bomb dropped on Hiroshima on August 6, 1945, the second on Nagasaki on August 9. Japan surrendered on August 14, 1945, and in the words of one of the war's most popular songs, the lights came on again all over the world.

The joy with which America greeted the news and welcomed its warriors home was unmitigated. Guns boomed with it, rockets burst with it, church bells rang with it, crowds cheered with it, wives and mothers wept with it. Never had America known such triumph and such relief.

It's little wonder that when a young, unknown designer named Christian Dior opened his Parisian salon in 1947 with a collection featuring full skirts that fell luxuriously to within 12 inches of the floor, pinched waists, and sloped shoulders, the "New Look" created a sensation. Men were to wear the "Bold Look," featuring long, rolled lapels, straight waists, stripes, plaids, and checks, wide ties, and wide-brimmed hats.

But though America hoped once again to be dressed for a party, shortages made the new clothes hard to find, and the rest of the decade was full of unexpected troubles. Once our troops were home, our erstwhile ally Russia seized the opportunity to annex or install puppet governments in East Germany, Latvia, Lithuania, Estonia, Poland, Hungary, Yugoslavia, Albania, Rumania, Bulgaria, Manchuria, and North Korea. The wartime British Prime Minister, Winston Churchill, warned that an iron curtain had fallen across Europe. The fall of Greece and Turkey seemed so imminent that President Truman asked Congress for $400 million of military supplies to assist them. Congress agreed, but Communists promptly seized control of Czechoslovakia. In 1948, the Marshall Plan was created to bolster the rest of Europe. Peacetime

$\mathcal{F}$ashion $\mathcal{E}$mphasis, 1940: Jive!

The youthful look was everywhere in 1940. The padded-shoulder women's suits and dresses of the late thirties had been given even broader shoulders and shorter skirts: the hat became as important a fashion feature as it was at the turn of the century, but with an emphasis now on playfulness. Hats might be large, they might be small, but they must nonsensically sprout feathers, plumes, fruits and flowers, ribbons, veils, pleats, folds, artificial birds and bright little animals. Men's suits were more often single-breasted than not, and the sportcoat-slacks combination had a resounding success.

During World War II, the government's L-85 ruling made the short, tight look obligatory: hems could not exceed two inches, there could be but one patch pocket per blouse, and cuffs were forbidden. The skirt could not exceed 72 inches at the hem and the belt could not exceed two inches in width. Men's clothes, too, were pared down. Vogue and Harper's Bazaar helped women with ideas for the basic suit, convertible for evening, and the coordinated wardrobe. In 1943 Eleanor Lambert created the first annual Coty American Fashion Critics' Award for excellence in American design. In 1944 she staged the first semiannual Press Week show, sponsored by the New York Dress Institute.

The teenagers who appeared during the war managed to achieve an effect of bulk by the simple expedient of buying clothes a size or two too large.

Both boys and girls favored men's shirts with the tails out, saddle oxfords or inexpensive copies of Loafers, white ribbed ankle socks (bobby sox), jeans rolled up at the cuff. There were Sloppy Joe sweaters and pleated skirts. After the war the junior market mushroomed; Seventeen was launched, junior departments were added to stores, cosmetics companies introduced lines specifically for teens.

Paris returned to the fashion scene when the war ended with a group of youthful new designers, Christian Dior, Pierre Balmain, Jacques Fath, Balenciaga. Dior's New Look was a sensation in 1947, with skirts falling luxuriously to within 12 inches of the floor, pinched waists made possible by a new Dior-designed foundation garment, and natural shoulders. Men were to wear the Bold Look, with long, rolled lapels, straight waists, stripes and plaids and checks, wide ties, wide-brimmed hats. Continuing shortages of materials made the triumph of the New Look gradual, and the Bold Look was a success only so long as shortages made it possible to sell anything manufacturers cared to make. As the shortages diminished, men were found to prefer the narrow-lapeled, natural-shouldered Ivy League style.

During much of the decade, shortages made merchandising, advertising, and manufacturing innovations unnecessary.

The trend of the decade was from youth toward elegance.

conscription was started to rebuild America's armed forces. China fell to Communists in 1949.

The reconversion from war production to civilian goods had proceeded rapidly, but demand was far in excess of supply. A wave of strikes made the shortages worse. The veterans taking advantage of the GI Bill to further their educations found wildly overcrowded classes and dorms and almost no provision for housing the married. Spies were discovered in some branches of the government, bribe takers in others. And in 1949 President Truman announced that Russia had developed its own atomic bomb.

1950–1960

Though the pundits predicted that the new decade would be "The Age of Anxiety," counterforces at work during the forties had ensured that the America of the fifties would not be anxious very long. A 1943 musical comedy was the first straw in the wind. With its integration of story, song, and dance, Rodgers and Hammerstein's *Oklahoma!* was so compelling an innovation that it started a revolution not only on the stage but in the American life style. *Oklahoma!* ran on Broadway for five years and toured the country for ten, and the only way you could see it was to get dressed up and go to the theater. *On the Town* joined it in 1944; *Carousel* in 1945; *Annie Get Your Gun* in 1946; *Allegro, Finian's Rainbow, Street Scene, Brigadoon,* and *High Button Shoes* in 1947; *Kiss Me, Kate* in 1949; *Gentlemen Prefer Blondes* and the incomparable *South Pacific* in 1949. By the end of the forties, this sunburst of creativity had flooded the radio with lush melodies like "Some Enchanted Evening," had filled the theaters and dance floors with men and women dressed with appropriate elegance, and had monopolized the general magazines with articles on the shows themselves and on their stars—Ethel Merman, Carol Channing, above all Mary Martin. By 1950, with the opening of *Guys and Dolls* and *Call Me Madam,* America was unmistakably in the middle of a festival.

By 1950, too, sanity had returned to labor–management negotiations. The Marshall Plan was clearly a success. The appointment in 1950 of the war hero Dwight Eisenhower as Supreme Commander of NATO in Europe stamped as final the determination of America to assume leadership of the Free World. 1950 also saw America's resolve to maintain atomic parity with Russia by development of the hydrogen bomb. And the invasion of South Korea by Communist North Korea on June 25, 1950, was immediately countered by United Nations troops under the command of General Douglas MacArthur. The landing of U.S. Marines at Inchon on September 15, 1950, stunned the world, because the entire North Korean army immediately collapsed. Though Communist China entered the war before the end of the year and the fighting developed into a stalemate, the North Korean collapse ended the myth of Communist invincibility and raised so many questions about the reliability of Russia's puppet-state armies in Eastern Europe that Russia was forced onto the defensive.

In 1952 leaders of both parties offered the presidential nomination to the immensely popular General Eisenhower. Choosing to run as a Republican, he campaigned as the soldier who would bring peace. When he won the election, he delivered the Korean armistice and brought America eight years of international successes and a domestic prosperity unequaled in memory.

The festival of Broadway continued through the decade—*Can-Can, Wonderful Town,* and *Pajama Game* in 1953, *Kismet, The Boy Friend,* and *Threepenny Opera* in 1954, *Damn Yankees* in 1955, *Fanny, Bells Are Ringing,* and the stupendous *My Fair Lady* in 1956, *West Side Story* and *The Music Man* in 1957, *Gypsy* and *Flower Drum Song* in 1959. There was also a boom in opera, symphonies, the fine arts. Office and apartment and hotel towers rose in the cities, and the towers were made of glass, demonstrating as nothing else could the confidence of America that it need fear no bombs. New superhighways swept across the continent, the jet age dawned, the first satellites circled the earth and soared to the moon.

Astonishingly, all of this hustle and bustle and burgeon and blastoff was the creation of a man whose name America would never hear, a man who had to be named collectively, the "man in the gray flannel suit." The corporations enlarged by the war and giantized by the peace were too vast to have owners any more. There were only stockholders, with individual holdings a tiny percentage of the whole, and the practically anonymous managers who ran the businesses day by day and who determined when to launch new products, buy subsidiaries, open branches, diversify. The shortages created by World War II had largely disappeared, and selling was important again; Madison Avenue, street of the advertising agencies, exerted an immense influence.

The man in the gray flannel suit made sure that his suit was *charcoal* gray. It was cut in the Ivy League style, with natural shoulders, slim, tapered trousers, and narrow lapels; hat brims and ties also became narrow, though the hat in the summer might be a dapper straw boater revived from the turn of the century. His wife wore Dior's New Look through most of the decade, with skirts at midcalf, lots of petticoats, a pinched waist, and natural shoulders. For evening the gown was strapless atop a gracefully billowing skirt. The hair was worn on the short side, with the poodle cut a favorite. Hats were obligatory. Women's sportswear featured Bermuda shorts, pedal pushers, short shorts, halter tops, and halter dresses. Pants were worn only as sportswear, usually in the form of blue jeans; but the decade being a dressy one, jeans were considered unsuitable except for activities such as participation in the "do-it-yourself" craze that was sweeping America. Around 1955 the fashionable man permitted a pink or heliotrope shirt to vary the ubiquitious white. Bermuda shorts, proper Bermudian over-the-calf socks, and a Madras jacket might be worn for informal social occasions in the summer. Coco Chanel returned to the fashion world in 1957 to revive the chemise, and other designers reintroduced the sheath and shirtwaist.

The majority of this strangely anonymous group of fashion leaders was moving to the suburbs; fresh air and lawns were thought desirable for the children. Cocktail parties, dinner parties, and barbecues were common entertainments, as well as luncheons and afternoons of canasta for the nonworking wives. But the group numbered in the tens of millions—80 per cent of America

considered itself middle class—and many activities obligatory to earlier upwardly mobile societies went by the board; for example, it no longer mattered very much whether you joined a country club. With factory workers earning an average wage of $2.22 an hour in 1959, social rankings of leisure activities were rapidly disappearing. And there was one notion about which all classes were unanimous: the children must be given "the advantages." These included—where they could be afforded—not only the finest, or at least the most expensive, schools that money could buy, but the Little League, and golf lessons, swimming lessons, riding lessons, sailing lessons, skating lessons, piano lessons, dancing lessons, *everything* lessons. Mothers drove the little ones from class to class, and the children never knew that childhood had once included the alternative blessings of jumping into leaf piles in the fall, throwing snowballs in the winter, building slushy dams in gutters during the February thaw, catching june bugs in their season, playing cowboys and Indians and hide-and-seek, and presenting their mothers with hand-picked mushrooms with the comforting knowledge that edibility would not be put to the test. The only sign of rebellion was at the cabana clubs, where the mothers banded together to demand that adults be permitted ten minutes of child-free swimming each hour.

The home was automated, and the advent of convenience foods and ready mixes started to make cooking effortless, if not quite as delicious as what Mother used to make. In the proliferating suburban shopping centers, the city department stores opened glossy new branches.

Television was abruptly everywhere, though many Americans were inclined to be apologetic about it. They had finally got a set, they said, to keep up with the football games and the cultural specials. The ratings nevertheless suggested that a good many of the apologists were chuckling over Milton Berle and Lucille Ball as much as the rest of the country, and sweating out the quiz shows, and cheering Mat Dillon, Paladin, and Cheyenne. In any event, they were very choosy about the movies they went to—only the blockbuster could be sure of a large adult audience. The sex goddess of the decade, Marilyn Monroe, had the good sense to see that standing around emitting steam was no longer enough. She developed a quick wit for interviews—"Didn't you have *anything* on?" gasped a reporter, during the furore over the discovery that she had once posed nude for a calendar. "Oh, *yes*," replied Miss Monroe, with a breathless air of explaining everything away. "I had the radio on." In pictures like *Some Like It Hot* she also demonstrated that she was an accomplished comedienne, and in

---

Fashion Emphasis, 1950: Suburban Style

Dior's New Look reigned supreme by 1950. The hemline stayed from below the knee to midcalf throughout the decade. Fashion emphasis fell on the natural shoulder, with a dolman or raglan sleeve, a full skirt with lots of petticoats, a pinched waist. For evening the gown was strapless atop a billowing, flowing skirt. Sportswear featured Bermuda shorts, pedal pushers, short shorts, halter tops, and halter dresses. Pants were worn only as sportswear, but were less popular than in the forties; shorts of various lengths, sport skirts, and sport dresses were preferred. Heels continued to rise, culminating in the three- to four-inch spikes of the late fifties that briefly wreaked havoc on the nation's carpets and floors. Hats and gloves were considered necessary accessories and jewelry made a strong comeback.

The charcoal gray Ivy League suit was the male uniform of the decade; the jacket was cut tight with natural shoulders and narrow lapels, the trousers were slim and tapered, vests were common, and ties and hat brims were narrow. By the middle of the decade, Bermuda shorts and Madras jackets were common informal summer wear and pink shirts made inroads at the office.

Teenagers, too, became comparatively dressy; they were not entirely out of jeans, but skirts, dresses, shorts, and pedal pushers made serious inroads in girls' wardrobes, and the boys often wore slacks or shorts and sport shirts. The bulky teenage silhouette of the forties disappeared altogether. Elvis Presley fans tended to leather jackets.

In 1957 Chanel reappeared on the fashion scene after a long retirement. She and other designers reintroduced the sack dress and the curveless chemise—a slim, waistless, tight, almost hobble-skirted dress that fell to midcalf.

The big fabric news was the introduction of Dacron. Blended with rayon or cotton, Dacron produced wash-and-wear clothing. Blended with worsted, Dacron made possible a summer suiting fabric less than half the weight of the tropicals of the 1930s.

Fashion merchandising was revolutionized by the proliferation of suburban shopping centers and by television. The largest of the city department stores became regional chains by opening branches in the shopping centers; the national chains previously existing underwent an enormous expansion. Discount stores such as E. J. Korvette and Alexander's appeared, while former bargain centers such as Sears strove to upgrade their images. Television brought instant nationwide exposure to fashion trends. The trends were largely controlled by Madison Avenue, which not only decided what actors would wear in television ads but largely controlled the selection and content of the programs themselves.

New York was beginning to challenge Paris with its own crop of designers: Hattie Carnegie, Lilly Daché, Mainbocher, and Pauline Trigère. The mass producers along Seventh Avenue were growing so fast that they launched a campaign to rename the street "Fashion Avenue."

The trend of the decade seemed to be toward ever-increasing elegance. This apparent unanimity was largely a mirage created by Madison Avenue, however, and Madison Avenue itself would soon be at the heart of the fragmentation that was to occur in the sixties.

FIGURE 1.19 *Elvis Presley was the idol of teens and subteens in the 1950s. (Courtesy of RCA Records.)*

others that she was a capable dramatic actress. Women confessed to their surprise that they *liked* her.

Like their parents, teenagers had developed upward mobility, and the country swarmed with them. They kept so exclusively to themselves that they were called the "silent generation," but though their uniform moved in the direction of their parents' elegance, with plenty of money to spend (babysitters got 25 to 50 cents per hour) they continued to create their own stars. Early in the decade, these included Guy Madison, Tab Hunter, and Tony Curtis, whose publicity shots concentrated on wholesome activities like romping at the beach and eating ice cream and whose movies, especially those made specifically for teenagers, were so awful that one forthright exhibitor concluded an ad, "Not recommended for adults." In 1955, however, the teenagers created a star that everyone admitted was genuine, James Dean, who in *Rebel Without a Cause* introduced America to the possibility that providing its young with the advantages might not be enough. By middecade, too, a music and dance called "bop" was filtering in from the coasts, and it quickly developed into rock and roll. A young Memphis truck driver named Elvis Presley adopted it and as a performer not only took the teenage world by storm but created the "teeny-boppers" among the subteen group. Mr. Presley accompanied his singing with a guitar and gyrations. When Ed Sullivan , host of a Sunday night family variety show on television, finally engaged "Elvis the Pelvis" to appear, he instructed the cameramen to keep the view decorously above the waist. Many boys copied Mr. Presley's heavily oiled ducktail haircut, but when their parents learned that he did not drink or smoke and was a model of rectitude as a draftee, they concluded that the craze was probably as harmless as the cult of bearded beatniks who were appearing on the West Coast.

The only major event to ripple the domestic tranquility of the Eisenhower years was the campaign for civil rights. In 1954, the Supreme Court ruled that public school segregation is unconstitutional and in 1957 it did the same for public bus segregation in Alabama. Martin Luther King's gospel of nonviolence and a 385-day boycott had resulted in peaceful integration of Birmingham buses in advance of the Supreme Court's decision, but in September 1957, school integration in Little Rock, Arkansas, was so violently resisted by whites that President Eisenhower sent troops to enforce the law. The troops maintained order and Central High was integrated.

1960–1970

One of the problems of being a leader, whether of fashion or of anything else, is that something is usually gaining on you. The middle classes entered the sixties seeing America in terms of John Kenneth Galbraith's *The Affluent Society*, presiding over the triumph of the computer, and predicting that the new decade would be overwhelmingly prosperous. Their prediction was accurate: the Gross National Product would rise from $504 billion in 1960 to $970 billion in 1970, and wages and salaries would double. But though in other decades it had often seemed that money and happiness were blissfully wed, the sixties were to bring them to the brink of divorce.

The decade began brightly enough, with the election of John Fitzgerald Kennedy as president. His victory over Richard Nixon was as narrow as the difference in their platforms, and the conservatism of the Congress elected with Mr. Kennedy made it evident that the voters expected the important things to stay about as they were. Mr. Kennedy talked of a new frontier, but America seemed much more interested in the glamorously young and handsome image of itself projected by the new President, his large and lively cluster of relatives, and his lovely wife. Though Mr. Kennedy wore a loose-cut two-button suit rather than the regulation natural-shoulder three, his style was otherwise that of the middle-class American of the fifties, even to the extent of playing touch football and tennis, enjoying skiing and swimming, and sailing his boat himself. Mrs. Kennedy was photographed water skiing in Capri pants. Her pillbox hats and sleeveless, collarless dresses cut with exquisite seaming and detail became the uniform of the smart young woman of 1960. The dresses were sometimes fitted, sometimes semifitted with a jacket, and always beautifully tailored. The skirts were a few inches below the knee. Both of the Kennedys shared the country's new enthusiasm for the arts, and as a result America's official entertainments were gratifyingly elegant. Not only were the interiors of the White House restored to their original period styles under Mrs. Kennedy's direction, but the nation was invited to join her on television for that traditional American ceremony, "the

Showing of the House." The stylish excitement of the Broadway musical *Camelot* seemed so appropriate to the new administration that reference to Camelot has ever since been used to convey its quality.

But the fifties were not to be replayed. The first unmistakable symptom of the coming revolution was, appropriately enough for America, a 1959 advertising campaign for an automobile. The car was the German-made Volkswagen, the agency was Doyle Dane Bernbach, the slogan was "think small." The beetle had been introduced in America as far back as 1949, and that year sales had totaled an unrevolutionary two. The new slogan, startling to a country priding itself on thinking big, made the car the phenomenon that launched the counterculture. Another German product, Thalidomide, provided the next jolt, for in 1961 it developed that this supposedly safe and heavily advertised new tranquillizer was responsible for the births in Europe of thousands of armless and legless babies. In 1962 Ralph Nader's book *Unsafe at Any Speed* shocked America with the advice that structural defects of its cars were responsible for thousands of deaths and millions of accidents. The shock increased when America learned that General Motors had chosen to react not by resolving to build safe cars but by poking into Mr. Nader's private life in the hope of finding dirt. Also in 1962, Rachel Carson's *The Silent Spring* launched ecology; we were told that our insecticides were poisoning us quite as efficiently as they poisoned insects. In 1963, Ms. Betty Friedan published *The Feminine Mystique*, denouncing the housewifely bustle of the fifties and proclaiming Women's Lib. And on November 22, 1963, came the ultimate shock: while motorcading through Dallas, Texas, in an open car with Mrs. Kennedy at his side, surrounded by friendly, applauding Americans, John Fitzgerald Kennedy was assassinated. Two days later, the suspected assassin was murdered on live television before the nation's eyes.

Vice-president Lyndon Baines Johnson had been sworn in as president the day Kennedy died, and he quickly attempted to restore the country's shaken confidence. He cut the budget, cut taxes, got President Kennedy's stalled civil rights bill passed by Congress, declared a war on poverty,

FIGURE 1.20 *The Beatles bounded through the 60s, influencing the life styles and fashions of youth all over the world. (The Bettmann Archive.)*

and proclaimed the Great Society. But the personal graciousness with which the Kennedys had managed to hold the country together was gone, and the young in particular looked elsewhere than to a White House that now was the scene of hootenannies and Texas-style barbecues.

The first object of youth's attention was a singing group from Britain, the Beatles. Formed in Liverpool in 1963, the Beatles overwhelmed England. With their arrival in America in January 1964, they created a full-fledged mania. Their heavily rhythmed music was called "beat," their lyrics were about love, their hair was long. They sold America one hundred million records that year, created thousands of rock groups in their image, and put most of America's boys and many of its young men into bangs or even longer hair. The general discontent with things American soon sent the young and not-so-young businessman out to buy European-style suits that featured wide lapels, wide ties, flared or bell-bottomed trousers, and nipped waists; even Brooks Brothers regretfully widened its lapels a Brooks-Brotherish eighth of an inch. In 1965, André Courrèges of France bared the feminine knee,

put feminine legs into boots, and discarded the bra. Mary Quant of London became the "high priestess of Mod" with the introduction of the miniskirt and the colored opaque hose of the "total look." King's Road and Carnaby Street became world-famous centers of fashion, as even middle-aged women began to sport skirts of utmost brevity. Discotheques were imported from London and Paris. A Supreme Court ruling that nudity in itself is not obscene started topless go-go dancers doing their thing. Boutiques featuring the latest eccentricities from abroad sprang up everywhere. In 1966 Yves St. Laurent of haute couture joined them with his first ready-to-wear boutique, Rive Gauche. There was the unisex look and the funky look and the psychedelic look, even a boom in second-hand theatrical costumes that the young wore to discos. Blacks declared that black is beautiful and began wearing African clothing and jewelry. The Afro hair style was worn by whites as well.

The beatniks of the fifties were replaced by the hippies and the street people, dropouts whose rejection of American values was total. By choice they lived in slums, refused to work and sometimes to bathe. Instead they held love-ins. The use of marijuana, pep pills, and speed penetrated all levels of society. Artists satirized America with paintings of Campbell Soup cans and comic-strip panels. Zen Buddhism attracted converts, as did Yoga and the Jesus Freaks. The 1966 Supreme Court decision permitting American publication of *Lady Chatterley's Lover* released a flood of pornography. Movie ratings, including "X," were introduced in 1968.

In short, the quiet, prosperous, and predictable life style of the fifties had at last left America, particularly young America, perilously bored. In the early sixties the Kennedys and Martin Luther King had channeled the yearning for something new into a massive crusade for civil rights; there were freedom rides to integrate public transportation and restaurants and lodgings in the South, voter registration drives, and the massive and magnificently dignified March on Washington in August 1963. The assassination of President Kennedy cost the nation not only its leader but that vision of a universal aristocracy the Kennedys had given America. America's energies were abruptly unfocused; the most telling thing about the sit-ins, student protests, and black urban riots that started in 1965 was that in the early days it was often impossible to determine what they were about. An administration building at a university would be seized, and then it would be necessary for the president and the trustees to wait for the occupiers to think up their nonnegotiable demands. Stores and homes in black neighborhoods would be burned by rioting blacks, and then the municipal authorities would have to wait until some community spokesman explained that the *real* cause of the riot was the lack of stores and homes. At one point, in Newark, the city's mobile maternity units were denounced by a community spokesman as a device for black genocide. The city hastily announced that the maternity units would be withdrawn. Whereupon Newark's black women unanimously demanded that the units be retained; what did the city mean by listening to "one loudmouth"? Planes were hijacked, banks and stores and offices were bombed, telephoned bomb threats caused the almost daily evacuation of hundreds of thousands of people from offices, factories, schools, and even homes.

But it soon became apparent that the number of full-fledged revolutionaries was very small indeed and that the media were not only exaggerating many of the incidents but creating others by providing coverage. Particularly in the colleges and universities, the hippie-radical-proletarian look was the rage. Students of both sexes wore tattered jeans, army fatigues and boots, long hair, beads, and bangles. Stenciled clenched fists replaced the fraternity and sorority pins of earlier generations. But "the look" was not the deed; most students were simply going along with a fashion. When one professor of economics asked a particularly villainous-looking graduating senior what he planned to do next, the professor was told to his astonishment that the fellow would join his father's stockbrokerage business. "I might as well be groovy while I can," the student added, with a mischievous all-American grin. And the newsmen who gave television coverage to the fifteen pickets at city hall somehow neglected to mention the 45,000 nonpickets watching the ballgame at the stadium.

There was no doubt, however, that the undeclared war in Vietnam was increasingly the focus of the disorder. In 1964 Lyndon Johnson was elected president in his own right, in part because he represented his Republican opponent, Barry Goldwater, as a dangerous radical who would escalate American involvement in Vietnam beyond the few thousand advisors sent by President Kennedy. Within a few months, President Johnson was doing all of the things he had warned America to expect of Goldwater. President Johnson gave his reasons, and at first the country accepted them. By by 1968 the protests were so tumultuous that neither President Johnson nor the members of his cabinet dared make a public appearance. President Johnson announced that he would not seek re-election, and the contest between Hawks and Doves turned the Democratic nominating convention in Chicago into a shambles. Richard Nixon, the Republican nominee, promised an honorable end to the war and won the election. Taking office in 1969, he proceeded to "Vietnamize" the struggle, turning over the ground fighting to the Vietnamese and bringing Americans home. America started to cool.

Fashion Emphasis, 1960: The Lull and the Storm

Fashion turned younger in 1960, with the pillbox hat and the sleeveless, collarless dress cut with exquisite seaming and detail. The dresses were sometimes fitted, sometimes semifitted with a jacket but always beautifully tailored. Skirts were a few inches below the knee. Pants were cut in the tight capri style and stopped at the ankle. Men's suits were a bit looser than before, with slightly wider lapels and two buttons instead of three.

The advent of the Beatles in 1963 put much of young adult America into the costume of the English teenager, with American elders following to the extent that the anatomy of age permitted. The skirt rose to above the knee, eventually reaching the brevity of short shorts. The legs were booted, sometimes to midthigh. The bra was discarded and Rudi Gernreich's topless bathing suit and the see-through blouse made a startling debut. Colored opaque hose added by Mary Quant to her miniskirt produced the "total look." Men's sideburns and hair grew longer and longer and moustaches became a rage. Lapels and ties were widened drastically, the waistline was narrowed, the bottom of the jacket was flared, and trousers were flared or bell-bottomed. Colors and patterns became electrifying; materials formerly considered suitable only for sportshirts were used for dress shirts and worn to the office. The shirt in the evening might be ruffled down the front and at the cuffs. Men also began wearing costume jewelry, not only rings but bracelets and necklaces, the latter with open shirts that also might appear in the evening and at the office. Boots encased the male foot and wigs were available for the male head. Hats for both sexes almost disappeared.

American teenagers, meanwhile, turned into cowboys and Indians (with the Indians in the majority): Levi pants and jackets were everywhere, often adorned with studs applied by the teenagers themselves. Fringed leather jackets, Indian headbands, and beaded moccasins enjoyed a vogue. Bibbed overalls were another rage. The unisex look also came in, with boys and girls dressed alike and wearing their hair in identical lengths; when the girls stopped wearing make-up, the sexes became nearly indistinguishable. Then, too, there was the "funky" look of the teen disco crowd, a deliberate combination of things that didn't go together, often employing secondhand theatrical costumes.

Collegians adopted the hippie-proletarian-radical look: army fatiques, tattered jeans, boots, long hair, stenciled clenched fists, no makeup for the coeds. Meanwhile, the real proletarians, the working young blacks, sported dazzling colors, high heels, platform soles, and Superfly hat brims. Other blacks created the "Black is beautiful" style, with African clothing and jewelry and "Afro" hair for both sexes.

The large manufacturers and stores discovered that they could not possibly keep up with so much profusion; boutiques appeared everywhere, each offering "something else," as fashion stopped coming from the designer's salon and started coming from the streets. Yves St. Laurent in 1966 joined the revolution by becoming the first haute couture designer to go into ready-to-wear with his boutique, Rive Gauche. Both St. Laurent and Courrèges introduced the pantsuit in the mid 1960s; and women, tired of deciding whether to wear the mini, midi, or maxi, turned to the pantsuit in droves. A large number of women stuck with the mini until 1972, however.

The fabric innovation of the decade was polyester double-knit, but denim was everywhere.

The trend of the sixties seemed to be in the direction of youth unbridled.

1970–

The seventies, the decade of America's bicentennial, produced a quiet America. The Vietnam War ended, relations with Russia and China improved, and inflation and recession sobered the young with the knowledge that a good job or even any job might be hard to come by. There was a clear trend to the natural and the traditional in life style. Make-up was subdued (the "natural look"), home cooking came back into fashion,

FIGURE 1.21 *The mid 70s revived the elegant look for women. This subtly fitted knee-length silk dress is from the house of Chanel. (Courtesy of the French Embassy Press and Information Division.)*

there was a rage for herbs and health foods, and for the first time in American history the great metropolitan areas began to lose population. The new magnets were smallish towns in rural regions such as New Hampshire, Idaho, Oregon, the South, and the Southwest. Older parts of cities meanwhile staged a comeback with the restoration of eighteenth- and nineteenth-century homes to their original graciousness. Having ended the confusion of maxi, mini, and midi dress lengths by opting for the pantsuit, by the middle of the decade women started wearing dresses again, with the hemline a bit below the knee and a feminine, soft look to the rest. Men moved away from bells and beads and into businesslike suits and ties. The button-down shirt, symbol of all that was up-tight in the sixties, in the seventies came back strong, and the dapper young executive sported a vest. America's air and lakes and rivers were growing cleaner, birds and other endangered wildlife staged a comeback, organic gardening and farming boomed, and colleges of agriculture and forestry reported a doubling in enrollment. The bicentennial celebration was marked by the magnificence of the Tall Ships and fireworks and a revival of national pride that left few Americans unmoved. By 1977, America had reached a point where Ms. Betty Friedan confessed to a passion for gourmet cookery, Rudi Gernreich of topless fame was designing underwear for Lily of France and "nonshock" clothes for Atelier 7 of Los Angeles, and the new president, Jimmy Carter, insisted on walking to the White House after his inauguration at the Capitol.

And what will the future bring? Looking back, we can see that the twenties, the forties, and the sixties were dominated by youth. Will the eighties be a decade when youth will rise again to command the fashion spotlight? Surveys of population trends made in 1977 indicate that, if birth and mortality rates continue to fall, the present median age of 28.9 will rise to 30 in 1981, to 35 by 2000, and to nearly 40 by 2030. There will be more than 52 million Americans—double the present number—over 65 by 2030. It's possible, of course, that the fashion for smaller families will be reversed by some unexpected development, but at present all the weight of the ecology

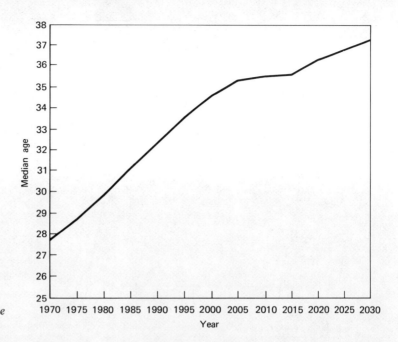

FIGURE 1.22 *Median age in the United States, 1970–2030.*

movement, economic trends, government policy, and public opinion is on the side of "the graying of America." An older America may very well choose to *look* young, as older Americans did in the twenties, forties, and sixties. However, it's doubtful that the young themselves will be permitted to determine for their elders which fashions bespeak youth. The bright and crisp models introduced by Paris in 1976–1977 suggest that a "youthful adult" look will be the fashion of tomorrow.

Fashion Emphasis, 1970: Straightening Out

The cooling of America during the seventies was the result of an extraordinary series of domestic and international sensations, and fashion, too, turned conservative by lurches. The decade began with the pantsuit dominating women's clothes, the "peacock look" men's. The winter of 1971 saw a rage for short shorts, rechristened "hot pants" and worn, sometimes with a slashed midi as a teaser, in the evening; with the arrival of summer, hot pants went out. The young wore patchwork and printed T-shirts that year. In 1972 the "costume look" disappeared; it was no longer the vogue to appear to be a cowboy, cowgirl, Indian,

Vietnamese guerrilla, or beggar. Women turned to classic, wearable clothes, and the button-down shirt was revived for men. Teenage boys, however, tottered about on high heels. The dress was revived in 1973 and young males had an understandable desire to look like Olympic hero Mark Spitz (the moustache was in, and so was Mr. Spitz's red, white, and blue star-spangled swimming suit). 1974 was a year of revivals, spurred by the publicity for the film The Great Gatsby; *full-cut white suits appeared on sooty city streets. In the nation's colleges, there was a rage for streaking—dashing naked through crowded pub-*

lic places. The leisure suit was a sensation of 1975; 1976 saw its passing. Red, white, and blue were the fashionable colors of the bicentennial year.

By 1977 the conservative trend was firmly entrenched. Paris, traditional center of fashion, produced three sensational collections, those of St. Laurent, Dior, and Givenchy. Skirts were at midcalf, colors were bright, and lines and materials crisply contemporary. Ira Newmark, president of Bergdorf Goodman, contracted in advance to buy the styles from all three collections and was hailed as a seer. Makers of men's clothing confirmed the dress-up trend. According to John D. Gray, chairman of Hart, Schaffner, & Marx, "There is a tremendous interest in dressing up, and young people who formerly showed no interest in shirts and ties are now wearing them." Levi Straus was pushing a line of vested corduroy suits. Checkrooms in fashionable restaurants reported that more men than women were wearing fur coats.

The entry of the famous designers into ready-to-wear continued during the seventies, with Alix Grès the only remaining exclusive designer of custom-made clothes in Paris. Many of the designers of women's clothing were also designing for men, and vice versa.

The boutique craze subsided during the seventies, as the designers and department stores once again assumed fashion leadership.

The trend of the decade was toward the traditional and the elegant.

CONCLUSIONS

In review, *fashion essence* is the emotion, the event, the vibration cast upon the waters of the pond; its *reflection* becomes the *fashion*. Fashion is a barometer of the times and for this reason, when doing a study of history, fashion becomes an excellent, additional resource. Anatole France, the writer and scholar, felt that if he could ever return to this world, he could know what it had done politically, socially, economically, and technologically by looking only at a review of the fashions.

Reading about the decades of the twentieth century enables you to develop an understanding of the changes that have come about in our life styles. These changes must be correlated with fashion changes. Fashion reflects what a culture is *thinking*; what it is doing, in politics, in work, and in its recreation; how people behave morally; and how financially stable or successful a country is.

Now that you have learned the first lesson of fashion, *reflection*, the next is to learn the fundamentals of fashion, *fashion concepts* and *fashion analysis*. You cannot do fashion analysis without understanding the *concept* of reflection. Reflection, very simply, can be read as what has been, but analysis and prediction are the life blood of the fashion business.

END OF CHAPTER GUIDE

Review, Discussion, and Evaluation

Study of this chapter should enable students to
A. Develop and give evidence of the following kinds of competencies:
  1. Awareness of the major changes that have come about in American life style over the last 75 years.
  2. Understanding of some of the social, cultural, political, economic, and technological changes reflected in the fashions of each decade.
  3. Ability to identify the impact of youth on the decades of the 1920s, 1940s, and 1960s.
  4. Ability to recognize certain fashion reflections related to the Depression of the 1930s and the years during and after World War I and World War II.
  5. Some ability to speculate on the fashion reflection apparent in the 1970s.
B. Develop and/or clarify concepts related to the following key words or phrases:
  1. fashion 2. life styles 3. social and cultural aspects 4. economic and political aspects 5. technological aspects 6. factory-made goods

7. Gibson Girl 8. women's suffrage 9. film industry 10. Broadway 11. Roaring Twenties 12. Prohibition 13. Temperance 14. movie palaces 15. jazz singers 16. flappers 17. stock market crash 18. Great Depression 19. FDR 20. New Deal 21. mass production 22. defense workers 23. WAVES 24. WACS 25. victory gardens 26. bobby-soxers 27. jitterbug 28. jukebox 29. Hiroshima 30. A-bomb 31. teenagers 32. suburbia 33. television 34. civil rights 35. The New Look "sack" dress; chemise 36. rock and roll 37. touch football 38. computers 39. the Great Society 40. hippie love-ins 41. flower children 42. Establishment 43. drug culture 44. black power 45. miniskirt 46. unisex 47. pantsuit

Extended Classroom Learning Experiences

A. Research fashion magazines since 1970 and collect illustrations to reflect the spirit of the decade.
   1. Consider some of the social, political, technological, and economic events of the 1970s and note your own fashion reflections.
   2. Write a paper presenting your findings and draw your own conclusions as to why fashion is the way it is today.
B. Select two decades and answer the following questions concerning the period. After you have answered the questions and have given the feel of the era, relate the economic, political, technological, and social events to the fashions of the decade and incorporate your own ideas as to their "why." You may not be able to answer every question about every decade.
   1. *Political*
      a. Were there any wars? If so, how did the nation respond?
      b. Was the president successful in advancing his programs and philosophies?
      c. Was the president well liked by the majority of the people?
      d. Did the administration pass much legislation? Of what nature?
      e. What did the general mood of the country seem to be?
   2. *Economic*
      a. How do you view the economic level of the decade? Depressed, prosperous, stable? Explain.
      b. What major production was occurring?
      c. What were the prime sources of income for the masses?
      d. How was the manufacturing industry progressing?
      e. How much spendable income did the masses seem to have? What were they buying?
      f. What was government money being spent on?
      g. How did you view the stock market during this decade?
   3. *Social*
      a. What was the woman's role in the decade?
      b. What social legislation was passed in Congress: Labor, civil rights, women's rights, education, others?
      c. What was the moral behavior?
      d. What were the work and social activities of youngsters, teenagers, and adults?
      e. How much leisure time did children and adults seem to have?
      f. What were the trends in housing?
      g. What events occurred in sports, music, dance, art, literature, and the movies?
      h. What were the religious patterns?
      i. Who were some outstanding people of the decade? Why?
   4. *Technological:*
      a. What type of inventions, discoveries, or progress was being made?
      b. Was there money available to spend on technologic advancements? Why?
      c. Did the decade seem to progress technologically as a whole? Why?
      d. What were the communication and transportation systems? How do they affect fashion?
C. If possible, visit a museum that has a costume collection. If this is not possible, study a history-of-costume book for examples to include in your report.
D. Read two or more of the articles listed here or research current periodicals or trade journals and select two or more articles related to one of the concepts suggested in "Review, Discussion, and Evaluation."
   1. Prepare note cards while reading each article.
   2. Using your note cards, write a brief summary indicating the relation of each article to concepts presented in this chapter.
   3. Using your note cards, give an oral report in your class and point out the important facts included in the articles.

Suggested Articles

DAVIES, JESSICA. "Can Fashion Be Immoral?" *Ladies Home Journal*, January 1965, pp. 92e–92h.

HARTMANN, GEORGE W. "Clothing: Personal Problems and Social Issue." *Journal of Home Economics*, June 1949, pp. 295–98.

JOHNSTON, MOIRA. "What Will Happen to the Gray Flannel Suit?" *Journal of Home Economics*, November 1972, pp. 5–12.

MACLEISH, ARCHIBALD. "Rediscovering the Simple Life." *McCalls*, April 1972, pp. 79–82.

ROSENCRANZ, MARY LOU. "Social and Psychological Approaches to Clothing Research." *Journal of Home Economics*, January 1965, pp. 26–29.

———. "The Communes Come to America," *Life*, July 1969, pp. 16–23.

WARNING, MARGARET. "Future Explorations in Clothing." *Journal of Home Economics*, October 1960, pp. 646–51.

NOTES

[1] "The Rag Business: 7th Avenue Goes to 20 Wall Street," *Forbes*, July 1, 1964, pp. 24–29.

[2] *Random House Dictionary of the English Language*, unabridged edition. New York: Random House, 1962, p. 487.

[3] *This Fabulous Century*. Volume 3: 1920–1930. New York: Time-Life Books, 1969, p. 30.

[4] *This Fabulous Century*. Volume 5: 1940–1950. New York: Time–Life Books, p. 70.

2

Fashion Concepts

Fashion—what is it all about? Why is it that the clothing we wear always seems right for our way of life at a given time? And why do we choose to wear what we do? A designer may produce thousands of designs—beautiful, elaborate, exotic, or elegant—but if they are not right for us in our particular moment in history, they will not be accepted. Design must reflect what people are thinking, feeling, and doing. Can anyone imagine Marie Antoinette moving about her palace in a pair of hip-hugger jeans? Certainly not, no more than we can imagine a teenager of today running around in an enormous hoopskirt and a 12-inch powdered pompadour wig. We wear what is right for our way of life.

Chapter 2 explores the realm of fashion, giving the necessary terms and definitions that relate to fashion and the fashion business—explaining, exploring, and probing the phenomenon of fashion itself.

THE IMPACT OF FASHION

Fashion, like music, is a universal language, accessible to everyone and innately understood. Fashion needs no interpreter to be an international communicator. It is a common denominator in the Western world. Non-Western cultures are bound by dress codes that have their own system of fashion communication.

Fashion contributes to an individual's emotional life as few other things can; the clothes we wear have the power to create feelings of exhilaration or moods of depression, cause conflict or approval between husbands and wives or parents and children, and arouse feelings of jealousy between friends. Fashion is the intangible force that encourages men as a group to wear their hair long or short, women to show a lot of leg with the miniskirt or to cover up with a midcalf length, and both sexes to select shoes with pointed toes or clunky platforms. Fashion is integrated into everyday life. Often we are as unaware of its impact on our lives as we are of the air we breathe.

The influence of fashion is seen in clothing, food, hair styles, architecture, automobiles, advertising, home furnishings, kitchen appliances, and packaging. It is seen in store windows, newspapers, magazines, television, movies, in everyone's home, and on everyone's back. Fashion surrounds us and there is no avoiding it. Those individuals who insist that they are oblivious to and unconcerned with fashion are only deceiving themselves; "antifashion" is itself a fashion. We live in an atmosphere of fashion related to our life style. It cannot be escaped.

This theory is reflected by our consumer purchases. The livelihood of merchants does not depend on our purchases for "survival needs." Rarely do we need fashion, in the sense that we need air, water, food; we buy to satisfy our individual emotional desires. The dynamic phenomenon of fashion has become an integral part of our lives.

We are creatures of change; we select a new color for a dress or our hair, a new design for pants or a car or a house, a new texture for a coat or a couch, a new pet to care for, a new hobby to consume our time—all on the basis of fashion. The things we *most often purchase we do not "need."*

Certainly you have noticed by now that fashion is not limited to clothing. However, fashion changes seem to occur faster and more often in apparel than, for example, in home furnishings, automobiles, or packaging design. For this reason, the term *fashion* has almost become synonymous with apparel and accessories. It is not: fashion is everywhere and is related to everything we do. Fashion reflects a way of life, and fashion changes occur in everything we use or enjoy, including all forms of music, literature, and the graphic arts. In the remainder of the text, however, we will be referring specifically to fashion in the apparel industry.

FASHION TERMINOLOGY

To be able to communicate in the fashion world, you must understand the terminology. As in every other specialized field, fashion has its own vocabulary. The most important definition to begin with is the word *fashion.*

For many years, people have been defining fashion—and each from his or her own vantage point. Sociologists see it as one thing, economists view it differently. Psychologists generally feel that there are indications of sexual impulses in the pattern of dress. Here are a few definitions from the perspective of various professions of the word *fashion:*

1. Dictionary: "(a) a prevailing custom or style of dress, etiquette, procedure, etc. . . . (b) conventional usage in dress, manners, etc."[1]
2. Economist: "Fashion is nothing more or less than the prevailing style at any given time."[2]
3. Economist: "Fashion, defined in its most general sense, is the pursuit of novelty for its own

sake."[3] ". . . change in the design of things for decorative purposes."[4]
4. Retailer: "Fashion is a conception of what is currently appropriate."[5]
5. Marketing professor: "Fashion adoption is a process of social contagion by which a new style or product is adopted by the consumer after commercial introduction by the designer or manufacturer."[6]
6. Home economist: "A manifestation of collective behavior and as such represents the popular, accepted, prevailing style at any given time."[7]
7. Sociologist: "A collective phenomenon and has an objective existence apart from any individual."[8]
8. Psychoanalyst: "Stripped to its essentials, fashion is no more than a series of permutations of seven basic themes, each theme being a part of the female body: the breasts or neckline; wasit or abdomen; hips; buttocks; legs; arms; and length or circumference of the body itself. Parts of the body 'appear' and 'disappear' as the theme of fashion changes, and one and then another is emphasized by succeeding styles."[9]

We prefer to adhere to the simple statement of fashion authority Paul Nystrom in 1928 that *"Fashion is nothing more or less than the prevailing style at a given time."*[10] This is the purest definition of fashion. Any additions or elaborations entering into the realm of the "why" of fashion will be discussed later in this chapter.

The concept of *style* is defined in various publications:

1. In *Clothing for Moderns:* "It [style], in dress or any other art, refers to the characteristic or distinctive form, outline, or shape an article possesses."[11]
2. In *Random House Unabridged Dictionary:* "A particular kind, sort, or type as with reference to form, appearance, or character."[12]
3. In *Inside the Fashion Business:* "A style of clothing is considered to be a product with specific characteristics that distinguishes it from another product of the same type."[13]

What has been said is that style in clothing is a particular characteristic of design, silhouette, or line. For example, there is the flared, the stovepipe, the capri, the slim jim, and the bell-bottom pant; the A-line, the pleated, the gathered, or the gored skirt; there is the capped, the leg-of-mutton, the bishop, or the straight sleeve; or there is the Peter Pan, mandarin, or cowl collar. Each of these possesses its particular design characteristics. Each is referred to as a *style*.

Fashion is the prevailing style at a given time. Style is the particular design. Often, the words fashion and style are used interchangeably, but they are not synonymous. A style, such as the hip-hugger jean, will not always be in fashion, but it will always retain the unique cut and design that makes it a hip-hugger jean. Its design characteristics will never change, but it may or may not be in fashion. It will not always be the acceptable or the "fashionable" thing to wear.

Other fashion terms are

Trend The visible direction in which fashion is moving, the style characteristics that are evident for a coming season. For example, the "naive chemise" was a trend introduced by couture designer Yves St. Laurent in 1974; the remaining season determined whether it would become a fashion.

Apparel In retailing, the term *apparel* applies only to outerwear (coats, suits, dresses, sportswear, etc.) for women, misses, and juniors. However, with common usage, it has come to be known as any fashion item that is worn or carried by men, women, or children.

Classic A style that endures over a long period of time. The classic may undergo minor changes. An example is the shirtwaist dress, a classic with variations in the type of sleeve or skirt.

Couture The French word for sewing. Reference is made to "the couture" as the design originator in the sense that the designer develops his or her own ideas.

Couturier The French word for dressmaker or designer, referring to the male.

Couturière The female designer in the couture house.

High fashion The innovation or introduction of a new style generally accepted by a limited group of elite customers. The design is usually very expensive and may be extreme.

Haute couture The French expression whose English translation is "fine sewing." It refers to high fashion, which the designer creates, produces, and presents.

Mass fashion The style at a given time that has been accepted by the mass market. It is produced and sold as a volume fashion item.

Fad A relatively short-lived fashion. A fad has quick acceptance and goes out with the same speed.

Ford A best-seller, also often referred to as a "runner" or "hot item." It generally has strong customer demand, and a good rate of salability; it is produced by many different manufacturers in a variety of price lines at the same time.

FASHION INDUSTRIES

Fashion industries refers to all of activities that surround the marketing process that provides the consumer with goods. The vast fashion industries encompass the various efforts of (1) the creators who provide the thrust of innovation; (2) the suppliers that supply or manufacture textiles, furs, leathers, plastics, findings, and trims; (3) the manufacturers that produce the actual apparel and accessories for the ready-to-wear market; (4) the sales representatives that are the market associations on a national, regional, and local level; and (5) the retail outlets. In addition there are many fashion-related services: pattern companies, magazines, trade journals, modeling agencies, advertising agencies, publicity agencies, consultants, buying offices, and others directly connected with the promotion and sale of fashion and fashion goods. (See Figure 2.1.)

FASHION CHARACTERISTICS

In reading and studying the theory of fashion, one realizes that fashion is an intangible entity. The question "What is fashion?" can be difficult to answer because there are so many things to say about it. It can become so elusive that one will

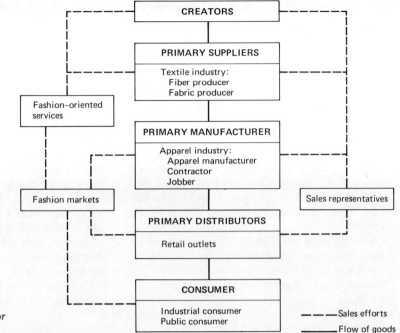

FIGURE 2.1 *Flow chart for the fashion industries.*

have to grope and stumble to find the right words. Fashion is an ever-changing facet of our being. However, the following discussion presents an organized, systematic method of identifying fashion characteristics.

Although fashion is an ever-changing force, there are certain statements that can be made about it that are *absolute*. These will be referred to as the *Four Absolutes of Fashion*. They are

1. Prevailing style . . . The "What is it?"
2. Reflection . . . The "Where does it come from?"
3. Change . . . The "Why does it change and how?"
4. Acceptance . . . The "How do you know it is a fashion?"

The Four Absolutes of Fashion

PREVAILING STYLE

Fashion is the prevailing style at a given time. This is not only the purest definition of fashion but it also is the first absolute of fashion. The statement can always be made comfortably, knowing that it is irrevocable. It can be determined for any given period of time, past or present. If necessary, the reader should review the difference between fashion and style.

REFLECTION

The answers to the questions "Why do we have it?" "Where does it come from?" and "What made it happen?" define the second absolute of fashion, reflection. In Chapter 1 the reflection theory is applied to the twentieth century—the life styles reflecting (1) the economic structure of our society; (2) social changes; (3) political situations; and (4) technological advancements. The premise is that these four factors influence fashion. They create a demand for specific fashions. Just about anything that happens can be relegated to one of these four aspects.

Fashion trends reflect the changes in what a culture is *thinking*, *feeling*, and *doing*, both in work and recreation; how an era is *behaving mor-*

ally; and how stable or successful a country is *financially*.

Some readers are surely thinking that it is not society that creates the fashions, but the designers. They may imagine the designers conjuring up designs in their salons, producing them, and then using the media to twist the consumer's arm to buy them. They also may think that the designer and the manufacturer deliberately make the consumer's closetful of clothing obsolete so that the customer will buy more. This view of fashion would make the lives of designers and manufacturers and retailers very easy indeed, but it is refuted by facts and figures. Consider the fate of the "Bold Look" for men at the end of World War II.

Regardless of how erratic it may appear at times, fashion is not an arbitrary or meaningless expression. It is the result of human behavior: "Fashion is sociology of the hoof."[14] It reflects a way of life.

The designer's role today is to sense what consumers want. The designer—and the retailer as well—must keep fingertips on the pulses of consumers each season to know what they want, what they will buy, whether they want more of the same or if they are ready for a change. The successful designer is then able to present designs compatible with the feelings of the society.

James Laver, a British social historian, states in his book *Taste and Fashion* that he feels there is a definite resemblance between women's fashions and the architectural design of any given period. If given a historical picture with a fashionable woman in it, Mr. Laver can date the picture to within one year in the nineteenth century, to within two years in the eighteenth century, and to within ten years in the seventeenth century. He is able to do this because the fashions are appropriate for their time.

How does a designer or retailer know if the time is right for a change or what the fickle con-

FIGURE 2.2 *The flowing tunic of ancient Greece reflects the designs of certain classical Greek architectural details.*

FIGURE 2.3 *Similarities of design in medieval European dress and architectural details.*

sumer will want? He knows by being *aware* of what the economy is doing; by being aware of what political events are brewing; by observing social happenings; by keeping up with the latest in technology; and by *interpreting* this knowledge into fashion trends. The sensitive creators of fashion act as a barometer for the fashion world by charting the climatic conditions; they produce what is desired.

To this point, generalities have been expressed. Now it is time to deal with the specifics of how to read the four environmental influences on fashion: economic, social, political, and technological.

Economic Influences. A country's general economic structure and economic vacillations influence both the speed of fashion changes and the trends themselves. Art historian Quentin Bell, in his work *On Human Finery*, relates the economic progress of a country to the length of retention of the traditional national dress. Bell

states that countries with high economic development abandon traditional national dress sooner than countries characterized by sluggish economic progress. England, the leader of the Western world in the industrial revolution, was the first country of the Western world to give up traditional national dress. Bell directs his attention to Greece, Russia, Spain, and Persia (now Iran), countries that demonstrated a slow rate of economic development. They retained national dress when countries such as Germany, Belgium, Denmark, and Japan were abandoning theirs. Perhaps, before advancing further, some economic terms should be identified to clarify population spending.

Gross National Product (GNP) Value of a nation's total output of goods and services in any calendar year.
Personal income The portion of a nation's income that reaches the individual.
Disposable income The amount of money an

individual has left after taxes are paid; commonly referred to as "take-home pay."

Discretionary income The amount of spending money left after providing for basic necessities.

DIFFUSION OF WEALTH. Fashion concentrates on the wealth of a nation—on the groups with the largest discretionary incomes. Those who have more to spend, spend more on fashion.

When studying historical costume, one places importance on the dress of the wealthy and the powerful. Little time is devoted to peasant dress. Historical costumes reflect the fact that fashion is dependent on those who control the greatest spending power of a society.

At the turn of the century, it was expensive to be fashionable. The nation's wealth was primarily controlled by a small group, "high society" and the merely "rich" on its fringes. Though most Americans could afford readymade versions of the latest styles, few could enjoy the indulgence of a high fashion that included such accessories as diamond tiaras. But the twentieth century was to bring many structural economic changes.

Over the course of years, with the growth and expansion of the great middle class, came a wide diffusion of wealth. Figure 2.4 shows the social-class breakdown of the total population, illustrating that 71 per cent of the population falls into the huge groups made up of the upper-lower, lower-middle, and middle classes. These three groups represent the steady earners who draw reasonably good to very good incomes and control the spending power of the country.

Another assumption that can be made is that the more liberated a society becomes, the greater is its economic development, which results in a more widespread diffusion of wealth, thus creating a greater demand for fashion items.

Many factors account for the economic rise of the middle class. The United States has a liberated middle class primarily because of its basic ideology. Although the middle class has been in existence for almost two hundred years, much of that time has been spent in learning how to use the freedoms that we have won. Herein lies the basis for our existing affluent middle-class society: the freedom of choice to pursue creative thought and work patterns; the freedom to speak

out; and the freedom of change and challenge. These privileges are conducive to the attainment of growth, wealth, and achievement. Thus, the peoples of the free world function in an environment of independent and collective productivity and accomplishment.

During the last three quarters of a century, we have watched vast changes in the economic structure of our country. Today, there are often two incomes in one family. There are shorter working hours for both the skilled and unskilled laborers. Advanced technology has given a tremendous boost to our economic growth. Minority groups—racial, ethnic, and women's—are being given equal economic opportunities in the labor force. The women's liberation movement and the racial strife and the youth revolt of the 1960s have had their impact on the economic structure. The credit system is flourishing, enabling people to purchase more and buy it "on time." Fashion has felt the influence of each of these.

Compare the fashion of the United States with that of Communist Russia. Americans are free to select or reject the fashions that match their desires. An American can buy what he can afford—and often what he cannot afford. We exist in a democracy that encourages freedom of choice and independence. In Russia, anyone who wears jeans is considered a potential traitor; an American tourist who sells or even gives away a pair of jeans is condemned.

ECONOMIC STABILITY. Fashion is affected by recession, depression, inflation, and the "good times" of the economy. During recession, depression, or inflation, discretionary income may become minimal or nonexistent. The individual may choose to invest or save his money and curtail the indulgences of life. People may buy fewer fashion items and use them longer. This may slow fashion changes and, in turn, slow the total marketing process, as was seen in late 1974 and 1975.

Skirt lengths, which affect dress design seem to correspond to the stock market—the economic highs and lows. When the market is down, so are skirt lengths. There are two theories on this phenomenon: one is *pragmatic* and the other is *hypothetical*.

The pragmatic theory assumes that when the

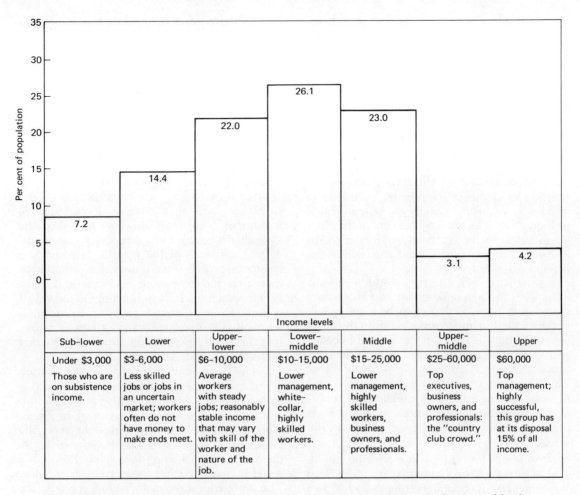

Sub-lower	Lower	Upper-lower	Lower-middle	Middle	Upper-middle	Upper
Under $3,000	$3–6,000	$6–10,000	$10–15,000	$15–25,000	$25–60,000	$60,000
Those who are on subsistence income.	Less skilled jobs or jobs in an uncertain market; workers often do not have money to make ends meet.	Average workers with steady jobs; reasonably stable income that may vary with skill of the worker and nature of the job.	Lower management, white-collar, highly skilled workers.	Lower management, highly skilled workers, business owners, and professionals.	Top executives, business owners, and professionals: the "country club crowd."	Top management; highly successful, this group has at its disposal 15% of all income.

FIGURE 2.4 *Distribution of families by income level. (From the* U.S. Fact Book, *prepared by the Bureau of the Census. New York: Grosset and Dunlap, 1974.)*

economy is depressed, the price of the fabric will decline. The trade is then in need of additional consumption to give it an economic boost. One way to solve this problem is to make skirts fuller and longer; this new style will create demand and money will be poured into a depressed industry. As the new lengths are accepted, the price of the fabric goes up. To compensate for the price increase and to keep cost figures within a reasonable price range, skirts will then become shorter.

The hypothetical, and somewhat psychological theory is that when the economy is depressed, so are the consumers. The image conveyed by a longer skirt is somewhat more "depressed" than the image conveyed by the shorter skirt. And consumers buy fashion according to their moods.

Life is more frivolous in times of an affluent economy. People are more carefree, spend more money, and spend it more recklessly, exhibiting very few restraints. More jobs are available and there is a lower percentage of unemployment. Classic examples of good times are the Roaring Twenties and the late 1960s and early 1970s. Skirts were high and so was living.

During the Depression of the 1930s, money

was tight, prices were down, and so were hemlines. Fashion focused on those with spending power. This small elite group was not financially crippled by the crash of the market in 1929. This segment of the population controlled the wealth of the country and dictated fashion.

The recession of 1974 coincided with a lengthening of skirts, but it did not correspond to the pragmatic theory. The 1974 recession was accompanied by inflation. Fabric prices, as well as all other prices, were high, but still skirt lengths began to come down. There was, however, a shortage of discretionary income in the large middle-class consumer segment, as represented in Figure 2.4. The lower 87 per cent of the chart was affected by the recession of 1974. Perhaps this particular economic period is related to the hypothetical theory.

FASHION IS NOT A PRICE. Although fashion reflects the economic situation, fashion does not relate to price. Fashion may be found in any of the smallest manufacturing plants in the small towns that dot the landscape from coast to coast, as well as in the gold-encrusted labels of the couture of Seventh Avenue or the salons of Paris. The American system of mass production and the existence of a liberated middle class makes fashion available to the masses. America leads the way in being the best-dressed country in the world.

Anyone can buy fashion at a price he can afford. A pair of woman's pants may sell for $8.95 at the corner family shopping center or $59.95 in a designer boutique. The quality of the fabric and construction may differ, but the fashion "look" can be the same. Fashion is no longer only for those with money.

Summary of Economic Influences
1. Fashion is influenced by the economic factors of recession, depression, inflation, and affluence and may be either accelerated or retarded by these developments.
2. Fashion flourishes in an economically progressive society.
3. Fashion focuses on the segment that controls the spending power of a nation.
4. The more money an individual earns, the more fashion goods he or she can buy.

5. A liberated middle class increases the economic development of a nation.
6. Fashion may be bought in various price ranges. Fashion does not relate to price.

Social Changes. There is a persistent trend of thought that fashion is social in origin—that it is neither a creative dream nor a business directive. Fashion truly does reflect the sociological mood of a time. Fashion reacts to sociological occurrences, demands by market groups, current events, and personalities of the time.

SOCIOLOGICAL OCCURRENCES. Education is both the foremost ambassador of fashion and a sociological occurrence. With the individual's freedom in a democracy and the increased affluence of the middle class comes a greater dispersion of education, for people have more time and more money to spend on it. Education accelerates fashion because the individual is more aware of what is going on in his environment. On the other hand, a lack of knowledge and of exposure to education is a factor that normally retards fashion.

Before the advent of television, the child from ethnic or religious groups that held strict clothing traditions might have spent his early years unaware of another way of dress until he began school. Also, the deprived child could be equally unaware if it were not for public education. By the simple act of going to school, the child's world is broadened and deepened by experience. The more education an individual receives, the broader his world becomes.

Another assumption that can be made of education is that the greater the amount of education received, the higher the desired standard of living. The accomplishment of this goal is directly related to greater economic development, thus resulting in more discretionary income for the individual who, in turn, has greater purchasing power.

Changes in geographic living patterns can influence fashion. A transient society creates a spread of fashion. With progress the keynote of the twentieth century, families move more frequently into new geographic locations, with the result that customs, practices, and fashion from all geographic areas are exchanged.

The move to the suburbs in the 1950s was another sociological occurrence that left its mark on fashion. To join the mass egress from the cities became a status symbol.

In the suburbs, women began to dispense with the "street dress" for shopping. Instead, they adopted sportswear for almost all occasions except the dress-up affairs of church, teas, weddings, funerals, and evening parties. Shopping centers began cropping up all over the country to accommodate this new suburban shopper and to cater to her demands.

Children became organized and needed fashion for everything. Little girls were provided with dancing costumes, leotards, twirler outfits, riding clothes. Little League was formed for boys, and manufacturers began turning out thousands of baseball, football, and basketball uniforms.

FIGURE 2.6 *Today women's tennis wear is simple, airy, and brief—designed to be functional and fashionable.*

FIGURE 2.5 *Women's tennis wear at the turn of the century—cumbersome full-length skirt, fussy blouse, hat. Only the footwear—sneakers—differed from everyday street dress.*

Another sociological phenomenon that occurs is the appearance of *crazes and fads*, the "attention getters" that attract the public's fancy: the Davy Crockett and hula hoop crazes of the fifties; the dances that the young adopt, such as the Charleston of the twenties, the jitterbug of the forties and fifties, and the rock and roll of the sixties and seventies. The games and toys of each decade that children respond to are a further instance, as is athletic hero worship such as that accorded Babe Ruth in the twenties and Hank Aaron in the seventies.

Current events are another realm of sociological occurrences that affect a person's particular world by influencing what he does and what he wears to do it in. Whether he is a spectator or a participant, current events can influence fashion trends; men watch golf matches in "Arnold Palmer" styles, for instance.

An individual's vocation will influence his or her fashion choices. Whether one works on Wall Street in New York City or in the coal mines of Pennsylvania makes an obvious difference in the clothes one wears.

The types of entertainment in which one participates also determine fashion choices. The working person has more leisure time now than in the early part of the century. What this individual does with the free time will determine the type of clothing needed or desired.

Participation in tennis, swimming, bowling, horse racing, football, and the Olympics requires specific clothing. Then, too, fashions change in athletic garments as well as in other fashion apparel. One chooses appropriate attire even as a spectator. College and pro football stimulated the production of jackets, rain gear, and dresses for the fans—often identifying with the team by either color or insignia.

The cultural aspect of current happenings of art, music, and literature can affect a person's life style and dress, particularly if he is a participant. The rock festivals of the sixties dictated a certain type of dress, as does an evening at the opera.

During the late sixties, an ecological movement was under way—in effect, an extended current event. People realized they were destroying their environments by a gluttonous and barbaric expenditure of the earth's resources. The United States, by virtue of its affluence, was one of the foremost leaders of waste. Youth again came to the front of this movement with a back-to-nature theme. People were encouraged not to buy or wear fur coats or use other products made from wild animals. They were encouraged to wear fake furs or furs from animals specifically grown for commercial purposes.

During the height of the ecology movement dresses designed with a peasant or country look appeared, and fabric design reflected the movement. The Western look was popular. Natural fibers again became strong on the fashion scene, with muslins and denims in the lead. Organic and natural foods became popular. Laws were passed requiring that detergents and plastic items be biodegradable.

FASHION DEMAND BY GROUPS Various consumer groups demand that certain fashion items be produced to meet their specific needs and desires. Examples of consumer groups are teenagers, the elderly, the handicapped, certain races, ethnic groups, young working singles, religious sects, street gangs, and clubs.

The youth movement of the 1960s is probably the most obvious example of dynamic group influence on life styles and fashion change that we have seen in the twentieth century. As stated in Chapter 1, the movement began in the early sixties when the Kennedys occupied the White House. There was a feeling of youth and vigor in the air. Everyone seemed to want to *feel* young and *look* young. *Women's Wear Daily* referred to the movement as "youth power" or "youth snap." The baby boom of the late 1940s created a consumer group. Teenagers and those in their early twenties were used to being indulged. One of the things they demanded was *fashion*. Major stores around the country began designating more square footage to Junior departments, placing them on the first floor and offering Saturday entertainment of music, dancing, and free Cokes to lure teenagers in to buy.

During the middle sixties, controversy over the Vietnam War and racial disturbances were beginning to incite rebellion in youth groups. Moral behavior began to deteriorate into "free love," premarital sex, and unmarried couples living together. Moral behavior in the sixties and seventies was reflected in such fashions as the topless bathing suit, the no-bra look, see-through tops and bottoms, the string bikini, mini- and microskirts, nudity on the beaches, and "streaking," first seen in the spring of 1974. Streaking, or running nude, except perhaps for a face mask, became a favorite college pastime. It always was done in front of a group.

The youth rebellion brought with it the use of drugs and the development of a culture referred to as "hip." The hippy impact on youth fashion was unprecedented. The culture first appeared in Haight-Ashbury in San Francisco in the early sixties and rapidly spread across the United States. The dress was anything found in grandmother's attic or pile of discarded clothes. Each hippy would put together his "look," his "thing," which became his signature. Over the next few years it evolved into the "jean look," reaping bil-

FIGURE 2.7 *As the 1960s progressed, so did the hemline. By 1967 the erogenous zone was at least six inches above the knee. Left: The "Twiggy" look that was popular in the mid-1960s. Right: A mini-skirted suit by Pierre Chardin (1967).*

lions of dollars for the fashion industry, which manufactured and sold millions of pairs of jeans over a 10- to 12-year period.

The *unisex look* appeared among the young later in the 1960s. The young men wore their hair long and dressed in jeans and T-shirts. The young women wore their hair long and dressed in jeans and T-shirts. If hair grew on a person's face, the person was assumed to be male. Unisex shops opened so the guys and gals could shop together and buy identical merchandise.

During the late sixties, fashion was almost completely dedicated to a youthful look. A mature woman found it difficult to find a skirt that would come to her knees. She was a neglected market segment during the miniskirt era. It was the youth market group that was spending the money, and fashion catered to it.

In the middle 1970s, manufacturing research groups began studying the youth groups of the market. In 1974 Bobbie Brooks did a research composite of statistics "Lifestyle—The Junior Customer and Bobbie Brooks" of the junior female population to determine the age mix, the size, and the rate of growth of this market segment. The Bobbie Brooks study revealed that the *junior customer* is between the ages of fourteen and twenty-four. This market group has increased by eight million from 1960 to 1974, an increase of 22 million girls. The *young teen* is between the ages of fourteen and seventeen; in 1974 this was the largest segment of the group, but it will decrease by 1980. The *young adult* is between the ages of eighteen to twenty-one; this group, the next largest in 1974, will be the most important group by 1978. The *career girl* is between twenty-two and twenty-four years of age and was the smallest segment in 1975, but the group will continue in growth and importance.

Racial strife in the sixties prompted the Afro hairstyle and African designs in fabrics and dress. The seventies produced the Indian movement, which sparked the popularity of Indian jewelry. Women's lib and the burning of bras helped the progress of the "braless" look. For professional women, the women's lib movement helped give the pantsuit an acceptable image.

Throughout the twentieth century, menswear changed very slowly and then with only minor stylistic changes in the design of a shirt collar, the cuff of a sleeve, the width of a lapel, or the vacillation between cuffs or no cuffs on the trousers.

But the male revolt, beginning with youth and filtering up to the mature man, in the 1960s and 1970s saw the male reappropriate many of the fashions that through the nineteenth century had been given up to women. The adult male tried the Nehru jacket, the ruffled or turtleneck shirt worn with a necklace for dress occasions, and leisure suits. His suits, shirts, and ties were in vivid colors and patterns, and he began to let his hair grow longer. Football star Joe Namath's fur coat started a vogue. Suits were redesigned to emphasize the male anatomy—broad shoulder, slim waists, flared trousers. The young male, of course, wore jeans and T-shirts; and a majority sported shoulder-length hair, beards, or mustaches. Some wore pony tails.

Dress codes became almost nonexistent during the 1960s. School dress barriers were almost completely torn down, except for some private schools that required uniforms. What started as a leisurely way of life in the 1950s with the move to suburbia was accelerated by the youth revolt in the 1960s and resulted in changing many traditional ways of dress. Women no longer wore hats and gloves to church, funerals, teas, and shops. They adopted pants for a more casual existence. Clothes were designed for comfort and function. A fashion way of life had yielded to the demands of social changes.

Women worshipers in Roman Catholic and Episcopal churches at one time could not enter the sanctuary without a head covering. However, this requirement has been abandoned. Many of the Amish and the Mennonites, have held to their dress regulations for both sexes. The clergy of many churches also wear specific garments during the worship service, some required by the liturgy, and this custom was subject to little change.

The elderly is another market group demanding a specific type of fashion. It is becoming a larger segment of the population because of the ability of modern medicine to prolong life. The needs of the elderly are different from those of other groups. A look of maturity is desired. Those among the elderly who are incapable of caring for themselves require special clothing designed for bed or wheelchair use.

The handicapped, either physically or mentally, form yet another group whose apparel needs must be met. The physically disabled must have specially designed clothing, and the mentally disabled need a type of clothing that provides for physical safety and comfort. This group is a small segment of the overall market, but a very great need exists here, one that has been neglected by the industry to some extent. In the general population there are those who are overweight or very tall or very short who often require specifically designed clothing as well.

City street gangs may adopt a uniform type of apparel as a means of identification and segregation from other groups. Such organizations as the Masons, college sororities, or women's clubs sometimes have a specific dress for initiation or public ceremonies. The armed forces of all countries create a great demand for manufacturers to fulfill their specific dress requirements, including winter and summer uniforms and formal and informal attire.

PERSONALITIES CREATE FASHION DEMANDS. The outstanding public personalities of each decade may inspire fashion trends: movie or television stars, dancers, comedians, singers, athletes, political figures, or members of the wealthy or elite group. Fashion personalities are chosen differently by decade according to the reflection theory.

In the 1920s and 1930s, for example, worship of the movie greats was common: Jean Harlow, Rudolph Valentino, Clark Gable, and Joan Crawford all launched new fashions. Debutantes such as Brenda Duff Frazier and other members of the wealthy elite controlled the spending power of the country and often set the fashions.

Since those days, fashion figures have become more scarce. Other factors have influenced fashion more than personalities, but there have been a few through the years: Frank Sinatra, Lana Turner, and Rita Hayworth in the forties, Marilyn Monroe and Elvis Presley in the fifties. Elvis did most, introducing the ducktail hairdo and the leather look. The early sixties had Jacqueline Kennedy, a political figure, who reflected a powerful image on fashion. The late sixties began with the Beatles, went from there to feeling the impact of youth, gave a nod to Twiggy, and went from her into a "do-your-own-thing" phase.

Summary of Social Influences
1. Fashion is influenced by sociological occurrences such as education, changes in geographic living patterns, life-style changes, crazes, and current events.
2. Fashion is demanded by different market segments: youth, elderly, racial, handicapped, ethnic, sex, religion, minority, or oppressed groups, clubs, and organizations.
3. Fashion is influenced by personalities.

Political Situations. Political happenings can influence fashion trends. Often it is difficult to differentiate the social, economic, technological and political aspects. Generally, if an event involves legislation it can be considered political, even though it may be social, economic, or technological in origin.

The three general political areas that can create an influence on fashion are (1) personalities in the White House, on Capitol Hill, or in political circles; (2) diplomacy; and (3) legislation.

PERSONALITIES. The personalities in the White House may or may not be fashion influencers. Usually they are not. Teddy Roosevelt in the 1900s was a dynamic man, and his personality alone was an influence. Jacqueline Kennedy in the 1960s exerted great influence on the fashions of the period. In the 1970s Betty Ford successfully stressed buying from conservative American designers to help the economy.

DIPLOMACY. Diplomacy, which includes trade and negotiations, definitely influences fashion. Trade with foreign countries brings in a flood of international influences. This is most noticeable, of course, when the government first opens trade with a foreign country. Through these diplomatic relationships, interest is created in the countries themselves and their products, as with Japan after World War II, Communist China in the 1970s, and Russia throughout the 1960s and 1970s. In 1974 the Russian influence in fashion was very noticeable, with the Russian cossack overblouse, the "big look," and the boot with a Russian design.

In the late 1950s educational interchange was established between the United States and several foreign countries. This created an influx of foreign fabrics, designs, and artifacts. Pakistan is a good example of such interchange.

In 1974 Gerald Ford's wife Betty wore a Chinese-designed dress made from Chinese fabric to an opening of a Chinese art exhibit in Washington.

LEGISLATION. Legislation is generally social in origin but may also be economic or technological. The civil rights legislation in 1963 was prompted by social movements to attain a legislative goal and for many years exerted a fashion influence over blacks, as reflected in the "Black is beautiful" movement.

The space program is technological but would be hard pressed for funds to become a reality without legislation. The space program of the 1960s and 1970s greatly influenced children's toys, foods, dress, and fabric design.

When Hawaii became the fiftieth state in 1959, there was a great influx of Hawaiian dresses and Hawaiian print fabrics to the mainland.

Wars, both political and social, are the result of legislation and are influencers of fashion. Olive drab and red, white, and blue are colors associated with wartime clothing in the United States.

During World War II, dress regulations were issued by the government to the garment industry in an effort to conserve fibers and fabrics. The amount of hem in a dress was specified, there were no cuffs on men's trousers, and the degree of fullness in skirts was designated.

Flammability retardance is a legislative and technological achievement first applied to children's wear in 1974. However, the flame retardant material Tris was banned in 1977 as a cancer-causing agent. The textile labeling law and the fur labeling law are other examples of legislation that affects the fashion industry.

The energy crisis of the 1970s is both technological and political because of the ability of the oil-rich Arab countries to enforce an oil embargo on the United States and other oil-using nations. Shortages of petrochemicals in 1974 for manmade fibers jolted the apparel industry. Natural fibers, as well as rayon and acetate, were used more. The switch to the natural fibers affected performance qualities as well as design. When the Arab oil embargo was lifted, more man-made fibers began appearing. These are examples of some of the kinds of legislation that can affect fashion.

Summary of Political Influences
1. Fashion can be influenced by political personalities.
2. Fashion can be influenced by trade and negotiations with foreign countries or diplomacy.
3. Fashion can be affected by legislation.

Technological Advancements. Technology, "a systematic knowledge of the industrial arts," is certainly a catalyst of fashion. Technology, as much as anything else, has made the fashion business what it is today.

Where would we be if it were not for the spinning wheel and the sewing machine? Both of these led to far more intricate and innovative equipment. *Mass production* is the result of technology. Through mass production, we are able to dress our country in fashion at an acceptable cost.

Research in the textile industry resulted in the development of man-made fibers, finishes, and knits. No longer do we have to wash, starch, and iron a cotton garment that when worn briefly will look as if it has been slept in. Performance qualities of "easy care" and neat appearance came with the new fibers and finishes.

The elasticity and the comfort knits offer have given a new dimension to the fabric world. Beginning in the late 1960s, a man or woman could dress entirely in knits from the skin out.

The development of transportation methods—the train, the automobile, the airplane, and the space vehicle—certainly has left the horse and buggy outdistanced. But travel demands specific clothing; lightweight, packable, and nonwrinkling garments are needed. Technology has made all of these possible. Travel also helps to spread fashion trends from state to state and country to country.

COMMUNICATIONS. The press, television, radio, and the satellites also are catalysts of fashion. Satellites and television bring instant worldwide visual communication. Fashion innovations are thereby instantaneously projected to viewers across the country. No longer do we need to wait for the monthly magazine or the seasonal catalog to see what the new season will bring.

KITCHEN APPLIANCES AND HOME INVENTIONS. Modern appliances such as the washing machine, dryer, steam iron, home sewing machine, and cleaning and cooking equipment shorten the time the homemaker must spend at household duties and take the drudgery out of much of it. They also have changed her wardrobe.

Summary of Technological Influences
1. Fashion is influenced by technological achievements: mass production, textile re-search developments, travel, communications, and inventions.

CHANGE

Fashion will change. This is the third absolute of fashion in a free society. We are a culture of change. We understand it and live with it constantly. Our heritage consists of change. Compared with the cultures of Europe and Asia our country is in its infancy. In Japan, for example, some of the artifacts, temples, and statues are thousands of years old. European structures date back many centuries. In 1976 the United States of America celebrated its two hundredth birthday. We are only toddlers in the great span of time—young, growing, and maturing. Along with our maturation go an eagerness and affluence that nurture change. For example, our inner-city areas are beginning to decay. Some cities are restoring our historical sites, while others call on urban renewal to tear down and rebuild.

People change jobs, houses, spouses, hair coloring, make-up, facial features, and automobiles. We live with change. If fashion adheres to the reflection theory, then we know that by virtue of the changes in our way of life, our clothing, too, is going to change.

The constantly changing cycles of our life style contribute to a greater dissemination of fashion. Estelle Hamburger, fashion consultant, made reference to the millions of people in the United States and their clothing needs in a talk in 1972 called "Clothes Now." In referring to mass life styles, she said, "all of which are profoundly changing clothes that serve life, express life, and enhance life. No longer a look, but a language—that is what clothes now are all about."[15] Our way of life is rapidly changing and so are our clothes.

Fashion Evolution. Even though our fashion changes seem rapid at times, fashion generally tends to be more evolutionary than revolutionary. A style will be introduced, and the fashion innovators will wear it. It is then seen by others and may be adopted by the masses. Thus, it advances in an evolutionary manner.

In 1947, Christian Dior, a young Parisian designer, showed his collection. His designs were a dramatic change from what had been worn during the clothing-restriction days of World War II. His cinched waist, long full skirts, and natural shoulder line took the fashion world by storm, and we witnessed a fashion revolution. Dior, who possessed an exceptional sense of timing, had taken the pulse of the people and felt they were ready for a change. This is a rare phenomenon in the fashion world.

The leisure suit for men was a sensation in the fall of 1974, but actually it was the third season that the leisure suit had been around. A derivation of the Western style of dress, most men noticed it for the first time in the fall of 1974. It thus had moved through the normal evolutionary patterns of fashion to reach acceptance. However, stocks were liquidated at distress prices during 1975, and by 1976 there were widespread reports that personnel departments considered the leisure suit inappropriate garb for job interviews even when the job to be filled did not require a suit.

The midi-length skirt was introduced in the fall of 1970. It did not cause a fashion revolution or even a mild tremor. At this time, women had almost completely rejected skirts and adopted a pantsuit way of life. Gradually, skirts did emerge—by the fall of 1974—with the longer lengths—again, through the evolutionary process.

Erogenous Zone. Skirt lengths had to come down. Beside the fact that they could not have gone higher, there is another reason for their predictable movement: James Laver writes that "psychologists have devised what they call the shifting erogenous zone,"[16] meaning that woman is a pleasurable thing but man simply cannot cope with all of her at once. It becomes one of fashion's duties to expose her a little at a time and to concentrate on one area.

In the late 1960s, it was definitely the legs that received exposure. Dior's "New Look" of the late forties emphasized the natural waist—and when the waist is emphasized, this automatically brings attention to the bustline.

Man's eye will soon become bored with the concentration of one area and the erogenous zone will shift. Mr. Laver also writes: "In 1925, I wrote in my diary that I found the newly exposed legs of women rather exciting. By 1930, legs were a bore and attention had to be directed elsewhere."[17]

Classic Compromise. As we watch the fashion pendulum swing between exposure of different parts of the female anatomy or between overdressing or underdressing, we often see, between the extremities, a "leveling off" period. It is called the *classic compromise.* Fashion is deciding what to do next. Business historian Dwight Robinson related it well when he wrote: "The safest thing that can be said of costume variation is that it veers between extremes of overdressing and underdressing, although there are many other variables. Perusal of the fashion journals suggests that when one of these extremes has been reached, the recourse that has typically proved most successful is swift return to a form of compromise, or golden mean, which lies about halfway between overdress and underdress. Such norms are loosely referred to as a 'classical' style in the dress trade."[18]

The classic compromise was in effect in 1972 and 1973. In the late 1960s, women had worn the miniskirt, styles next focused on the pantsuit, and by 1972 the dress with the skirt length around the knee was beginning to be popular. Fashion was trying to decide where to go.

Fashion Cycles. Styles periodically will be reborn and accepted as fashion. Often this happens after a classic compromise period. Designers will sometimes resort to the museums or costume collections for ideas. A style will strike them as being right for the time, and they will recycle it in whole or in part.

Then too, if the socio-economic and political vibrations of a decade or era are similar to another, the earlier era's clothes also may seem right for the later time. Affluent periods lend themselves to one style of clothing, whereas depression reflects another.

In the recycling or the recurrence of a style, often only a sleeve, a collar, a skirt, or a type of pant leg may return and not the complete style. The symbol of remembrance of a time gone by may resurface and become fashion once again.

If a style is going to be recycled, it generally must wait out an interim of twenty-five to thirty years. This has led Laver to write: "The same dress is indecent ten years before its time; daring one year before its time; chic (contemporarily seductive) in its time; dowdy five years after its time; hideous twenty years after its time; amusing thirty years after its time; romantic one hundred years after its time; beautiful one hundred and fifty years after its time. It would have been quite impossible to revive the fashion of the mid-twenties until thirty years had elapsed. Thirty years elapsed and behold! Those fashions or modes very like them came back again."[19]

Nostalgia during the middle 1970s brought back some of the forties styling of women's jackets and the thirties soft looks of shirring, gathers, and the bias. During the early seventies high school students were having "50s Days" at their schools. The fifties styles were worn as a spoof, however, as "camp," and not accepted as fashion. It was too soon for the fifties fashions to return.

Fashion, then, has movement—sometimes slow, sometimes rapid. Often, it will even fall into patterns over the years and styles will repeat themselves, and thus it can be studied according to its cycles.

As all have observed, as fashion is introduced, it may become popular and then fade away. It has progressed through its fashion cycle.

Every style presented has a fashion cycle or fashion process through which it is presented to the public for either acceptance or rejection. The public acceptance or rejection will determine what the particular fashion cycle will be. Figure 2.8 shows the six stages that an average style progresses through in the fashion cycle. At any point in the fashion cycle, the style may be rejected and end in obsolescence. As Paul Poiret, the top couturier in Paris in the 1920s, so adroitly phrased it, "All fashion ends in excess." When a style is finally rejected by the public, it is obsolete. At this point, it is in excess, whether it is hanging in an individual's closet or on the merchant's rack. Anyone in the fashion business must understand this.

Table 2.1, "Fashion Diffusion Chart," shows the diffusion of fashion by consumer types and motives as well as the types of manufacturers who participate in the stages in the fashion cycle.

STAGES IN THE FASHION CYCLE. The fashion cycle moves from innovation, rise, acceleration, general acceptance, decline, and obsolescence.

The innovation, inception, creation, or introduction of a fashion is the beginning of a fashion cycle. Major fashion trends are usually started by a creative designer who has the ability to forecast a trend by sensing what the public wants. A keen sense of timing and sensitivity to social changes, economic situations, political events, and technological advancements, as well as a background of history, a familiarity with museums, and ex-

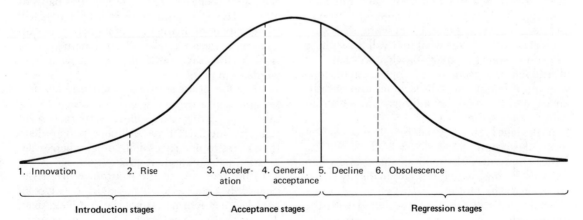

FIGURE 2.8 *Stages of the fashion cycle.*

TABLE 2.1 Fashion Diffusion Chart

Stage of the fashion cycle	Consumer type	Consumer motive	Manufacturer	Type of store
Introduction stages				
Innovation	Fashion innovator	Desire for distinctiveness and high fashion	Creative designer	High-fashion couture salon, specialty stores, and boutiques
Rise	Fashion specialist	Sophistication, good taste, and appreciation of what is new	Adaptor, line-for-line, good imitations	High-fashion stores, department stores, specialty stores, and boutiques
Acceptance stages				
Acceleration	Fashion realist	Emulation as a wardrobe builder; receptivity to change	Popularization knock-off, stylists	Department stores and specialty stores
General	Fashion fundamentalist (mass acceptance)	Practicality; need for durability and fashion at a price	Mass production	All stores
Regression stages				
Decline	Necessity group	Economic		Discount houses, chain stores, and special sales
Obsolescence	Deprived	Sheer necessity		Clearance and close-out outlets

perience in travel are necessary adjuncts to a fashion designer's success.

A creation produced by this type of fashion designer is usually called "high fashion," is purchased by the *fashion innovators*, and is carried in specialty, high-fashion, and other stores on a test basis.

The fashion innovator has been identified in a study done by fashion researchers G. B. Sproles and C. W. King. Their research refers to the fashion leader or innovator as the "fashion change agent," depicted as being "generally higher in education, income, and occupational status than the less fashion-oriented segments of the population." These authors further state that fashion leaders possess "fashion innovativeness, opinion leadership, and interest characteristics." They are "social participants" and possess traits of

"assertiveness, competitiveness, self-confidence, and attention-seeking behavior."[20]

The study suggests that there are more people in this group than traditional theory has implied. Perhaps as much as one third of the mass consumer market are fashion change agents. This could account for the rapid adoption of fashion in the last few years.

During the rising stage of the cycle, a style is being adopted. The fashion innovators have worn it and have communicated it visually to others within their social stratum. A fashion can very easily be rejected at this point and die a quick death.

If a fashion continues to rise, it is purchased and worn by the fashion specialist who likes the "new look" as opposed to the existing fashion mode. The fashion specialist is a sophisticated consumer who travels and vacations frequently. Home and wardrobe reflect good taste and status consciousness. Clothes are only a part of a total environment. Such people help to further spread the creative design. During this stage of the cycle, a fashion creation may be carried by those stores willing to experiment with new ideas.

At the point of acceleration, generally, the style will be on a definite upward swing. The manufacturer will be one that is quick to pick up new prospective trends and do "knock-offs," or a stylized version of the original. The original design is often simplified to make it more acceptable to the mass audience.

The fashion realists will wear the accelerated-stage style. These are wardrobe builders, receptive to solid fashion changes that allow clothing to express personality. They select a fashion that they are sure will be accepted by their peers.

A style can truly be said to have become a "fashion" when it reaches a peak of general acceptance and has been produced on a mass level by a mass producer. The *fashion fundamentalist* will buy it and wear it. The fundamentalist is interested in fashion at a price. The home is modest and styles are basic. There is a strong interest in durability and practicality.

Almost all stores will stock the style when it is in demand. However, stores will continue to buy fashion merchandise only so long as the fashion cycle is working upward or is at the top and exhibits an elongated general acceptance span. The smart store buyer must know when to stop reorders on a style that is past its prime. Remember, "All fashion ends in excess."

When a style reaches its saturation point of consumer interest, decline sets in. Almost everyone has worn it, the eye has become bored with it, the wearer has tired of it, and so a style hits the downward slump of the fashion cycle. New styles and creations are introduced that are refreshing to see.

When a style ceases to be manufactured and stores no longer are buying it, it will still be worn and used by the consumer who has previously purchased it and the consumer who is buying it from the markdown rack out of economic necessity. The obsolete style is no longer a fashion; it is finished. (See Table 2.1.)

BROKEN FASHION CYCLES. Broken fashion cycles occur when fashion abruptly changes for some reason. There are generally three categories into which broken cycles fall: *seasonal*, *catastrophic*, and *revolutionary*. Cyclical fashion movements can be altered when the society is experiencing unrest.

The broken fashion cycle referred to as seasonal occurs at the end of a season when an item is no longer desired for climatic reasons. The bathing suit is usually not in demand in the fall, and there is very little demand for winter coats in June. Seasonal shoes, furs, fabrics, and accessories will usually react the same way. It is important to note, however, that trends tend to recur; a style that was selling well at the end of one spring will tend to be in strong demand when the next spring arrives.

Catastrophic events also may break the fashion cycle. A war can create a fabric shortage; an energy crisis can change the kind of fabric that is popular; widespread economic recession or depression can curtail the buying of a particular fashion, such as evening wear. Political upheavals can cause breaks in the natural progress of a fashion cycle as well. World War II greatly disrupted fashion progress, particularly in Europe, and America's disorders of the late 1960s disrupted a fashion cycle in dresses and brought in jeans.

Fashion revolutions are rare but can occur if the consuming public wants them—as it wanted Dior's New Look in 1947 to bring an end to the styles that had been imposed partially by war regulations. It is difficult for a designer or manufacturer to create a fashion revolution arbitrarily; revolution usually comes from the streets.

During any period when fashion is being interrupted, it becomes a difficult task for the fashion analyst to make long-range predictions.

Fashion-Adoption Theories. For a style to go through the fashion cycle, it must have a mechanism of diffusion, a means by which it is spread. These theoretical mechanisms are called *fashion-adoption theories*. True, it is fashion-conscious people who will spread a style, but adoption is the route it will take. Each of these theories has merit.

TRICKLE-DOWN THEORY. The traditional adoption theory projected in the fashion diffusion chart is called the trickle-down theory. This is the pyramid theory in which the top of the social stratum first adopts a style and then it trickles down to lower socioeconomic levels. When it finally reaches the general-acceptance stage, the fashion innovator will no longer desire it.

This theory is based on economic and social realities: Those who can afford originality and true creativity in dress are generally in a high income bracket. Of course, an accomplished home sewer can have the same look without the exorbitant costs.

The fashion innovator's high economic bracket usually corresponds with social level.

The trickle-down theory held true until World War II. After the war, the great dispersion of wealth into the middle class, rapid communications systems, and great technological advancements speeded up fashion diffusion. This change brought the trickle-across theory.

TRICKLE-ACROSS THEORY. The trickle-across theory was proposed by Charles W. King in 1963. It is a *horizontal-flow concept* adhering to the principle that rapid communication allows the public to know immediately what the fashion innovations are. Mass production can introduce the new style simultaneously in all price ranges. Therefore, each social class has the opportunity to accept or reject the new idea at the same time.

Paris, London, and American high fashions are copied so quickly by the mass manufacturers that often the elite have not had time for couture designers and tailors to make their new clothes by hand; when London tailors revived the Edwardian silhouette for upper-class Englishmen during the late fifties, the style in inexpensive copies became the uniform of the English working-class teenager.

From the study done by Sproles and King on the consumer fashion-change agent, there appear to be fashion innovators within each socioeconomic group. The style will be adopted by the innovators and spread simultaneously.

King maintains that no longer will the mass producers or the mass market wait for the approval of the elite market to make its decision to adopt a particular style.

It seems likely in reviewing the trickle-across theory to speculate that perhaps the tremendous youth influence of the late fifties, the sixties, and the early seventies must have some impact on this mechanism of fashion diffusion. Youth, eager, ready, and impatient, wants to try the new and does not want to wait for the new to be tried by someone else.

BOTTOM-UP THEORY. Youth definitely plays a role in the bottom-up theory, which was presented by Doyle Dane Bernbach, a New York advertising agency. The assumption behind this theory is that lower-income youth groups are much freer than any other social groups in their adoption of new styles. This group has few inhibitions and traditions and little social prestige or position that might hamper decisions and actions. At the same time, the young from the elite social groups are so secure that they, too, feel free to adopt unusual dress patterns. The middle class is truly thrust into a middle situation with the new trends of dress coming from the bottom and the top at the same time.

The fifties reflected this theory, with the Beatniks mingling with the art crowd at the top of the social heap. The street gangs and their black leather jackets led to Elvis Presley, and the "leather look" became a reality. *West Side Story*, a Broadway musical popular in the fifties, supported the street gang fashion.

In the late 1960s, the hippie craze, which began at the bottom, rose to the top and completely engulfed the middle class. In 1970 the American Indian movement began at the bottom and circumvented the middle class. Movie star Marlon Brando and others supported it. In fashion the movement popularized Indian jewelry which was completely accepted by the mass market, as well as fringed leather jackets and beaded headbands and moccasins for teenagers. It closed in on the middle class from both the upper and lower classes.

GEOGRAPHIC THEORY. The geographic theory is supported not by research but by acute observation of the three major markets in the United States: New York, Los Angeles, and Dallas. Over the years, the authors have observed the types of clothing shown in the store windows on both coasts, in stores in the middle section of

America, and on the backs of consumers in different parts of the country.

The New York market area is the oldest and largest of the three major markets. It is innovative in philosophy and sophisticated in execution and design. Many of the major American couture designers have their salons along Seventh Avenue. The atmosphere in the streets convinces people that New York is the focus of fashion and that there is no other place like it in the world.

The Los Angeles market is set in an environment that is youthful, innovative, and vital. It specializes in extremely casual leisure clothing and sportswear, at-home wear, and the ultraglamorous formal and evening wear that is required by the movie industry. Because of the unusual characteristics of the consumer market segments in California, this area is considered to be a testing ground for new, and sometimes radical, styles, fabrics, and colors for both men and women. The California theory is "Try it and you might like it."

The Dallas market is very important for the moderate-priced manufacturer. The market is held in a building called the Apparel Mart; the entire market exists under one roof. It is done "Texas style," which is big and flamboyant. It is not particularly innovative but definitely serves the needs of middle America by offering accepted fashion looks.

As buyers from across the United States go to their particular market area, they buy what they think their customers will buy. Representatives from small stores usually go to only one market area.

The Dallas market in the past has not shown the number of innovative styles that New York and Los Angeles feature. Therefore, the majority of the stores that go to Dallas do not take home to their customers the high fashions. If they do, it is on a limited basis.

High fashion appears in New York and Los Angeles and jumps from coast to coast. When it appears to be an accepted style, it filters into middle America.

Although many people in the middle part of the United States do not like to think they are fashion laggers, in reality they are. This section of the country, as a whole, is slower to pick up the trends. However, fashion certainly moves more rapidly now to small towns in the middle part of the country than it did 10 to 20 years ago. This is a demonstration of the trickle-across and the bottom-up phenomena.

ACCEPTANCE

A *style* does not become a *fashion* until it has been accepted—that is, purchased and used by a major portion of the population. This is the final absolute fact of fashion. No matter how beautiful a design or creation is, unless the public likes it and wants to wear it, it will never be a fashion.

Fashions are not business-created but people-created through acceptance. Perhaps the best example of nonacceptance of a fashion is that of the midi in 1970. John Fairchild of the trade publication *Women's Wear Daily*, decreed 1970 the year of the midi. And so it was, for *Women's Wear* is read extensively in the trade by retailers and manufacturers. In the fall of 1970, through *Women's Wear*, they were exposed to virtually nothing but the "longuette" or midi-length skirt.

Designers, manufacturers, and retailers were caught in the squeeze of choosing the outdated miniskirt or a midcalf length that might not sell. Many in the industry listened to the daily projections *Women's Wear* made and produced the midi. It proved to be a disaster. The American woman simply did not accept the midi. It was worn in high-fashion circles and only there. Instead of making a decision on skirt lengths, women turned to the pantsuit. John Fairchild had wanted to spawn a fashion revolution, but the time was not right. Only the consumer makes fashion, not the designer or manufacturer.

Many factors control acceptance. Acceptance does not necessarily mean that the style is worn by everyone. Acceptance can also be limited to a special group. Sports participants, for example, will accept a particular design of clothing. Tennis, in the early 1970s, became a major sport. Tennis dresses, shorts, warm-ups, and assorted paraphernalia appeared, and certain designs were accepted as fashion by the tennis crowd.

College students wear clothing to class that they would not wear to church. The clothes that college students wear to dances are not the accepted dress of the social elite. During the bitterly cold winter of 1976–1977, ski clothes became so popular on the nation's campuses that they became a fashion. There may be a style trend that threads its way through each group, but it is adapted to the consumer group's needs.

Whatever the controlled conditions may be that make a fashion acceptable, there is one other that must be considered: the psychological aspect of clothing selection. An individual wants to feel good in a garment and often wants to project a self-determined image: the suburban matron look, the rising young businessman look. Of course, there are many other psychological factors that enter into clothing selection that will not be discussed in this book. But, all in all, the consumer must *like* it, *desire* it, or *need* it for some reason in order to make the purchase. When enough consumers purchase a particular style and use it, it becomes a fashion through this process of mass acceptance.

Fashion Is Big Business

The best way to grasp the size of the fashion industry is to try to envision its vast productivity. Hundreds of thousands of items are produced every day for men, women, and children—shoes, belts, jeans, pants, sweaters, coats, shawls, blouses, shirts, skirts, gloves, scarves, ties, T-shirts, underwear, gowns, robes, furs, socks, hosiery, hats, slips, bras, bodysuits, umbrellas, sunglasses, wallets, and key cases.

For apparel manufacturers to be able to produce these goods, textile and related industries must supply fabrics of all kinds, colors, and descriptions as well as plastics, furs, leathers, buttons, zippers, threads, trims, laces, embroidery, and all of the other products required to make a garment.

For the textile manufacturers to produce the goods for the garment makers, they must have the raw materials—natural fibers (cotton, wool, silk, and linen) and the many man-made fibers. Somehow these fibers must be processed into a usable form. The colorist must determine the colors for that season, and the textile designer must determine fabric patterns. Every one of

these operations throughout the industry requires special technical and often computerized equipment to do the job.

Distribution begins with the raw materials, continues through the manufacturers, and goes on to the markets where the apparel makers show their lines to the buyers for the retail outlets. The distribution and marketing process will terminate with the consumer who purchases fashion goods.

This gigantic, complex industry is geared to a synchronized system of mass production and distribution incorporating many people and many machines.

There is no need to wonder whether the fashion business is big business. It is indeed, so big that in 1973, $69.8 billion was spent on apparel. The American consumer spent an average of $332 per person on clothing and shoes: 8.7 per cent of personal income.[21] In the spring of 1976, teenage girls alone spent $3.5 billion replenishing their wardrobes: 24.4 million sweaters, 47.8 million shoes, 59.4 million pants, and 80.7 million pairs of hose. Fashion is truly big business.

END OF CHAPTER GUIDE

Review, Discussion, and Evaluation

Study of this chapter should enable students to
A. Develop and give evidence of the following kinds of competencies:
  1. Awareness of fashion as a universal communicator and as a powerful force in the environment.
  2. Ability to describe the characteristics that relate to each of the four absolutes of fashion.
  3. Ability to identify the stages in the fashion cycle as each relates to the innovation process.
  4. Ability to relate the concept of fashion diffusion to the various stages of the fashion cycle.
  5. Ability to recognize the implications of various fashion-adoption theories in terms of fashion acceptance.
B. Develop and/or clarify concepts related to the following key words or phrases:
  1. fashion 2. style 3. trend 4. apparel 5. classic 6. couture 7. high fashion 8. mass fashion 9. fad 10. ford 11. fashion industries 12. fashion characteristics 13. fashion absolutes 14. prevailing style 15. reflection theories 16.

gross national product (GNP)   17. personal income   18. disposable income   19. discretionary income   20. diffusion of wealth   21. economic stability   22. pragmatic theory   23. hypothetical theory   24. sociological influences   25. ecology movement   26. fashion demand   27. consumer groups   28. fashion personalities   29. political influences   30. legislation and diplomacy   31. technological advancement   32. erogenous zone   33. classic compromise   34. recurring fashions   35. fashion cycles   36. fashion introduction   37. fashion acceptance   38. fashion regression   39. broken-fashion cycles   40. trickle-down theory   41. trickle-across theory   42. bottom-up theory   43. geographic theory

Extended Classroom Learning Experiences

A. Make a collection of current examples of the following fashions:
   1. classic   2. high fashion   3. mass fashion   4. ford   5. couture.
B. Relate each of the preceding five terms to the reflection theory through political, social, economic, and technological comparison.
C. Summarize your findings in a report that includes your examples.
D. Make a collection of three or more mass-acceptance fashions.
   1. Review the four adoption theories and draw conclusions relating to the fashion-diffusion pattern of each.
   2. Summarize your study in a written report.
E. Follow the nation's leading political figures for a period of two months in a trade publication, such as *Women's Wear Daily*, and your own newspaper. Consider whether these political personalities have any impact on changes in fashion.
F. Contact a local retailer or businessman and inquire about any new technological developments that might affect fashion in the future.
G. Read two or more of the articles listed here or research current periodicals or trade journals and select two or more articles related to one of the concepts suggested in the "Review, Discussion, and Evaluation."
   1. Prepare note cards while reading each article.
   2. Using your note cards, write a brief summary indicating the relation of each article to concepts presented in this chapter.
   3. Using your note cards, give an oral report in your class and point out the important facts included in the articles.

Suggested Articles

BOSWORTHY, PATRICIA. "Who Killed High Fashion?" *Esquire*, May, 1973, pp. 124–127, 214–218.
GRINDERENG, MARGARET. "Fashion Diffusion." *Journal of Home Economics*, March 1967, pp. 171–174.
BERGLER, EDMUND, M.D. "A Psychoanalyst Looks at Women's Clothes." *Cosmopolitan*, February 1960, pp. 95–96.
BRITTON, VIRGINIA. "Clothing and Textiles: Supplies, Prices, and Outlook for 1974." *Family Economics Review*, Consumer and Food Economic Institute, Agricultural Research Service, U.S. Department of Agriculture. Washington, D.C.: Government Printing Office, Spring 1974.
LAVER, JAMES. "Fashion, A Detective Story." *Vogue*, January 1959, pp. 77–79.
LAVER, JAMES. *Taste and Fashion.* New York: Dodd, Mead, 1938.
ROBINSON, DWIGHT E. "The Rules of Fashion Cycles." *Horizon*, March 1959, 4.
"Understated Elegance." *Time*, July 6, 1962.

NOTES

[1] *Random House Dictionary of the English Language*, unabridged edition. New York: Random House, 1967.
[2] Paul Nystrom, *Economics of Fashion.* New York: Ronald Press, 1928, p. 4.
[3] Dwight E. Robinson, "Fashion Theory and Product Design," *Harvard Business Review*, **36**: 126–138 (November–December 1958).
[4] Dwight E. Robinson, "The Economics of Fashion Demand," *Quarterly Journal of Economics*, **85**: 376–398 (August 1961).
[5] Alfred H. Daniels, "Fashion Merchandising," **in** Jeanette A. Jarnow and Beatrice Judelle (eds.): *Inside the Fashion Business.* New York: Wiley, 1974.
[6] Charles W. King, "The Innovator in the Fashion Adoption Process," **in** L. George Smith (ed.): *Reflections on Progress in Marketing.* New York: American Marketing Association, 1964.
[7] Marilyn Horn, *The Second Skin.* Boston: Houghton Mifflin, 1968, p. 13.
[8] Kurt Lang and Gladys Engel Lang, *Collection Dynamics.* New York: Thomas Y. Crowell, 1961, p. 470.
[9] Edmund Bergler, "A Psychoanalyst Looks at Women's Clothes," *Cosmopolitan*, February 1960, p. 95.
[10] Paul Nystrom, op. cit.
[11] Mabel D. Erwin and Lila A. Kinchen, *Clothing for Moderns.* New York: Macmillan, 1969.

[12] *The Random House Dictionary of the English Language*, unabridged edition.

[13] Jeanette Jarnow and Beatrice Judelle, *Inside the Fashion Business*. New York: Wiley, 1974, p. 3.

[14] Daisy Goldsmith, "Fashion Closes the Gap," in Jeanette Jarnow and Beatrice Judelle (eds.): *Inside the Fashion Business*. New York: Wiley, 1974.

[15] Estelle Hamburger, "Clothes Now," in Jeanette A. Jarnow and Beatrice Judelle (eds.): *Inside the Fashion Business*. New York: Wiley, 1974.

[16] James Laver, "Fashion, A Detective Story," *Vogue*, January 1959, pp. 77–79.

[17] Ibid.

[18] Dwight E. Robinson, "The Rules of Fashion Cycles," *Horizon*, March 1959, p. 66.

[19] James Laver, op. cit., p. 78.

[20] G. B. Sproles and Charles W. King, *The Consumer Fashion Change Agent: A Theoretical Conceptualization and Empirical Identification*. Purdue University, West Lafayette, Indiana, November, 1973, pp. 59–61.

[21] Virginia Britton, "Clothing and Textiles: Supplies, Prices, and Outlook for 1974, *Family Economics Review*, Spring 1974. Washington, D.C.: U.S. Government Printing Office, 1974.

3

Fashion Analysis

Fashion analysis is the process of examining and evaluating the interrelationships of the variables of fashion, the fashion influencers, and fashion changes in order to predict fashion trends. Not only have people been analyzing fashion for many years, but analysis is one of the most vital functions of the fashion industry. The substance of this chapter is the multifaceted process of the prediction of fashion. The emphasis moves from analyzing the fashion variables to predicting fashion trends. The beginning of the chapter is concerned with the *fashion variables,* the tools of fashion analysis; we will concentrate on their use in fashion analysis. The remainder of the chapter relates to the processes of *fashion prediction,* the muscle of fashion analysis. It incorporates the fashion influencers that are a part of reflection, one of fashion's four absolutes, with the fashion variables. The beginning student of fashion analysis needs a sound knowledge of the elements and principles of design.

FASHION VARIABLES

Interpreting the Fashion Variables

The word *variable* means "that which is changeable, diverse, likely to change in direction." Any discussion of the variables of fashion must, then, relate to the components of fashion that are subject to change: line, color, and texture. The fashion variables are the art elements that relate to fashion change and allow one style to be distinguished from another. Line, color, and texture, called the tools of fashion, will be used to identify the variables. Interchangeable terms for *line* are *style* and *design;* for *texture, materials* and *fabric.* However, it is the *basic* art elements that are manipulated to achieve harmony in a style; and for this reason the terms *line, color,* and *texture* will be used.

Let us say that a woman is describing a dress to a friend. She will probably mention its outstanding *line features*—for example, the cut of the skirt, the length of the sleeve, the type of collar, and the amount of fullness in the bodice. Most likely, she will mention its color and something about what the dress is made of, its *texture.*

She has described a fashion by using the fashion variables. This same process is performed daily by consumers, fashion commentators, buyers, coordinators, analysts, tailors and seamstresses, salesmen, and manufacturers—everyone involved in the fashion business.

The use of changeables, or variables, in fashion is a necessary ingredient in fashion communication. The fashion variables make fashion the universal language that it is. Fashion analysis can be a simple process, but it is absolutely essential to the textile and apparel industries. Through the use of the variables, the fashion analyst is able to evaluate style changes and predict fashion trends. However, the prediction process is not simple; in fact, it can be extremely risky.

Without fashion interpretation, the industry could not manufacture massive quantities of apparel and have them available for consumers. The primary producers work so far in advance of the actual season that interpretation and prediction are necessities. The textile colorist may work approximately two years in advance of a season. The fabric specialist works with the colorist. The leather and fabric colorists coordinate in an effort to produce the same "color look." The designer works nine months to a year ahead of a season, producing a line for the buyers to view six months ahead of the season.

Each is examining and evaluating the variables and analyzing society in an attempt to predict a fashion trend. Without interpretation of the variables and fashion analysis there would be no excitement, no "pizzazz," no challenges, and no ulcers.

LINE

Line is by far the most important variable.

The line, style, or design of a garment can make a designer famous, a manufacturer wealthy, a buyer confident. Line is either lauded or denounced by the press. There is rarely any neutrality of feelings over line—either it is liked or it is not. Line is most important—what the consuming public is most interested in and the variable that is altered the most frequently. Line wields the power in the industry.

Purpose of Line. The number one variable, *line,* has two major features: the *silhouette line* and the *interior line.* These two types of line combine to make a composite of the overall design or style. They are defined in the following ways:

1. *Silhouette lines:* Lines forming boundaries.
2. *Interior lines:*
   a. Lines creating optical illusions.
   b. Lines dividing areas into shapes and spaces.
   c. Lines developing rhythm in a design, causing an emotional response. (A favorable emotional response is the desired goal of a design.)

In clothing design, the most important lines are those that form the silhouette, outline, or general shape, because these create the lasting impression.

Silhouettes fall into three main types: *straight,* or *tubular; bouffant,* or *bell-shaped*; and *triangular,* or having *back-fullness.* Each of these silhouettes has its counterpart in a geometric shape. The rectangle can be seen in the tubular outline; the oval, triangle, and hourglass shapes in the bouffant; and the triangle where there is back fullness. Historically, line has repeated these three basic shapes.

The lines that form the interior design express any sensation the designer chooses by manipulating the direction of a garment's lines. The interior line in apparel design has three major functions.

LINE CREATES OPTICAL ILLUSIONS. Sometimes it is difficult to believe that "seeing can be deceiving," but it can be, and for this reason it is necessary to understand optical illusions.

The eye is influenced by the direction that a line takes. The eye can be carried upward, making the line appear taller, as in Figure 3.1(a). The eye can also be stopped and brought downward, making the line look shorter.

As for the rectangles in Figure 3.1(b) the one divided vertically looks narrower than the one with the horizontal division. The rectangle in Figure 3.1(c) with the stripes closer together looks narrower than the one with the stripes farther apart. Figure 3.1(d) shows the diagonal breaking the rectangle: the one with the line beginning at the top looks narrower than the one with the diagonal beginning at the side.

A basic rule of line to remember is that lines that carry the eye in a vertical direction make one look taller; in a horizontal direction, wider; in a diagonal direction, taller or wider, depending on where the line begins.

Now that we know that the eye is influenced by the direction a line takes, look at Figure 3.2

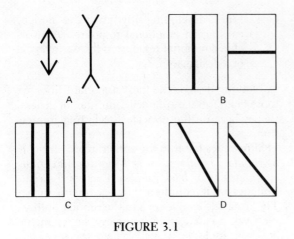

FIGURE 3.1

and study the example. Each vertical line is the same length, but the line direction creates an optical illusion by stopping the eye with a horizontal line in (b), by creating an illusion of shortness in (c), and by producing an illusion of greater height in (d).

The importance of studying optical illusion is that these principles are used in dress design. The proper use of optical illusions can create any effect the designer chooses.

LINES DIVIDE AREAS INTO SHAPES AND SPACES. Spaces create illusion as well as line though, of course, spaces are created by the line placement. The manner in which the area of a design is divided by lines influences its appearance. (See Figures 3.1(b), (c), and (d) and observe the spaces that have been created by line placement.)

When an area is divided into smaller sections, the reaction of the eye must always be considered. In Figure 3.1(c), the rectangles are divided by lines that form panels. The narrow panel makes the rectangle appear narrower because the

eye travels upward between these lines, paying little attention to the rest of the design. However, when the wider panel is used, the eye moves back and forth between the lines, giving an impression of width to the figure.

Although the general principle of line is that vertical lines make an object appear taller and horizontal lines wider, there are times when the effect is reversed—when pleats, tucks, repetitive patterns, or striped fabrics are used.

LINE DEVELOPS RHYTHM IN A DESIGN. "One of the most vital facts uncovered by scientific study is the existence of basic rhythms throughout nature. Any good design is based on some sort of rhythm." "These principles are not restrictions imposed upon the designer, but basic truths blending all of existence into a related whole."[1]

In design, rhythm patterns are established by line, form, color, and texture. The rhythm of the design is the flow of the pattern that the eye follows, the stimulus that causes the eye to move from one part of the design to the other and helps to stabilize the visual emphasis and attention.

In order to use line to produce rhythm correctly, it is important to understand that line has both functional and emotional significance. Although there are only two types of lines, *straight and curved*, they offer infinite variety.

Straight lines may follow a vertical, horizontal, or oblique direction; they can be continuous or broken and combined into angles. Straight line seems still and unrelenting to the point of seriousness or sternness. However, the direction the straight line takes influences the mood of the design: Vertical lines give the feeling of dignity and sophistication, whereas horizontal lines signify calmness and gentleness. Oblique lines are a satisfying combination of both, when the qualities of dignity and sophistication are modified to give a more relaxed feeling.

Curved lines can be round as a full moon or they can appear almost straight. Curved lines are considered to be more graceful than straight lines. However, the curved line must be controlled if it is to achieve its effect. The most graceful curved line is one that runs in a diagonal direction, as in the soft folds of material or in the edges of a soft ruffled collar. Curved lines can be

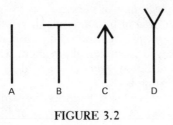

FIGURE 3.2

luxurious, long, graceful curves or intense little restless circles.

It is important that lines be combined so that they are harmonious with each other and conform to the lines of the body. Lines may repeat each other as in forming angles. Transition lines may be used to bring horizontal and vertical lines together in harmony. For example, the V-neck can be a transitional line between the vertical front line and the horizontal shoulder line.

Through the application of straight and curved lines a design is born. These lines develop the rhythmic, or eye, flow of the design. It is the lines and their rhythmic flow in a design that create the emotional response.

The Components. To play the fashion game of design, the player must have the proper pieces. The components of fashion design are the basic style characteristics of the individual areas of a costume: sleeve, collar, skirt, pants, bodice, jacket and the correct fashion name for them.

STYLES REPEAT THEMSELVES. Because styles repeat themselves, the fashion interpreter must be familiar with style characteristics and their historical names. True, the fashion designer will probably give the new creation an up-to-date fashion name, but it is necessary for analyzation purposes for it to be identified by its original name and characteristics. Many of these are given in Appendix 1.

Summary of Line

1. Line is the most important variable.
2. Line consists of two major parts:
   a. Silhouette (outline)
   b. Interior line
      • Creates optical illusions
      • Divides areas into shapes and spaces
      • Develops rhythm, which causes an emotional response
   c. Line has component parts that recur in fashion.

COLOR

The variable that is talked about with the most excitement in the fashion world is color. At first glance it is the most noticeable. Generally, color is the first impression one receives when looking at a fashion.

It is probably color in a store window that catches a person's eye, color that encourages one to walk across the floor of a store to look at a mannequin, color that makes someone stand out at a party. Everyone has probably used color in an effort to describe someone, saying something like, "Who is the dark-haired man wearing the yellow and white tie?"

Color, a very complex element in design, can be spectacular, easily noticed, and extremely stimulating. But all in all, color helps make fashion and color helps sell fashion. For these two reasons, color is extremely important to the fashion industry.

Projecting Color Trends. Twice a year the fabric and fashion world goes through the trauma of color selection, with shoe and fabric colorists working at least two years in advance of a season. For example, the colors for the 1976 bicentennial year were projected and planned in late 1973 and early 1974. This was a known event, and historical research was involved in the 1976 colorations.

All color projections are not as easy as this one was because obviously it is not often that an event of such magnitude occurs. The professional colorist must project color trends based on:

1. The study of color fashion cycles.
2. The knowledge of color chemistry.
3. Aesthetics and taste.
4. General observations (experience).

Color Fashion Cycles. The colorist must research color fashion cycles. Accurately predicting economic stability, the political situation, and technological advances too far in the future cannot be done by the colorist, although he or she will be able to observe some positive indicators of social change. However, the study of color fashion *cycles* is a worthwhile enterprise. The colorists review which colors have been fashionable in certain seasons.

Colors seem to recur, often with new names. A color that might have been called "apple green" or "chartreuse" in a past season may reappear with the name "tropic" or "lettuce" green. New colors also attract attention as well as new names.

Color choices are limited to the color range predicted and manufactured for that season. If an individual desires a color that is not within the fashion color range, it will be difficult to find it in ready-to-wear items or on the piece goods market—it simply may not have been produced. Although there is a wide range of colors every season, there are times when a specific color is difficult or impossible to find.

Color Chemistry. The colorist must have practical knowledge of how colors actually work, how they interact with each other, and how they are affected by different fabrics as well as theoretical knowledge of color chemistry, which involves:

1. Color properties.
2. Color and light.
3. Principles of color harmony.

Color has three properties, or dimensions, that identify and control its emotional and aesthetic aspects: hue, value and intensity. *Hue* is a term used in art to give the *name of the color* tone. Many names of colors are derived from nature or things made from natural resources: flowers, trees, woods, foods, spices, fruits, vegetables, wines, liquors, stones, metals, birds, furs, animals, earth, fire, and water. There may be well over a million different color names. Some of nature's color names are burnt sienna, bronze, sage green, slate, mistletoe, pimento, peat brown, emerald, eggshell, cornflower, nutmeg, and cinnamon. The list is endless.

Value is the *lightness or darkness* of a hue. The value scale runs from white to black. A darker value is referred to as a shade; a lighter value, a tint. For example, in the red hues, wine would be considered a shade and pink a tint.

Intensity, or chroma, is the *brightness or dullness* of a hue. In the red hue, shocking pink would be at a high-intensity level, and soft pastel pink would be considered low.

To discuss color and light, it must first be said that color is the result of a reflection of light as it strikes a surface. Different colors reflect light differently. Color is everything seen by the eye. We see a tree because it is in contrast to the sky, because tree and sky are each reflecting light differently.

Lighter and brighter colors reflect more light than darker and less intense colors. Because of this light reflection, color can create optical illusions, as does line. There are some general color-illusion rules relative to apparel: the lighter the color, the larger the human figure will appear; the darker the color, the smaller the figure will appear; the brighter the color the larger the figure will appear; the duller or less intense a color the smaller a figure will appear.

Color may change under artificial lighting. Different light sources are differently colored, and the color of the light affects the color of the object or fabric. A yellow dress may take on an orange cast under an incandescent electric light because the light bulb has a reddish hue (red + yellow = orange). Under some fluorescent lights, the same yellow dress may take on a greenish cast because fluorescent light often has a blue hue to it (blue + yellow = green).

Two colors that are chemically different may appear to match under a specific source of light because of the addition of the light's color. When the two colors are removed to a natural light, they may clash.

A *color wheel* displays the many possible color combinations, or color harmonies. It is truly a wheel of the color spectrum, beginning with the *primary* colors, red, blue, and yellow. These are also called simple colors because in their pure form they are irreducible. Through mixing primary colors, three *secondary* colors appear: violet, green, and orange, also called compound colors. The secondary colors fall between the primaries and are thus made up of the two primary colors on either side of them. Red and blue make violet, blue and yellow make green, and yellow and red make orange. The mixing of colors continues on the color wheel to develop many hues.

Attractive color combinations are obtained by applying the principles of color harmony. There are eight generally accepted color harmonies, or color combinations, that are developed by their positions on the color wheel:

1. Monochromatic.
2. Complementary.
3. Double complementary.
4. Triadic.
5. Analogous.
6. Analogous complementary.
7. Adjacent complementary.
8. Split complementary.

There are other color harmonies, the only limitation being in the eyes of the color creator. Colorists and designers are forever creating new and exciting color combinations.

There was a time when discordant colors were identified and were forbidden by the color community to be used together: pink and orange, red and pink, bright red and dark red, fuschia and bright red, blue and green, orange and cerise, bright pink and yellow. Today, however, some of the loveliest color schemes or harmonies come from these combinations. This is the point at which the professional colorist must use his aesthetic sense, good taste, and experience to determine and create unique color harmonies.

Color and acceptable color combinations can now be achieved by instruments and computer techniques much more quickly and accurately than by the human eye and hand.

When involved in a comprehensive study of color and the intricacies inherent in it, one soon becomes aware of color's psychological impact. In viewing the aggressive warm colors and the receding cool colors, psychological contrasts appear.

WARM COLORS: RED, YELLOW, AND ORANGE. Red signifies hearty life, love, romance, valentines, courage, martyrdom, danger, fires. It also gives the feeling of warmth, and connotes enthusiasm for life, excitement, and vigor. Yellow and orange suggest sunlight, warmth, openness, friendliness, gaiety, even glory in the church; yet, yellow is the least popular of all the colors, perhaps because of its use in slang to denote cowardice.

COOL COLORS: BLUE, GREEN, AND VIOLET. Blue signifies coolness, aloofness, fidelity, and suggests the cool blue sky and the calm blue sea. In the church it stands for piety. It is the favorite color of men. But it is also the color of inner life and is symbolic of introverted people.

Green is cool, pleasing, the most restful of all colors; it suggests peace, the olive branch, newness, freshness, growth, and is the symbol for hope. School and hospital rooms are so often painted in a soft green, however, that many people find the shade depressing; "renter's green" is similarly dismal.

Violet is a subtle color, suggests the retiring, subdued life.

These cool colors are adjacent to blue on the color wheel and reflect the same psychological coolness as does blue.

The greatest psychological impact is felt when one enters a room decorated in the warm earth tones. Warmth and comfort spread through the room, and one may find oneself sinking into a chair and relaxing. A room decorated in the cool colors does not lend itself to this immediate comfort and relaxation. It is psychologically cooler and projects a more formal image.

Our whole existence has been steeped in the emotional impact of color. Specific colors call for specific emotional responses. For example, a yellow flag is flown on a ship with disease, and yellow is the sign of a coward (a yellow streak down his back); aristocrats are referred to as bluebloods, or a friend is "true blue"; black signals terror, pirates, and mourning; white is for purity and brides; and we are "green with envy" or we "see red."

Events in our lives cause us to attach emotional feelings toward particular colors. Colors at certain times clearly indicate a person's state of mind as well. An economic depression will usually be reflected by somber colors, and prosperity will bring forth vivid colors.

Nothing is more representative of the power of color than the fashions we wear. We have only to think about our daily clothing selections. Some days we select a bright color that is full of life. On other days, we may choose to wear a duller color. If we were to reflect on this, we find that our selections relate to mood, occasion, climate, or the specific weather outside.

Color seems to be one answer for man's search for beauty and expression, a primary universal need. It has a social and spiritual importance exemplified in the use of colorful flags for all sorts of occasions, uniforms, festivities, and rituals that can be joyful or sad. We express much emotion through the use of color in our lives.

General Observations (Experience). Colors can create a point of emphasis, control rhythm, determine proportion, stabilize balance, and create harmony or havoc in a costume.

Apparel colors are generally considered to be seasonal. Usually, we think of lighter and brighter colors for spring and summer, darker and duller colors for fall and winter, and pastels for Easter. During the late 1960s, colors adopted a transeasonal approach. Winter white and many light colors became popular for women's clothing, and men wore white shoes and belts the year around. The accepted color cycles were violated. However, after a few seasons of this, the standard pastel and bright colors for summer and darker shades for winter apparel reappeared.

The fashion public is very sensitive to color and color change. People tire of colors as well as styles. Colors do run in cycles and trends, but the individual's color choices are as varied as are style choices. Color choices are related to one's personality, hair, skin, age, and taste and to the classification of merchandise: that is, one may choose one color for a sportswear item and another color for evening.

Color may be the most noticeable of the fashion variables, but if a design is out of fashion, no color in the world can make a person want to wear it.

Today, more than ever, the use of color is extravagant. There is an increasing dependence on excellent color reproduction in magazines, newspapers, and, of course, television. There is a greater scientific understanding of color and its use in the movies. We see flamboyant use of color in offices and industry. New hospitals are startling everyone with their brightly decorative colors. Psychologists even suggest the use of color to relieve fatigue. Stores are presenting an array of color in interior store design to stimulate the sale of merchandise. Also, color is used in all types of packaging as well as in cosmetics.

Summary of Color

1. Color is the most noticeable variable.
2. Color helps make fashion and sell fashion.
3. Color trends are projected by fashion cycles, color chemistry, aesthetic sense, taste, and experience.
4. Colors follow cycles in fashion.
5. Color has three properties: hue, value, and intensity.
6. Color is a result of light reflection.
7. Color creates illusions.
8. Color may be combined in many diffrent ways.
9. Color creates psychological moods.
10. Color stirs emotions.
11. Color preference seems to be seasonal.

TEXTURE

Texture or fabric, dictates the silhouette and defines the general characteristics of design. Without fabric there would be no fashion.

The designer or manufacturer knows which fabrics can be cut and sewn into which designs. Each fabric has its own personality and characteristics. It will perform in its own way. A chiffon flows and drapes, a denim is sturdy, a velvet is luxurious, and a cotton flannel gives softness and warmth. Each has its affinity for a particular type of design.

Most fashion-conscious consumers look first to the new lines of a season, then to the new colors, and last to the fabric, which is often considered of least significance. If a consumer can find the desired line or color, the fabric may not matter.

This, of course, is not the most desirable method of selecting clothing. Workmen and mothers shopping for children's clothing are more conscious of fabric performance factors than teenagers are. They want the fabric to launder and wear well. Travelers may shop for clothing with specific fabric requirements—nonwrinkling properties and very lightweight, packable textures. There are certainly other times when specific fabric qualities are desired by the consumer.

Texture experiences fashion cycles, as do line

and color. In the late 1960s there was a surge in the popularity of denim fabrics that extended into the late 1970s. Evening fabrics recur in fashion demand over the years. Fabric and line usually correspond in fashion cycles. If a style returns to popularity, it will usually look best in the original fabric. The bias cut of the twenties will always need to be cut in a fabric that will lend itself to the bias. It is impossible to make a body-conscious, slithery gown out of a heavy tweed.

Often the color and fabric design provide the emphasis for the style of the garment. The pin-striped suit for men that was fashionable in the thirties returns periodically, with much the same line as the original design and with a remarkably similar pin stripe.

Texture creates illusions, as do line and color. The heavier, the more textured, the shinier, or the crisper the fabric, the larger a person generally will appear. The softer, thinner, or smoother the texture, or the duller the surface, the smaller the individual will seem to the viewer.

Texture Terminology. Texture in fashion is basically referred to as fabric, fur, or leather—the primary resources of the textile industry. However, the expansion and creativity in the industry are so great today that plastic, paper, wood, rubber, and metal should be included in the list.

Texture is the surface appearance or "feel" of a substance. It is referred to as the "hand" and relates to the qualities that influence the tactile sense: namely, the body, the fall, the drapability, and the weight of a fabric.

Because there would be no fashion without fabric, it is essential to know some basic facts about fabric. To anyone involved in any facet of the fashion industry—textile production, designing, manufacturing, coordination, or retailing—some fabric knowledge is a must; and for the consumer, it is vital.

For those who have not had a basic textile course, the following information about fabric, minimal as it is, will help to establish a base for fabric analysis.

Fiber A pliable, short, hairlike individual strand. Sometimes referred to as a filament, fibers are used to make yarns. There are *natu-ral, synthetic* (noncellulosic), and *man-made* (cellulosic) fibers. (See Chapter 5.)

Yarns A group of fibers laid or twisted together; characterized by being continuous.

Fabric A structure from yarns, fibers, or substances such as plastic, rubber, metal, paper, or wood. The two main types of construction are weaving and knitting. Others are braiding, knotting, crocheting, felting, bonding, and laminating.

Finish Anything done to fiber, yarn, or fabric either before or after weaving or knitting to change its appearance (hand, and/or performance).

Hand How the fabric feels to the touch.

Almost no fabrics are ready for use as they come from the weaving or knitting machine. First, they must be dyed or printed and finished.

Summary of Texture

1. The texture of a fabric defines the general characteristics of a design.
2. Texture is the surface appearance, or feel, of a fabric.
3. Although texture is considered to refer to the primary resources of the fashion industry of fabric, fur, and leather, others should be included, such as plastic, paper, wood, rubber, and metal.
4. Textures recur in fashion as do color and design.
5. Fiber is the beginning of all cloth.
6. Yarns are used to make fabrics by two basic constructions: weaving and knitting.
7. Finishes are applied to fibers or fabrics to change appearance, hand, or performance.

The Variables as Fashion Tools

Line, color, and texture are the tools of fashion prediction. Fashion analysis is the process of examining and evaluating the interrelationships of variables of fashion and fashion influencers for the purpose of predicting fashion trends.

The individual, whether working in a facet of the fashion business or as a consumer, should have some knowledge of the function of line and style as they relate to fashion, of kinds of lines and what they do, of the illusion created by line, of the component parts of a style, and their fashion names.

Knowledge of color is important in fashion to understand the emotion and illusion color can create. Knowledge of texture and textiles is important in all segments of the industry. Also, fabric information is vital to understanding the performance of a fashion: what a fabric will do and how to care for it.

A thorough working knowledge and understanding of the tools of fashion are imperative for the individual in the fashion business . . . to predict the fashion trends.

FASHION PREDICTION

Interpreting Fashion Prediction

Fashion prediction—What does the phrase really mean? Who can predict? What educational background and training must one have? What professional experience does one need to become a fashion analyst or predictor? Does this individual have special, innate perceptive ability? What does he or she actually do? How does he or she do it?

To predict is to tell in advance, to prophesy. A *fashion prediction is telling in advance what the predictor thinks the fashion trends will be for the coming season.* This term is used interchangeably with *forecast*, which is to form an opinion beforehand or to have foresight in planning.

A trend is "the general course or a prevailing tendency." The *fashion trend is the prevailing style characteristics that are being seen in a season.* It is the visible direction in which fashion is moving.

The fashion predictor, or forecaster, is usually referred to as a fashion analyst. *The fashion analyst evaluates the fashion variables and the fashion influencers to predict fashion trends.*

Who can be a fashion analyst? The fashion analyst may be any of the following:

- a colorist for a fabric or shoe manufacturer
- a designer
- a buyer for a buying office that services small stores
- a buyer for department stores
- a fashion coordinator of a multiunit organization
- an owner or manager of a small store
- *you*, anyone who must make decisions about his or her personal wardrobe.

The fashion analyst may be anyone in the fashion business or functioning around it. Anyone can be a fashion analyst, but, of course, the theories will be practiced in varying degrees of expertise. The principles of fashion analysis are the same for whoever chooses to use them. They are relative to the amount of dollars that one has to spend and the audience at his or her command. The analyst may be projecting a major fashion trend for the country or a fashion for his or her private use. The analyst should, however, use the same basic principles for prediction.

Of course, the professional fashion analyst will have an extensive background and available information to assist with decision making. An analyst works six months to two years ahead of a season, depending on the segment of the industry with which he or she is involved. The individual consumer is usually concerned with the present or preceding season.

If a person wants to learn the principles of fashion analysis, what must be known? The professional must have an acutely developed sense of fashion and timing, must be able to feel the vibrations of the incoming and outgoing trends. This is an innate ability that is difficult to develop. Other qualities can be learned and refined as necessary. The analyst must be able to sense and evaluate the public's desires and needs. To do this he or she must be completely familiar with the four absolutes of fashion and must unequivocally absorb the reflection theory. Above all, the analyst should be sensitive to changes in different aspects of life and should learn to evaluate the economic situation, social changes, political events, and technological advancements. She or he must comprehend the movement of fashion according to the fashion cycles and be able to predict the changes. The analyst must completely understand the acceptance theory and the customer, whoever or however large that segment may be.

An educational background in fashion, art, business, history, and the humanities is necessary to the professonal; but experience is the best teacher. There is no substitute for the experience of being on the selling floor, meeting the customer on his or her terms, and watching trends develop and fade away. These experiences aid the professional in acquiring initial insight into prediction.

Fashion prediction is a hazardous, exciting challenge. Even though the analyst strives for perfection, no one is 100 per cent accurate; yet, it must be recognized that the more successful the predictor, or analyst, the larger the profits. Prediction, or forecasting, is the name of the fashion game and it is the lifeblood of the industry. All of the people involved in the business of selling fashion at a profit are involved in the business of predicting or trying to predict the trends of fashion for coming seasons. Now, how is it done?

Predicting Fashion

All predictions require study, forethought, and evaluation. But certain *awareness factors* and *measurements or indicators* can be used to analyze and make predictions.

The astute forecaster will be sensitive to several awareness factors, such as the latest (1) fashion innovations, the impact of (2) current situations, (3) sales promotion efforts, and any (4) acceptance elements.

Measurements and indicators that can be vital to the analyst, depending on the facet of the industry in which he or she works, are (1) sales records, (2) the fashion count, and (3) cyclic patterns of stylistic changes. Both the awareness factors and measurements can help analysts predict fashion trends.

Awareness Factors

Fashion Innovation. All professional fashion analysts are aware of the innovative styles presented each season. They are also aware of the acceptance or rejection of the new styles by the fashion specialists who wear the fashion looks in the rising stage of the fashion cycle.

During the innovative stage of the fashion cycle, there are some styles that are considered prophetic styles—they are destined to become a fashion. The accomplished analyst, buyer, or coordinator will be able to sense much of the time which styles are prophetic. This is based partially on the innate ability to perceive mentioned previously. One's educational background and experience in knowing *what* the consumer wants and *when* it is wanted must come into play here.

The trade publications in the textile, manufacturing, and retail world are very helpful to the analyst. Every possible resource must be used to make the right decisions on the innovative style presentations by the creative designers and to predict the trends.

Impact of Current Situations. Current situations here refer to the reflection theory and the four major influencers of fashion: Economic stability must be considered when predicting trends. The question "How does the current economic situation affect the fashion industry?" must be answered every season.

Social changes must be analyzed. In which direction are the people moving? What social occurrences are taking place? What insight is the analyst receiving about major social change? What national and local sporting or other major events are on the horizon?

What is the political situation, domestic and foreign? Is there legislation before Congress that can affect the fashion business? Are there negotiations with a foreign country that could influence fashion? What is the energy situation?

Are there future technological advancements that will influence the textile world? What will it mean in direction of style, fabrics, or colors?

It is imperative that the analyst be aware of the immediate and forthcoming events in each of these four areas to be able to predict trends.

Sales Promotion Effort. Nystrom in *Fashion Merchandising* feels that the amount of publicity and promotional effort given a style or fabric may affect the acceptance of the product by the masses.

For example, when Dupont introduced Qiana, a new nylon fiber produced to imitate silk, a great national sales promotion effort was put forth by the company. Millions of dollars were spent to inform the trade and the public of the properties and attributes of Qiana.

The analyst must evaluate the sales promotion effort and be able to project whether the product will attain the anticipated mass acceptance. This evaluation will help in predicting the trend. Will Qiana be a fashion fabric with mass acceptance, or will it plod along in a semiaccepted state? This is another awareness factor for the analyst to consider.

Acceptance Factors Reviewing sales records and the fashion count, being aware of fashion innovation and its projection, and all of the preceding factors will help determine which styles will be accepted.

Certainly season, geography, and timing are acceptance factors. Designers and analysts are aware of them and will not present or predict trends in conflict with them.

Nystrom also suggests that accepted canons of art, custom, modesty, and utility must govern new styles in order to accurately predict trends.

Obviously, in 1964 Rudi Gernreich's topless bathing suit could not reach mass acceptance. It was not only in direct conflict with the canon of modesty and good taste at that time, but required a physical perfection that most women could not meet. The naive chemise of 1974 was not accepted. It conflicted at that particular time with the canon of art. It made women look big. Bigness was not fashionable then. Thus, an important measurement for prediction is that "Accepted canons of art, custom, modesty, and utility are most easily accepted, go further, and last longest."[1] Fashion cannot go against what is fundamental.

MEASUREMENTS AND INDICATORS

Retail Sales Records. Sales records can be obtained on a national, regional, local, individual store, or department basis. The fashion analyst will use the level that is more relevant to her or his position.

For example, a buyer preparing for a trip to the spring market will view sales records of the past spring's sales. The buyer will look at the *classifications* (or types of clothing) he or she carries—pants, tops, skirts, accessories, and so on. Classifications will be tabulated by the purchase and sales records of the previous year. The buyer will do this by the *number of units* (pieces) purchased and sold in the categories of:

- Style number (description).
- Color.
- Cost per unit (purchased).
- Cost per unit (sold).
- Fabric.
- Resource (manufacturer).
- Size.

and any other measurement that may be pertinent to the store. The data will be evaluated on what percentage sold well and what percentage was placed on the markdown rack. The units that were put on the markdown rack must be evaluated as to the causes of their failure to sell. A primary cause could be one of the fashion variables. Perhaps the fabric was not the right weight or not durable enough. Perhaps the color was bad or an off-color blend. Perhaps the style was unacceptable for some reason. Perhaps the sizing was faulty. A very probable cause could have been that the *resource* was shipped late to the buyer, thus causing the merchandise to be in less demand than if it had arrived three weeks earlier. There are a multitude of problems that plague the buyer. When items fail to sell, one responsibility of a buyer is to figure out "Why?"

Sales records must be analyzed to make a market plan. It should be mentioned here that chain stores and many multiunit stores use computers to obtain these sales records. Single-unit stores can subscribe to a buying office that will computerize their sales records for them.

The fashion analyst who is predicting overall trends for a large national chain such as Penney, Sears, or Ward may look at national and regional sales records. These are the questions to ask:

- Did this particular style sell?
- Was it good on the East Coast only?
- Did it surface in the Middle West?
- Was this color just beginning to make headway?
- Was the new fabric successful?
- Is denim going to be strong again? Why or why not?

The fashion coordinator who works for a regional multiunit store—such as Foley's in the Houston, Texas, area—will concentrate his or her queries on a regional basis in order to be aware of and alert to national sales figures and trends. The questions asked will be the same, but will be focused on the coordinator's immediate location.

The fashion coordinator may primarily be interested in presenting a total projected fashion image of the store's policies and philosophies. One of the coordinator's responsibilities is to see to it that all of the departments' and stores' buyers present that image. The coordinator may, also, be budgeting advertising dollars for overall advertising to project certain fashion "looks."

The individual shopper does not work nearly as far ahead as the professional fashion analyst. In order for the consumer to make wise personal choices he or she should have some knowledge of incoming and outgoing fashion trends. The consumer will not have sales records, but he or she can subscribe to fashion magazines, a newsletter, or newspapers to keep informed.

The Fashion Count. The fashion count is an organized plan of counting and classifying the fashion variables of designated items of apparel. The count shows the relative importance of different styles, colors, and fabrics as worn by a specified group. Through the use of the fashion count, current fashion looks can be defined.

If repeated at frequent intervals, the count will show the styles, colors, and fabrics that are nearing the acceptance stage in the fashion cycle and those that are approaching the regression stage in the cycle.

The items that can be counted best are those in the outer-clothing field, which include dresses, suits, coats, hats, shoes, hosiery, neckwear, jewelry, and handbags. Colors may be counted as well as fabrics.

Fashion counts may be made at random in any place where people congregate. The selected place should be one in which the individuals observed are of the same social class and are interested in what is fashionable, relative to their tastes.

Decision can be given as to which segment of the fashion cycle will be accentuated: the introduction, acceptance, or regression stage. If interested in high fashion, the counter should select high-class restaurants, clubs, hotels, theaters, and social events such as opening nights to count.

Student styles should be counted at schools or colleges. The styles worn by the fashion-conscious at popular social events, resorts, hangouts, and dances should be considered. Mass acceptance counts can be held in a classroom or anywhere on campus.

Steps in a Fashion Count
1. Decide on the *variable* to be counted: color, fabric, or style. (It may be all three of these.) The list is endless: pants, tops, dresses, skirt lengths, sleeve design.
2. Decide on the *group* to be counted: high-fashion women, college women, college men, junior high school girls, businessmen.
3. Decide on the *location*; it should be appropriate to the specified group.
4. Decide on the *fashion-cycle emphasis*: introduction, acceptance, or regression stages. This may or may not be applicable to the count.
5. Decide on a *time* for the count to be made. This will, of course, be relative to an event, if selected.
6. Formulate a *tabulation sheet* for specific needs to hasten the count when it is in progress. This will also help to tabulate data. You should be sure to include on the tabulation sheet the questons for written evaluation.
- Did you note an important classification not included in the original list? Explain.
- Did you have any difficulties in making the count? Explain.
- Do you feel that the percentages calculated

on your sheet fairly represent the relative importance of the characteristics? Explain.

7. *Proceed* with the count. Each counter should observe at least fifty samples in the selected group. Be as accurate as possible in the tabulation.
8. *Study the data* and carefully tabulate it.
9. *Record the results* by percentages. Analyze the data in relation to the fashion-cycle position of the style, color, or fabric of the selected item.

The major value of the count is to help the counter determine the styles that are being accepted, have been accepted, or are being rejected. The method is a very simple means of doing a fashion count, but it can be most helpful in measuring fashion change and defining current fashion looks. The analyst can use this as another measurement for predicting trends.

Cyclical Patterns of Style Changes. The professional analyst must be aware of the fashions of the past. He or she must possess a firm knowledge of at least twentiety-century fashions and their movements to be able to predict current fashion trends. Knowing what was current in the thirties, forties, or fifties also will be a great help in forecasting fashion trends.

Quantitative analysis is a step-by-step process to determine the stylistic changes in dresses from 1900 until now. This format can be used to measure any stylistic change in fashion and can be a great help in fashion prediction. This process is given in Appendix 2, p. 258.

END OF CHAPTER GUIDE

Review, Discussion, and Evaluation

Study of this chapter should enable students to

A. Develop and give evidence of the following kinds of competencies:
   1. An understanding of the manner in which each fashion variable is used as a tool to analyze and predict fashion changes.
   2. A knowledge of the various elements unique to each fashion variable: color, line, and texture.
   3. An ability to utilize each of the fashion variables to analyze and describe current fashion trends.
   4. An understanding of awareness factors and measurement indicators used in predicting fashion trends.

B. Develop and/or clarify concepts related to the following words or phrases:
   1. fashion variables 2. line 3. silhouette 4. interior line 5. line and optical illusions 6. straight lines 7. curved lines 8. design component 9. basic style characteristics 10. color components 11. color properties 12. primary colors 13. secondary colors 14. warm colors 15. cool colors 16. texture 17. fabric hand 18. fibers 19. yarns 20. fabric 21. finishes 22. tools of fashion 23. fashion prediction 24. fashion influencers 25. fashion analyst 26. awareness factors 27. measurement indicators 28. fashion count

Extended Classroom Learning Experiences:

A. Review the examples of optical illusions in the use of lines and select illustrations from current fashion magazines of two or more designs in which use of lines creates optical illusions.
B. Review the basic style characteristics in Appendix 1, p. 255:
   1. Search through historical fashion periodicals for examples of five or more illustrations of classic style features such as leg-of-mutton sleeves, empire waistline, bell-bottom pants, and so on.
   2. Search through current fashion magazines and collect five or more advertisements of classic style features that are in fashion.
   3. Compile your findings in a brief report.
C. Make a collection of five woven fabrics and five knitted fabrics and briefly analyze the difference.
D. Make a collection of three color hues in varying degrees of values, intensities, and textures.
   1. Analyze each collection under artificial light and under sunlight. Observe the differences in color appearances in each situation.
   2. Analyze the differences in the effect of each of the values, intensities, and textures in relation to your own skin tones.
   3. Write a brief summary of your findings and conclusions.
E. Examine the differences in the hand of the following kinds of fabrics: wool crepe, moiré taffeta, chiffon, Qiana, Ultrasuede, wool jersey, polyester double knit.
   1. Describe the hand of three or more of these fabrics from a source such as your wardrobe, a friend's wardrobe, a nearby store, or the like.

2. Suggest an appropriate style for a garment in three or more of these fabrics. Sketch or clip a picture that represents these styles.
3. Write a brief report, including a summary of your findings and the illustrations you collected.
F. Make a fashion count according to the procedures described in this chapter. Write a brief report describing your findings and make predictions relative to your conclusions about the fashion you counted.
G. Review the quantative analysis section in Appendix 2, p. 258, and carry out a project of this nature.
   1. Formulate a graph depicting the cyclic pattern of change in a style over a 25-year period.
   2. Summarize your findings and make a prediction as to the acceleration or decline of the cyclic pattern of a future period.
I. Read two or more of the articles listed here or research current periodicals or trade journals and select two or more articles related to one of the concepts suggested in the "Review, Discussion and Evaluation."
   1. Prepare note cards while reading each article.
   2. Using your note cards, write a brief summary indicating the relationship of each article to concepts presented in this chapter.
3. Using your note cards, give an oral report in your class, pointing out the important facts included in the articles.

Suggested Articles

Birren, Faber. "Color Comes First." *House and Garden*, September 1957, p. 178.
De Long, Marilyn Revelle. "Analysis of Costume Visual Form." *Journal of Home Economics*, December 1968, pp. 784–88.
Shearer, Lloyd. "Mini–Midi–Maxi—How Ridiculous Can Fashion Get?" *Parade*, March 29, 1970, p. 5.
Rudofsky, Bernard. "The Fashionable Body." *Horizon*, Autumn 1971, p. 56.
"What Fashion Designer John Weitz Sees Ahead." *Textile World*, April 1968, p. 199.
Gernreich, Rudi, "Fashion for the 70's." *Life*, January 9, 1970, pp. 115–118.

NOTE

[1] Marjorie Bevlin, *Design Through Discovery*. New York: Holt, 1970, p. 14.

4

Fashion Creation

At least twice a year, American buyers, journalists, and merchandisers gather in Europe to see the best of the European couture collections. This influential group of Americans arrives with authorized credentials in hand to view, criticize, evaluate, and perhaps make or break the designer for that season—or even for a lifetime.

Even now, when all but one of the major designers have gone into ready-to-wear, the seasonal openings of each couture house are surrounded with an aura of excitement, suspense, and expectation. As the mannequins move through their paces with the customary air of professional hauteur, the viewers have the opportunity to see fashion innovation at its best. The buyers of fashion and the press see the fruits of the true fashion makers. They see the presentation of the seed of an idea, the creative thought of the designer, the innate aesthetic sense that the *good* designer possesses, and the courage that it takes to suggest fashion change to the fickle public. This is the apex of fashion creativity.

As they sit through showing after showing, they may see the most outlandish designs, or the most beautiful, the most overdone, the most exquisite. Perhaps somewhere in this maze of human inspiration they will see the birth of a major fashion change, although major fashion innovations do not necessarily occur each season. Of all the cities in Europe presenting fashion collections, it is Paris that after centuries is still the cradle of the fashion world. The major high fashion changes are born there.

In the preceding chapters, much in-depth discussion has been presented about fashion, fashion innovation, fashion changes, and fashion motivation. In this chapter the focus is on fashion creation: Who are the creators of fashion? Where are they? How do they work? Why are they held in such esteem? Why do we look to Paris for inspiration? What role does the American couture play in the fashion business?

ROLE OF THE FASHION CREATOR

The fashion creator is the genesis of the fashion business. The creator gives birth to ideas; he or she is the beginning, the prime mover, the one who inspires change in high fashion.

The couture, whether European or American, is exclusive, and so expensive to produce (not to mention to buy) that all of the high fashion designers but Alix Grès have gone into ready-to-wear, usually through licensing arrangements with mass manufacturers. The ready-to-wear fashions are said to be designed first, with the high fashion collection a publicity and prestige earner, as well as a kind of trial balloon for the following year's styles.

The creator provides his services for those who want uniqueness, quality, service, and a name, as well as for the fashion innovator, the fashion leader who wants the newest and latest in design. This quality of attainment is called prestige.

But how did it all begin? We constantly hear that "Paris is the fashion capital." What events built this dynasty of designers that has flourished for three centuries? Why is it Paris that has attracted Englishmen, Belgians, Spaniards, Russians, Italians, Swedes, and Americans to seek fame and fortune in the design world?

TERMINOLOGY AND PRONUNCIATION

To continue a study of couture, it is necessary to clarify some vocabulary. Most of the words are French, and many are used in this country in the fashion world. Some are specifically reserved, however, for the French couture.

Adaptation A copy of a garment having features like that of the original.

Atelier (*ah-tel-yay*) A workroom where the models are made and duplicated.

Boutique (*boo-teek*) A shop where accessories and separates are sold.

Chic (*sheek*) Smart, stylish.

Collection The group of models shown by a designer.

Commissionaire (*ko-me-see-ohn-air*) A firm that handles purchases for both manufacturers and stores.

Copy Reproduction of a model, made outside the house that originated it.

Couture (*ko-tour*) A collective term used for design houses.

Couturier (*ko-tour-ee-ay*) A male designer.

Couturière (*ko-tour-ee-air*) A female designer.

Croquis (*kro-kee*) Sketch.

Haute couture (*ot-ko-tour*) The top houses, regarded as creators.

House Abbreviation for a dressmaking house.

Line-for-line Exact copy of a style originated by a foreign designer.

Maison de couture (*may-sahn-duh ko-tour*) A dressmaking house.

Mannequin In France, this word currently means the professional model who shows the clothes in a collection.

Midinette (*me-de-net*) A seamstress. There are classifications of midinettes: first hands, second hands, and apprentices.

Model In France, a term referring to the garment itself, not to the mannequin who wears it.

Modelliste (*mow-day-leest*) One who designs in a house but whose designs are shown under the name of the house.

Modiste (*mow-deest*) Milliner.

Needle trades Includes the industries of dressmaking, millinery, and the manufacture of accessories, notions, and many types of soft goods.

Openings The first showings of the new collections. Usually referred to as "the openings."

Original A design created for showing in a collection. For customers, a duplicate is made to order. Each additional order is a *repeat*.

Premier (*pray-me-ay*) The male head of a workroom.

Première (*pray-me-air*) The female head of a workroom.

Prêt à porter (*pret-ah-por-tay*) Ready-to-wear.

Salon (*sa-lohn*) A spacious room where the collections are shown.

Toile (*twall*) Muslin that in line duplicates an original.

Vendeuse (*van-does*) A saleswoman.

Pronunciation of Designers' Names

Balenciaga: *Bah-lehn-see-ah-gah*
Balmain: *Bal-mehn*
Bohan: *Bo-hahn*
Cardin: *Car-dan*
Castelbajac: *Cah-stel-bah-jahc*
Chanel: *Chah-nel*
Courrèges: *Coor-redge*
Dessés: *Day-say*
Dior: *Dee-or*
Fabiani: *Fah-bee-ahny*
Fath: *Faht*
Forquet: *For-kay*
Galitzine: *Gal-it-zeen*
Givenchy: *Gshe-vahn-shee*
Grès: *Gree*
Griffe: *Grief*
Heim: *I'm*
Kenzo: *Kin-zo*
Lanvin: *Lahn-vahn*
Laroche: *La-roshe*

Lelong: *Luh-long*
Miyake: *Mi-yah-kee*
Molyneux: *Mol-ee-no*
Patou: *Pah-too*
Poiret: *Pwah-ray*
Pucci: *Poo-chee*
Ricci: *Ree-chee*
Rodriguez: *Ro-dree-gez*
Rykiel: *Ri-keel*
St. Laurent, Yves: *Sahn Lawrahn, Eave*
Schiaparelli: *Scap-ah-rel-ee*
Simonetta: *See-mo-netta*
Ungaro: *Uhn-gah-row*
Valentino: *Val-ahn-tee-no*
Vionnet: *Ve-o-nay*

THE FRENCH COUTURE

French Fashion Supremacy

Often it is said that there is something in the air in Paris that makes it an environment of true creativity. Many forces have combined to make Paris the center of the fashion apparel industry: (1) the history of the country, (2) governmental protection of the industry, (3) the auxiliary industries, (4) the splendid needle trades of France, and (5) the geographic location and climate of France.

In the past, the English were noted for architecture, diplomacy, and government; the Japanese for producing silk that supplied the world markets; the Germans for their scientific accomplishment and research; the Italians for their painting and sculpture; the Venetians for their navigators; and the Americans for their construction, machinery, and transportation. But it is the French whose cultural development in the last several centuries has led to the fashion leadership of the world.

HISTORICAL SIGNIFICANCE

Eighteenth-century France was noted especially for its fashion influence; but even before that time, events had shaped the fashion history of that nation.

Two great universities were formed in the 1200s, the University of Paris and the Sorbonne. Culture, art, and religion flourished during the Renaissance. By the 1600s, France was unified, prosperous, the most powerful nation on earth and the *established* center of culture and learning.

French culture during the reign of the Bourbons from the 1600s and into the era of Napoleon III in the middle 1850s, set the world's standard of elegance. The Palace of Versailles, built by Louis XIV in 1661, was the model by which all other palaces were judged.

At that time the fine arts and related arts were reaching a high degree of development. The world's wealthy patronized the Sèvres porcelain factory, the Lyons silk mills, the Gobelin tapestry works, and the French lace industry. The needle trades flourished.

Famous names in fashion began to appear in the 1700s and 1800s: Marie Antoinette, her dressmaker Rose Bertin, Mme. du Pompadour, Mme. du Barry, the Empress Josephine, and the Empress Eugenie. Each of these women had her own special flair for fashion, and each imparted her own special influence to fashion. Their extensive wardrobes reflected the periods in which they lived.

Charles Fredrick Worth, an Englishman, was twenty years old in 1846. He left London for Paris in that year with the desire to make clothes for the wealthy women of France. In that same year, Elias Howe patented his lockstitch sewing machine in the United States. Young Worth soon realized that customers could be persuaded to buy a creation that was already designed, constructed, and shown to them. He is credited with being the father of modern couture. He developed a new way of selling clothing: he showed it on a live model. The most beautiful live model that showed his clothes soon became his wife. He and his model-wife were so successful that in 1860 Empress Eugenie appointed him the court dressmaker. He began attracting foreign trade buyers, as well as a private foreign clientele. Charles Worth was a business innovator as well as a fashion innovator. The "princess" style, often revived today, was designed by Worth for one of Queen Victoria's daughters. The wedding dress was also created by Worth.

FIGURE 4.1 *Opulent French ball gowns. The satin and net gown at the left (1887) is by Worth; the other (1900), embroidered in an Art Nouveau motif, is by Doucet of Paris. (The Metropolitan Museum of Art.)*

Couture houses began springing up all over Paris, attracting both French and foreign designers. The charm, beauty, and imperial power of Paris attracted the wealthy of the world, and the wealthy attracted fashion creators to establish couture houses in Paris. *Harper's Bazaar*, first published on November 2, 1867, appeared in both Paris and the United States. The famous *Godey's Lady's Book* prints and *Leslie's Weekly*, the first popular American illustrated magazine, kept American women informed of the latest Paris modes.

GOVERNMENT PROTECTION OF THE INDUSTRY

Throughout the history of France, the government has given both financial and legislative support to the creative ventures of designers and those in the needle trades.

As far back as the fifteenth century, the rulers of France became patrons of the arts and protected the work of French artists. French fashion was very important in the country's economy. Dressmaking was considered a profession of great importance. For example, in the nineteenth century Napoleon I established the Legion of Honor, to be given for outstanding military or civil service; in our century Christian Dior, designer; Rodier, fabric manufacturer; and Mme. Lanvin, designer, all have received it. Dressmakers and mill owners always have been accorded prestige. An American designer explained what it is like to work in Paris: "Everything is arranged for couturiers in Paris. When you design in Paris, you know that everyone understands what you are trying to do and wants to help."[1]

Into the twentieth century, workers were guaranteed old-age pensions and social insurance. The designs of artists were protected by the government, in recognition of the financial importance of an original design to an artist. In France, copyists were prosecuted, whereas in the United States it is difficult to protect original apparel designs.

AUXILIARY INDUSTRIES

Cooperation has been the keynote of the relationship between the mills, the designers, and the auxiliary industries of buttons, findings, furs, embroiderers, and accessory items. The couture designers of France could design a one-of-a-kind garment because a mill was willing to make the required amount of fabric necessary for the design. Button makers would create exclusive fasteners, and the same enthusiasms existed for the designer in every facet of the apparel industry in France. "Anytime you want a special buckle in France, someone will run it up for you. They don't have to make a die and cast a thousand of them."[2]

In the United States, mass production is a deterrent to the one-of-a-kind creation. The need for assured volume sales handicaps any outstanding new design. Textile mills produce a specific fabric in thousands of yards, whereas in France a fabric producer would weave a small piece of yardage for his client.

This feeling of working together in France is another reason for the fashion supremacy that France has enjoyed for so many years. Designers work in an unconstricted atmosphere, with superb textiles and trimmings close at hand.

THE NEEDLE TRADES OF FRANCE

The French designer flourishes in an environment of splendid workroom cooperation, pride in production, and the magnificent sewing techniques of the French women.

A French workroom is an exciting place to see. All who work there have a tremendous sense of loyalty to the "house," a respect for the fabrics and designs, and a love for and a pride in the work they do. Drama and intrigue envelop those feverish days when the collection is being prepared for the opening.

The staff views the collection at a dress rehearsal, and the couturier often says to his audience that "without les mains de France ("the hands of France"), he himself could do nothing."[3]

French women respect each other's abilities in the needle trades. This respect is instilled early in their lives, because both public and parochial schools teach sewing, millinery, and other crafts on a nationwide basis. Those who excel are encouraged to study further.

THE GEOGRAPHIC LOCATION AND CLIMATE OF FRANCE

Paris is situated on a natural trade route, for all the other capitals of Europe form a circle around it. There is a saying that "All roads lead to Paris." France is about four fifths the size of Texas, and Paris is not far from other capital cities. This is one of the reasons that it is an international market patronized by women of wealth from all over the world. It is easy to get to France; and once Paris was the established fashion center, it became "the place" to go for the international market.

Even the weather offers a sympathetic atmosphere for creativity of France. The climate is without extremes of heat or cold. Seldom do the French experience blizzards, heat waves, hurricanes, or other severe weather conditions. The pleasant weather allows people to wear beautiful clothes without being bundled up or burning up.

TWENTIETH-CENTURY HERITAGE

In 1900 Paris was still the undisputed fashion capital of the world, having been in the fashion lead for centuries. From 1919 until World War II, the role of the Parisian couturière was at its height. Throughout the twentieth century, many famed houses have risen and fallen.

Some of the great names from the early part of this century to which much contemporary styling can be attributed are Madeleine Vionnet, Paul Poiret, Jeanne Lanvin, Coco Chanel, Lucien Lelong, Edward Molyneux, Elsa Schiaparelli,

Jean Patou, Christobal Balenciaga, Alix Grès, and Christian Dior. These are but a few of the great Parisian creators of fashion, but they have become legends. Although of various nationalities, they all chose Paris as their designing home.

Madeleine Vionnet (French). One of the fashion world's great innovators died in March 1975, at the age of ninety-eight. She was the last survivor of the golden age of the Paris couture. Vionnet will be remembered as the master technician who created the bias cut of the 1930s. She said everyone else was doing straight cuts and she felt the need for something different. She produced suppleness, seductivity, and the modern feminine body. Vionnet was a loner who did not participate in social life. She closed her design house in 1939, but during her reign she dressed all of the queens of Europe and many other wealthy women.

FIGURE 4.3 *Ensemble by Paul Poiret, 1918.*

Paul Poiret (French). One of the great figures of the French dressmaking world, Paul Poiret was an interesting, exciting personality, a leader in his social set. His enthusiasms carried over into his professional endeavors. He gave extravagant parties, often costume parties. He established the School of Decorative Arts and wrote his own story in a book entitled, *The King of Fashion.*

One of Poiret's innovations was the harem skirt. He also received much publicity and criticism for taking his mannequins to the races in slacks. His life was spiced with excitement and achievement, but unfortunately he lived the last ten years of his life without funds, supported by friends made in better days.

Jeanne Lanvin (French). Mme. Lanvin was solely responsible for her designs; she never received financial aid or subsidies from the government or from a partner. She was the sole owner and sole creator of her house. She was unique in

FIGURE 4.2 *Evening dress by Vionnet, 1938. Silk with gilt. (The Metropolitan Museum of Art, Gift of Ann Payne Blumenthal, 1941.)*

FIGURE 4.4 *Evening gown by Lanvin, 1961. (Courtesy of the French Embassy Press and Information Division.)*

being the dressmaker who first created a shop for men, featuring suits, shirts, and accessories.

Lanvin is credited with having raised the haute couture to the rank of an industry that brought prestige and fortune to France. In 1926, she received the Croix de la Legion d'Honneur; in 1936, she was named an officer of the Legion d'Honneur.

Her designs had a youthful look; she borrowed ideas from all periods and countries. Many of her designs looked like works of art taken from paintings, and she will be especially remembered for her embroideries.

Gabrielle Chanel (French). Known to everyone as Coco, Chanel was an amazing woman, full of ideas, energy, and initiative. She brought the French woman into the full thrust of the business world as head of her own big business.

It was Coco, in the 1920s, who shortened skirts to match short hair and in the early twenties introduced her famous Chanel No. 5 perfume. She was the first to use jersey for women's clothing. She made acceptable the use of costume ("junk") jewelry as fashion, particularly long strands of fake pearls.

In 1935, she opened her own fabric factory, and her red and beige woolens became known internationally. She closed her couture house in 1939, only to reopen it again in 1954, saying that she could no longer endure idleness. She was seventy at the time.

FIGURE 4.5 *The classic Chanel suit and hat. This version, shown by the house of Chanel in 1973, is almost identical to suits designed by Coco Chanel herself decades ago. (Courtesy of the French Embassy Press and Information Division.)*

She considered being copied one of the greatest compliments. She said, "Imitation makes fashion." She died in 1971 at the age of eighty-seven while preparing for the opening of her January collection. Some called her the most influential designer of the twentieth century.

Lucien Lelong (French). A brilliant designer and decorated French war hero of World War I, Lelong's success came quickly after the war, a time when the Parisian couture flourished.

During the depression after 1929, Lelong, a good businessman, created his "edition" department, comparable to the designer boutiques of today.

At the onset of World War II, the Paris couture was closed. In 1947, Lelong came to America with a few models to stimulate and re-open the fashion traffic and trade across the Atlantic. He wanted the United States to know that Paris was her creative self again.

Lelong will be remembered for his use and understanding of fabrics. He felt that fabrics had their own personality and a behavior he likened to that of a temperamental woman.

Edward Molyneux (Irish). Molyneux was a gifted artist who rose to the rank of captain in the British Army during World War I. In 1919, he opened a salon in Paris that achieved immediate success. He dressed the English court from the salon he established in London. During his time as a couturier he offered tremendous service in financing schools for French workers in the dress-

FIGURE 4.6 Lucien Lelong, 1930s look of classic lines cut on the bias. He liked to create a feeling of movement in his skirts.

FIGURE 4.7 *The house of Molyneux is famous for beautifully executed tailored designs. (Courtesy of the French Embassy Press and Information Division.)*

making field. He gave money, time, thought, and effort to promote the required training for students who showed promise in the field.

Molyneux had a fetish about the number 5. His showings always opened on the fifth of the month, and his most famous perfume was named Number 5. His birthday was September 5, and his salon was at number 5 on the street. He is best remembered for his severe elegance and purity of line. His collections were conservative, yet distinguished.

Elsa Schiaparelli (Italian). Schiaparelli was a true innovator with touches of the daring, the dramatic, and the aloof. It was not uncommon for Schiap, as she was nicknamed, to tell a customer that her clothes did not look right on her or to tell a store's buyers that they simply did not understand her and that she would rather not sell to them.

Shocking pink, a vibrant color, was always associated with her name. She also introduced ticking as a fashion fabric. Her reputation was built on the spectacular. Her colors were the purest, her designs the starkest, her decoration the most embellished. She combined her knowledge, timing, and sense of daring in the presentation of her designs, colors, and fabrics.

In 1954, she presented her last collection in the haute couture, feeling that she was out of step with the times. However, she continued to design for her boutique.

Jean Patou (French). Patou was a man of courage, great inspiration, and dynamic personality. When Patou believed in something, no amount of effort was too great. He approached his work in the couture with this philosophy.

In 1924, after a visit to the United States, he returned to Paris with six beautiful American

FIGURE 4.8 *Jean Patou, 1970.*

mannequins, to the shock and dismay of the Parisian couture. From that time, he always included American women in his groups of mannequins.

Patou produced sports clothes, and during the Roaring 20s, designed some extremely short skirts; in 1929, he went to the other extreme and greatly lengthened the hemline. Patou felt that the dress should be part of the woman, that they should move as one, neither overpowering the other. He ran his house with flair and instilled great pride, loyalty, and artistry in the people who worked there.

Patou died suddenly in March 1936. Raymond Barbas continued in his place, retaining the name of the House of Patou.

Christobal Balenciaga (Spanish). Balenciaga was a Spaniard, who was the leading couturier in

FIGURE 4.10 *Grès, 1972. Grès drapes and shapes her dresses with exquisite detail, feeling, and movement.*

Barcelona, Spain, until 1937, when he answered the call of Paris and established his successful house there. He was a master of elegance and line, of taste and temperament. Balenciaga rarely made sports clothing; he specialized in the sophistication and drama of exquisite dresses.

He was a simple man who, in his later years of designing, would not allow the press into his showing. This decision cost him greatly. Neither would he allow himself to be photographed. Many times black or blacks and browns predominated in his collections. He manipulated lavish laces superbly. He also used heavy braids, fringes, and tassels, in keeping with his Spanish heritage.

Alix Grès (French). Grès is most noted for her ability to drape. Many of her designs reflect a strong Grecian influence. She conceives all of

FIGURE 4.9 *Balenciaga, 1960. A master tailor and superb dressmaker as well.*

FIGURE 4.11 *Dior, 1961. This A-line jacket-dress shows the elegance and sophistication that made Dior a success at every opening. (Courtesy of the French Embassy Press and Information Division.)*

draping and pinning with her nimble, accomplished fingers. Grès possesses boundless energy, loves work, gives attention to details, and is a good businesswoman; the last of the great designers to ignore ready-to-wear, she is president of the Chambre Syndicale and is widely revered.

Christian Dior (French). Dior was the master of timing, sensing accurately when the fashion public was ready for a change. He is most famous for his fashion revolution, the New Look, of his 1947 postwar collection. In the fall of 1954 he presented his H line and in 1955 the A and Y lines.

He said he benefited from knowing the work of other designers: "Molyneux' style, Chanel's restraint and omissions, Vionnet's techniques, Lelong's working knowledge of and respect for fabrics."[4]

Dior's love of work was paramount in his life, and he developed the largest couture house in Paris. Reading was a form of relaxation for him, and he accumulated a large library in his home. Dior was a superstitious man, who insisted on having a mannequin carry a bouquet of fresh lilies of the valley at each opening. He would never see the first show from the salon but would watch from behind the scenes.

His name became a household word in the United States after World War II. At the height of his career, he was certainly the most well-known French designer in the world. He died in 1957, and his duties were assumed first by Yves St. Laurent and later by Marc Bohan, who is still the head designer in the House of Dior.

At present, the House of Dior is the largest of the high fashion houses, with American sales outstripping those of the whole French auto industry. Franchised ready-to-wear, perfumes, and accessories account for most revenue.

The Haute Couture Today

STRUCTURE

Haute couture in France is a highly structured and prized industry, as we know from its history. One of the major sources of its strength and organization is the *Chambre Syndicale de la Couture*

her designs herself and constructs each one on a mannequin. Along with Chanel, she helped bring jersey into the fashion spotlight. Jersey flows as she directs it to, in her designs.

She possesses the qualities of a sculptor and has the ability to accentuate the feminine form,

Parisienne. The United States has nothing comparable to this in her gigantic, sprawling textile and apparel industry.

The Chambre Syndicale de la Couture Parisienne has been a stabilizing force for the French couture since 1868. It was formed at that time on the model of the old guilds that had existed in medieval days. Its original objectives were to deal collectively for its members in problems concerning taxes, wages, and other administrative matters.

The Chambre Syndicale has grown strong in France by providing many services for the French dressmaking industry.

1. The Chambre Syndicale *represents* all members, which include the haute couture as well as the mass producers of the trade, and *advises* on law, taxes, and on every aspect of employment.
2. It *lobbies* by carrying on negotiations with the various branches of government that cover the industry. It also polices the industry itself to prevent misuses of creative design.
3. In 1929, the Chambre Syndicale established an *educational system* that ensures training for every girl and boy in France who shows an aptitude for the needle trades or allied arts. It is a part of the Ministry of National Education.
4. It *coordinates* openings by setting the days, dates, and hours to avoid an overlapping of designers' showings in France and in other countries.
5. The Chambre Syndicale establishes the *delivery dates of pieces* ordered by the trade buyers. These are usually shipped thirty days after their showing. It also *regulates press release dates*, which are set approximately six weeks after showings. This gives the buyers of expensive models time to get copies made.
6. The Chambre Syndicale *issues credentials* for authorized buyers and the press for both French and foreign groups.
7. The Chambre Syndicale *registers designs* and thus serves as the protection agency against fashion piracy. A garment made by a Syndicale member, is photographed from the back, front, and sides, and the design is registered with the Chambre Syndicale. If a registered design is copied in France, the act is punishable by law.

ORGANIZATION OF A COUTURE HOUSE

Each couture firm is referred to as a house and contains a design area and sewing rooms. It is generally located in an exclusive residential area or perhaps in an old palace, as is the case with Emilio Pucci's house in Florence, Italy.

The name of the house usually carries the name of the head designer, except in such instances when the head designer–owner has died and the management chooses to retain the original name and hire a new head designer. Marc Bohan is head designer at Dior's and Michael Goma at Patou's.

Houses vary in size, but there is a ranking hierarchy of personnel that exists in each.

Première   Responsible for reproducing the work of the design department; a very skilled technician in charge of the midinettes.

Midinettes   The women who do the sewing.

Directrice   Supervises the line mannequins on whom the samples are made and shown. She is also in charge of the selling showroom and the saleswomen.

Vendeuse   Saleswoman.

Some houses have extensive business offices and sales promotion divisions, depending on their size.

Until 1950, the French government subsidized the couture houses from a tax levied against French fabric firms. To qualify for this, a house would have to use 80 per cent of its fabrics from French textile producers. Since this subsidy has been discontinued, designers have looked to other sources to help achieve financial stability. In January 1976, however, the French government contributed $500,000 to revive the house of Pierre Balmain.

The economics of the couture is changing, and many couturiers are involved in other businesses beside the actual creation of garments. Couture productions and collection openings are terribly expensive. To supplement the business, enterprising couturiers may manufacture or license others to manufacture and sell perfumes, jewelry, lingerie, handbags, and other accessory items. Others have outside financial backing from large textile firms, or they deal directly with pattern companies in design work. Dior has a manufacturing firm on Seventh Avenue, and others have them in other parts of the world as well as in New York.

COUTURE OPENINGS

With the strength of the Chambre Syndicale de la Couture Parisienne, world prestige and publicity, and a great history, the haute couture moves twice a year into its openings in January and July. The atmosphere is tense, charged with electricity and anticipation, and the grand presentations are done with finesse.

The press generally views the openings shortly before the trade buyers but is pledged not to publish coverage for six weeks. The press comes to evaluate what will create fashion news. The professional buyers represent manufacturers as well as retail stores. They come in search of innovations in silhouette, fabric, trim, and color. They are looking for an idea to copy or stylize (some major retail stores will do "line-for-line" copies). It will take the American entourage approximately two or three weeks to view the openings on the continent and in London. A few weeks later, the couture has a showing for its private clientele.

The trade buyers come to the openings with the ultimate purpose of copying, and it proves to be expensive for them. At each house, the buyer is charged a *caution fee*, for any idea he might take with him in his head. The trade buyer has an acutely trained eye for detail and will remember a lot; thus, the buyer will leave with more than is actually purchased. The caution fee is a source of protective income for the designer. The fee can be anywhere from $500 to $3,000 and is deducted from any purchases made from the house. The trade buyer will pay more for the same dress than the private customer will pay. The increased cost is for the copying rights. After all the designers' collections are viewed, the

buyers head for home, sometimes exhilarated about what they saw—and always exhausted.

In the last few days of February, after the January showings, the French imports begin to dribble in through the customs to the Seventh Avenue showrooms. These were the purchases the trade buyers made to copy. The first United States showings of French clothes are customarily staged by The Fashion Group in an elaborate performance in the grand ballroom of the Hilton Hotel. Many fantastic creations that are not bought by American trade buyers are flown to this country for this special showing. The "influentials" of the American garment industry view the French fashion innovations.

It is thus that French fashions are presented for all the world to see—to either accept or reject. So the cycle goes, while the couture houses again begin to get ready for the showings in another six months.

STATUS

After World War II in 1946, the French couture reopened its doors. Dior, Balenciaga, Jean Dessès, Jacques Fath, Hubert de Givenchy, Nina Ricci, Schiaparelli, and others are famous for their leadership in the design world at that time. During the 1950s, France managed to maintain its fashion supremacy.

Schiaparelli, in 1954, was one of the first to realize that the haute couture was out of step with the world's fast pace and mass production techniques. Thus, we saw major changes in the couture during the 1960s and the 1970s.

Ready-to-wear clothes have been produced in France since 1903. The industry was small, but in the 1960s couture designers, one, by one, began moving into the field. The couturier was interested in the *prêt-à-porter* for greater volume and profit. It was becoming evident for several reasons that the haute couture collections were not commanding the attention that they once did; haute couture in 1977 had only 3,000 clients, as compared with 15,000 just after World War II.

In 1977 a full-scale production of a collection cost around $500,000. This automatically raises the cost of a garment. Another important factor to be considered is the time involved. There are few women who have the time or the patience for four fittings. Even the wealthy want their clothes immediately. Furthermore, fashion cycles are changing more rapidly than they once did, and a dress may be stylish for only one season. Who can afford an $8,000 dress for one season? Priorities and values have been reassessed at all economic levels.

For years several designers had boutiques on their premises through which they sold their factory-produced, less-expensive garments. During the early 1970s, however, nearly all of the couture went into the prêt-à-porter, franchising boutiques in Europe, in Japan, and in the United States.

In 1971 Yves St. Laurent shocked the fashion world by announcing that he no longer would do a haute couture collection. From 1960 to 1970, twenty couture salons had been forced to close, and even Dior had reduced his workroom in 1971 from nineteen rooms to five. However, the fashion world was still not ready for St. Laurent's decision.

At 35, after being at the top for fourteen years, he said that he couldn't participate in the fashion "circus" any longer: "I saw it all as fake and with every passing season it got worse." He announced that he was "hopelessly out of touch," that "fashion comes from the streets." He wanted to be a part of it.

The first Rive Gauche, a ready-to-wear boutique, opened in Paris in 1966. Another opened in New York in 1968. By 1977 St. Laurent had franchised 112 boutiques around the world and worldwide sales totaled $200 million. Although he has re-entered haute couture and is considered by many to be the "golden-haired darling of Paris fashion," the most influential designer in the world today, he shattered tradition by showing his 1976 fall collection at the big, commercial Hotel Intercontinental rather than in his elegant couture house on the Avenue Marceau.

Courrèges, Cardin, Lanvin, Ricci, Givenchy, and others have established ready-to-wear boutiques all over the world and are realizing the benefits of fast-selling fashions. The couturiers have joined the mass-production system and have greatly raised its standards. The French couturier now offers men and women well-styled clothes at comparatively reasonable prices. The designer boutiques featuring prêt-à-porter are still by no means inexpensive. They are in the $100 and up range, but they are considerably less expensive than the haute couture.

FRENCH COUTURE PERSONALITIES

Following are brief descriptions of some of the most outstanding contemporary French designers.

Yves St. Laurent. St. Laurent has given us the trapeze, the tunic, the midi, city pants, and a large dress called the naive chemise. This fashion genius has outfitted us as Robin Hoods, Mondrian paintings, gangsters, and cowboys. In the fall of 1974, he presented his collection in America for

FIGURE 4.12 *Yves St. Laurent's double-breasted pant suit in pinstriped wool shows an important part of his daytime philosophy for 1976.*

the first time. The clothes were expensive, even though they were from the prêt-à-porter.

Kenzo Takada. Kenzo Takada is a superstar. He was born in Osaka, Japan, in 1944 and is today a prêt-à-porter designer whose style is distinctly contemporary. He had had three years of style training and four years of sketching in Japan, before he went to Paris on a vacation and decided not to return home.

In 1970 he opened his own Paris boutique. He is innovative—one of the most innovative of today's designers. His clothes are fresh, natural, and fun to wear. He had a great influence on the smocks of the early 1970s and is responsible for the dolmans, cap sleeves, smocksweaters, and deep-sleeved battle-jacket of 1972; the Great Gatsby look of 1972; and the low-slung Chinese look that was popular in the fall of 1975.

FIGURE 4.14 *A balloon bat-wing top over a matching skirt with knit trim. Pierre Cardin, 1977.*

Pierre Cardin. One of the wealthiest couturiers, Pierre Cardin is definitely a trend-setter who became well known for his bubble silhouette in the late 1950s. Born in 1922 he has exerted a great influence on the fashion world. Cardin feels that the idea of couture where a seam is studied for an hour, where a woman should look elegant and refined is dead. Cardin is an intellectual designer whose creations are avant garde and sometimes extreme.

In 1960 he was the first to begin a complete line of women's ready-to-wear fashions, and in 1964 he began a full line of custom-made and ready-to-wear fashions for men. He has shown mannequins in crash helmets, matched short skirts and colored stockings, and futuristic space suits for both men and women.

André Courrèges. Courrèges is best known among designers for his architectural influence

FIGURE 4.13 *Kenzo did the "Great Gatsby" look in 1972. He began the idea with a tennis look in swimsuits and the innovation grew.*

FIGURE 4.15 *Courrèges, 1971. This hooded white coat, designed to be worn over a bathing suit, is typical of the "architectural" look of Courrèges' designs. (Courtesy of the French Embassy Press and Information Division.)*

of the 1960s. His most important design concept is that "beauty is logical."

Marc Bohan.   Bohan was born in Paris in the early 30s and had apprentice experience with Piquet, Molyneux, Madeleine de Rauch, Patou, and then worked at Dior's. At Dior's death, Yves St. Laurent was put in the position of head designer at the House of Dior. He and Bohan had worked together there. Yves left for the army, and when he returned in 1961 Bohan was firmly situated as head designer, having had a tremendous success at his first showing. He still holds this position and supervises other branches in London, New York, and South America. Bohan is noted for fine craftmanship but is not particularly innovative. He does, however, strive for elegance and simplicity.

on the clothes of the 1960s. Courrèges is noted as the man who did the most for the "flying hemline." He is a former disciple of Balenciaga, from whom he separated in 1961 to open his own house. Soon afterward he became known as the trouser king, for his slit at the bottom of slacks and formal trouser suits. Then, in 1965, when his girlish-figured mannequins stepped on stage in severe white dresses three inches above the knee, the high-flying hem was born.

Courrèges prefers white, but he sometimes combines it with a sharply contrasting hue. He felt that he could make women happier by bringing more white and more color into their lives. He also played a part in the innovation of boots for women. (He thinks high heels are as preposterous as the ancient Chinese practice of binding women's feet.) Courrèges felt that boots were more practical and went well with the short skirts

FIGURE 4.16 *Marc Bohan, 1976. His weightless raincoat in tissue-weight silk taffeta is worn over a crepe de chine dress.*

FIGURE 4.17 *Givenchy concentrates on quality and detail. His spring/summer 1976 collection was filled with meticulous touches and intricate pleat treatments.*

Hubert de Givenchy. Givenchy was born in 1927. He is a tall, lean man—a man of experience and judgment. During the 1950s and 1960s, he was considered one of the greatest of the French haute couture. As a small boy he began designing clothes and at seventeen began working for Jacques Fath. He then moved to Piquet, Lelong, and Schiaparelli. In 1952, at the age of twenty-four, he opened his own salon. He was greatly influenced by Balenciaga, whom he met in 1953. Givenchy took up where the great technician left off as the master of line, cut, and elegance. He maintained this philosophy of design throughout the latter sixties and the period he called the "vulgar shock." He said, "There are not 36,000 ways to do couture. There's only one way to do it well. Balenciaga found it."[5] Givenchy operates boutiques in Europe and the United States.

Future of the Haute Couture

Late in 1971, the French televised a round-table discussion concerning the haute couture. Included in the discussion group were three of France's leading couturiers: Pierre Cardin, Andre Courrèges, and Marc Bohan.

Bohan said, "It's sad to say, but I have been all over the world and I must confess that Paris no longer holds the first place it once had." However, he further stated, "Nothing will change for us. The buyers and the private clients need these prestige presentations. Our ready-to-wear line is an entirely different order."

Pierre Cardin said, "No woman in her right mind wants to pay $1,500 for a dress these days. Anyway, it's madness to risk one's reputation twice a year."

In an interview, Michael Goma at Jean Patou said, "We are going to stay in the ranks of the haute couture. But we are not unmindful of the importance of the ready-to-wear clientele."

The old faithful of the haute couture will certainly be mindful of the fast-rising ready-to-wear industry. American buyers are flocking in ever-increasing numbers to the prêt-à-porter openings held in October and April. Many innovations are launched during these openings.

The tradition of French fashion leadership is being employed to boost the importance of the French prêt-à-porter.

In spite of social and economic changes, the *prestige* of the couture is still evident. Couture showings attract worldwide attention and help the designers promote the more profitable businesses they may be engaged in, such as franchised ready-to-wear, perfumes, hosiery, accessories, pattern companies, and the designing of linens.

These is still a small *private clientele* that patronizes the couture. For elegant dresses, ball gowns, and furs, this group looks to the couturier. St. Laurent not only retains his private trade but has 750 faithful customers—not bad at $7,000 to $8,000 a dress.

Trade buyers will continue to come to openings, if not to buy, then to look, to sum up, to assess, to be aware of what the innovators are showing and where fashion is headed.

Paris is still Paris. The creative climate that has existed for three centuries is still there. The small quantities and excellent quality of textiles, accessories, findings, laces, and embroideries are still available. The thousands of dedicated and skilled seamstresses are still eager to work. The French still appreciate and honor their artists. The return to traditional values that seems to be the trend in America in the late 1970s seems to be signalling a revival of the elegance that is the Parisian trademark. In 1975, the couture business produced $1.5 billion, a 15 per cent increase over the year before. Another 15 per cent gain was projected for 1976. The number of Parisian haute couture houses in 1976 rose by two to 26.

THE AMERICAN COUTURE

Twentieth-Century Heritage

At the beginning of the century, American women were trained to think of nothing but Paris when thinking of fashion. Americans were also accustomed to a cheap form of mass production before World War II. Only the wealthy could afford appealing individual designs, and the wealthy could and did shop in Paris. American mass-produced knock-offs of fashions were necessarily simplified, and definitely not chic. The situation presented a frustrating dilemma for the American designer, who did not receive any prestige, glamour, or individual fame. The thing that the American designer did receive was financial recognition—this was the motivation.

At the outset, the American couture was wholesale-oriented in concept, whereas the Paris couture was a retail institution. Haute couture had been developed with the idea of satisfying the demands of the wealthy through twenty to twenty-five first-class designers and their shops. American couture was developed to sell primarily to stores across the country, thus, putting it into a wholesale situation.

Some of the designers of note during the embryonic days of American couture were Nettie Rosenstein, Clare Potter, and Hattie Carnegie, all wholesale designers. The Hollywood greats were Adrian of Metro-Goldwyn-Mayer and Howard Greer and Travis Banton of Paramount. Some retail designers had their own shops; and there were also designers for such specialty stores as Bergdorf Goodman, Saks Fifth Avenue, and Bendel. Many of the American designers went to the Paris openings. The Paris designers were the outstanding originators, but the Americans were proving themselves adept at providing variations of the Paris themes.

During World War I, the American fashion magazines began promoting American designers, and Americans were forced to stop, look, listen, and learn about the American designers and what they had to offer. After World War I, in around the early 1920s, the United States' appetite for French finery was so great that Paris could not meet the demand: the designer could not design fast enough and the seamstress could not sew fast enough. This opened the way for the birth of American couture, aligned with the American department store.

In March 1932 the Manhattan retail establishment of Lord & Taylor bought newspaper space to advertise dresses made by American designers, a first in this country. Other stores quickly followed; the Depression made it popular to "buy American." Although there had been American designers for many years, no one had paid attention to them or even knew their names. Another result of hard times was that the homemaker, the career woman, and the college woman were beginning to rebel against some of the extreme styles coming out of Paris, on the well-known principle that "If you have to buy it cheap, buy it *plain*."

In 1940 Lord & Taylor opened a designer shop in their store for original, popular-priced American dresses. As a form of challenge, a Texan, Stanley Marcus, owner-president of Dallas's Neiman-Marcus, stated, "The American garment industry is now in a position to prove whether it can make a silk dress or a sow's ear."[6]

Then came World War II, and in 1941 the Parisian couture closed. This was the second and biggest push that the American designers received. They had been productive, but only in an atmosphere of following the giants of the fashion world, housed in their towers of fame and charisma, flaunting their leadership role in the face of the fashion world. This was hard competition, but when France fell to the Nazis, American design had to stand on its own and produce for American society.

On January 23, 1943, in the main hall of the Metropolitan Museum of Art in New York City, the first American Fashion Critics' Award was presented for outstanding contribution to American fashion. The award had been conceived years before by Eleanor Lambert and was presented by Mayor La Guardia of New York. The immediate object was to show the rest of the country that New York City would continue to be the fashion center of the world. The mayor beamed as he handed $1000 in war bonds and a gilded bronze statuette called the "Winnie" to a dark-haired, dapper young designer who was to gain world-wide recognition in the next few years, Norman Norell. He received the first "Winnie" and created a "Hall of Fame" for three-time winners.

In 1947 Eleanor Lambert helped create the Coty awards for excellence in design.

During the peak of haute couture, between World War I and World War II, elegance was a major criterion—though, as we have seen, elegance tended to the playful in the twenties and to the casual in the thirties. After World War II, the mushrooming suburbs lent themselves to a more casual life style. The huge middle class was emerging. The American couture was coming alive.

THE COUTURE TODAY

Status

On March 14, 1963, in the Grand Ballroom of the Waldorf-Astoria Hotel in New York City, the elite of the American fashion industry—over 1,500 men and women—came to watch the best of the latest French haute couture collections, and for the first time two American designers were included in that prestigious showing. The two were Norman Norell, born in Indiana and designing out of New York, and James Galanos, born in Philadelphia and designing in Los Angeles. American couture had arrived.

American couture has a different set of goals from that of France. America does not have trained personnel to do the fine sewing of haute couture, and the intention of American couture is not to dress one individual, but to clothe many. Labor costs are high, and we have a very sophisticated system of mass production. American couture serves as a trend-setter for the apparel field in line, color, and texture. It is definitely a ready-to-wear system of garment production, but not on the scale of the huge mass producers.

Before World War II, there were a dozen or more couturiers in New York doing custom work, but they have long since vanished as American women have assumed a new set of values.

Between 1963 and 1974, Americans suffered through a great deal of political and social turmoil. The traditional haute couture of Paris lost some of its luster and life was too hectic to fit custom clothing into the picture. Thus, the American ready-to-wear began to thrive.

Structure

There are three major fashion centers in the United States today where couture designing is done: New York, Los Angeles, and Dallas. New York, of course, is still at the fashion pinnacle in the United States, but it is currently besieged by many problems such as rising labor costs, living costs, rent costs, crime rates and the encroachment of organized crime.

SEVENTH AVENUE

New York is the oldest and most comprehensive fashion market in the United States and serves manufacturers and retailers with a full range of apparel and textile products for men, women, and children as well as related industries. "New York is where it's at." Seventh Avenue—or Fashion Avenue, as the city of New York has named it—manufactures and markets in a very small area always referred to by the trade as Seventh Avenue. The four blocks on either side of Seventh Avenue and Broadway, between 36th and 40th Street, constitute the New York dress business. It is innovative in philosophy and sophisticated in execution of design.

When one walks the streets of Seventh Avenue in the garment district, one knows that there is no other place like it in the world. It is *the* center of the garment industry in America, with its frantic, frenetic pace and impassable streets. One is always being pushed, shoved, and walked into by workingmen thrusting large racks of clothes down the sidewalks or yelling at people to "move it" so they can get through with their mountainous rolls of fabric. They know they own the streets, but visitors at least can feel that they are at the throbbing heart of the industry. New York does not have the beauty, the serenity, and the history that Paris offers; instead, it offers the hustle, bustle, and sheer madness of the American at work and the American way of "making a buck" in the "rag trade," and the American couture takes part in it as well as the mass producer. Seventh Avenue in New York is the top of the fashion world on this side of the Atlantic.

Many top designers have their showrooms along Seventh Avenue. As visitors enter these, they are engulfed by another world. They are elevated out of the confusion of the streets into the sophistication of the designer salon.

Most of the familiar names of couture operate out of New York. Geoffrey (pronounced "Jeffrey") Beene, Bill Blass, Oscar de La Renta, Pauline Trigère, Halston, Norman Norell (d. 1972), Donald Brooks, Stephen Burrows, Stan Herman, Anne Klein, Calvin Klein, Betsy Johnson, Maurice Rentner, and Oleg Cassini are a few who work out of New York.

LOS ANGELES

Los Angeles is a truly unusual fashion market in an innovative, young, and vital environment that specializes in leisure sportswear and at-home wear and the ultraglamourous formal and evening wear influenced by the movie industry. The California climate is better than New York's; the atmosphere is more relaxed than that of Seventh Avenue. There are many good seamstresses who come from the area's Oriental population.

Due to the unusual characteristics of the consumer market segments in California, Los Angeles is considered to be a testing ground for new and sometimes radical styles. There are startling new fabrics and color combinations for both women and men. The California theory is "Try it, you might like it!"

The work of California couture designers reflects both casualness and the extremes of luxury. Some of the best-known California designers are Rudi Gernreich, who presented the topless bathing suit in 1964—and to his amazement had 1,000 orders for it; James Galanos, who specializes in extravagant ball gowns; of course, the movie and television designers. Probably the most famous of these is Edith Head, seven-time Oscar winner, who was with Paramount for many years and is now with Universal Studios. Actually, the film industry opens a completely new category for the creative designer, and many prefer working in it.

DALLAS

Dallas is the area that is important for the moderate-price manufacturer. Couture designers are few in the Dallas area, but Les Wilk, Randy Randazzo, and Victor Costa manage to keep couture alive there.

A huge couture wing was recently added to the Apparel Mart which has brought some glitter to the Dallas fashion center and has helped its fashion image. A new showroom, opened for the April 1975 market, is called Design Concept. This group shops the European market and offers a collection of couture lines to the small buyer who usually does not go to New York, much less Europe.

Developing the Collection

Fall is the major season for couture, both French and American. The majority of the major fashion changes are presented in these collections. Holiday and resort lines are next and then the spring and summer lines. In the summer, a small collection of sometimes under fifty units is generally presented because it is difficult to convince the American woman that she should spend $200 for a summer cotton dress.

Each designer has his own "thing." It may be a special technique with fabrics, a way with line, or an ability to say it with color. And each designer has his own way of arriving at the ideas for new creations. Some may use a very simple sketch, some will do elaborate pencil and paper designs, and others will work directly with the fabric on a model and drape it to get the feel of it. But each will do some sort of visual presentation of the idea.

After these designs are created, samples are made in muslin or other fabric, and changes are made until the designer is satisfied. Then the pattern is cut and it is perfected in the chosen fabric. This process continues until the designer has anywhere from 30 to 150 pieces, what is called a collection or a line.

SHOWING THE COLLECTION

Buyers flock to New York for a two- to three-week period for the couture showings. Fall–winter showings begin in late April and run into May. Spring–summer showings are in late October or November. These follow the Paris prêt-à-porter openings, which show fall–winter collections in late March and spring–summer collections in early October. Usually, before the buyers leave New York, The Fashion Group takes over and presents an edited version of the creations of domestic designers with great flair in the Hilton Hotel ballroom. This gives the audience an overview of what the season looks like.

The Fashion Group has been highly responsible for bringing together all aspects of the fashion business. The interchange that has resulted from the formation of The Fashion Group has helped to benefit the entire fashion industry. In 1928, some of the pioneers met on a stormy night at Mary Elizabeth's Tea Room in New York City. It was decided that a "club" or organization of some kind was definitely in order for women working in fashion. The organization was to serve as a clearing house for information about what was going on in the business. It was to be a sharing of problems and exploring of ideas.

By 1930, the "group" was not as yet formed but 45 women met at the Women's City Club in New York to hear Marcia Conner (then associate editor of Vogue) talk about the importance of a fashion guild. The Fashion Group was born in 1931 when 75 women attended a luncheon at the Hotel Pennsylvania. Its original purpose was to promote good taste and serve as a clearing house for current problems and new ideas. Extensive research and comprehensive programs have been included over the years and greatly benefit the fashion business.

Today, The Fashion Group has over 5000 members with regional chapters in 24 cities and five foreign countries. Women are elegible for membership when they have worked as executives for at least three years.

Press Week, established in 1940 exclusively for the women of the press, brings approximately 200 editors to New York for the top New York couture showings. There are two Press Weeks a year, in June for fall–winter and in January for spring–summer. It is quite a week for the press, including not only the showing of fashions from many designers and manufacturers but enormous amounts of wining and dining. The participating designers and manufacturers pick up the entertainment tab in return for nationwide communication with the fashion public.

Most of the American couture designers show a resort-holiday line to keep their manufacturers and their showrooms busy. Some designers produce a line during all of the five market seasons, as do the mass producers.

When the buyers are at the showings, they "leave paper," or place orders, for the styles. If a couture designer gets 100 orders, it will be considered a *good* cutting; 250 orders will mean the production of a real winner. He or she may cut the style with fewer orders, too. Reorders are important to couture because stores do not buy in volume. Most couture designers are eager to cut reorders even in small numbers.

Personalities of American Couture

Norman Norell. Although Norell has been dead since 1972, his influence still lives in the American couture. He was called the dean of fashion and was a three-time Winnie winner, which elected him to fashion's Hall of Fame.

Norell began as a Hollywood designer in the early 1920s, created costumes for vaudeville and

FIGURE 4.18 *Norell was the American master of proportion and cut patterning his work after Balenciaga's tailoring. The sketch shows one of his outstanding designs.*

FIGURE 4.19 *This skirt with vest and cape shows Trigére's special flair for achieving elegant results from simple elements (1975).*

burlesque shows, worked for Hattie Carnegie and Teal Traina, and in 1961 formed Norman Norell, Inc.

Through the years he perfected a remarkable product known as a "Norell." "A Norell is a coat, suit, or dress that is a triumph of simplicity, fabric, painstaking workmanship, and fashion news."[7] His clothes retailed from $250 to $2,500.

Pauline Trigère. If Seventh Avenue can claim one true dressmaker, it is Pauline Trigère. She was born and reared in Paris and came to the United States on her way to Chile at the beginning of World War II. However, she never made it to Chile even though her possessions did.

Trigère has a special way with fabric in a dart or a drape. She drapes the final fabric and never

uses muslin. She makes sketches, but says she can never find them—says they are like shorthand notes to her. She has an expert knowledge of cutting and works well in the bias. Her clothes are simple and yet dramatic and sophisticated.

Calvin Klein In June 1975 Calvin Klein became the first designer to win a third straight Coty Award. His career really began in 1968 when he approached Bonwit Teller's president, Mildred Custin, to show her his line. She advised him to raise his prices by $10. He did and walked away with a $50,000 order. In 1975, at the age of thirty-two, he grossed $12 million, with projections of $20 million for 1976.

Klein's work is best described as exemplifying purity of line and simplicity of design. He takes the clean-cut, all-American look of sportswear and executes it with the elegance of couture. He

FIGURE 4.20 *Calvin Klein, 1976. Evening tunics of luxurious ivory crepe de chine are worn over crepe de chine pajama pants. (Courtesy of Calvin Klein.)*

has the ability to proportion the "fantasies of France" to American taste and come out with a profit in the cash register.

His critics view him as an adapter rather than an innovator. Creator or adapter, it doesn't matter much, for Calvin Klein designs for the American woman and she likes it.

Oscar de la Renta. De la Renta designs with the woman over 30 firmly in mind. His silhouettes are loose, clean, and classic and with no gimmicks. As early as 1972, Oscar de la Renta was predicting an era of elegance for the fashion minded. He does a full fashion collection from day dresses and separates to evening wear and is probably most recognized for his party dresses. In addition to the women's apparel, he also designs for men and does jewelry, wigs, raincoats, bridal gowns, leather purse accessories and even mattresses . . . the ticking, that is.

Bill Blass. Blass, a versatile man who owns his own firm, produces a couture collection and a sportswear line called Blassport. He designs

men's wear, grooming aids, sheets and towels, and writing paper. He won the Coty Award in 1961, 1970, and 1971, thus qualifying him for the Coty Hall of Fame.

Blass feels that fashion is no longer a cut or a seam but a "look." He takes his collection on the road over the United States to get the feel of what the American is looking for in a garment.

Geoffrey Beene. President of Geoffrey Beene, Inc., since 1962, Beene not only does his couture collection but a sportswear line called Beene Bag. He won the Coty Award in 1964 and 1966, the Neiman-Marcus Award in 1965, and was the first designer to receive the Ethel Traphagen Award, in 1966 from the Traphagen School of Design. His clothes are structurally simple, original, and contemporary.

Halston. Halston began to manufacture in 1972. Orders surpassed the $3 million mark during the showing of his first three collections during a nine-month period. This feat was unheard of for so young a firm in such a short time.

FIGURE 4.21 *Oscar de la Renta. A light mohair dirndle with embroidered border, combined with a crepe de chine blouse and matching shawl. From Oscar de la Renta's Warm Weather Collection of 1978. (Courtesy of Eleanor Lamber, Inc.)*

Roy Halston Frowich is the real name of the young man who simply calls himself Halston. He says of himself, "I'm a craftsman. I know my craft. I've been immersed in the business of design for over twenty years. What am I doing? I'm giving women what they want. Women want to be comfortable and they want to look sexy. It's as simple as that."[8] He feels that clothes must be elegant, well made, and as casual as sportswear, with an utter lack of contrivance. His clothes are often zipperless and buttonless.

Halston won the Coty Award in 1972 for his flowing matte jersey and tie-dyed caftans. He has become well known for his use of ultrasuede.

Victor Costa. Costa is a product of Texas who studied at Pratt Institute in New York and Ecole Chambre Syndicale de la Couture Parisienne in Paris and later settled in New York. By the summer of 1965, he had outfitted some 35,000 "Costa brides" in the United States for Murray Hamburger, a bridal line. Later he joined Suzy Perette. After eighteen years as a successful Seventh Avenue designer, he moved to Dallas to brighten the couture scene in that area. His collections underscore his ability to bring a high-fashion look to the "aware woman who knows quality but doesn't want to spend everything on clothes."[9] Costa's warmth as an individual and astuteness as a designer have won him the "most likable" award for those who meet him and, from the industry, the Young Designer Award by the Hecht Company, the Mayda Award by the May Company, and the Stix, Baer and Fuller Golden Award for fashion excellence.

OTHER DESIGNERS OF THE 1970s

After the shake-up of the late 1960s and the turmoil in the fashion world, a new wave of designers began to emerge who emphasized youth and timelessness. Young and less oriented to the Paris tradition, they designed casual, often fun-loving attire for the life of the 1970s. Outstanding designers of the new clothes were both men and women who were striving for their place in the sun.

Carol Horn of Seventh Avenue began her own firm of Carol Horn's Habitat and showed her tal-

FIGURE 4.22 *Three models from the 1975 Bill Blass collection—tailored wools in subtle colors lavishly scarved and furtrimmed. (Courtesy of Bill Blass.)*

ent in timeless clothing. She won the Coty Award in 1975.

Stephen Burrows, a Coty Award winner is usually known for his slithery, clingy knit jersey designs. He introduced the "lettuce edge" finish.

Betsey Johnson began designing the funky fashions in the fantastic 1960s for Paraphernalia boutiques. She then hit with her own Alley Cat, a mass producer of a junior line. She is a 1971 Coty Award winner and is now doing children's wear in an upper East Side boutique in New York.

Clovis Ruffin first designed knit T-shirts and later lengthened them into T-shirt dresses. He works simplicity in with sophistication and has come a long way from the T-top.

Willie Smith became known for his separates called "Digits," a junior line. He designs in a loft, has a Seventh Avenue showroom and works in both separates and dresses with a contemporary look.

Sonia Rykiel has done her own thing with knits. She shows in the Paris *prêt-à-porter* and has clothes loaded with style and new shapes. In the middle seventies, Rykiel had boutiques in four U.S. cities and a great number all over Europe.

Dorothée Bis has had one of the trend-setting boutiques of the 1970s in Paris. Her designs are young, always high fashion, and usually futuristic.

Jean Muir began in London when it was the

FIGURE 4.23 *Geoffrey Beene, 1975. Ready-to-wear corded-yoke pants and matching shawl in wool sweater knit.*

swinging fashion center of the 1960s. She designs pretty clothes mostly in wovens, with lots of detail which make them expensive. They are forward looking but with the good dressmaker look of times past.

The Future of Couture

All indications are that the American couture, which is a ready-to-wear institution rather than a custom one, is growing by leaps and bounds as it serves the needs of the American public. It has become fashionable to "buy American."

OTHER FASHION CENTERS

Many free countries around the world might produce creative designers, but often there is no

FIGURE 4.24 *Halston's 1976 designs included this evening sarong in printed chiffon. (Courtesy of Halston.)*

government or national support, financial support, creative climate, and organizations under which to work, such as the Chambre Syndicale in France. However, since World War II, the trade and export of goods have become very important to many countries, and fashion is a source of trade.

Certainly, no country has achieved the fashion

FIGURE 4.25 *Evening separates by Victor Costa—matte jersey mandarin-collared shirt with matching fur-trimmed skirt. (Courtesy of Victor Costa.)*

Europe

ITALY

Italy is known for its beautiful fabrics, especially its silks. The country has established its own echelon of couture designers. Some of the most well known are Valentino, who works in Rome; Emilio Pucci, in Forence (whose house is in his family's palace); Veniziana of Milan; and Simonetta, Fabiani, Fontana, Galitzine, and Mila Schoen.

The couture is definitely smaller than that of Paris and is not concentrated in one geographic area. Each year, the openings are in a different city in Italy, but most buyers go from Paris to Italy to see what the Italian couture is offering.

The government of Italy does not subsidize couture, but it does sponsor showings in the Pitti Palace and the Strozzi Palace in Florence for sales transactions.

The Italian couture is having its financial problems, as is France, and designers are being lured into ready-to-wear. Valentino joined the ready-to-wear ranks in the early 1970s, and others have since joined.

ENGLAND

London is the fashion center of England, and for centuries the famed tailors of Bond Street and Saville Row have dressed the Englishman with trend-setting distinction. The great dandy Beau Brummel, launched the trend toward plainness in men's clothing that started at the beginning of the nineteenth century. Lord Chesterfield's overcoat, the Earl of Cardigan's sweater, Baron Raglan's sleeves, and Prince Albert's coat and Balmoral shoes, like Sherlock Holmes' deerstalker cap and checked cape, in their day set the style of the world. The natural shoulder suit of the 'teens was an English innovation, and so was the trench coat, created during World War I. The Duke of Windsor dominated men's fashions during the thirties. English women's fashions, however, have tended to be very conservative, perhaps never having recovered from the deliberate dowdiness of Queen Victoria.

Captain Molyneux highlighted the couture efforts in the early part of the century, with houses

prominence and status of France, but many countries have done quite well: countries in the Far East and in Scandinavia and Canada, Israel, Spain, England, Italy, Ireland, Greece, and Australia.

However, if a flair exists anywhere for creativity, the American buyers will seek it. The Fashion Group, an international organization based on the promise to support and promote fashion, periodically sponsors shows throughout the United States from other foreign countries besides France. In the last few years Israel, Australia, and Greece have been represented.

Following is a brief description of some of the creative activities of the major countries, their specific advancement, and current situations.

in Paris and London. He dressed the royal family in London. Norman Hartnell dressed Her Majesty Queen Elizabeth and the Queen Mother for many years, but always with very conservative taste, in keeping with the middle-class virtues the British expect of their royalty; there is an invariable rule, for instance, that royal ladies must wear pastels on public occasions, to increase their visibility.

It was not until Mary Quant rose to prominence as the "high priestess of the Mod cult and the mother of the miniskirt" in the 1960s that London was given much attention. Then the buyers of women's fashions felt it was worth their time to cross the English Channel to London from Paris.

Quant was definitely a ready-to-wear designer and became an instant success in the sixties, following the rages for the Beatles singing group and Twiggy, the skinny model with the large cocker spaniel eyes. The designers of Carnaby Street and Chelsea's King's Road launched exciting, uninhibited, and sometimes controversial fashions for men. London was finally having its day. During this time Paris couture often seemed dull and stiff.

Spain

Spain's *Alta Costura* ("haute couture") is situated in Madrid where it is highly subsidized by the Spanish government. There are approximately fourteen members of the Alta Costura. Among these are Pertegaz, Elio Berhanyer, Herrara y Ollero, and Redro Rovira.

Near East

Israel

Israel sponsors a school similar to New York's Fashion Institute of Technology (FIT) that trains young people in fashion careers. Young designers in Israel have been nurtured by the former Mrs. Moshe Dayan, and through her perseverance shows of Israel's designers have been presented in the United States by The Fashion Group.

The Israeli government supports a marketing organization in New York for Israeli products and provides subsidies for apparel exports.

Far East

Japan, Hong Kong, the Philippines, and Taiwan

These countries are considered *suppliers* rather than creators of fashion items. Apparel manufacturers in the Orient have been able to produce inexpensive volume fashions for specific American orders. These orders are placed well in advance of a season and will include the sizing and styling for the American market. They are mass-produced fashions such as tops, shirts, underwear, blouses, and great quantities of knitwear. There is a low degree of fashion innovation.

Many American manufacturing firms have established production plants in various countries of the Orient because production proved to be cheaper there. Manufacturers *build* plants there to cut and sew, then *export* to the United States, rather than produce in this country, primarily because of labor costs and availability.

The inflation of the middle 1970s in Japan, particularly, has hurt this method of fashion production. In 1974 in Japan the textile and apparel industry virtually came to a standstill for a few months. Costs have been rising everywhere.

The seamstresses and tailors of the Orient have always enjoyed a fine reputation for their exceptional and intricate handwork. A high-quality custom-tailored garment for both men and women can be purchased in most of the free Oriental countries for much less than in the United States. Hong Kong and Japan are particularly noted for their tailors. A customer can have any design reproduced by giving the tailor a picture of the garment. The workmanship is superb. Very fine beading, cutwork, and embroidery have been perfected by Oriental seamstresses.

END OF CHAPTER GUIDE

Review, Discussion, and Evaluation

Study of this chapter should enable students to:
A. Develop and give evidence of the following kinds of competencies:
  1. Describe the role of the fashion creator in terms of innovation and prestige.

2. Pronounce and define the fashion terms and designer's names listed in this chapter.
3. Explain five reasons for French fashion supremacy during the twentieth century.
4. Recognize the importance of the prêt-à-porter collections in the growth of the French fashion industry in the last two decades.
5. Discuss the contribution of five or more prominent French designers in relation to the heritage of fashion in the twentieth century.
6. Describe the contributions of La Chambre Syndicale de la Couture Parisienne to the development of haute couture in France.
7. Trace the growth of American couture from World War I to the 1970s.
8. Trace the development of a couture collection from the creation of the designs to the clientele showings.
9. Identify the particular contributions of five or more prominent American fashion designers since World War II.
10. List four world fashion centers.
B. Develop and/or clarify concepts related to the following key words or phrases:
1. fashion creator 2. adaptation 3. atelier 4. boutique 5. collection 6. couturier 7. vendeuse 8. haute couture 9. french fashion supremacy 10. couture houses 11. copyists 12. auxiliary industries 13. needle trades 14. Chambre Syndicale 15. couture openings 16. prêt-à-porter 17. trade buyers 18. Coty Awards 19. American couture 20. American fashion centers 21. showing collections 22. American designers 23. world fashion centers

Extended Classroom Learning Experiences

A. Prepare a written report with illustrations of Marie Antoinette and her dressmaker Rose Bertin and their impact on fashion at the time.
B. Write to the Chambre Syndicale de la Couture Parisienne and inquire about the current educational opportunities for the young person interested in the needle trades in France. The address is 102 Rue du Faubourg St. Honoré, Paris 8, France.
C. Using *Women's Wear Daily* or some other fashion publication, do a study of one or more of the following:
D. Review materials in the Job Analyses Series Appendix 6, pages 279–289.
E. Summarize briefly the responsibilities, personal characteristics, and employment opportunities for one or more of the following:

(1) designer (2) assistant designer (3) production coordinator.
F. Do a profile on three fashion designers. Inquire about their educational background and professional training, their professional beginnings, their philosophy of design, the fabrics they prefer to use, whether they have diversified into other activities, and the price ranges of their designs.
G. Read two or more of the articles listed here or research current periodicals or trade journals and select two or more articles related to one of the concepts suggested in the "Review, Discussion, and Evaluation."
1. Prepare note cards while reading each article.
2. Using your note cards, write a brief summary to indicate the relation of each article to concepts presented in this chapter.
3. Using your note cards, give an oral report in your class and point out the important facts included in the articles.

Suggested Articles

"American Couture: Toujours Trigère." *Clothes*, July 1, 1968.
"Chanel No. 1." *Time*, January 25, 1971.
Dryanaky, G. Y. "The Couture: Not What It Was, but Still a Power." *Women's Wear Daily*, January 26, 1973.
"Kenzo Takada." *Mademoiselle*, July 1972.
Shab, Diane K. "Haute Couture's High Priest Presents Collection in U.S." *The Sunday Oklahoman*, 17 November 1974.
"Yves in New York." *Times*, September 27, 1968.

NOTES

[1] Elizabeth Hawes, *Fashion Is Spinach*. New York: Random House, 1938, p. 16.
[2] Ibid.
[3] Mary Brooks Pickin and Dora Loues Miller, *Dressmakers of France*. New York: Harper, 1956, p. 5.
[4] Ibid., p. 105.
[5] "Understated Elegance," *Time*, July 6, 1962, p. 44.
[6] Phyllis Lee Levin, *The Wheels of Fashion*. New York: Doubleday, 1965, p. 219.
[7] "Understated Elegance," *Time*, July 6, 1962, p. 44.
[8] Patricia Bosworthy, "Halston Looks," *New York Times Magazine*, Feb. 11, 1973, pp. 72–73.
[9] Victor Costa, talk given to Fashion Associates, Southern Methodist University, June 17, 1975.

PART Two

Fashion Makers

*I*MPORTANT concepts and facts about fashion interpretation and the fashion creators were presented in Part One of this book. A basic knowledge of fashion interpretation—what it is, when it happens, where it is, and who creates it—must be acquired before one can understand the multifaceted operations involved in making fashion goods.

Fashion is big business. The mass producers are responsible for a tremendous variety of operations in the process of providing fashion for consumers. In Parts Two and Three our emphasis will be on the diversified fashion industries and the role each plays in this complicated network.

The fashion industries are sometimes considered only as the textile-apparel complex; however, in this text they will include all of the activities that surround the marketing process in providing goods to the consumer: (1) the creators, who provide innovation; (2) the suppliers, who supply and manufacture textile products, furs, leathers, plastics, findings, and trims; (3) the manufacturers, who produce the actual apparel and accessories for the ready-to-wear market; (4) the distributors, the sales representatives and the market associations at the national, regional, and local level; and (5) the retailers, who sell the merchandise to the consumer. The marketing process involves many fashion-oriented services: pattern companies, magazines, trade journals, modeling agencies, advertising agencies, publicity agencies, consultants, buying offices, and others directly connected with the promotion and sale of fashion and fashion goods. The Fashion Industries Flow Chart, page 57, depicts the processes that an innovation must go through to reach the consumer of fashion goods.

Mass producers of fashion exist at every level of textile and apparel production—men's, women's, and children's wear, accessories, and findings. The mass producers adapt the creative ideas of the innovators and convert them into merchandise for the mass consumer market.

Whereas the mass production system turns out tremendous amounts of goods, the creators of fashion are the originators of line, color, and texture. The creators of the fashion variables establish the beginning of the fashion cycle. They are the couture designers, the colorists, and the textile researchers. Couture designers service a small percentage of the population with actual merchandise, but they offer the excitement of innovation.

The work in fiber research centers goes on for years and years to perfect serviceable and extraordinary fabrics that often revolutionize our way of life and dress. The textile mills establish the seasonal fabric trends for the mass producers of apparel.

Chapter 5, "Fashion Suppliers," deals with the producers of the raw materials of fashion, the firms and companies that provide the fibers, furs, leathers, plastics, findings, trims, and other supplies for fashion. Who are they? Where are they? How they do their work?

Chapter 6, "Fashion Manufacturers," discuss the producers of finished fashion goods, those firms and companies that perform such various operations as purchasing, designing, cutting, sewing, and finishing fashion apparel and accessories. How the goods are made? Where they are made? What kinds of problems are encountered in mass production?

Chapter 7, "Fashion Marketing," explains the giant step from producer to consumer in marketing terms: the flow of goods, the channel of distribution, and the marketing process. The impact of seasonal timing on marketing problems: availability of the right goods, at the right place, at the right price, at the right time.

Chapter 8, "Fashion Market Centers," describes the seasonal fashion markets—and relates the forces that accelerate the flow of fashion goods from the apparel manufacturer to the retailer, the excitement of fashion—the buying activities, and the inner workings of the market facilities. The unique characteristics of major fashion markets in the United States are summarized.

5

Fashion Suppliers

Stripes and plaids, reds and yellows, wovens and knits, cottons and nylons, zippers and threads, furs and leathers, buttons and buckles, feathers and sequins—these are only a few of the raw materials used to create the very essence of fashion. They are produced in astounding quantities by the millions of pounds, thousands of yards, and hundreds of dozens annually. The producers of these raw materials are known as *suppliers*. They are the cornerstone of the fashion industries. Because of the significance of this branch of fashion, we need to identify fashion suppliers, define raw materials, and understand the processes involved in supplying raw materials for the fashion industries.

The suppliers, as the source of the raw materials, are the starting point of the fashion industries. A vital component in fashion is the substance from which an article is made. In the overall structure of the fashion industries (see Figure 2.1), the suppliers are at the uppermost level—where fashion begins. Two major types of suppliers are considered important in the fashion industries: primary suppliers and secondary suppliers.

Producers of textile fibers and fabrics are *primary suppliers*. The mass producers of apparel and accessories are dependent on the complex textile operations for the raw materials of fashion. *Fiber production* includes both the companies that process cotton, wool, and other natural fibers and the firms that produce rayon, poly-

ester, and other man-made fibers. *Fabric production* involves yarn-spinning mills, weaving and knitting mills, converters, dyers, and finishers. As indicated in Figure 2.1, each of these textile operations is an integral part of the process of supplying raw materials for the giant fashion industries.

Many of the fashion products used by today's consumer are made from textiles. However, other primary suppliers may be involved in making fashion. The leather and fur industries produce some raw materials for apparel and accessories. Also, some plastic, paper, and nonwoven materials are produced for use by fashion makers.

Secondary suppliers play an important role in fashion. Notions, trims, buttons, interfacing, thread, zippers, beads, sequins, and hundreds of other items may be a part of the seasonal fashion picture. If fashion decrees buttons and lace, some supplier will produce them.

THE TEXTILE INDUSTRY

What is the textile industry? The term has been used in various ways, usually relating to the making of cloth. For the purposes of this book, however, the *textile industry* is the *primary supplier* of fibers and fabrics for the apparel and accessory industries. Thus, the textile industry involves the various operations in the processing of fibers—natural and man-made—from raw prod-

124

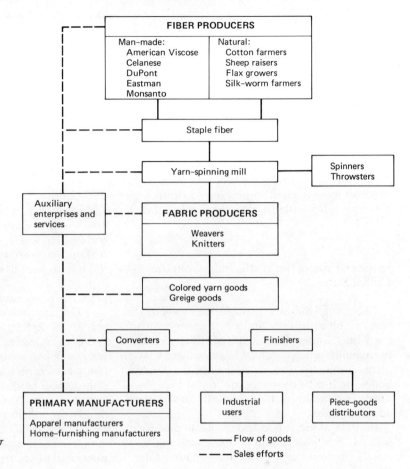

FIBER PRODUCERS

Man-made:	Natural:
American Viscose	Cotton farmers
Celanese	Sheep raisers
DuPont	Flax growers
Eastman	Silk-worm farmers
Monsanto	

Staple fiber

Yarn-spinning mill — Spinners / Throwsters

Auxiliary enterprises and services

FABRIC PRODUCERS

Weavers
Knitters

Colored yarn goods
Greige goods

Converters — Finishers

PRIMARY MANUFACTURERS

Apparel manufacturers
Home-furnishing manufacturers

Industrial users

Piece-goods distributors

———— Flow of goods
- - - - Sales efforts

FIGURE 5.1 *Flow chart for the textile industry.*

uct to finished fabric. It includes both fiber producers (producers of staple fibers and spun yarns of both natural and man-made made types) and fabric producers (producers of knitted and woven fabrics, and converters including dyers and finishers).

These textile suppliers form the upper level in the structure of the fashion industries in the United States. The flow of each of these operations is presented in Figure 5.1.

Economic Importance of the Textile Industry in the United States

In the early 1970s the sales of textile products soared beyond $23 billion per year, and estimates indicated that the $30 billion mark would be reached by the end of the decade.[1] The textile industry is an integral and important part of the American economy. The size and location of textile factories have considerable impact on the economy. This complex industry is considered the third largest in the United States in terms of the Gross National Product (GNP) with only food and oil ranking higher. One out of every eight persons employed in manufacturing industries in the United States works in the textile or apparel industrial complex.[2] Nearly one million workers in the textile industry are involved in such processes as the spinning of yarns; the weaving, knitting, or tufting of fabrics; and the bleaching, dyeing, finishing, or printing of an incredible variety of fabrics.

There is virtually no end to the kinds of products made from woven and knitted fabrics. Among the fashion products made from textiles are women's wear, men's wear, children's wear, sleep wear, casual wear, sportswear, outer wear, and lingerie. Other products influenced by fashion are piece goods, carpets, rugs, hosiery, draperies, towels, sheets, pillowcases, bedspreads, blankets, upholstery, industrial fabrics, ribbon, tapes, threads, and many decorative items.[3] It is almost impossible to imagine how the textile industry produced enough fibers and fabrics to make all these items. It is necessary to think big. If fashion is big business, then the textile industry is big business.

Scope and Size of the Textile Industry in the United States

The textile industry is made up of over 700 firms involved in fiber and fabric production in the United States. Over 7,000 plants are located throughout some 46 states.[4] Most of these textile plants are in the eastern section of the United States, with a heavy concentration of manufacturing facilities in North and South Carolina and adjoining states.

In 1974 alone, these textile plants processed over 11.09 billion pounds of fibers and produced over 17 billion yards of fabrics—approximately 83 yards of fabric for every man, woman, and child in the United States.[5] Approximately 12 billion linear yards of woven fabrics were produced in 1973, as well as 1.16 billion pounds of knit fabrics.[6] Carpeting, tire cord, and tire fabrics are also produced by the textile industry, but on a smaller scale. As shown in Table 5.1, the United States's textile industry output is used for industrial and military purposes, medical supplies, and export purposes, although the major portion is used for apparel and home furnishings.

A summary of some facts about the scope and size of the textile industry follows:

SIZE
700 companies
7,000 plants
$33 billion in sales annually
1 million workers

TABLE 5.1 U.S. Textile Industry

Users	Output (in %)
Apparel products	37
Home furnishings	30
Industrial	18
Military purposes or medical supplies	12
Export purposes	2.6

Source: Estimates, Springs Mills, Inc., 1971.

PRODUCTS
12 billion linear yards of woven fabrics
1 billion pounds of knitted goods
680 million square yards of carpeting yarns
600 million pounds of tire cord and fabric
9.4 billion pounds of fibers

Of the fibers used in the production of fabrics in 1974, approximately 70 per cent were man-made, including both cellulosic and non-cellulosic. Cotton, the most important natural fiber, supplied approximately 29 per cent.[7] Other natural fibers such as wool and silk accounted for only a small percentage of total consumption.

Just as the American consumer is tremendously dependent on the textile industry, so the textile industry is tremendously dependent on the American consumer. The separation of the producer and the consumer by the long process from raw fibers to yarns, to finished fabrics, to apparel products, to markets, to retailers, to consumers is an age-old problem in the textile industry. This time-lag makes it difficult for consumers to communicate their needs and wants to the suppliers of the raw materials of fashion. When the consumer decided to wear knits instead of woven fabrics in the 1960s, it took almost a decade to get enough knitting machines into operation to produce the variety of patterns and the amounts of knit goods needed to satisfy demand.

The following terms and definitions are associated with this long process from textile suppliers to consumers:

Fiber producers Man-made fiber companies and natural fiber suppliers.
Mills A manufacturer of fiber-to-fabric products; spinners, weavers, knitters, and dyers.

Greige goods Unfinished fabric.

Converters A contractor who purchases greige goods from a mill and arranges finishing, bleaching, dyeing, etc., as required by a manufacturer.

Jobber A converter on a small scale.

Manufacturer Producer of anything from cloth.

Retailer Department stores, specialty stores, and other outlets selling to the consumer.

Consumer Ultimate user of textile products.

STRUCTURE AND SEGMENTS

The primary suppliers in the textile industry are made up of two major kinds of firms: *fiber producers*, who are the source of the raw materials, and *fabric producers*, who transform the raw fibers into basic fabric forms. Shown in figure 5.1 are the various operations at the two levels in the textile industry: fiber production and fabric production.

The Fiber-production Level

Natural fibers have historically been used in the construction of materials for clothing and for other basic needs. Strawlike materials have been used to form protective coverings for the body and to provide shelter from heat, cold, and rain. The twentieth century has witnessed the development of many substitutes for natural materials. Although consumers still use many products made from natural fibers (such as cotton, wool, silk, and linen), the advent of man-made fibers in the 1930s changed the textile industry.

NATURAL FIBERS

Most people have seen cotton growing in the field and have looked at sheep grazing in the countryside. Most consumers have used products made from natural fibers such as cotton, wool, silk, and linen and may recognize other natural fibers, such as jute, hemp, sisal, and henequen. Only cotton and wool are considered to have major significance in world production of textile fibers.

Cotton Fibers. Eli Whitney's invention of the cotton gin in 1793 accelerated the growth of the textile industry in the United States, as did the advancement of mass production and mass distribution at the turn of the nineteenth century. The textile industry in the United States was dominated by cotton until the 1930s.

Currently, the United States has the largest cotton crop in the world, 20 per cent of the total world production. Texas has the largest cotton acreage in the nation.[8] In some ten other states cotton is a major crop. The Carolinas are the center of the cotton textile industry. Our labor costs are high compared with other cotton-producing countries, and the government subsidizes cotton exports to enable our cotton to compete on the world market.

Because of the size of the cotton segment of the textile industry, cotton is one of the major agricultural crops in the world. Brazil, Mexico, Turkey, Pakistan, and the Sudan have become major cotton-fiber producers in recent years; however, only China and the USSR produce cotton crops on a scale like that of the United States.[9]

Wool Fibers. As a fiber, wool has never greatly influenced the textile industry of the United States. Imports from Australia, New Zealand, and Argentina provide the wool for consumption in the United States. Wool fabrics are more expensive than cotton, because the costs of converting wool fibers to fabric are much higher. Some coarse wools are produced throughout the world. However, these are suitable only for carpets and other nonapparel uses. B. W. Hirsh reports that Argentina, China, India, and the USSR are the major wool-producing countries today. During the early 1970s, Japan replaced Britain as the world's largest importer (consumer) of wool fibers, and the United States is currently the third-largest buyer of the world's export wool.[10]

Other Natural Fibers. Several other natural fibers are produced and consumed in small quantities in the textile industry. Silk was a major Japanese industry before World War II and is still an important textile in Japan. Advances in technology enabled the silk industry to remain stable during the last two decades, and silk continued to command high prices on the consumer market, even with recent challenges from synthetic fibers having silk-like qualities.

A number of other natural (vegetable-based) fibers are used in the textile industry. Jute, flax, and hemp are characterized by a soft-fiber cellulosic structure. Jute probably is used the most in the textile industry and is the most important of this group from an economic point of view. Sisal and henequen are hard-leaf fibers. Several of these fibers have been used since the beginning of civilization for clothing and other purposes.

MAN-MADE FIBERS

The consumer may not know how *rayon*, *nylon*, or *polyester* are made, but the terms are in common household use in the United States and in many other countries. Nevertheless, there are two distinct kinds of man-made fibers: cellulosic and noncellulosic.

In 1886, the French Count Hilaire de Chardonnet invented rayon, using a fiber made from *natural cellulosic* substances. "Artificial silk" was soon being manufactured in the United States. After World War I, the cellulosic fibers known as viscose rayon and acetate rayon were introduced.[11]

Noncellulosic Fibers. Commonly called synthetic, noncellulosic fibers are a product of twentieth-century America. In the 1930s, nylon was discovered in the DuPont laboratories. About the same time, a process for making polyester was discovered in England; this led to the development of Dacron in the DuPont laboratories.[12] Later, acrylics and other synthetic fibers were developed. (See Figure 5.2.) These two groups of man-made fibers, cellulosics and noncellulosics, are of major importance in world production of textile fibers.

Man-made Cellulosic Fibers. The first real competition to natural fibers was rayon. Wood pulp and cotton linters are the main raw materials used in its production. Through a chemical process, a multifilament continuous yarn, or cellulosic fiber, known as viscose rayon is formed. An inexpensive process was developed to chop up these continuous filament yarns and produce a cellulosic staple fiber that competes economically with cotton. A later development by the Dreyfus brothers in England was cellulose acetate.[13] In both the viscose and acetate processes, a cellulose solution is pumped through spinnerets to produce filaments, or continuous fibers. There was a rapid rise in production and use in the United States after World War II. By the 1970s, the production cost of cellulosic fibers and yarns had been reduced to equal that of cotton.[14]

Man-Made Noncellulosic Fibers, or Synthetics. The synthetic fiber story started in 1935 with the development of nylon by W. H. Carothers at the DuPont laboratories. The synthetic fibers are created chemically out of oil, coal, water, and air by a process that ends in forcing the fiber substance through small holes, producing filaments of the desired size, or *denier*. Since the invention of nylon, fabrics of both acrylic and polyester fibers have been developed. Both filament yarns and staple fibers have been produced to compete with other man-made fibers and with natural fibers in performance and in cost. The use of man-made fibers has increased rapidly since 1950.

World Production and Consumption of Textile Fibers

The spectacular growth of world production of textile fibers, as seen in Figure 5.3, indicates the importance of man-made fibers (cellulosic and noncellulosic). The high rate of growth of man-made fibers compared with cotton is apparent, as is the comparative insignificance of wool.[15]

The rate of growth of the polyesters and acrylics has been greater than that of nylon in the last decade.[16]

Figure 5.4 makes another significant comparison of the four major fibers in respect to United States textile fiber mill consumption. The rapid rise in the use of noncellulosic fibers is dramatic when compared with the sharp decline of mill consumption of cotton. Cellulosic fibers and wool are of lesser importance in terms of the total

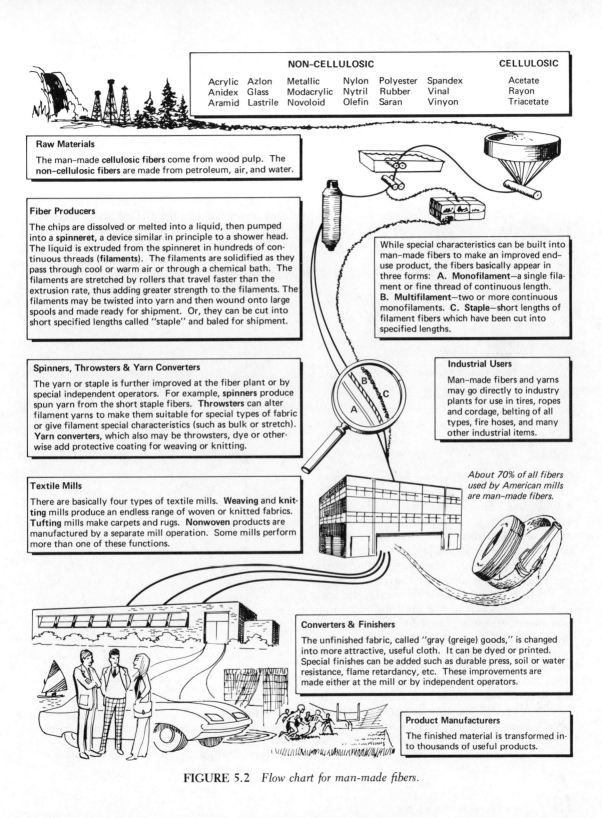

NON-CELLULOSIC						CELLULOSIC
Acrylic	Azlon	Metallic	Nylon	Polyester	Spandex	Acetate
Anidex	Glass	Modacrylic	Nytril	Rubber	Vinal	Rayon
Aramid	Lastrile	Novoloid	Olefin	Saran	Vinyon	Triacetate

Raw Materials

The man–made **cellulosic fibers** come from wood pulp. The **non-cellulosic fibers** are made from petroleum, air, and water.

Fiber Producers

The chips are dissolved or melted into a liquid, then pumped into a **spinneret**, a device similar in principle to a shower head. The liquid is extruded from the spinneret in hundreds of continuous threads (**filaments**). The filaments are solidified as they pass through cool or warm air or through a chemical bath. The filaments are stretched by rollers that travel faster than the extrusion rate, thus adding greater strength to the filaments. The filaments may be twisted into yarn and then wound onto large spools and made ready for shipment. Or, they can be cut into short specified lengths called "staple" and baled for shipment.

While special characteristics can be built into man-made fibers to make an improved end-use product, the fibers basically appear in three forms: **A. Monofilament**—a single filament or fine thread of continuous length. **B. Multifilament**—two or more continuous monofilaments. **C. Staple**—short lengths of filament fibers which have been cut into specified lengths.

Spinners, Throwsters & Yarn Converters

The yarn or staple is further improved at the fiber plant or by special independent operators. For example, **spinners** produce spun yarn from the short staple fibers. **Throwsters** can alter filament yarns to make them suitable for special types of fabric or give filament special characteristics (such as bulk or stretch). **Yarn converters**, which also may be throwsters, dye or otherwise add protective coating for weaving or knitting.

Industrial Users

Man-made fibers and yarns may go directly to industry plants for use in tires, ropes and cordage, belting of all types, fire hoses, and many other industrial items.

Textile Mills

There are basically four types of textile mills. **Weaving** and **knitting** mills produce an endless range of woven or knitted fabrics. **Tufting** mills make carpets and rugs. **Nonwoven** products are manufactured by a separate mill operation. Some mills perform more than one of these functions.

About 70% of all fibers used by American mills are man-made fibers.

Converters & Finishers

The unfinished fabric, called "gray (greige) goods," is changed into more attractive, useful cloth. It can be dyed or printed. Special finishes can be added such as durable press, soil or water resistance, flame retardancy, etc. These improvements are made either at the mill or by independent operators.

Product Manufacturers

The finished material is transformed into thousands of useful products.

FIGURE 5.2 *Flow chart for man-made fibers.*

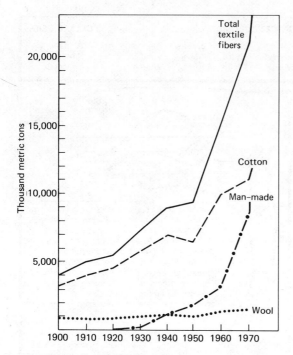

FIGURE 5.3 World production of textile fibers. (*From* Introduction to Textile Economics *by B. W. Hirsh and Peter Ellis. Manchester, England: The Textile Press, 1972, p. 13. Reprinted by permission.*)

fiber picture, although output of cellulosic fibers has more than tripled since 1940.

One more comparison of the world's usage of the four major fibers is made by Table 15.2, which lists the metric tons of fiber mill consumption in the United States, Japan, Germany, Britain, and the U.S.S.R. The consumption of cotton and cellulosic fibers in the U.S. and the U.S.S.R. is almost equal.[17] However, there is a dramatic difference in the fiber mill consumption of noncellulosic fibers by these same two nations—1,593 thousand metric tons were consumed by the U.S. and only 194 thousand metric tons by the U.S.S.R. The American consumer's ready acceptance of synthetic fibers is reflected in this tremendous difference. It is significant that Japan's fiber mill consumption of noncellulosic fibers is already half that of the United States and considerably above that of the other three countries.

The total fiber mill consumption of these four fibers in the U.S., 4,069 thousand metric tons, is greater than the U.S.S.R.'s, 2,775 thousand metric tons, although the population of the U.S. is less.[18] Of note is the population of Japan compared with the U.S. and the U.S.S.R. and the fiber mill consumption of the four fibers by Japan. This reflects the tremendous increase in production in the textile industry in Japan in the last decade.

A brief consideration of the end use of these four major fibers in the United States is given in Table 5.3. The greatest use of cotton is in men's and boys' wear and in home furnishings.[19] The greatest use of noncellulosic fibers is in women's and children's wear and in home furnishings. The total consumption of cotton by all end-use

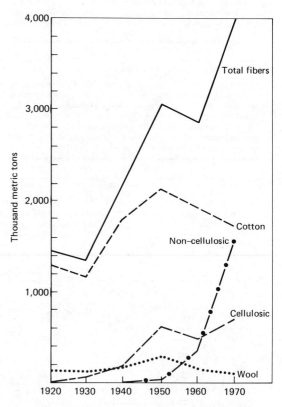

FIGURE 5.4 U.S. textile fiber mill consumption. (*From* Introduction to Textile Economics, *by B. W. Hirsh and Peter Ellis. Manchester, England: The Textile Press, 1972, p. 25. Reprinted by permission.*)

TABLE 5.2 Fiber Mill Consumption in 1970 (thousand metric tons)

Fiber	U.S.	Japan	West Germany	Britain	U.S.S.R.	Total as % world
Cotton	1,707	723	252	172	1,742	39
Wool	105	183	70	153	323	50
Cellulosic	664	353	178	190	516	54
Noncellulosic	1,593	838	322	272	194	65
Total	4,069	2,097	822	782	2,775	
Population (in millions)	208	104	62	56	243	18

Source: B. W. Hirsh and Peter Ellis, *An Introduction to Textile Economics*, Manchester, England, The Textile Press. 1972, p. 23.

classifications is slightly less than the total use of noncellulosic fibers. It should be noted that home furnishings as an end use for all fibers is considerably higher than either of the two apparel categories; however, if the two apparel categories are considered as one, then fiber consumption for clothing is greater.

These various charts tell a story about the present status of fiber production and consumption. Cotton continues to be an important fiber in the textile industry of the United States and of the rest of the world; noncellulosic fibers, such as nylon, acrylic, and the polyesters are gaining a prominent place in fiber production and consumption both in the United States and in Japan. The U.S. fiber mills consume more fibers per capita population than Japan, West Germany, Britain, or the U.S.S.R. According to end use, the fiber consumption of both cotton and noncellulosic is greater for the combined men's and women's and children's wear group than for home furnishings.

Thus, we might conclude that, in terms of fiber production and consumption, the textile industry in the United States is the greatest in the world; and in terms of the production and use, cotton and noncellulosics account for the greatest amount of total fibers consumed by textile mills. We should be alert to the downward trend of the textile mill consumption of cotton in the United States and the upward trend in the use of noncellulosic fibers such as nylon, acrylic, and polyester. Also, we should watch for continued increases in the textile mill consumption of both cotton and noncellulosic fibers by Japan.

The production of fibers is the initial step in the process of making fabric, whether the raw material comes from a cotton plant, a sheep or a test tube; it must be transformed into filament yarns or *staple fiber* in order to be processed into

TABLE 5.3 U.S. Fiber Consumption by End Use—1970 (thousand metric tons)

	Cotton	Wool	Cellulosic	Noncellulosic	All fibers
Men's and boys' wear	463	51	35	277	826
Women's and children's wear	229	48	180	344	801
Home furnishings	544	40	158	597	1,339
Other consumer-type products	219	15	165	193	592
Industrial uses	233	4	87	410	734
Total consumption	1,688	158	625	1,821	4,292

Source: B. W. Hirsh and Peter Ellis, *An Introduction to Textile Economics*, Manchester, England, The Textile Press. 1972, p. 23.

fabric, the major end product of the textile industry. The production of filament yarns and staple fibers is the function of the fiber producer.

The Role of the Fiber Producers

It was at the fiber production level that the first marketing changes came about in the textile industry. Before the man-made fiber producer entered the textile scene, the role of the producers of cotton and other natural fibers was simple. The annual cotton crop was raised, picked (often by hand), baled at the local gin, and the grower's or producer's job was done until the next cotton season. These cotton producers were not involved with what happened to the cotton. They were not concerned with fiber production, the actual making of raw materials into staple fibers that could be used to produce yarns for weaving or knitting fabric. They certainly had no thought of the garment maker or the consumer. They were concerned with growing cotton in heat, rain, floods, and droughts, and these problems were enough for them.

All this was changed by the producers of man-made fibers. A whole new textile world opened up with this new concept of *creating* whatever kind of fiber was wanted or needed by the consumer. Suddenly, the consumer gave the all-important answer to the man-made fiber producer's questions. If man could make almost any kind of fiber, what fibers should be made? The logical answer seemed to be to find out what the end use of the fiber would be: Who was going to be the ultimate user of the fiber, and how was it going to be used? No longer limited to what Mother Nature could provide, man-made fiber producers had a unique advantage that proved to be not only a challenge, but a boon to the textile industry.

Operating on the theory that fibers can be *made* and can be *changed*, producers saw that research and development efforts were aimed at planning the production of man-made fibers to meet consumer demand. A fiber could be given whatever characteristics were desirable from a performance, as well as an aesthetic, point of view. A new age had descended on the textile industry and the consumer was to be the chief benefactor.

There was yet another revolutionary aspect: new fibers meant new markets, or users. These new markets had to be identified, developed, and educated to use the new fibers. Of course, nylon led the way. Never had the consumer been so receptive and excited over a textile product. Nor had the consumer been so well informed about a fiber. Nylon had almost everything the consumer wanted and needed—it had drip-dry, wash-and-wear, and several other so-called performance qualities. These technological breakthroughs were just the beginning for the man-made fiber producers.

The new fiber technology that led to wash-and-wear was followed by numerous other performance- or convenience-oriented features for the consumer. No-iron was on the way. Not only were these advances readily received by the consumer, but each new development was a stimulus to the 8,000-year-old textile industry.

After World War II, product development became an integral part of fiber production; this meant better performance, better prices, and newer textures. Markets and sales soared! Excitement penetrated the textile industry. Spurred by the research-and-development concept (make what the consumer wants), the fiber producer joined with the fabric maker and the garment maker in a unified effort to plan in terms of the end use of raw textile materials. New ideas resulted from this coordinated research approach. Improved fibers and techniques in production were passed on from fiber producers to fabric producers, and on to the manufacturers of apparel and other textile products. Thus, the multifaceted activities of the man-made fiber producers stimulated advances in all phases of the textile industry. The research and development at the fiber level made it possible to have desired finishes on certain fabrics. Coordinated efforts at the fabric production level by converters, dyers, and finishers further developed the process, and permapress finish was created along with numerous other improvements. However, garment makers still had some experimenting to do before the consumer was satisfied with the performance and appearance of the new fabrics in terms of their end use.

The competitive, experimental environment initiated by the man-made fiber producers spread into the natural-fiber area. Growers of cotton, wool, and other fibers began to group together, and united efforts were made to compete with the man-made segment of the textile industry. The National Cotton Council, The Wool Bureau, The Silk Industry, and other organizations worked to improve natural fibers and promote their use. The ultimate goal thus became one of satisfying the consumer through the planned and controlled production of textile fibers, both natural and man-made. The textile industry was revolutionized from within, and this revolution started at the top, at the suppliers' level, with the raw materials of textiles. All this took place before our eyes. Actually, in little more than a quarter of a century, from 1950 to 1975, the textile industry integrated its forces, revamped its operations, realigned its goals, and redefined its customer—the ultimate consumer, the end user of textile products.

This excerpt, from an article written in recognition of the twenty-fifth anniversary of nylon, notes the change that occurred in the textile industry:

> Industrial research, relatively rare when nylon was born, is expanding today at a record pace. In the hunt for useful and profitable products, industrial managers have neglected neither synthetic fibers nor engineering plastics. . . . Many new fibers and plastics . . . have been carefully tailored to fill specific end uses. Nonetheless, broad-purpose nylon continues to enjoy a growing market.[20]

Some of the companies responsible for fiber production in the United States are listed in Table 5.4 and Appendix 8, p. 291. Many *suppliers* of raw materials for the textile industry are also seen among the well-known man-made fiber producers—DuPont, Celanese, American Akzona Corporation, Monsanto, Eastman, and American Viscose. Fiber producers sell man-made fiber by the pound either as a continuous filament or in a chopped or staple fiber form, depending on the customer's needs. The fiber producers' customer is a fiber mill, which will spin the raw fiber into yarns that can then be used

in constructing fabrics or for such purposes as carpet making.

Fabric Production Level

Textile mills of various types are the major consumers of both natural and man-made fibers. As can be seen in Figure 5.5, this fabric production process is somewhat complex. First, staple fibers must go to the yarn-spinning mill, sometimes referred to as the fiber mill; fibers in continuous filament form may go directly to the fabric mills. Next, the yarn spun from the raw fiber goes to the fabric mills, the knitters or weavers of greige goods.

Because the term *greige goods* means unfinished fabric, the next logical step in the production of fabric is the converting or finishing process.

The converter is the fabric mill's customer (see Figure 5.5), and as such is a vital component at the primary supplier's level. Dyeing, printing, and other forms of finishing greige goods may be necessary to convert the fabrics into the form desired by the converter's customers: the garment manufacturer or cutter—or the *needle trades*, as this customer level is often called in the textile industry.

YARN-SPINNING MILLS

Yarn-spinning mills are actually intermediary operations at the supplier's level, for they operate between the raw fiber producers and the fabric producer. Before the advent of man-made fibers, the yarn-spinning mill was absolutely essential. It was here that the short lengths of cotton and wool were straightened and laid side by side in an orderly, parallel manner and then processed into spun yarns. Today, man-made fibers are made in a continuous filament, much like silk. Some man-made fibers are chopped into staple fiber form and go to the yarn-spinning mills, as do cotton and wool fibers; however, the filament form may bypass the yarn process and go directly to the knitter or weaver.

Yarns and Fibers. Most consumers do not know the difference between the terms *fiber* and

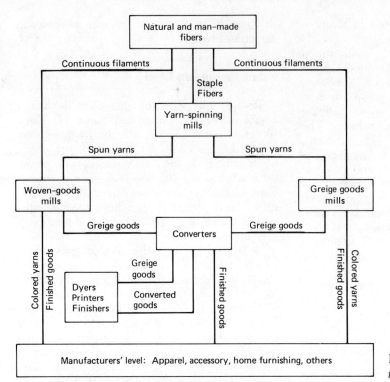

FIGURE 5.5 *Flow chart for fabric production.*

Flow chart labels:
Natural and man-made fibers

Continuous filaments — Continuous filaments

Staple Fibers

Yarn-spinning mills

Spun yarns — Spun yarns

Woven-goods mills — Greige goods mills

Greige goods — Converters — Greige goods

Colored yarns / Finished goods

Greige goods

Dyers Printers Finishers — Converted goods

Finished goods

Colored yarns / Finished goods

Manufacturers' level: Apparel, accessory, home furnishing, others

yarn. Nevertheless, a tour through a yarn-spinning mill soon makes the difference obvious. Above the thunderous roar of highly specialized machinery, a visitor watches the complicated process of making tons of raw fibers (bought from perhaps DuPont or Beaunit) into miles of twisted yarns to be wound onto cones (huge spool-like containers) ready to be shipped to a fabric mill for the weaving or knitting process. Some yarn-spinning mills produce yarns for fabric construction and some produce yarns for other uses, such as for carpets and industrial purposes. Most of these yarn mills are in the eastern part of the United States near the major fiber and fabric producers. There are, however, a few yarn mills in the central part of the country to serve the increasing number of customers west of the Mississippi River.

FABRIC MILLS

Designed for weaving or knitting fabrics, fabric mills are a mechanical engineering feat in the world of mass production. Thousands and thousands of yards of fabrics are constructed each day in the United States. The giant weaving looms and knitting machines, operating at the direction of computers, consume the yarns from hundreds of cones, noisily producing greige goods. Two kinds of mills produce fabrics: woven goods mills and knitted goods mills.

Woven Greige Goods Mills. Woven greige goods mills account for less than half of the fabric production in the United States today. Weaving is the construction of cloth by interlacing two sets of yarns at right angles to each other. The first successful automatic loom was not developed until the end of the nineteenth century. Major changes in woven fabric production have paralleled the economic and technological advancements that followed the two world wars in this century.

Since the 1950s, the invention of shuttleless looms and the computer has led to a tremendous advance in automation. (See Figure 5.7 for the

FIGURE 5.6 *Open-end spinning. (Courtesy of Burlington Industries, Inc.)*

design of a shuttleless loom.) These improvements in weaving machines have increased the financial investments necessary to operate weaving mills. Weaving was virtually the only way cloth was made until the early 1960s, when knitting began to enter the fabric scene on a major scale.

Knitted Greige Goods Mills. More than half of the fabrics consumed in the apparel industry today are produced by knitted greige goods mills. Knitting is the construction of fabric by forming rows of interlocking loops through which new loops are drawn in a continuous formation. Until the 1900s, the process of knitting was the domain of the hosiery and sweater industries. In the decade between 1960 and 1970, the knitting industry tripled in size. The popularity of double knit was primarily responsible for this acceleration. Since then circular knitting machines have been developed to produce intricate patterns at the command of computers. Electronic technology promises even more advances in the future. Knitting machines can produce fabric at a much higher rate of speed than the weaving process and jacquard and raschel knitting machines can produce more elaborate designs automatically.

FIGURE 5.7 *The Sulzer weaving machine, an example of the shuttleless loom. (Courtesy of Springs Mills, Inc.)*

FIGURE 5.8 *Circular dou-bleknit machine. (Courtesy of Burlington Industries, Inc.)*

It is true, that much woven and knitted fabric must go through some type of finishing process; however, some mills may produce fabrics ready for manufacturing operations or for the ultimate consumer. For example, pre-dyed yarns are often woven into plaids, herringbone, or stripes, and sold to apparel manufacturers or to consumers in the form of piece goods. The silk industry, as well as the wool industry, tends to handle fabric-making operations in this simplified way. For cotton and man-made fabrics, the finishing process is sometimes a separate operation completed through the activities of the converter, who is considered one of the fabric mills' customers.

FABRIC CONVERTERS

The role of the fabric converter is to keep greige goods flowing from the mills to the finishing plant's customers. The converter is a nerve center of the textile industry, directing the process of converting greige goods to printed, finished cloth in varieties of floral designs, stripes, solid colors, naps, and corduroys. The converter controls the fabric designs, colors, and finishes of fabrics from season to season in response to and in anticipation of consumer demand. He contracts for the finishing, bleaching, dyeing, and other operations necessary to convert greige goods from the mills into finished fabrics for his customer—the apparel or garment manufacturer. The converter thus works as the go-between for the weaving and knitting mills and the garment manufacturers, or cutters. He buys the greige goods, talks to his cus-

tomer (the cutter), finds out what kinds of fabrics are wanted for the next season, and then sends appropriate amounts of greige goods to a dyer and finisher on a contract basis. Finally, he sells the converted fabrics to the cutter. Some well-known names in the converter phase of the textile business are Cohn-Hall-Marx, Everfast, and M. Lowenstein.

This is such an intricate process that sometimes, when the converter has more than he can do, a jobber is contracted to do some of the converter's work. The jobber usually deals with small jobs of a specialized nature or works with a major converter on big jobs.

FABRIC FINISHERS

Finishers are highly skilled in the specialized and technical area in which they operate. *Bleaching* the greige fabric is usually the first step in the finishing process. The *dyeing* process is a chemical operation, particularly where man-made fibers are involved. *Color specialists* are required. They need to be in contact with the fashion world—they need to know what tones, hues, shades, and tints are in the fashion picture for the coming seasons. They have to know not only how to combine colors, but how to obtain desired color combinations through dyeing and printing processes. They are responsible for the fashion look—that is, the aesthetic appearance of the fabric.

Finishers may be called on by converters to provide various textures to a fabric that is in the

FIGURE 5.9 *Photo-finishing process. (Courtesy of Burlington Industries, Inc.)*

woven or knitted yardage stage. One important technological advancement is heat transfer printing, or the *sublistatic process* as it is called in the textile industry. Textile product development is responsible for the myriad of finishes that impart ease of care and other functional characteristics to fabric. Sanforizing, introduced in 1928, to control shrinkage of cotton, led to a multitude of post-World War II finishes: waterproofing, wrinkle resistance, wash-and-wear, and permanent press, to name a few. Some companies noted for the soil-release finishes are Deering Milliken, which created Visa; 3M, which introduced Scotchgard; Graniteville, which promoted Exit; and Klopman, which originated Clean. Dow Corning also makes textile finishes, and Cranston is a well-known textile printer. These are just a few of the wide variety of finishes that may be applied, depending on the type of fabric and the anticipated consumer demand. Our third generation of man-made fibers is engineered specifically for end-use performance, because soaring sales were the result of such technological breakthroughs as wash-and-wear, stretch, permanent press, and bonded fabrics.

Some of these processes at the fabric-production level are performed by small operators, but in recent years the larger companies have increasingly incorporated many or all of the operations. Burlington Industries, J. P. Stevens & Co., Dan River, Reeves Brothers, Deering Millikan, M. Lowenstein, and Greenwood Mills are examples of multifaceted operations in the textile industry.

Production Scheduling and Mill Liaison. Whether large or small companies are involved in the fabric production processes, production scheduling and the mill liaison activities play an important role. It is vitally important to coordinate salesmen's orders from garment makers with the fabric mill's production, with delivery dates, and with employee output. This kind of coordinating action makes it possible to operate on an even, year-round basis. Decisions must be made concerning color assortments, yardage, patterns, loom capacity, anticipation of new styles and obsolescence of old ones, introduction of new lines, geographic demands, seasonal demands. The entire textile industry depends on the competent functioning of the network of interrelated decision-making activities at the fabric-production level.

GROWTH AND PRESENT STATUS OF THE TEXTILE INDUSTRY

The fiber and fabric producers are major components of the textile industry. The entry of man-made fibers into the textile world in the 1930s and the impact of World War II on the supply-

and-demand picture were the prelude to change in the textile industry in the United States.

The Textile Giants

The trend in the textile industry in the last three decades has been toward integration and diversification. These two changes in the operation and structure of textile companies have produced giants. Small firms and big mills, once highly specialized in only one phase of the fiber-to-fabric process, started to spin, weave, or knit, finish, and even sell fabrics; this is known as vertical integration. This trend, already apparent in other industries, began to make inroads in the textile industry—giantism resulted.

The growth patterns of six major companies in the textile industry appear in Table 5.4.

Burlington Mills started in the South weaving cotton. Next the company got into synthetic fiber production, went on to set up finishing plants for greige goods, and then developed its own converting and selling organizations. Today, Burlington, the giant of the textile industry, operates at all levels: as supplier, manufacturer, and distributor. It is virtually a fashion industry in itself. As a form of public relations and consumer education, Burlington dedicated the lower floor of its midtown Manhattan office building to the visual story of its vertical integration.

Similar cases of vertical integration are companies that started as converters, such as Cohn-Hall-Marx, and firms that originally were sales agents, such as J. P. Stevens.

More recent trends in the textile industry are indicative of another form of bigness: *diversification of products*. An extreme example was the announcement in early 1973 of the purchase of a frozen-food company by Springs Mills, one of the leading producers of fabrics and household linens.[21] In spite of the use of couture designers, household linens have been relatively low-profit items for many years; most Americans can and do wait for the twice-yearly sales. Springs Mills's entry into the frozen-food business may be explained as an effort to add a quick-turnover, high-profit line. The same investment in fabric production facilities would have produced a lower return. Other examples are given in Appendix 9, p. 294.

Some of the advantages of combined facilities through mergers and acquisitions of other companies follow:

1. Increased product mix and more profit potential for the corporate group.
2. More efficient use of all line and staff functions—departments or divisions serving the entire corporate group.
3. More efficient use of all line and staff personnel—specialists serving the entire corporate group.

Thus, the corporation has a stronger base on which to work, more available money, better research development and distribution facilities, more promotional funds, and, thereby, a healthier and perfectly legal position from which to compete in the industrial market place.

Mergers and acquisitions brought about by vertical integration or diversification have

TABLE 5.4 Growth Pattern of Six Major Textile Companies, 1948–1974.

Company	Annual sales in millions of dollars				
	1948	1960	1965	1972	1974
Burlington Industries	288.2	913.0	1,313.3	1,816.1	2,329.9
J. P. Stevens & Co., Inc.	287.3	512.7	759.9	947.6	1,264.1
United Merchants & Manufacturers	211.5	468.2	559.7	787.0	1,015.0
Springs Mills, Inc.	154.0	200.0	252.0	398.9	555.8
M. Lowenstein & Sons, Inc.	120.1	253.3	288.7	470.0	551.6
Dan River Mills, Inc.	103.6	156.9	246.3	366.6	439.7

FIGURE 5.10 *Mock-up of "The Mill" at Burlington House in New York City. Here, visitors can observe the machines and operations that turn yarn into woven and knit fabrics. (Courtesy of Burlington Industries, Inc.)*

changed the textile industry at the supplier's level. Now, huge, publicly owned enterprises dominate the textile world. The 20 largest textile firms are listed in Appendix 10, p. 296.

Present Trends and Future Directions

Technology in textile production has been developed intensively in only a decade or so. The results have been new and improved fibers, fabrics, and finishes, in addition to modernized, automated, and computerized weaving and knitting processes. Much of the research and development has moved toward functional improvements in fiber and fabric production in direct response to consumer demand and acceptance patterns. Many new performance characteristics have been engineered and marketed, not the least of these being wash-and-wear and nonflammable finishes.

As a result of the new emphasis on developing performance characteristics in response to predetermined consumer desires, the influence of life styles is paramount. In many ways, the future will be an extension of these technological advances; however, there are other factors which relate to the trends and directions on the horizon.

GROWTH RATE

A continued growth for the production and consumption of textile fibers has been predicted on the basis of estimates of increased world population and economic development. A world population of 7,000 million has been projected by the year 2000, almost double the world population of 1975. A major portion of the increase will be in economically poorer areas of the world—Africa, India, and the rest of Asia. A huge market just beginning to affect the rest of the world is the People's Republic of China. The following predictions are based on observable facts and trends.

Consumption of Textile Fibers. As the basic needs of more and more people are met, more and more textile products will be consumed and more and more fibers will be required. The consumption of textile fibers is expected to increase by 45 per cent between 1970 and 1980 and slightly less after that.[22] As the disposable income of the consumer increases, there is usually an increase in the expenditures for textile items other than clothing—home furnishings, accessories, and the like. Usually, as the expenditures for these kinds of textile items get larger, the monies spent on clothing decrease slightly.

Increased Production of Fibers. The production of both natural and man-made fibers will expand to meet the increasing demands for clothing and other textile products by consumers around the world. Of course, the potential for growth is unlimited in the area of man-made fibers, whereas natural-fiber production is affected somewhat by factors beyond the control of producers—available acreage, rain, flood, heat, cold. Total world fiber production is expected to more than double in the next twenty-five years, and the production of man-made fibers is projected to nearly triple by the year 2000.[23] Synthetics increased from 11 per cent of the world fiber production in 1965 to 29 per cent in 1973; during this time total fiber production increased 40 per cent. Worldwide acceptance of synthetic fibers is somewhat behind United States consumption, which is now 50 per cent of the total. It should be noted, however, that the synthetic fiber industry is almost completely dependent on petroleum products for basic raw materials. Synthetic fiber production may be severely affected in years to come because it is an oil-based product.[24]

Knits. Knits are projected to grow at a faster rate than wovens because they have several advantages: (1) knitting remains the least expensive and the quickest method of producing cloth; (2) in periods of shorter and shorter inventories, and buying goods at the last possible moment by both garment makers and retailers, the flexibility and speed of knitting are assets; (3) knitting gives the best price value to the customer; (4) consumers like knits; this factor may be the most important of all. The future holds many possibilities for technological improvements—new fibers, new patterns, more desirable performance characteristics. Predictions for the future of the knit segment of the textile industry include:

1. Large companies, with their economies of scale, will drive out unspecialized small firms.
2. Small knitters that specialized previously in yarn-dyed jacquards will survive and continue to produce decorative knits to meet increasing demands for newness and novelty.
3. Large and small knitters will survive *only* if competitive in quality of finished goods, because the same yarns and same machines are available to all.
4. Vertically integrated knitters will have a big advantage because, by ownership of dyeing and finishing facilities, the mill gains increased control over the finished product.

5. Knitters will look around for new markets in which to sell their products: first, to try to recoup the moderate-to-better-priced women's business lost in the early 1970s; and second, to explore markets in which they have not sold before—juniors, young men's, and infants, for example.[25]

Consolidation

A continued move toward consolidation in the textile industry can be anticipated. Major companies, no doubt, will become increasingly competitive, and, as other textile firms attempt to grow, specialization will tend to give way both to vertical integration and to diversification. Restrictive merger guidelines for textiles were relaxed by the Federal Trade Commission (FTC) in 1975. Some directions are noted in the following discussion.

Quality and Costs. Internal ways to insure quality and cost control in every phase of production and distribution will be foremost in the minds of the producers of fibers and fabrics.

Modernization. Of necessity, modernization will continue to be a major concern in textile operations. Machinery and facilities must keep up with rapid growth in production and consumption of textiles. New technology (automated and computerized systems and processes) will be a keynote. Some smaller companies will continue to operate efficiently by working closely with others to share costs of research and computer-based marketing services or rely heavily on the research of other, bigger firms or trade associations in the textile industry.

Government Constraints and Controls. Growth that might tend toward monopolies in the industry will continue to be deterred by government. Strictness is to be expected in the enforcement of fair competition and honest product representation. There will be continued monitoring of mergers, acquisitions, and other types of conglomerate growth.

Foreign-based Operations. American textile exports and imports will continue to be monitored by the government in an effort to maintain the balance of trade.

Multinational Companies. Multinational companies now control 15 per cent of the gross world product. In the future, there will be some controls and one can envision a controlled multination—an attempt to rationalize distribution of world goods and markets.

TECHNOLOGY AND MARKETING

Technological and marketing advances are expected to continue to generate major changes in the textile industry. For the consumer, the future holds new fibers, new finishes, new fabrics—woven and knitted—suggested by present breakthroughs.

Printing and Finishing Processes. The processes of printing and finishing have received great impetus from the new heat-transfer method that appeared on the textile scene in the late 1960s. Two major companies have been alert to technical developments in this area: Lowenstein and Singer. Mills and fabric stylists have attempted to accelerate this revolutionary new printing idea—the first big change in printing in fifty or sixty years. One of its most significant advantages is the application of nearly any design, in any size, onto fabric faster than any other method known to man. Then, too, there is increased flexibility for the industry both in sampling fabric designs and in shifting vigorously with new fashion trends. Low labor costs add to the advantage of heat transfer, which is not a complex process, and are of great importance in the labor-intensive textile industry. Fashion and the ultimate consumer will be the beneficiaries of this breakthrough.

Woven Goods. As if not to be outdone by advances in printing and finishing, the woven goods segment of the textile industry has taken another giant step—open-end spinning.[26] This new technological development is a revolutionary high-speed yarn-spinning process that produces greatly improved fiber. Advantages are speed in producing yarns and adaptability to automation, which makes it much less labor intensive and much more economical. It is also a much cleaner operation than the former method (known as ring spinning in the textile industry).

New consumer life styles mean new fashions. The future is change. On the basis of what has happened in the textile industry in the last quarter of a century, some interesting and imaginative ideas about things to come in the years 1974 to 2001 were published in the one hundredth issue of the *American Fabrics and Fashions* magazine (see Figure 5.11).

OTHER PRIMARY SUPPLIERS

The textile industry is not the only one that supplies raw materials to the American apparel industry. Many smaller, more specialized producers of raw materials are also subjected to the seasonal fluctuations inflicted on fashion makers. Trade cycles with these smaller primary suppliers may start suddenly and end abruptly or may accelerate slowly and decline with the obsolescence of the fashion requiring the raw material. For example, the fur and leather industries are usually called on to make important contributions to fashion making during the fall and winter seasons. A revival of furs and leather as an important raw material of fashion in the 1970s has generated more vitality in these industries.

The Leather Industry

Leather, a raw material of fashion, is used in making shoes, handbags, gloves, jackets, and numerous other items and trims, according to the seasonal demands of fashion makers. The major portion of the leather produced in the United States comes from cattle. Goats and sheep (kids) are a second source of leather; however, these leathers are imported from South America, Europe, Africa, and countries in the Far East. The skins and hides of animals are usually a byproduct of the meat industry.

TANNING

Tanning is a process by which leather is produced. Small animals—calves, kids (sheep), and goats—are classified as skins in the tanning trade.

THE NEXT 100 ISSUES

THINGS TO COME 1974–2001

In the next 27 years, AFF with depth and imagination will report on the wondrous developments which lie ahead—a virtual fabric/fashion odyssey of technological and marketing wizardry. The mainstream of the future will change our lives and our businesses.

STAY TUNED TO THIS STATION FOR:

- The development of a *new generic fiber* which will have the ultimate properties. This Dream Fiber will combine the best properties of both the naturals and man-mades; the comfort of cotton, the loft and warmth of wool, the dye brilliance of silk, the performance and ease-of-care of polyester. It will be antistatic, lightweight, soil & flame retardant.

- There will be *hollow-core yarns* with programmable tubular funnels—color cores which can be changed; mechanical or chemical programming which can achieve a dazzling variety of characteristics: filtration, thermostatic/heat exchange, optical diffusion.

- A *"swell"-fiber*, with variable geometry, which can dilate or contract achieving a fabric which regulates air-passage: a breathing cloth. This opening-closing of the weave or knit would modulate escape or capture of body warmth.

- The *ultra-dry fiber*—a fiber or yarn construction which achieves super-dry moisture evaporation. Possibly, a combination of special super-porosity/hollow-core (osmosis) and thread-like screw spirals which will physically transport moisture molecules away for evaporation. This *dry fiber* will have a specific wicking scale range—high for toweling, socks, gloves—mid and low for other end-uses.

- *Photo-optic color*—activation by light-wave or laser radiation achieving of photo-latent dye characteristics programmed into fibers/fabrics which can be instantly colored and decorated, as easy as projecting a film slide.

- Home Furnishings will rid itself of the "own it for life" syndrome. *Reprogrammable color variation* will permit owner to change room decor electronically, or through new *Super-Dyes*, which can be color modulated by owner at will.

  Floor coverings will be reprogrammable. You will buy a "generic" covering, decorate and redecorate it yourself. Floor covering prints and patterns will be as intricate and lovely as couture fashion.

  Color and light ambiance programming for interior spaces will be a reality where the color-light-intensity factors of a room will be modulated for pleasing values for morning, mid-day or night.

  Furniture retailing will change drastically to emphasize decorative acces-

sories as more furniture gets built into rooms/walls.

- *In-home cleaning.* Clothes will be cleaned at home in a *microwave closet*, where a high frequency wave or electrical charge will polarize and reject dirt, not unlike NASA's decontamination process for spacesuits.

- *Direct fabric formation* (non wovens) will achieve parity with knit/woven fabrications and create a new level of production *economics* and style *aesthetics*.

- *Automated custom clothes* will be ordered at retail counters. Your size will be electronically recorded and stored, and the product will be computer-produced for prompt delivery. Electronic knitting or rapid direct fabric formation will produce full fashioned/contour molded custom fit products *on the spot*.

- *Nuclear texturing* of fibers; electron bombardment in the pre-extrusion phase will organize new polymer arrangements for varied product specifics.

- *Rented fashions:* a dramatic increase in *non-ownership* will take place. Wardrobes will be rented on a monthly basis for year-long joy of many new things to wear. Fashion product boredom will be long dead and the *psychological* importance of clothes will be fully understood. You will wear your ego and id.

  On another scale, commercial and residential interiors will also be serially rented-leased, achieving a pleasant 4-season change of decor.

- *The soft room;* fabric on floor, wall and ceiling—a sensuous and quiet departure from the square hard-walls which now encase us. Pleasing variations will come with the *reshapable soft room* with an inner fabric shell randomly shaped to achieve any desired functional or aesthetic effect.

- *Shopping revolution.* The store comes to your home. Retailers will bring products to you via electronic presentation—video, film, holographs, samples will showcase products through two-way cable/microwave hookup, store-to-home.

  Computer line connections will tie-in to manufacturers warehouse terminals, instantly updating inventory simultaneous with sale. The consumer's purchase action will trigger a computer controlled network which will transmit a chain-

reaction encompassing sales transaction information, in-store item replenishment, shipping orders to field warehouse and re-order command to manufacturer. The era of the order-taking salesclerk will have passed.

- *Local retail credits* will finally catch up to broadcast data—videoreceivers will decode and flash local retail store credit on merchandise whereabouts right down to the store up the block. Gone will be the Connecticut T.V. viewer seeing a commercial with a store credit for a New Jersey outlet.

- *A global retail satellite* will link stores around the world to vendors via microwave transmission network—a "store-in-the-sky."

  Satellite microwave transmission service will relay soft goods data to regional earth terminals, which will be interconnected with multi-point transmission facilities throughout the world.

  Thus, corporations will link together dealers, branch offices, plants and customers into "narrow-cast" networks for management communications, information systems, marketing, education, training and direct sales at minimum user cost.

- Corporate ownership of industrial communications equipment will see business letters processed through computers and typed-out at addressee's terminal, eliminating high-cost U.S. postal service.

- Magazines, newsprint will be custom ordered and teleprinted in your home or office, reducing the cost of printing and postal delivery.

- Business communications will undergo a revolution with emphasis on color coding of key words, 3-dimensional photographs, pictorial communications.

- Marketing emphasis will shift from share-of-market to share-of-mind.

  The most important business fact will be not how many people you reach but how effectively you reach each one.

  Feeling, the sense of touch, the impact of color, will be crucial marketing and product facts to grasp and understand.

  Color will be the most important long-range human/product ingredient to understand. It's the basis of sight which is the crucible of perception and knowledge.

FIGURE 5.11 American Fabrics and Fashions, No. 100, Spring 1974, p. 86. *(Reprinted by permission.)*

Large animals—cows, horses, and buffalo—provide hides. Calfskin, kidskin, and morocco (goat) leather have traditionally been produced in fine qualities for use in fashion accessories—gloves, shoes, handbags, belts, wallets, and the like. Other exotic leathers may be used as a raw material of fashion—deerskin, elkskin, ostrich, and various reptile skins. Today ecologists are bringing about a decrease in the use of skins from endangered species.

The tanning trade is another small, highly specialized operation. Approximately five hundred plants are located in the United States, most of which employ fewer than one hundred persons. But some 30,000 workers are involved in the leather industry in the United States. The value of products in the leather industry is approximately $1 million annually. Some 24 million hides and 11 million skins are processed each year in this country.[27] In the decade from 1965 to 1975, there was a tremendous increase in use of imported leather in the shoe industry.

The tanning operation may be an integrated part of the meat-packing industry or may be performed on a separate contract basis. In the latter case, a converter functions as he does in the textile industry; he obtains hides and skins and contracts for tanning them.

Like other suppliers of raw materials of fashion, the leather suppliers have made a tremendous effort to raise the quality of their product in recent years. In the 1960s and 1970s, a soft, supple leather was produced for clothing items—for shirts, slacks, and jackets. Research and development in the leather industry have been directed toward attaining a wash-and-wear leather product; machine-washable leather garments can be expected in fashion markets by the 1980s.

Leather making is a slow, time-consuming, and highly specialized process. Because of the time factor, the leather industry traditionally has had to anticipate and predict trends in advance of other fashion suppliers. Leather producers must make commitments to colors, finishes, and production some eight months to two years in advance of use of leather by apparel manufacturers. The coordination of colors, textures, and other fashion variables is vital to the leather industry. In the past, other fashion makers have often looked to the leather industry for leadership in color directions and for long-range forecasts.

The Fur Industry

Prestige, luxury, elegance—these terms have traditionally spelled fashion in the fur industry. Fur as a status symbol has been adopted by the middle-income consumer in the United States. Although inexpensive "fun" furs have become important in the fashion market, the prestige of sable, chinchilla, and mink has not declined.

The fur industry is another billion-dollar supplier of raw materials for fashion. Mass production of some species of mink, fox, chinchilla, and other animals has been successful in the United States. New colors are produced through mutations or cross-breeding. The fashion makers in the United States also import many furs. Nevertheless, there are some 1,300 plants in and around the New York area alone, employing 8,500 workers to supply the furs for fashion.[28] A reasonable estimate of the retail value of this industry's products would be more than half a billion dollars annually.

The fluctuation in the demand for particular furs is fashion oriented; price is influenced by this fickle factor. Whatever is in fashion usually becomes more expensive for a season or two.

The fur industry requires highly skilled craftsmen. Fur skins, or pelts, as they are called in the industry, are graded for standardized qualities and sold in bundles. The pelts are first dressed—a process that enhances the most desirable qualities and characteristics of each pelt. The dressed furs are then ready for the makers of fashion. The manufacturing stage is still far from mass production, for fur apparel and other fur products continue to require a great many hand operations.

As the fur and leather industries have moved to meet the challenges of the fashion industry, suppliers of man-made furs and leathers have entered the fashion arena. These fake furs sometimes called "fun furs" and leathers can be quickly produced at moderate prices. Rather than acting as a competitive factor, the man-made products tend to accelerate consumer demand for the real thing; if many consumers are sporting

FIGURE 5.12 *Seen in the fur merchant's storerooms are pelts from American farms, fields, and forests, as well as specialties from every other continent. Fox, mink, squirrel, muskrat, and Persian lamb are being inspected by a fur buyer. (Courtesy of the Fur Information and Fashion Council, Inc.)*

"leather-look" fashions, the upper segment of the fashion leaders will choose real leather—an example of the bottom-up theory. Thus, the use of nonwoven and various plastic products has increased. Fake furs and leathers can look amazingly real, even in the eyes of their competitors, the traditional fur and leather industry.

Nonwoven Textiles

Plastic "leather" is only one example of the nonwoven textiles. Cheap paper clothing and disposable paper underwear were being marketed in the 1970s. Early in the 1960s, researchers experimented with the use of paper for making clothing. The present nonwoven paper products are made in an adhesive bonding process. Although it has been estimated that the world production of nonwovens will triple before 1980, it is not likely that this raw product will present a serious challenge to the traditional woven and knitted fabric segment of the textile industry.

The real impact of the nonwoven material could be a technological breakthrough in the fiber-to-fabric-to-garment process that has traditionally complicated activities in the fashion industry. Current developments in the nonwoven field may make it possible to shorten the route from the fiber producer to the fabric producer and, thus, to the manufacturer of apparel for the consumer.

The nonwoven industry supplies the raw material for numerous products on today's market.

Two classifications have already emerged in the nonwoven (or should we say nonknit?) industry: (1) durable products and (2) disposable products. The key to the classification is not durability, however, but end use. Consumer acceptance has been rapid, but even more stimulating to the nonwoven producers have been industrial and medical uses. The search for end-use markets for non-wovens has been going on since the best-forgotten disposable dresses of the mid-1960s.[29] Nonwoven is a capital-intensive and labor-light business, unlike many other portions of the textile industry. Only five mills had serious commitments to the field by the mid-1970s: Stevens (which includes Kimberley-Clark), Burlington, West Point Pepperel, Kendall, and Chicopee.

DURABLES PRODUCT MARKET
20% interlinings
15–20% carpet backing
7–15% furniture and bedding
7–15% coated fabric materials
7–15% automotive and furniture padding

DISPOSABLE PRODUCT MARKET
50% disposable diapers
30% sanitary napkins
10% medical and surgical supplies
10% wipes, packages, headrests

What would be left of the textile industry, as we know it today, if the potential of the nonwoven process were realized? Would it be possible to develop the direct production of a garment from a mass of raw fibers? Modern technology makes even this seem feasible in the minds of some experts in the textile and apparel industries. Is a process of producing garments automatically without fabrics and without cutting or sewing possible? Plastics, for example, do provide a feasible source for experimenting with fabric construction.

Certainly, primary suppliers in the fashion industries may indeed be different tomorrow, but this prediction may not greatly affect the progress of today's primary suppliers: the textile industry, the leather industry, the fur industry, and many other small suppliers of the raw materials of fashion.

SECONDARY SUPPLIERS

The seasonal fluctuations and trade cycles that affect primary suppliers affect makers of buttons, thread, zippers, interfacing, sequins, and hundreds of other makers of trims.

Ruffling, lace, buttons, bows, and ribbons all were a part of the fashion scene for both women's and men's clothing before the seventeenth century. Diamonds and other precious and semiprecious stones were used in buttons and in trims for men's coats, women's gowns, and headdresses in the courts of Europe. Their use of silk ribbons and feathers earned fashion leadership in the world for French dressmakers in the eighteenth and nineteenth centuries.

Buttons. Today the button industry, although small in size, mass produces thousands of buttons and other ornamental trims to meet the functional and decorative needs of clothing consumers. The New York City area is the center for most button suppliers, and production is concentrated in that area of the United States. Tremendous varieties of buttons are available for the makers of fashion, many imported from Europe.

Zippers. The zipper belongs to twentieth-century America. A long-desired wish of the fashion makers came true with the invention of the first commercial zipper: a method of closing and opening a seam or placket in a fitted garment. Presto, the zipper did it and has continued to do it in apparel for men, women, and children for almost half a century! Other methods have been experimented with, and buttons continue to be used, but zipper suppliers are firmly entrenched in the fashion industries.

New materials—metals and plastics—and improved designs in zipper production have been lauded by both garment makers and home sewers. Today it is almost impossible to tell which seam or placket has the zipper; only the consumer who wears the garment knows. There is no question about the convenience and ease this functional invention provides to the millions of users.

Trims. Suppliers of trims that enhance the beauty of a garment—such as lace, ribbons, and sequins—are often victims of the on-again, off-again whims of consumer demand. Traditionally or European make, vast supplies are imported. However, the American lace industry, along with American makers of ribbons and other trims, is centered in the New York City area. Highly automated techniques have replaced some of the hand operations in these small, highly specialized trades.

Thread.   Threat suppliers are not entirely separate from the textile industry, although they are considered secondary suppliers. Thread is defined as a tightly twisted ply yarn used in sewing. Progress in the production of thread for the needle trades has paralleled advancements in the textile industry. Sewing threads have the qualities imparted by new and improved fibers and blends and by new techniques in the yarn-twisting and spinning process.

Interfacing.   Suppliers of interfacings are also a part of what has traditionally been considered the textile industry in the United States, yet they are considered to be secondary suppliers. According to one of the leading suppliers of interfacings, both for the apparel and home-sewing industries, "Interfacings have been important to fashion since the beginning of recorded time—no garment can be better than its inner construction."[30]

Various woven construction forms of interfacing have provided shape and fashion features for men's and women's clothing for decades. The men's tailoring industry has been one of the most important users of interfacings in the past. But with the birth of nonwovens, a new era has dawned. The miracle happened with the production of lightweight interfacings with body enough to shape the fashion, subtlety enough to be unobtrusive, pliability enough to be worn comfortably, and flexibility enough to fit into fashion's variety of uses. One of the suppliers of note here is the Pellon Corporation, an operation based in Germany, with a large division in the United States. Only seventeen years old, this firm makes a nonwoven interfacing with many of the qualities desired by fashion makers. Crinolins, hair canvas, and other long-used woven interfacings were virtually left behind by the late 1960s. This particular firm has been responsible for much of the research in the industry. Stay-put kinds of interfacings were achieved in Pellon-type nonwoven products that were also fuseable, washable, drycleanable, light weight, porous, resilient, nonwrinkling, and nonraveling. The plus for the manufacturer in figuring cost of yardage is a featured quality: the interfacing can be cut and sewn in any direction.

In addition to these advancements in nonwovens, Pellon Corporation has contributed in another way to the fashion industries. It has set an example of cooperation and coordination. Pellon has not been satisfied with just producing a product. This organization has consistently aimed at supplying a product that will function wherever it is needed in the fashion industries. Hours and hours of research and development time have gone into providing technical assistance and know-how for apparel manufacturers and others using the product. The manufacturers' problems are Pellon's problems—experimentation and problem solving are vital components of progress. The permanently compatible marriage between the shell and the interfacing that the Pellon Corporation has achieved may be an omen for the giant fashion industries. Pellon, along with several other firms at the supplier level, has set the stage for working together among interdependent operations. These kinds of activities are vital to progress in the fashion industries.

FEDERAL LEGISLATION GOVERNING FASHION SUPPLIERS

Any person involved in the fashion business needs to be aware of federal legislation. It is the responsibility of manufacturers and retailers as well as consumers to know what to expect from goods and to know the law.

Textile, fur, and leather legislation have been passed over the years to protect the consumer from false advertising and mislabeling of fiber content, furs, and leather. The Flammable Fabrics Act was passed to protect the consumer from fire hazards. In fact, much important legislation has resulted in response to specific needs.

Textile Fiber Products Identification Act

This act was signed by President Eisenhower and became law March 3, 1960. It covers wearing apparel and household textiles. *Textiles must be labeled or otherwise identified by percentage of each fiber present, by weight, in amounts of 5 per cent or more.* Fibers must be listed in order of prominence, and each fiber designated by its generic name (unless a natural fiber—cotton, wool, silk, or flax). Man-made fibers use their generic names, given according to chemical composition: acetate, acrylic, anidix, azlon, glass, lastrile, metallic, modacrylic, nylon, mutril, olefin, polyester, rayon, rubber, saran, spandex, triacetate, vinyl, vinyon, aramic, and novoloid. There may be several trade names for one generic fiber.

Flammable Fabrics Act of 1967

This act amended a 1953 piece of legislation. It expanded textile legislation to include the Department of Commerce Flammability Standards for certain textile products. They are enforced by the Consumer Product Safety Commission. In July 1973, fabrics intended for children's sleepwear (sizes 0 to 6x) were made subject to these standards. Also controlled by the same laws were carpets, rugs, mattresses, and mattress pads. Since that time, children's sleepwear from sizes 7 to 14 has been included, however, in 1977. Tris, the flame-retardent chemical, was banned by the federal government because of its cancer-causing effects. Textiles that meet the various standards may char, burn very slowly, or not burn at all under the testing condition. Testing conditions simulate household situations in which textiles will burn. Care instructions on flame-resistant textiles should be strictly followed. The flammability characteristics can be drastically changed by improper care.

Wool Products Labeling Act of 1939

This act required fiber-content labeling by wool type:

Wool Fiber from the fleece of the sheep or lamb or hair of the Angora or Cashmere goat (or hair of the camel, llama, alpaca, and vicuna) that has never been reclaimed from any woven or felted wool product.

Reprocessed wool Fiber that previously was manufactured into a wool product but was not used in any way by the ultimate consumer.

Reused wool Fiber reclaimed from wool products that were used by the ultimate consumer.

The term *virgin wool* was later defined as new wool fiber not previously processed.

Fur Products Labeling Act

This act, which became effective August 9, 1952, designated that (1) the true English name of the animal must be as prominently printed in advertisements and labels as any other words used. (2) No other animal's name could be used to describe any dye or process. (3) The geographic origin of the fur had to be accurate. (4) The origin of all imported furs had to be noted on the label, which had to be 1¾ by 2¾ inches in size. (5) Any waste fur or used fur had to be mentioned. (6) If the fur had been dyed or tip dyed, it had to be labeled "dyed rabbit" or "tip-dyed mink," for example.

The FTC issued rules in September 1941 controlling the labeling of leather products. The rules required that a label or tag be attached to luggage or such leather goods as wallets to indicate that split leather has been used. The tag could be labeled split cowhide. If a portion of the leather product is split leather, the label should read, "top-grain cowhide gussets." The English name of the leather must be used. Often, leather is embossed to imitate another texture, leather, or hide. Proper labeling helps the salesperson and the consumer know more about the quality and expected durability of the product.

In July 1972, a new FTC ruling went into effect requiring care instructions to be permanently affixed to garments—the label could be sewn in, stamped, or otherwise adhered to the garment. The consumer of piece goods should be handed stamped care-label instructions at the time of purchase. The consumer should take the responsibility to check to see that the instructions match those on the end of the bolt of fabric.

Importance of Labeling

Much time and effort on the part of the government, consumer action groups, manufacturers, and retailers have gone into labeling legislation to protect the consumer. Often, consumers never even read the labels, and many do not understand them when they do. But consumers should realize that proper fabric care can ensure longer life and better prformance for the fashion goods.

The consumer must have a basic knowledge of fiber, fabric, finishes, and care requirements to understand labels. Certainly, fashion personnel must have the same or even greater knowledge to design, buy, and sell fashion goods for the ultimate satisfaction of the consumer.

Apparel labels should give the consumer the following information:

1. The fiber content (required by law, generic as well as trade name).
2. Finish (any special treatment to change appearance or performance).
3. Care instructions (sewn in or otherwise adhered, required by law).
4. Manufacturer (trade or brand name).
5. Construction (weave or knit, not always included).
6. Size.
7. Price (sometimes included on national brand merchandise).

END OF CHAPTER GUIDE

Review, Discussion, and Evaluation

Study of this chapter should enable students to
A. Develop and give evidence of the following kinds of competencies:
   1. An understanding of the functions and relationship of the textile industry in the total structure of the fashion industries.
   2. A knowledge of the various factors that indicate the size and importance of the textile industry and other suppliers of raw materials for the fashion industries.
   3. An awareness of the functional operations involved in the production of fabrics for the consumer, as well as for industrial users.
   4. An ability to recognize the trends in world production and consumption of textile fibers.
   5. An ability to relate changes in the textile industry to recent trends and growth patterns of major firms.
   6. Recognize federal legislation that has impact on the labeling of textiles and other raw materials used in fashion products produced for the consumer.
B. Develop and/or clarify concepts related to the following key words or phrases:
   1. primary and secondary suppliers 2. fiber production 3. fabric production 4. textile industry 5. natural fibers 6. man-made fibers 7. leather industry 8. fur industry 9. nonwoven industry 10. button industry 11. zipper industry 12. suppliers of thread and trimmings 13. fabric mills 14. weavers and knitters and spinners 15. fabric converters and finishers 16. jobbers 17. fiber consumption and end use 18. greige goods 19. textile giants 20. textile legislation 21. consumer care guide 22. fur products labeling 23. leather products labeling

Extended Classroom Learning Experiences

A. Develop a flow chart indicating the process involved in producing a textile item (blouse, skirt, jeans, etc.), describing the stages from consumer product *back* to the raw material. (Use the flow chart of the textile industry on page 125 for a guide.)
B. Make a collection of brand names used by fabric producers in advertising or labeling clothing and other textile products (towels, linens, draperies, carpets, etc.)
   1. Search out information in advertisements in current magazines or newspapers and on labels or hang tags on products in local stores. Compile a list of names that indicate brand and fiber or fabric producers.
   2. Summarize your findings briefly, including the list you compiled for number B.1, and noting any names of fiber or fabric producers listed in this chapter.
C. Arrange an interview with the manager or buyer of one or more fabric stores or the piece goods departments of a local department store.
   1. Ask the following kinds of questions:
      a. Which are the major fabric companies supplying fabrics for the department or store?

b. What are the brand names of fabrics currently popular with consumers?
c. What kinds of fabric finishes does the consumer ask for most frequently in purchasing piece goods?
2. Write a brief report of your interview and include a summary of the information you received.
D. Write to one or more of the trade associations listed in appendix 7, page 290, and request current information about these primary or secondary suppliers or about related organizations.
E. Make a study of the fiber content of clothing and other textile products.
1. Look at several items of clothing in your wardrobe and list the fiber content on the labels. How many items do you have that are cotton? Wool? Man-made? Blends?
2. Visit one or more stores and check the hang tags on items of merchandise in two of the following departments: women's and children's wear, men's and boys' wear, home furnishings. Note the fiber content on at least ten items in two different departments. How many items did you find that were cotton ____, wool ____, man-made ____, blends ____?
3. Write a brief report summarizing your findings and draw conclusions related to the information presented in Table 5.3, page 131.
F. Read two or more of the articles listed here or research current periodicals or trade journals and select two or more articles related to one of the concepts suggested in "Review, Discussion, and Evaluation."
1. Prepare note cards while reading each article.
2. Using your note cards, write a brief summary indicating the relationship of each article to concepts presented in this chapter.
3. Using your note cards, give an oral report in your class and point out the important facts included in the articles.

Suggested Articles

Loving, Rush. "What the U.S. Textile Industry Really Needs," *Fortune* (October 1970), pp. 84–87, 161–63.
Mecklin, J. M. "Asia's Great Leap in Textiles." *Fortune* (October 1970), pp. 77–83, 138.
"Toward the Multinational Textile Company." *American Fabrics*, Summer 1972, pp. 59–61.

NOTES

[1] U.S. Census Bureau, Office of Labor Statistics and Office of Textiles, 1974.
[2] Marshall Doswell, "Architects of Change." Fort Mill, N.C.: Spring Mills, Inc., 1972, p. 2.
[3] Ibid.
[4] Department of Commerce, *U.S. Industrial 1975 Outlook*. Washington, D.C.: U.S. Government Printing Office, 1975, p. 217.
[5] Department of Agriculture, *Textile Report*. Washington, D.C.: U.S. Government Printing Office, 1974.
[6] U.S. Census Bureau, Office of Labor Statistics and Office of Textiles, 1973, p. 88.
[7] *Focus*. Washington, D.C.: Man Made Fiber Producing Association, Inc., Spring, 1976.
[8] B. W. Hirsh and Peter Ellis, *An Introduction to Textile Economics*. Manchester, England: The Textile Trade Press, 1972, p. 61.
[9] Ibid.
[10] Ibid., p. 66.
[11] Ibid., p. 89.
[12] Ibid., p. 30.
[13] Ibid., p. 92.
[14] Ibid., p. 30.
[15] Ibid., p. 13.
[16] Ibid., p. 15.
[17] Ibid., p. 23.
[18] Ibid., p. 23.
[19] Ibid., p. 31.
[20] "Nylon, The First 25 Years." Philadelphia: E. I. DuPont Publication, 1963, p. 2.
[21] *Forbes*, January, 1975, p. 21.
[22] Hirsh and Ellis, op. cit., pp. 140–158
[23] Ibid.
[24] "Fibers and Petrochemicals," *American Fabrics and Fashions*, Fall, 1974. New York: Doric Publishing Co., 1974, p. 45.
[25] "New Markets for Knitters," *Clothes*, April 15, 1975, pp. 61–67.
[26] "Open-End Spinning," *American Fabrics and Fashions*, Summer, 1974. New York: Doric Publishing Co., 1974, p. 52.
[27] Department of Commerce, *U.S. Industrial 1975 Outlook*. Washington, D.C.: U.S. Government Printing Office, 1975, p. 233.
[28] Census of Manufacturers, U.S. Department of Commerce, 1971.
[29] "Non-Wovens," *American Fabrics and Fashions*, Summer, 1974. New York: Doric Publishing Co., 1974, p. 39.
[30] "Interfacings," *Clothes*, December 1, 1967, pp. 9–13.

6

Fashion Manufacturers

Billions of pounds of fibers, millions of yards of fabrics, and trillions of items of apparel—these extravagant figures signify fashion en masse. Mass producers of ready-to-wear are the major consumers of textile fabrics in the United States. The apparel industry manufactures clothing and accessories for women, men, and children; this multibillion-dollar industry has grown up in less than a century. The apparel industry is big business. In this chapter we will discuss just how big it is, where it carries on its work, how it grows, and what kinds of problems it encounters in producing fashion for millions of Americans. (See Figure 6.1.)

Consideration is given first to the scope, size, and economic importance of this industry in the United States. Next, the various types of manufacturing operations are discussed, along with the organizational responsibilities within apparel firms, and some trends and future developments within segments of the industry. Noted in the latter part of this chapter are some related industries that manufacture fashion accessories, such as shoes, handbags, gloves, belts, hosiery, millinery, and lingerie.

When the word *fashion* is mentioned in the United States, the consumer thinks of ready-to-wear, the apparel industry, Seventh Avenue, New York, and mass production. These terms are not synonymous, but they reflect the idea of big business. *Fashion* for 75 million women, for example, has to be mass produced, and that

means big business. When other market segments of the apparel industry are added—that is, men's, boys', and children's wear, plus the accessory firms, then the fashion business becomes big almost beyond comprehension.

These various apparel manufacturers style, cut, sew, and ship an unbelievable variety of garments each season to retail outlets across the country. In a year's time, apparel manufacturers in the United States produce:

204 million blouses
 60 million skirts
 23 million coats
226 million dresses
629 million men's shirts
 48 million men's work shirts
 17 million men's suits
174 million pairs of men's pants
218 million pairs of work pants
643 million women's and children's panties
210 million bras and bralets

These figures, compiled in 1974 by the International Ladies Garment Workers Union (ILGWU), indicate only part of the total items mass produced in our country.[1] American consumers, young or old, rich or poor, male or female, spend all their waking hours (and most sleeping hours, too, for that matter) wearing clothing of some kind or other. "Clothing for every man, woman, and child in the United

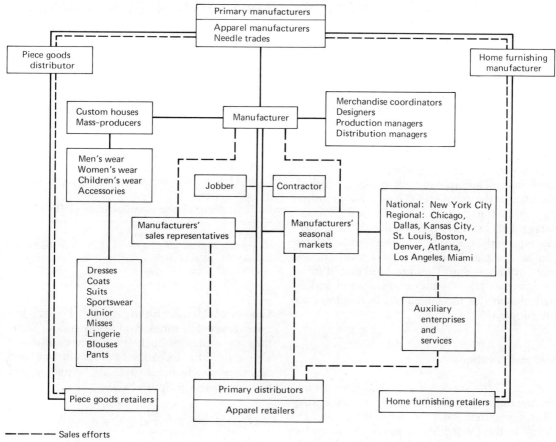

FIGURE 6.1 *Flow chart for the apparel industry.*

States" could well be the *slogan* of the mass producers of apparel. During the coming year, about 7.5 per cent of each consumer dollar will be spent on clothing.[2]

Nowhere else in the world is there such a tremendous assortment of clothing and such a wide range of prices to meet the needs and desires of people of all ages within each of the various income groups. In the United States, mass produced ready-to-wear is fashion. Seasonal clothing in an assortment of styles, colors, fabrics, sizes, and prices has been largely responsible for the tremendous increase in sales in the United States. This multibillion-dollar industry has grown up in our country in less than a century.

Confirming Shakespeare's observation that fashion wears out more apparel than the man, the apparel industry has flourished in the twentieth century. In the United States, the apparel industry is defined as clothing and accessories for women, men, and children, manufactured by garment makers in the needle trades. In most factories, apparel is designed, fabric is purchased from the textile industry, patterns are made, samples are finished and shown to retail buyers, and selected styles are cut, produced, and shipped directly to the retailers.

The apparel industry operates at the middle level in the overall structure of the fashion industries. The couture and design firms, discussed in

Chapter 4, are the real creators of fashion—the originators, the innovators, the life's blood of fashion. In this chapter the focus is on mass produced ready-to-wear, with particular attention to the apparel industry in the United States.

THE APPAREL INDUSTRY IN THE UNITED STATES

The apparel industry consists of those business establishments that take care of all aspects of apparel, from designing garments to selling finished products to the retail trade. It is a big industry, bigger than the textile industry. Some 22,500 apparel plants are spread across the country, employing nearly 1.5 million workers (these figures can be compared with the 7,000 textile plants that have fewer than 1 million workers). It must be remembered that the textile-apparel industrial complex is the largest single employer in the country.[3]

Size and Location

Big and *little* are commonly used terms in the apparel industry. It depends on who is measuring what. Some facts about the size of the apparel industry in the United States and the most recent statistics available are listed in a somewhat random manner in Table 6.1.[4] First, consider the size of apparel firms in terms of the number of employees. Nearly three fourths of the firms are small, with fewer than fifty employees. However, there are a few giants. Twenty of the largest firms have a sales volume of $10 to $15 million annually.

Sales volume of the apparel industry is over $30 billion per year. Comparisons with other industries are impressive: compared with the tobacco industry, the apparel industry is nearly $4 billion bigger in sales; compared with the two largest industries, food and fuel, apparel is often ranked third in size. In the last decade, the American Apparel Manufacturing Association (AAMA) has been a reliable source of information about the apparel industry. Other sources of statistics are the United States Government

TABLE 6.1   United States Apparel Industry Summary of Size*

22,696 plants
   1.3 million workers
   250 firms with $5–10 million volume
    20 firms with $10–15 million volume
   70% firms with fewer than 50 employees
   $32 billion, total sales (apparel manufacturers)
   $46 billion, total consumer expenditures for clothing
   $53 billion, total worth of apparel industry
   $10 billion, women's and children's segments alone
   $50 billion, annual contribution to GNP

* Approximate figures or estimates
Source: Department of Commerce, *U.S. Industrial Outlook, 1975* (Washington, D.C.: U.S. Govt. Printing Office, 1975) pp. 224–231.

Census of Manufacturers and the Federal Reserve Board Industrial Production Index. Some data are routed through the Office of Business Economics, the Department of Commerce, and other federal agencies. The 20 largest apparel firms are listed in Appendix 11, p. 297.

CAPITAL AND STYLING

The size, as well as the organization, of individual firms is dependent on the amount of capital investment and on the styling of the goods produced. *Manufacturers* are the largest of the firms and require the greatest capital outlay; they control the product from its design to its delivery to the retail customer. *Contractors* have a smaller investment. They only cut and/or sew and finish garments for jobbers and, thus, usually need only machines and work facilities. *Jobbers* buy fabric, design garments, sometimes make patterns and cut fabrics, and then contract the sewing of the garments. They also sell the finished goods. However, their greatest outlay of money is for materials and labor. Jobbers and contractors are usually much smaller than manufacturers, yet they account for a large percentage of plants with fewer than fifty employees.

Size of apparel firms also is influenced by the

styling of the product. The more extreme the style, the greater the risk and cost in manufacturing, and the more urgent the timing element. Generally, firms producing high-fashion goods are the smallest in size and least complicated in organization. Staple goods are handled best by large manufacturing operations, especially where the durability and price of the product outweigh styling and seasonal timing.

INTEGRATION OF PRODUCTION

An important factor in the size of apparel firms today is the trend toward the horizontal and vertical integration of production. *Horizontal integration* involves an increase in manufacturer's product lines and, thereby, an increase in sales volume. *Vertical integration* results when the apparel manufacturer expands to include the textile mills that supply materials and the retail outlets that sell directly to the consumer. Thus, a large firm may be a combination of numerous small operations that represent each level of the fashion industries: suppliers, manufacturers, and retailers.

In the last decade the number of individual firms in the apparel industry has decreased while the number of employees per firm has increased. In the late 1960s, 72.2 per cent of apparel firms had fewer than twenty employees; by 1975, only 70 per cent had fewer than fifty workers.[5] Slightly more than 2 per cent of the companies employed 250 workers or more. It is significant to note that the size of firms by number of employees differs in the various segments of the industry. The men's apparel firms tend to be two or three times larger in size than the firms in the women's segment.

LOCATION

New York City remains unchallenged as the center of apparel production in the world. New York produces more than 69 per cent of the women's and children's wear sold in the United States and more than 40 per cent of the men's and boys' wear.[6] Major cities where apparel production is concentrated in the United States are listed in Table 6.2. Information about apparel in any state or regional areas is available from the

TABLE 6.2 Production of Women's Apparel by Major Cities in the United States (in %)

New York City	62.1
Los Angeles	6.2
Chicago	3.8
Philadelphia	3.3
Boston	2.6
Dallas	1.4
St. Louis	1.2
Cleveland	1.1
Kansas City	1.0
Miami	.8
Baltimore	.3
Other	16.2

Source: Research Division, ILGWU, 1974.

state departments of commerce and industrial development.

Apparel manufacturing in the United States tends to concentrate in the vicinity of major market areas as shown in Figure 6.2. It is estimated that three fourths of apparel firms are located in the East or the Atlantic Coast area.[7] The heaviest concentration is in the New York area, which includes New York City and Boston and Philadelphia. Apparel firms dot the Carolinas, eastern Tennessee, Georgia, and Florida.

Fewer than 10 per cent of the apparel firms are located in the middle central area of the United States, including Chicago, St. Louis, Kansas City, and Dallas. An increasing amount of apparel is produced on the West Coast; both Los Angeles and San Francisco have apparel firms of national importance.

Structure of the Apparel Industry

The types of apparel firms in the United States are usually described in terms of the three official industrial classifications designated in the United States Census of Manufacturers: apparel manufacturers, jobbers, and contractors.

THE APPAREL MANUFACTURER

Apparel manufacturers perform each of the following operations in factories of their own:

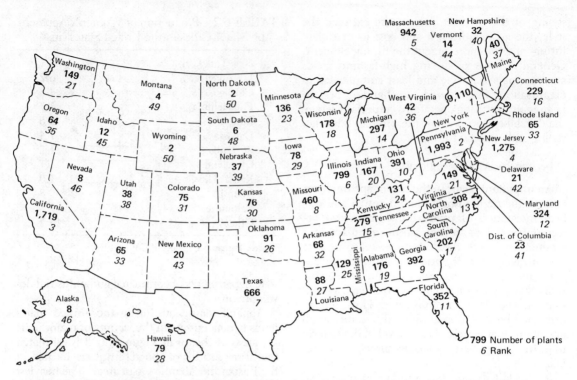

FIGURE 6.2 *Apparel manufacturing plant distribution in the United States. (Source: Dun & Bradstreet, Inc., 1969.)*

they either (1) purchase fabrics from textile converters or directly from mills in some cases or, in cases where there is vertical integration, manufacture and finish their own fabrics; (2) design the styles and the patterns to be used in making garments; (3) show the styles to potential retail buyers and obtain orders for specific numbers of garments; (4) cut each of the pieces in the pattern layouts from the fabrics designated; and (5) sew and assemble the finished garments for shipment to the retail trade.

THE JOBBER

Jobbers may perform any of the following operations: they (1) design the style or styles of the garments to be produced; (2) make arrangements to have cutting and sewing done in some independently owned shop (contractor); and (3) store and ship finished garments to their customers.

THE CONTRACTOR

Contractors may perform any of the following operations: they (1) cut the garment pieces using the specified pattern layout and fabric designated by the manufacturer or jobber; and/or (2) sew and assemble the finished garments according to the specifications of the firm that hires them.

Although these official terms suggest the traditional structure of the apparel industry, they do not accurately interpret the diverse nature of firms operating within the industry. Two other terms are needed to explain the structure of the apparel industry, *inside* and *outside* shops.

Inside Shops. Inside shop operations are common. As previously mentioned, more staple-type clothing items (underwear, some men's wear, and children's wear) are made by firms that perform all the necessary operations to produce the finished garment within their own factories.

Outside Shops. Outside shop operations, in the apparel trade, are limited to one or more operations, usually cutting and/or sewing. They are contractors available for hire. Some manufacturers own outside shop operations themselves, in distant locations, and thus may be said to operate their own contract business.

The production of ready-to-wear in the United States is a thriving business. The apparel industry epitomizes mass production: it is a myriad of manufacturers, jobbers, and contractors, some side by side, some large and some small, some "inside" and some "outside"—nearly 23,000 units in all. Fewer than three hundred of these factories are considered to be large—by number of employees or dollar volume of sales. The majority are small manufacturers, jobbers, or contractors. As presented in Table 6–1, approximately 70 per cent of these firms employ as few as fifty workers. This is one of the features that makes the apparel industry unique, compared with other industries in the United States. It remains a stronghold of the small, independent business operator.

Organization of Apparel Firms

Apparel firms are often organized in an individual manner, depending on the type of operation, how the company began, and the pattern of growth of the production or product lines. It has been said that an apparel firm is what happens when a salesman and a production man get together. Many partnerships in the apparel business started this way, and some still do. The initial investment used to be nominal: "In the old days, anyone who thought he could design a dress could get the money to do it."[8] Recent estimates suggest that at least $50,000 in personal capital is needed to start an apparel factory today. However, *factoring*, whereby financial arrangements are made by agents who loan capital, is a common practice in the apparel industry.

Regardless of the type of firm, there are certain functional responsibilities involved in its organization and operation. Along with the need for *capital* and *facilities*, the owner(s) must have designers, production managers, pattern makers,

sample hands, fabric spreaders and markers, cutters, sewers, finishers, pressers, inspectors, and shippers or distribution managers. All of these operations may be performed in one factory, if it is an inside shop; in the case of an outside shop, bundles of cut pieces of garments may be transferred to sewing plants owned by the firm or to a contractor's sewing plant. In some parts of the country, contractors tend to do both cutting and sewing on a job basis, especially when dealing in certain kinds of merchandise (sportswear, for example, in the Southwest). Sometimes, large apparel firms with normal inside shop operations contract for cutting and/or sewing at peak seasons or for highly specialized work—for instance, when certain types of machines are needed for a small amount of work or for short periods of time. Machines must be used on a continuous schedule if they are to be profitable. Examples are bound-buttonhole machines, which are used in the women's segment of the industry, and double- and triple-needle machines for decorative stitching (as opposed to the single-needle machines used in the normal production of staple goods).

THE DESIGN FUNCTION

Designing may be done by one of the owners in a small apparel firm. Usually a salesman–owner, in a partnership like the one mentioned previously, is more aware of style trends than is a production-oriented owner. In larger organizations, the designing may be done by one person or by a staff. It is also possible to use free-lance designers, who operate out of their own studios on a job-by-job basis.

What are the design responsibilities? The firm owners expect the designer(s) to provide a group of styles at least two or three months in advance of a seasonal market period, which is six to nine months in advance of the consumer season. This collection of styles should be representative of the fashion trends in line, color, fabrics, and design details and should be within price ranges and classifications of merchandise appropriate for the firm's retail customers.

What may appear to the novice as creative designing is to the mass producer of ready-to-wear a seasonal collection that will, of economic necessity, include a majority of styles that are merely new versions of the "best sellers" from the last season. This may mean that the designer revamps the most popular previous styles, or he or she may copy (or "knock-off") the competition's most successful styles. Today, the trend of most mass producers, as well as of some couture houses, is less toward fashion tangents and more toward classic styles that appeal to volume market segments in the United States.

The designer may work from a creative idea sketched on a drawing board and go on to an original in muslin made by an assistant or by a sample hand. Expert seamstresses usually work closely with the designer in making up the sample of a new style. In apparel firms where less emphasis is on originality, the designer may work from a sketch, a picture, or from a garment purchased for the purpose of copying.

The Seasonal Line

At this point, often the owners or a team of the company's executives will make the final decisions as to which of the designer's styles will or will not be included in the firm's line or collection, for the coming season. Each garment will be considered in terms of its cost, its potential for sales, its production feasibility, and its fabric requirements. One style may look attractive but will require more fabric than is justified by the price policy of the firm. Another style may be too advanced for the firm's retail customers. Some styles are classic and are proven best sellers in retail stores, and these will stay in the line, but there may be some changes here and there—buttons, pockets, or pleats added or omitted as the season's fashion decrees. Changes in the design may occur along the way if the garment is to stay in the collection. In some firms, the reactions of key or regional sales representatives may be considered. Even the opinions of major retail buyers may be solicited before the line is finalized for an important season.

The Pattern Maker. Next, a *production pattern* must be made for each style that is to be a part of the firm's collection. Pattern makers make up the

garments in the sample size after checking and testing for possible revisions and corrections. These patterns are often made up in muslin rather than the actual fabric. The pattern is checked finally by the designer and is used to make the necessary number of samples of each style needed by the sales representatives to show the firm's line to the retail buyers.

The Showing of a Seasonal Line

Company executives and sales representatives are responsible for showing the sample line for the coming season to the retail buyer. The line is normally shown at seasonal markets in New York City and in other showrooms in apparel markets across the country—in Chicago, Atlanta, Kansas City, Dallas, and Los Angeles. This *seasonal market system* will be discussed in detail in Chapter 8. For our purposes in this chapter, it is enough to note that mass production of the garments in a firm's seasonal collection usually does not begin until *after* the retail buyers have placed a sufficient number of orders for any one style to justify its mass production. In some less style-oriented firms, the production department may make decisions as to which numbers will be produced, and in what quantities, on the basis of realistic estimates of consumer demand. An example might be men's undershirts or even dress shirts. However, for the most part, in the women's apparel business cutting decisions and production schedules are projected from actual retail orders. The signed orders specify numbers of units in each size, color, and fabric and designate delivery dates for the shipment of the merchandise. These production decisions are made after the seasonal markets are held across the country, six months or more in advance of the actual season in which the apparel will be offered to the consumer. When the final cutting decisions are made, it may be that out of 150 or more styles in a season's collection, only two thirds or less may be put into production schedules.

It is possible that a firm may decide to produce as few as fifteen to twenty pieces of a style, but more normally the cutting decisions are held up until orders are received for a total of one hundred or more garments in one style.

The Pattern Grader. Until recently, the next step in production involved a pattern grader who took the sample size of the pattern and converted it into precise mathematical proportions for each size to be produced—that is, 10, 12, 14, and so on. Automation is taking over this highly skilled task. Smaller companies may continue to use pattern graders as long as they can hire or train efficient ones, but many firms that cannot afford the expensive automated grading equipment are sending their patterns out to be graded on a job or contract basis. Because the skillful pattern grader has been difficult to find in recent years, this job may soon become extinct in mass-production circles in the United States.

The Pattern Markers. The pieces of the pattern for each garment must be arranged as economically as possible on the fabric (the *layout*). This process is first done on long sheets of paper by the pattern markers, who make sure all the pieces of the pattern are placed in the proper direction—on the bias or straight—and that the most advantageous use is made of fabrics such as plaids and naps. Two square inches of fabric saved in cutting each dress style will be a saving of many square yards if 6,000 garments are cut. In the apparel industry it has often been said that the profit is made or lost on the cutting table. Technological advancements have given us computer markers, thereby saving time and increasing efficiency.

The Cutter. We are now ready for the skilled cutter who, using the marker or pattern layout for a guide, may cut through hundreds of layers of various colors and kinds of fabric with a mechanized cutting knife: 6,000 garments or 48,000 pattern pieces or more at once! As one might imagine, the cutter is a highly paid skilled worker.

The Sewers. The bundles of garment pieces are assembled and marked and then moved along to the sewing section in an inside shop operation or transferred to a contractor if an outside shop operation is involved. As has already been indicated, the contractor may do the cutting as well as the sewing, depending on the contract agreement.

In either case, the sewing of the garment, in

FIGURE 6.3 *Operators sewing finished apparel. (Courtesy of Hanes Corporation.)*

most factories, is an assembly-line operation. The sewing machine operators are paid by the number of pieces they sew. This is called piece-work in the apparel industry: one machine operator may sew facings in place, another may turn the collar, another may sew the sleeves in the armscye, and so on. Each will be paid on the basis of the number of pieces finished in an allotted time. Sometimes there is an additional rate for the person who works the fastest. Rates also vary with the difficulty of the sewing operation.

Quality Inspectors. Usually, there are quality inspectors at the end of the assembly line for each finished garment. If a mistake is found in the sewing, the operator who was responsible for sewing that piece of the garment will have to resew the piece, or it may become a "second" or "irregular." Thus, some time may be lost and additional pay will not be realized by the worker.

The Finishers. Certain machines necessary for the styling of one garment may not be needed in another (that is, buttonhole machines or pleating and gathering machines). In this case, the sewing operations are reassigned periodically. Though a person might think that operating the same machine and sewing the same pieces of a garment all day, day after day, would get monotonous, a sewing room supervisor recently commented that the workers did not like to be moved because it took time and was frustrating to change operations. Time means money in a piecework operation. A slowdown is expensive for the worker, as well as for the production or sewing room manager.

Finishing, pressing, and inspection are end-of-the-line operations in today's mass production of apparel. In the past, pressing and inspection operations were included at several stages in the sewing process; this is simply not so today, except in couture houses. Technology, mechanization, and plain old economies of time and money have reserved the pressing operation for the end of the process, and in lower price ranges of merchandise this step may have been eliminated altogether. *Finishing* may mean adding buttons, snaps, trim, belts, and buckles, or clipping of hanging threads; however, the latter responsi-

bility may be assigned to the inspector and packer for some kinds of apparel. This last step in assembling finished garments for distribution to retailers is coordinated with the delivery dates on the shipping orders.

This is mass production of ready-to-wear. This is garment making today. This is the apparel industry. All kinds of apparel, styled in the fashion trends of the season, and produced in a variety of colors, sizes, and fabrics in an effort to meet the needs and desires of the ultimate consumer. And, significantly, too, these items are manufactured in a wide range of prices for distribution in the various types of retail outlets.

SPECIALIZATION IN THE APPAREL INDUSTRY

Thus far we have considered apparel manufacturing as a single industry. In the trade, it is often identified as three separate industries: the women's segment, the men's segment, and the children's segment. These three segments have some similarities, but each is unique in many ways. The differences are attributed in part to the degree of specialization that has developed in the nature of the merchandise and in the production processes. We will focus briefly on some of the differences in each segment. Trends related to these differences will be reviewed later in this chapter.

Women's Wear

One of the unique characteristics of the women's apparel industry is the intensity of seasonal change. Styling is an important competitive factor that results in style piracy—in knock-offs. Copying a popular style is a common practice in the women's segment. The more a firm is mass production oriented, the greater the tendency to copy and make in volume the styles already proven to be best sellers at the retail level.

Another characteristic of this segment is the high degree of specialization in the production of various kinds of apparel, size ranges, and price lines. Traditionally, one manufacturer may

TABLE 6.3 Per Capita Consumption of Women's Wear (includes home-sewn garments)*

Age	1969	1970	1971	1972	1973
5–13	38.1†	39.3	38.6	41.4	39.5
14–24	32.8	32.0	31.7	31.6	30.2
25–34	36.5	33.6	32.0	33.1	33.0
35–44	29.5	31.5	31.0	32.4	31.7
45–54	31.4	33.8	34.1	37.1	37.3
55+	25.1	24.6	26.4	26.1	29.2
Total	193.4	194.8	193.8	201.7	200.9
% Change vs prior year		+0.7	−0.5	+4.1	−0.4

* Includes outerwear, intimate apparel, home-sewn garments; excludes hosiery and accessories.
† All numbers are in clothing units purchased at retail in year indicated.
Source: DuPont Marketing Report, 1974.

make only women's coats or dresses, not both, in a particular size and price range. This is especially true in the junior market that developed in the 1960s. This emphasis on junior wear is not expected to persist, on the basis of the consumption patterns for women's wear. In Table 6.3 it is apparent that the fourteen to twenty-four age group has decreased slightly in clothing consumption on a per capita basis. A decrease is also apparent in the twenty-five to thirty-four age group. However, in the forty-five to fifty-four age group there was a decided increase in clothing consumption. These consumption patterns are a basis for anticipating size ranges, along with other trends that affect the women's segment of the apparel industry. Population forecasts are also meaningful to the apparel manufacturer of women's wear. Population forecasts for the 1980s suggest an even greater change in the consumption patterns for the twenty-five to thirty-four-year-old female group.

A firm that makes dresses to retail for $16 to $35 probably would not vary from this price range other than in a normal process of year-to-year upgrading of the line—or, as in the 1970s, because of inflation. Consequently, retail buyers would consider this manufacturer a possible resource only when the price range was compara-

ble with the price "image" of their particular store.

Other specialized tendencies in the women's wear segment are evidenced by firms that make only women's half sizes, companies that make only lingerie, and a few garment makers who cut and sew in knits only. Some manufacturers are known as sportswear firms, some as swimwear makers, and so on.

In the last two decades, a specialization of a different nature has appeared in the Dallas manufacturing area. Firms in this region have developed predominantly to serve the several national chains. They mass produce according to specifications of these retailers—500 to 1,000 or more of a single number or style. Chain stores cultivate the Dallas women's wear manufacturers because they have an advantageous labor situation and understand the price structure. Some of these manufacturers also serve small specialty stores in the central and southern parts of the country, through the efforts of traveling sales representatives. The major department stores do not tend to buy from these manufacturers in the Dallas area.

One labor organization unites the myriad of women's apparel firms: the International Ladies Garment Workers Union (ILGWU). This group has served the industry in many ways, particularly in terms of labor relations, workers' benefits, and research and development.

Men's Wear

In previous discussions, the focus has concentrated on the women's segment of the industry, which has been recognized for having generated much of the fashion excitement and many of the technological advancements in this century. Now it is time to take a brief look at the manufacture of men's wear and consider the several ways in which it differs from the women's segment: the nature of the segment, its size and location, and its structure and organization.

THE NATURE OF THE MEN'S WEAR INDUSTRY

The term *tailoring* in the men's clothing trade probably says it all when it comes to the differences between men's and women's wear. *Webster's* definition for the term is "the making or adapting of something to suit a particular purpose," further stating that the verb *to tailor* means "to make or fashion a garment with trim straight lines and finished handwork like that of a tailor on men's garments." So it is evident that this term is closely associated with men's clothing.

The nature of the tailoring operation influenced the size and location of the men's clothing industry in the United States. Before the apparel trade was industrialized, men's clothing was made in tailor's shops—small retail stores where tailors made suits "to measure" for the men in the vicinity. As the small tailor shop produced more and more suits, in a way it became a small factory. This was the beginning of the men's wear trade. Thus, the men's wear industry started as a "made-to-order" or "made-to-measure" operation.

The small men's wear factory, or tailor shop, moved across the country, as did other merchants. These small tailor shops became "jobber" or wholesale operations eventually, as men's clothing factories began mass-producing suits. The growing ready-made segment of the men's wear trade needed distributors, and the tailor shops across the country served this function. The term "store bought" clothes was in use in the United States before 1850. At the retail level, the tailor continued to make or adapt men's suits individually for each customer. Even today this "custom-tailoring" operation is a part of the retailers' function, particularly in the higher-priced men's clothing stores.

SIZE AND LOCATION

There is a considerable difference between the size of the men's and women's segments of the apparel industry in the United States. The men's wear trade is not so large as the giant women's ready-to-wear segment. There are approximately 3,500 firms producing some $8 billion annually in men's and boys' clothing. Over half a million workers are employed in some 4,100 plants across the country.[9]

Another factor that can be compared is the size of firms. Although there are many small men's wear factories, 80 per cent of the firms employing fewer than fifty workers, there are some giant firms. Five to ten large firms do approximately one third of the total men's wear business at the manufacturing level in this country. Two well-known examples of these dominant men's wear firms as Cluett, Peabody, known to the consumer as the maker of Arrow shirts, a company that also produces suits and sportswear of various kinds; and Hart Schaffner & Marx, known to the consumer as a men's clothing (suits) firm, yet one that also produces other men's wear items. Each of these firms, along with several others, has moved toward or exceeded $500 million in annual volume in the mid-1970s.

In terms of location, the men's wear industry is not concentrated in the New York area to the same extent as the women's industry. This difference is attributed, in part, to the manner in which the men's wear trade developed across the country with the tailor shop. Small men's wear factories appear throughout the United States. However, as shown in Table 6.4, 42 per cent of men's wear, is produced in the New York City area. Smaller percentages of the total output are in various other areas. The area round Atlanta, Georgia, has become important in this respect in recent years.

Although the production of men's wear is not concentrated in New York City as much as is the

TABLE 6.4 Men's Wear Industry in the United States

Area	Production (%)
New York City (Middle Atlantic region)	42
Atlanta (Southern Atlantic Coast, and eastern and south central)	27
Los Angeles (Far West)	8
Chicago (eastern and north central)	7
Boston (New England)	6
Dallas (western and south central)	5
Kansas City (western and north central)	5

Source: U.S. Department of Commerce, *Census of Manufacturers*, 1973.

women's wear industry, the marketing center for the men's wear trade has traditionally been there. Most of the men's wear firms have offices, showrooms, and sales representatives in the Empire State Building and several other buildings along Broadway between 23rd and 36th streets. This is probably because of the close association of men's wear and textile firms. The Amalgamated Clothing Workers of America (ACWA) is the largest industry union. With headquarters in the New York City area, this union organization continues to monitor labor problems and to work for arbitration in the men's wear industry.

STRUCTURE AND ORGANIZATION

The men's wear trade differs greatly from the women's wear segment in terms of structure. The major divisions of the men's wear trade are recognized both at manufacturing and retail levels. The term *men's clothing* has traditionally referred to the suit and coat trade. The other broad term is *men's furnishings;* this classification covers the remainder of the men's wear trade—shirts, separate trousers, ties, jackets, undergarments, and so on. In Table 6.5 the influence of these traditional divisions can be seen, as well as the size of each by the number of plants.

Not reflected in this data is the tremendous growth of the trousers and slacks division and the trend to jeans, included in the classification with work clothes in Table 6.5.

The organization of the manufacturing operation for men's wear also differs greatly from the women's wear segment. The inside shop system

TABLE 6.5 Men's Wear Divisions

Classification	Number of plants
Suits and coats	846
Shirts and nightwear	722
Separate trousers	610
Work clothes and jeans	492
Outerwear, sweaters, and miscellaneous	525

Source: U.S. Department of Commerce, *Industrial Outlook 1975.*

dominates the men's wear industry, for there are fewer contractors and jobbers at the manufacturing level. In the men's wear trade there are counterparts for the designer, the pattern maker, the cutter, and the sewers, but usually the type of operation differs greatly. At the sewing stage, for instance, traditionally we have found the complicated tailoring process known only to the men's wear trade. However, with this exception, the mass-production process has been more highly developed in the men's wear segment. This was made possible in the past because of less emphasis on styling and seasonal change. However, since mass production is best suited to basic styling, the more rapid changes in men's fashions since the 1960s have wrought havoc both at the manufacturing and retail level.

Some of these problems are evidenced in the organizational changes that have come about in the last two decades, such as the linking up of the men's wear segment with the women's apparel segment. Following are some examples of this kind of horizontal integration—adding and combining product lines.

1. Cluett, Peabody: A men's wear corporation that also owns Van Raalte, a women's lingerie and accessories firm.
2. Manhattan Industries: A men's shirt firm that also includes Lady Manhattan, a division that makes women's shirts and blouses.
3. Kayser-Roth: A women's apparel firm that also owns five men's wear divisions.

The men's wear trade has continued to maintain its traditional link with the retailer. Many large men's wear corporations are vertically integrated, having their own retail outlets: examples are Botany, Cluett, Peabody, Hart Schaffner & Marx, Manhattan, Phillips-Van Heusen, and Genesco. Though highly specialized at the manufacturing and retail level, the men's wear industry also produces for the department store trade and family clothing store.

National brand names are another characteristic that is more a part of the men's wear segment: for example, Arrow shirts, Jockey underwear, and Botany suits.

Another important characteristic in manufacturing men's clothing, particularly suits, is the range of size variables. This affects the production operation as a whole, as well as the distribution pattern. For example, each style of suit will be cut in many sizes, as determined by men's chest measurements (37–38, 46, 48, etc.) and by men's figure types (short, regular, long). In the dress shirt segment, sizing is done by neck diameter and sleeve length.

Recently, the sportswear or leisure-clothing styles for men have reduced some of the fit problems as well as lessened the sizing factor in some areas of production. In this segment of the industry much of the tailoring element has given way to leisure and casual wear in the mid-1970s. Sport shirts are often sold in small, medium, large, and "X-large" sizes.

There has been a fashion revolution in men's wear. The trend to the plain launched by Beau Brummel at the beginning of the nineteenth century was reversed during the 1960s. For the first time since the eighteenth century, men's sense of fashion was stimulated by radical new styles, colors, textures, and *change* in general. Suddenly men's fashion sense came to life, and this spelled bedlam in the men's wear industry. Wigs, necklaces, bracelets, colognes, platform heels, "body" (suppressed-waist) and see-through shirts, boots, turtlenecks, fur coats, bell-bottoms, flares, wide lapels and *no* lapels—all burst onto the male fashion scene. Dior, Cardin, and St. Laurent joined such Americans as Bill Blass in designing and franchising ready-to-wear suits and accessories.

Double-knit fabric has replaced much of the woven goods in men's wear in the last decade. The textile industry naturally joined the men's wear firms in their quest for an answer to what men wanted in fabrics and fashion. Even men's shoes moved in the direction of change: from no-lace slip-ons to boots to patent leather in white, black, and *red*. On the men went, and in the late 1970s, the verdict seemed to be that *men like fashion!*

It could be, then, as a result of this revolutionizing discovery, that the men's and women's segments of the apparel industry will continue to move toward related operations. In terms of the industry, this may mean continued growth via horizontal integration. Giants in the apparel industry may be here to stay.

Children's Wear

The manufacture of children's wear is another part of the giant apparel industry. However, the production of children's wear remains a small-factory operation. Found in various sections of the United States and often family-owned, the majority of factories produce small volumes of children's clothing in a specialized area. For example, infants' wear firms usually make a line of layettes, a line of little girls' dresses, and a line of little boys' clothes; other firms make buntings and coats for infant sizes. For children over six, the trade is usually divided into girls' wear and boys' wear; one company may make only girls' dresses sizes 6 to 12, and another firm will make corresponding sizes in pants and shirts for boys.

In the last two decades, the move into the pantsuit has greatly affected the girls' segment of the children's wear industry, even down to in-

FIGURE 6.4a *Child's dress with crewel-work embroidery, 1700s. (The Metropolitan Museum of Art, Rogers Fund, 1954.)*

fants in some cases. The consumers, mothers, and children, expect to find fashionable styles, colors, and fabrics in children's wear departments and specialty shops. Across the country, children's wear firms have been trying hard to satisfy the consumers' expectations. But it is not easy to succeed in making such changes in the tradition-bound children's wear industry. The colors and patterns in fabrics for children's wear were not fashion oriented to start with; children have traditionally been dressed as children, rather than as stylish little adults. Many of the fabric producers were not accustomed to selling to the children's

FIGURE 6.4c *Boys' wear, 1970s. (Courtesy of Donmoor, Inc.)*

trade—and, of course, that trade is not a volume fabric purchaser because it takes little yardage to make clothes for the "little people." Then, too, the infants' wear firms were accustomed to buying and using large quantities of lace and ruffles, buttons, and other trims. The change did not come easily, but that it is taking place can be seen by a visit to any nearby retail store that sells children's clothing. Boys' wear followed the direction of girls' wear—like father, like son. More than any other single factor, of course, the baby boom made this revolution in children's wear a real "happening" in the apparel industry. However, the recent decline in the number of babies and the wearing of jeans has forced children's dress companies to expand into sportswear.

PRESENT STATUS OF THE APPAREL INDUSTRY

The various segments within the apparel industry were traditionally distinct because of the

FIGURE 6.4b *Girls' wear, 1970s. Materials and methods have changed, but little girls' dresses today and yesterday seem to reflect similar ideas. (Courtesy of Baylis Brothers Co.)*

high degree of specialized skills and business acumen required to succeed in a particular aspect of the business. Some specialization still exists, and various segments may be distinguished in one or more of the following manners:

1. Type of merchandise produced—women's wear, men's wear, children's wear, etc.
2. Kind of garment manufactured—dresses, coats, suits, sportswear, etc.
3. Price line of apparel produced—low- or budget-priced, moderate- or volume-priced, high- or upper-priced, etc.
4. Size range of garment made—junior, preteen, petite, misses (common in the women's apparel segment of the industry but even more pronounced in the men's wear trade).

We have considered each of the segments of the apparel industry separately. Each has its own peculiar differences as well as problems. Nevertheless, some of the characteristics, changes, and trends in the apparel industry are relevant to one or more of these various segments.

Four Unique Characteristics of the Apparel Industry

The apparel industry continues to be unique in many ways when compared with other contemporary industries in the United States.

STYLING

The apparel industry is unique in that it is dominated by the *element of style* (fashion). Basic styling versus high styling, short-lived styles versus staple styles—these contrasting forces must be dealt with to some extent in each segment of the industry. It is safer for a firm to produce more classic, middle-of-the-road styles that appeal to a broad consumer market segment. However, in order to be competitive, some style distinctiveness is vital. A high degree of manufacturing efficiency is not technologically possible in highly styled products, resulting in increased prices. Changes in methods of manufacturing styled products are more costly than for staple goods.

This, too, results in increased prices of high-styled products. The styling element that characterizes the apparel industry is commonly known as fashion and as such is often heralded as the life blood of the garment trade. The women's segment of the industry has traditionally been affected more by the variables of fashion—that is, color, line, fabrics, and consumer acceptance, as well as by fashion cycles. In any segment of the apparel industry, the greater the influence of fashion—the styling element—the greater the business risk for the manufacturer, as well as the retailer. Thus, there is constant pressure in the apparel industry to bring about some balance between style goods and classic apparel in order to lessen the risk of doing business and to increase the possibility for profits by appealing to a broader, more predictable consumer market.

SEASONS

The manufacturer has to contend with a *seasonal element* in the production and distribution of apparel. This characteristic is unique to apparel, compared with other industries. Styled merchandise more than staple goods is subject to seasonal trends in consumer demand. Efficiencies of operation and profit in the apparel trades often reflect the vital importance of timing. Highly styled garments must be delivered to the retailer immediately, as the item might go out of fashion when the season changes.

In recent years, timing has become a greater element in the men's outerwear industry. Quick delivery of garments to the retailer has become essential so that highly styled garments will not be left in stock when they are no longer in seasonal demand. Thus, the men's wear industry has taken on some of the merchandising techniques that were considered particular to the women's wear business.

MARKETING

Another unique aspect of the apparel trade is the *direct method* by which manufactured goods are matched with their markets. There is no true wholesale operation that dominates the distribution system in the apparel industry as it does in most other industries in our country. The apparel manufacturer produces garments in direct response to the orders placed by retail buyers, and the merchandise changes hands and ownership only once, when it is shipped directly to the retail store designated by the buyer. Today, in the large chain-store operations and in multiunit department and specialty store organizations, there may be provisions by the retailer for a distribution center within a local or regional area. For the most part, apparel is virtually made to order for individual retailers by the manufacturer. Shipped directly from the factory sewing rooms to the receiving rooms in stores across the country, apparel is immediately available for purchase to the local consumers for whom it was ordered. This direct marketing system is characteristic of most of the segments of the apparel industry.

Size

Even in an era of giants in business, *small firms* still manufacture a major portion of the garments for men, women, and children in this country. Small manufacturers, jobbers, and contractors continue to operate effectively, side by side with the giants—Puritan, Jonathan Logan, Bobbie Brooks, and others.

Changes in Management

It is important to consider the present status of the apparel industry in light of certain changes that have come about in the last decade. To do this we logically look first at what has happened and is happening in the center of the garment industry—Seventh Avenue, New York City, which was renamed Fashion Avenue in early 1972. Everywhere on this avenue there are push carts, clothes on racks, sidewalk hawkers, hot chestnuts, and bagels. The apparel trade, sometimes called the needle trade, looks much as it did in the early 1900s: garments, textiles, furs, and leathers are being transferred to and fro, from supplier to manufacturer: The carriers of the materials of fashion fill the streets and sidewalks, the stairways and elevators, from morning until night, week in and week out. During peak hours

of the day and at peak seasons it is difficult just to move about in the garment district.

The traditional apparel trade was known for its small, family-owned establishments, operated by intuition and trial and error, referred to as "seat of the pants" operations. Each owner did what he thought he had to do to make a living or to keep from going bankrupt. The contemporary apparel firm is larger. Some small companies grew bigger as they succeeded; some went out of business or were driven out by the industry's fierce competition. Today's larger companies have more professional management. Although some are still family operated, they are based on second- and third-generation experience. Today a college degree and even an MBA (a master's degree in business administration) may bolster the family holdings. A much more sophisticated apparel business now exists, as is evidenced by some trends that developed in the industry in the last decade.

Trends in the Apparel Industry

Some major trends are concerned with (1) broader product-mix concepts; (2) emphasis on classic styling for volume markets; and (3) vertical integration, consolidation, and diversification in organizational structure.

Broadening the Product Mix

Both large and small companies are considering the marketing concept of broadening the product mix as opposed to the previous policy of a high degree of specialization within the various segments of the apparel industry.

Adding Product Lines. Adding other product lines is one way of achieving product mix. For example, firms that formerly had made only misses dresses within a given price range and for a specific or narrow market may decide to diversify within the women's segment to reach a broader market in terms of sizes, styles, and prices. Misses dress firms may add a junior line or a pantsuit line or even a men's wear line, as did Kayser-Roth. Kayser-Roth traditionally had been a women's hosiery and sportswear operation, but in the early 1970s it added five men's wear divisions. The company broadened the product mix in response to a *marketing gap* that was not being filled—that is, medium-priced boys' and men's wear.

Adding Price Lines and Labels. Adding other price lines and labels is another way to obtain product mix. A firm might broaden its product mix by adding another price line—lower or higher (depending on an identified market need)—and sell the new line under another label. This has occurred in couture houses, in firms that serve national chain organizations, and in independent department stores. High-fashion and designer firms have tended to scale down the fashion look of the season both in terms of price and extremes of style and sell these versions under another label in a price range that is more competitive in the retail market place—witness Blassport, Beene Bag, Halston, and others.

REACHING A BROADER MARKET

In the apparel industry, where fashion has been the rallying cry that set the competitive edge, many firms are following a safer "make what the majority wants" policy.

Volume Retail Markets. In terms of style merchandise, volume means *classic looks* that appeal to a broad market segment. In the industry it is called staying on top of the market, or keeping production in line with consumer buying patterns. Reaching the middle-of-the-road consumer market is the *focus of mass merchandising* and *mass distribution*. National chain retailers have been instrumental in encouraging the apparel manufacturer along this road to *mediocrity*, or democratization, so to speak. Making thousands of shirtwaist dresses a day in the sewing room is less risky and less expensive than making 200 or fewer highly styled garments. Sometimes, the retail buyer does not buy a style because similar styles had to be marked down in the preceding season—or, in the words of the trade, the buyer had to "eat them." They were considered the buyer's mistakes.

This new focus on broader market segments may indicate the tendency toward market research, actually determining the consumer demand curve for a product or a style. This consumer-oriented marketing expertise is replacing the age-old method of operating by intuition in the apparel industry. The garment industry is facing up to the fact that there is a real live, flesh-and-blood customer out there who has to be catered to.

Best Sellers. Emphasis on best sellers is related to this concept of reaching a broader market. The idea is to determine the best sellers and exploit them by recutting large quantities for a reorder trade. The risk and expense involved in producing styled garments may be overcome by the manufacturer who is able to capitalize on reorders for the best sellers in the line. The *margin of profit* for the apparel maker may be determined by the speed in production and distribution of a seasonal line and/or the reorder business.

INTEGRATION

In the last decade, some of the major firms in the apparel industry have moved toward integration in growth patterns and organization structure. Some of the most successful efforts have been in what is known as *backward integration*— the use of consolidations, acquisitions, and mergers with fabric mills to give garment makers more control over product quality. Apparel firms and textile mills have a long history of poor communication. Backward integration allows management to have complete control of the product from fiber to finished garment. Efforts of this type may increase the degree of sensitivity among suppliers, manufacturers, and retailers—and the consumer may be the benefactor of this new relationship. Jonathan Logan's ownership of the prestigious Butte Knitting plant is one example of successful backward integration. This apparel firm is "less vulnerable than companies that depend completely on outsiders for fabric sources." [10]

Success has not been totally achieved in the attempt to include the retail level (*forward integra-*

tion). Botany and several other manufacturers followed Genesco's lead in acquiring retail outlets. After a brief period, losses were suffered at both wholesale and retail levels. The chance for double profits turned suddenly into double loses. Retrenchment has been the final recourse on the part of several of these companies.

However, one retail device has been somewhat more successful; this is the operation of a factory outlet for the odds and ends and overruns that every manufacturer has each season. The factory outlet replaces the previous practice of finding a bargain basement or discount operation to take each season's leftovers. So far this operation has proved to have the advantages without the problems of retail—no rent, no delivery, no returns, no weekend store hours, little advertising expense, no adjustments and no complaints.

DIVERSIFICATION

At the same time that some apparel firms have been following the concept of vertical integration, there has also been a move toward another growth pattern, diversification. Consolidations and acquisitions are producing conglomerate-type companies with subsidiaries that handle a diversity of products. Genesco, one of the industry's giants, acquired a great many small companies, some at the *retail level*, some at the *manufacturer's level*, and some at the *suppliers' level*. Thus, the company incorporated stores, wholesalers, producers of a variety of industrial products, and even raw material suppliers other than textiles. Genesco followed the concept that big means best, and the business was highly successful until the early 1970s, at which time it was plagued by management and marketing problems that resulted in profit sag.

Conglomerates and Consolidations. Other firms pursued a course similar to that of Genesco, some successfully up to the present time. These growth companies have developed *information systems* and have moved into more *sophisticated marketing activities.* Research and development efforts have contributed greatly. Nevertheless, there have been some warning signals in respect to consolidation. Although con-

solidation has revolutionized the apparel industry, some feel that big does not necessarily mean best, as Genesco seems to have learned.

Specialization and Concentration. A few companies have tried to grow larger by adopting a basic style or a particular look. Villager, one of the experimenters with this concept, succeeded for a short time, then profits decreased; fortunately, Jonathan Logan came to the rescue.

Another way of growing bigger and better is through concentration and specialization. Act III is a division of Jonathan Logan, an example of this concept in action. Expansion through the addition or development of divisions within the company allows management to attain a high degree of specialization. Each operation is something of an autonomous unit.

In these various ways, the apparel industry has grown in size and prestige, and along with these have come some advantages: (1) economy of size and scale of operation as well as decreased costs of facilities and management and (2) marketing leverage at the supplier's level as well as at the retail level.

RELATED FASHION INDUSTRIES

Manufacturers of fashion accessories are an essential segment of the apparel industry. In truth, the giant fashion industries depend on the manufacturers of products that serve as accessories, such as shoes, handbags, gloves, belts, hosiery, jewelry, scarves, and millinery. Whereas some fashion accessories are primarily functional in use, others serve to enhance the aesthetic purpose of fashion by being decorative.

Functional Accessories

Leather or leatherlike fashion accessories— shoes, handbags, gloves, and belts—are often considered to be functional accessories.

SHOES

In the early 1970s shoes became a focus of fashion. Any way the workmen cut the uppers or stacked the heels, shoes were news. The surprising aspect of this fashion was the distinctive styles that imports gave to the fashion mix. Innovations in heels, soles, leather, styles, and colors were introduced for both men and women. Shoes, which had previously been basic, functional accessories, were increasing in numbers of pairs in the consumer's wardrobe.

Until the late 1960s, leather was the raw material most used in making shoes; then, along came corfam. Corfam was a man-made leatherlike material, and though it proved to be too stiff, hot, and slippery-soled to win ultimate consumer acceptance, it did serve to motivate the consumer to accept shoe materials other than leather. This meant a drastic change in a very tradition-oriented industry.

The Shoe Industry: A Small-unit Operation. Many firms in the shoe industry employ only a few highly skilled craftsmen. As many as two hundred or more operations may be performed in the process of making shoes. The industry, with its long history of specialized production, was slow to advance technologically until recent years. Today, with numerous styles of shoes to choose from, the average consumer considers the right shoes as a part of the total fashion look.

Although New York City is the center of marketing activities for the shoe industry, the major production centers are located in the New England, Great Lakes regions and in the St. Louis area. Mergers and acquisitions have been prevalent. Along with vertical integration, some diversification has taken place. As a matter of fact, mergers between apparel manufacturers and shoe producers have contributed coordinated efforts for total fashion looks. As a consequence, the shoe industry has grown to such an extent that shipments of shoes and slippers were valued at $33.2 billion in 1974.[11]

HANDBAGS

Purses, pocketbooks, bags, totes, carryalls, whatever the name, the purpose of the item has been functional. For centuries women, and sometimes men, have toted money and other useful things about in some manner. In the fifteenth century, both men and women carried elaborate little purses. Today men may use the attaché case, but women use all sorts of bags. One idea of a well-balanced handbag wardrobe includes a casual carryall, an expandable shopping bag, a tailored daytime bag, a more elaborate bag for luncheons, and a small purse for evening.

Some handbags continue to be made of quality leather in various textures and are usually expensive. Leatherlike materials sometimes fool even a leather expert, and vinyl products often withstand the wear and tear test more like iron than leather. Now as in the past, fabrics, other exotic materials and metals are used in making handbags and purses—brocade, silk, faille, tapestry, velvet, silver and gold mesh, and straw. Various styles of handbags have been fashionable over the last two decades—tote, pouch, beach, duffle, envelope, and clutch. However, the shoulder-strap bag, often identified with the WAVES in World War II, has become a necessary utilitarian item for today's female, who goes everywhere.

Producing Handbags. Craftsmanship is essential in producing handbags because a well-constructed bag requires numerous hand operations. Most handbags are constructed from several raw products: the outside layer is made of leather or other materials, reinforcement gives shape or support, the lining is often silk or rayon, and the frame and handle may be of metal or some other sturdy material. Hand assembly of the metal and hardware attachments makes this industry a labor-intensive trade. Imports account for some of the raw materials, and also for some of the more unusual handbag styles on the market in the United States today—straw bags from the West Indies and the Orient, gold-tooled leather bags from Florence, Italy.

Small firms concentrated in the New York City area produce nearly 70 per cent of the handbags sold in the United States. In 1975 the output of the total industry was estimated to be over $400 million annually.[12] Little research and development have taken place in this industry, particularly in exploring fashion trends or pursuing technical advancements. It is somewhat an "every man for himself" trade. However, lately, the larger handbag makers have been placing more emphasis on coordinating their lines with the important fashion trends, in terms of colors, styles, textures, and details.

GLOVES

Today, gloves play a more functional role in the fashion world than they did during the first half of this century. The contemporary consumer knows little about glove lengths, such as four-button and eight-button lengths. Gloves are worn when they are needed to keep hands warm, in contrast to former years when they were worn according to rules of etiquette. When Emily Post said to wear gloves, women wore gloves and furthermore, they wore the exact button length she decreed.

The materials used in glove production may be leather, leatherlike products, or fabrics—mostly knits and some meshes—or they may be crocheted. Cold-weather gloves, of course, must be of heavy materials, often lined. Some furs, rabbit and lambskin, are worn for warmth, for fun, for fashion, or for all three. Knits and stretch fabrics have been a boon to the glove industry because they eliminate one market problem: differences in size. In the past, variances in hand sizes—from large to small, from thick to thin—made it difficult to achieve "one size that fits all." Today that is possible. The result is greater consumer satisfaction when purchasing gloves.

Traditionally, *hand-made gloves* were a status symbol for the wealthy and the fashion-conscious consumer. Gloves are still made in a step-by-step process that requires craftsmanship. The craft originated in Europe, and some high-fashion stores in the United States continue the policy of sending their glove buyer to that continent several times a year to select merchandise. In 1975 the output of the glove industry in the United States was estimated to be more than $100 million annually.[13]

Gloves are made in Gloversville, where else? Gloversville, New York, is the location of the major producers of gloves in the United States. The production of leather gloves is highly specialized, to the point that each operation is distinct and is contracted to separate firms for the cutting, stitching, and finishing. Fabric glove making has tended to involve a more mechanized process. Few firms produce both fabric and leather gloves. Some efforts in research and development in the glove industry have resulted in progress in the marketing of domestically manufactured products. Improvements have also been made in the washability of leathers and the production of colors and styles is in tune with fashion trends and consumer demand cycles.

BELTS

These accents at the waistline may be made of leather, leatherlike materials, macramé, or whatever else is inspired by fashion, such as chains, Indian concho medallions, and beads. In the beginning, belts served a specific purpose: they held two pieces (upper and lower parts) of a garment together or in place. In the last decade dresses have been beltless for the most part, or loosely belted. Now it is pants that have belts—whether one wears fitted waistlines or hip huggers, belts are usually worn. Huge, wide belts and buckles and tiny strips or strings are being offered; the consumer is expected to follow his or her fancy.

This is another industry of small firms that operate according to the anticipated needs of the rest of the fashion industries. Season by season, a few workers produce belts according to the specifications of garment companies in a contract type operation.

Decorative Accessories

Jewelry, scarves, and other fashion accessories are classified as decorative accessories, as opposed to the more functional accessories previously discussed.

JEWELRY

Necklaces, bracelets, earrings, brooches, clips, rings, hair ornaments, and watches enhance both the male and female image. Fine jewelry is usually defined as those articles made with precious stones and metals. Costume jewelry is truly twentieth-century American in origin, though the fashion was generated by the French designer Coco Chanel in the 1920s.

A significant milestone in the last decade has been the move of the middle class and the male into the fine jewelry market. This changing market has resulted in the upgrading of costume jewelry. These factors have resulted in a tremendous boom in fashion jewelry, antique jewelry, and contemporary jewelry. In fact, the phenomenal interest in jewelry, which started with the gold and silver charm bracelet craze of the 1960s, occasioned a return to the primitive idea of adorning the fingers with as many rings as possible. Ethnic jewelry fashions have become so popular that the supply can scarcely meet the demand. Even imitation American Indian jewelry had its appeal.

The jewelry industry is another New York City-based operation. In 1974 the total value of the industry shipments reached nearly $2 billion.[14] Skilled craftsmen work in specialized operations, often on a one-man basis. Design and creativity play an important role. Craftsmen from Europe and other continents contribute to the importance of the trade in the United States.

Scarves are used to accent a dress or blouse, to soften a neckline, and to cover or protect the head. The designers or stylists in companies that make scarves may spend most of their time trying to invent new ways to use scarves.

Scarves are either mass produced and machine finished, or decorated and finished by hand. Today, most hand-finished scarves are imported because the cost of labor is a factor in the United States. Before the late 1960s, few consumers considered paying $50 or more for a single scarf. Noted French and American designers cashed in on that idea and not only developed a profitable market, but also gained some promotional value from the signature fashion of the 1970s.

The scarf industry is scattered from New York to California, to Hong Kong, to Paris, and to London, where Liberty silk scarves have been worn by royalty for centuries and have become collectors' items for middle-class Americans since World War II.

MILLINERY

Millinery, long the queen of the fashion accessories industries, lapsed into oblivion in the 1960s, but there are some indications of a return performance in the mid-1970s.

Other Items of Apparel

Lingerie, bras, and other underpinnings have been enjoying fashion prominence in recent years. Lingerie has assumed a much more important role in the feminine world. Emphasis on leisure time and casual life styles has generated a consumer market for "at-home" fashions. Traditional firms in the apparel trade have been slow to realize the future potential of the trend. Even lingerie firms did not accept the challenge in the loungewear area readily. Sportswear, the less structured, less traditional segment of the apparel industry, had the vision to introduce "separates," which found a receptive consumer market in the 1960s and 1970s. The possibility of a fashion explosion in loungewear remains on the horizon.

HOSIERY

The hosiery industry has functioned as a separate entity since women started showing their legs in the 1920s. Silk was fashion in hosiery in the twenties and thirties; rayon was fashion in hosiery in the late thirties and forties. Not until the 1950s did nylon come into common use for hosiery; pantyhose were the innovation of the 1960s. With the advent of the latter, there was a drastic change in consumer demand and in the pricing concept in the hosiery industry. One dollar was a competitive price for a pair of hose in the traditional stocking era; however, many consumers paid $5 for three pairs or $3 per pair for pantyhose in the 1970s.

Because legs received so much attention in the 1960s and 1970s, fashion experts have attempted to attract the consumer by focusing on "the total look." Nylon seems to be the best raw material.

FIGURE 6.5 *Specialization in the women's apparel manufacturing industry. Quality control of hosiery to check for machine defects. (Courtesy of L'eggs Products, Inc.)*

The "bare legs" look appeared before the introduction of the miniskirt; then textured, colored hose became popular. In the 1970s, with the advent of the natural look, there was a return to the "barely there" fashion in hosiery, which is predominantly pantyhose. Another attractive feature of nylon is that its quality can be measured in terms that women can understand—sheers, semisheers, and service weights. A quantity of styles are offered in nylon, including pantyhose labeled toe-to-waist and regular and knee-high hose. Each has special features such as sandal foot or reinforced toe and heel to accommodate shoe fashions.

Hosiery is known as a brand-oriented industry. Many different brands may be produced by one company for a variety of retail outlets. Color and grade specifications are important factors in packaging and merchandising hosiery.

More often than not hosiery is produced by a division of one of the big textile companies. A majority of these firms are located in the textile areas of the Carolinas, although the market center for hosiery is New York City. Approximately eight hundred mills make hosiery in the United States; the output of the hosiery firms is nearly $2 billion annually. Thus, the hosiery industry makes a significant contribution to the total output of the textile industry.[15]

The $2 billion notion industry is another fashion-oriented trade.[16] Sewing, personal care, and household notions are relatively inexpensive and serve a myriad of consumer needs. Fashion's influence is evidenced in many of these products.

END OF CHAPTER GUIDE

Review, Discussion, and Evaluation

Study of this chapter should enable the students to:
A. Develop and give evidence of the following kinds of competencies:
1. An understanding of the flow of production in the apparel industry, from the various kinds of manufacturers in the needle trades to the retail outlet.
2. A knowledge of the scope and size of the apparel industry as compared with the textile industry and as a part of the giant textile-apparel industrial complex.
3. An awareness of the scope and size of the men's wear and children's wear industries, as well as the nature of some of the related industries that manufacture fashion accessories.
4. A knowledge of the various functional operations involved in the process of mass-producing women's wear.
5. A recognition of some of the unique characteristics of the apparel industry and of the changes that suggest trends in this industry.
B. Develop and/or clarify concepts related to the following key words and phrases:
1. ready-to-wear 2. apparel industry 3. apparel manufacturer 4. needle trades 5. garment makers 6. apparel contractors 7. apparel jobbers 8. inside-shop operations 9. outside-shop operations 10. factoring 11. designing 12. seasonal line or collection 13. pattern makers 14. sample line 15. pattern graders 16. pattern markers 17. cutters and sewers 18. finishers and inspectors 19. machine operations 20.

broadening the product mix 21. backward integration 22. diversification 23. specialization 24. functional accessories 25. decorative accessories

Extended Classroom Learning Experiences

A. Review the list of major cities where apparel is produced in the United States in Appendix 11, p. 297. Chances are if you live near one of these cities, you will know something about apparel making. Maybe you have visited an apparel factory and have observed the various operations. In your state or in your regional area you may find information about the apparel firms from the state department of commerce and industrial development.
  1. Write at least one source for information about apparel production in your state or regional area.
  2. Draw a map of your state or regional area and locate the towns where manufacturers are producing apparel.
  3. Write to one of these manufacturers and arrange to visit a factory.
B. Contact a local merchant or store buyer concerning apparel manufacturers that ship merchandise to their store.
  1. Ask for the location of the apparel firms from which the store purchases women's wear, men's wear, and children's wear. Note each of the cities mentioned and ask for the specific address for one or more apparel manufacturers.
    a. Write for additional information about the production of apparel.
    b. Prepare a brief summary of the information you received and include your letter, the reply, and the materials you received from the manufacturer.
  2. Ask for information about the location of several manufacturers of fashion accessories. Note the cities and obtain the address of one or more manufacturers.
    a. Write for information about the production of one or more fashion accessories.
    b. Prepare a brief summary of the information you received and include your letter, the reply, and the materials you received from the manufacturer.
  3. Ask if sales representatives from apparel firms call at a local store. Make arrangements to have an interview with a sales representative when he or she is in the area; or, arrange with your teacher to have a sales representative speak to your class.
C. Prepare a cost factor sheet for one or more items of ready-to-wear.
  1. Work out the cost *components* on one or more items of clothing in your wardrobe, using information in Appendix 4, p. 267.
  2. Summarize the data you have prepared and include it in a brief report on the cost of ready-to-wear.
D. Review the career areas on fashion manufacturing in the job analysis series in Appendix 6, p. 279.
  1. Consider the personal characteristics and the educational background for one of the following jobs: pattern maker, dressmaker, production supervisor, grader, spreader, marker, cutter, machine operator, finisher.
  2. Research the employment opportunities in this career area in your state or in nearby states.
  3. Write a brief report summarizing your findings.
E. Read two or more of the articles listed here or research current periodicals or trade journals and select two or more articles related to one of the concepts suggested in the "Review, Discussion, and Evaluation."
  1. Prepare note cards while reading each article.
  2. Using your note cards, write a brief summary indicating the relationship of each article to concepts presented in this chapter.
  3. Using your note cards, give an oral report in your class and point out the important facts included in the articles.

Suggested Articles

BENDER, MARILYN. "Why Your Clothes Cost So Much." *McCall's*, (May, 1970), p. 94.
"Apparel in a Billion Dollar Conglomerate." *Clothes* (September 1, 1970).
MCQUODE, WALTER. "High Style Disrupts Men's Wear Industry." *Fortune*, February, 1971, p. 70.
"The Surprising Story of Career Apparel." *American Fabrics* (Winter 1971), pp. 55–66.

NOTES

[1] Research Department, International Ladies Garment Workers Union, New York, 1974.
[2] Department of Commerce "Annual Estimates of Personal Consumption Expenditures." Washington, D.C.: U.S. Government Printing Office, 1974.

[3] Marshall Doswell, *Architects of Change*, Fort Mill, N.C.: Springs Mills, Inc., Feb. 1972, p. 2.

[4] Department of Commerce, *U.S. Industrial 1975 Outlook*. Washington, D.C.: U.S. Government Printing Office, 1975, p. 224.

[5] "Focus, Economic Profile of the Apparel Industry." Arlington, Va.: American Apparel Manufacturers Association, Inc., 1974, p. 6.

[6] Research Department, ILGWU, loc. cit.

[7] Research Department, Dun and Bradstreet, Inc., New York, 1969.

[8] "The Garment Trade Learns Sophisticated Selling," *Business Week*, September 22, 1973, p. 86.

[9] *Industrial Outlook*, 1975, p. 225.

[10] *Business Week*, September 22, 1973, p. 85.

[11] Industrial Outlook, 1975, p. 237.

[12] Ibid., p. 241.

[13] Ibid.

[14] Ibid., p. 256.

[15] Census of Manufacturers, Department of Commerce. Washington, D.C.: U.S. Govt. Printing Office, 1971.

[16] Ruth Tolman, *Guide to Fashion Merchandising Knowledge*. New York: Milady Publishing Corp., 1973, p. 365.

7

Fashion Marketing

The giant step from the producer to the consumer, presented in marketing terms, follows a pattern of development: the flow of goods, the channel of distribution, and the marketing process. In the fashion industries, the flow of goods from raw materials to the consumer is unique. Seasonal timing and changes in styles, colors, and textures complicate the making of fashion merchandise, but once the product is completed, the finished goods zoom straight to the retailer where they are immediately available to the customer to see, to touch, and to own. Thus far in Part Two we have focused on supplying raw materials, and manufacturing apparel. Now it is time to consider the nature of the *marketing activities* involved in making fashion goods available to the consumer—the right goods, at the right time, at the right place, at the right price, and in the right amounts to satisfy consumer demand. These are *marketing problems*, and they present a tremendous challenge in the fashion industries.

In this chapter, the focus is on the fashion marketing concept: the professional timetable and selling targets at each level of the fashion industries, the fashion-marketing process and sales efforts at each level of the fashion industries, and other activities that accelerate the flow of fashion goods to the consumer.

THE FASHION-MARKETING CONCEPT

The term *fashion marketing* must be defined before we advance to an explanation of marketing concept. Marketing has been defined in numerous ways. As you read the following five definitions, you will note that the first three, made in the 1960s, are rather general in nature. The fourth is a broad concept representing the approach to marketing in the mid-1970s. The fifth statement defines textile marketing in more specific terms. However, it is apparent that in each of the five statements marketing includes those activities involved in moving merchandise in a profitable manner from producer to consumer.

1. Marketing is a comprehensive system of business action that directs the company's activities to meet customer needs and desires profitably.

It is no longer possible for a company to prosper merely by producing goods and services and attempting to sell them. In today's competitive marketplace, organizations must start with the resources of the company toward meeting these needs with a profit. This philosophy of business has been called the marketing concept. . . . the process of converting the idea to reality. This approach to marketing has become a necessity . . . not only for corporate growth, but often for survival as well[1] (American Management Association).

174

2. Marketing is the total of all the phases of business activity directed toward, and resulting in, the flow of goods from the original producer to the final consumer. In the broad sense, this includes not only selling, but advertising, packaging, research, and other nonmanufacturing activities[2] (Directory of Business and Finance, Harvard School of Business Administration).

3. Marketing has been defined as a business process by which products are matched with markets and through which transfers of ownership are effected[3] (Sills and Cundiff, authors in the marketing field).

4. Marketing includes all the operations of a business that determine and influence existing and potential demand in the marketplace and that activate the supply of goods and services to meet this demand[4] (Lipson and Darling, authors in the marketing field).

5. Textile marketing is more than selling. It starts with market research to discover present and potential profit opportunities for the company and its customers; plans a strategy of exploiting these opportunities; creates and prices the needed products and services; and distributes by methods which enhance relations with present customers and with new ones[5] (Willard C. Wheeler, an expert in the textile field).

Based on these five statements we can define *fashion marketing as the various activities involved in stimulating and maintaining the profitable flow of seasonal fashion goods from the raw product to the manufacturers and on to the retailer for purchase and use by consumers.*

Thus, the primary goal of the fashion industries is evident: the right merchandise, at the right time, at the right place, and in the right assortments and amounts to satisfy the consumer seasonal demands. However, there are numerous problems in this fashion marketing system. Because of the unique nature of fashion, who knows *today* what styles, colors, or fabrics the consumer will want *tomorrow?* Many people in the fashion industries had to know the answers to these questions *yesterday*. Apparel makers decided several months ago—anticipated or guessed—what the consumer wants today; the fabric producers had to answer these same questions many months before that; and the fiber producers were projecting answers several years ago in order that the consumers' needs could be met today. These are some of the timing factors that complicate the marketing process for fashion goods.

The Professional Timetable for Fashion

First, it is essential to realize the importance of the professional timetable that controls, stimulates, and maintains the flow of seasonal goods in the fashion industries. The seasonal timing and the selling targets are indicated in Table 7.1 for each level of marketing activities.

FIBER PRODUCERS

The fiber producer's selling target, or customer, is the spinning mill and/or weaving and knitting mill. Billions of dollars are spent on research and development activities at the fiber production level in an effort to create new or improved fibers for the decades ahead. Some man-made fiber producers are presently working on technical advances that could make it possible to change the color of a room or a dress by the flip of a switch.

Other activities at the fiber production level are aimed at a closer target—two or three years ahead. For instance, efforts are presently being made to sell fabric mills and apparel manufacturers on the tremendous range of uses for new fibers. Successful efforts of this type could mean that in a year or so the consumer will find new or improved fibers in an assortment of colors and textures in both ready-to-wear and piece goods at a nearby shopping center. Remember, the *product emphasis* at this level is the development of new or improved fibers that can be produced in staple and filament forms for use in making yarns and/or fabrics. The role of the fiber producer in the marketing process is discussed in detail later in this chapter.

FABRIC PRODUCERS

The fabric producer's selling target, or customer, is actually the garment maker, but the

TABLE 7.1 Fashion Industries Professional Timetable

Level of marketing activities	Lead time required	Selling target (customer)	Product emphasis
1. Fiber producers	2–3 years or more	Spinning mills Knitting mills Weaving mills	Staple and filament fibers for yarns and fabrics
2. Fabric producers	15–18 months	Cutting and needle trades; Converters and apparel manufacturers	Sample lengths and swatches of finished fabric
3. Apparel manufacturers	10–12 months	Retailers	Manufacturers' seasonal sample designs available for orders
Seasonal fashion markets	6–8 months	Store buyers	
Sales representatives	4–6 months	Store buyers	
4. Retailer	2–3 months	Consumer	Seasonal fashion goods for sale
5. Consumer	0–1 months	End user	Items to replace or supplement wardrobe

converter often serves as a middleman at this level. Marketing activities are projected approximately 15 to 18 months in advance by the fabric producer. Spinning mills and weaving and knitting mills may be producing greige goods more than a year in advance. However, the converters and finishers can work much closer to the demand of the apparel maker they are supplying. New printing and finishing techniques are being developed today that could shorten the lead time considerably between the converter and the garment maker.

Sample lengths, swatches, and color cards are available more than a year in advance in order to show the apparel manufacturer the assortment of fabrics projected for production in future seasons. Fabric companies now have fabric libraries in New York City and in other fashion centers across the country. These fabric libraries make it possible for a variety of professional people in the fashion trade to see the fabric colors, textures, and construction that will be available on an advanced seasonal basis; these people are the fashion coordinators, stylists, and representatives for retailers, magazines, newspapers, buying offices, trade associations, and related industries.

Remember that the product emphasis at this level is on the production of sample lengths, swatches, and color cards representing fabrics that can be produced in quantities for making garments.

APPAREL MANUFACTURERS

The apparel manufacturer's selling target, or customer, is the retail buyer. Marketing activities at the garment-making level are highly seasonal by nature and are initiated 10 to 12 months in advance of the actual season in which the consumer will be buying fashion goods.

The apparel manufacturer produces a number of sample lines to show to retailers in an effort to obtain orders for specific styles before mass production is started for a season. These sample lines are presented to retailers at seasonal markets six to eight months in advance of a consumer selling season.

Most apparel firms have one or more sales representatives. Each salesman has his own sample line; his activities are usually concentrated four to six months in advance and are aimed toward maximizing sales to retailers in a given region. The combined efforts of the apparel firm executives and salesmen are concentrated in the glorified fashion market system. Remember the *product emphasis* at this level is on the design and

FIGURE 7.1 *Fabric libraries such as this one in New York City play an important role in textile product development. (Courtesy of M. Lowenstein and Sons, Inc.)*

production of styles in colors and fabrics that can be mass produced at a profit for both retailers and manufacturers. The role of the seasonal fashion market is discussed in detail in Chapter 8.

RETAILERS

The retailer's selling target, or customer, is the utlimate consumer. Finally, the flow of fashion goods reaches the consumer. An appropriate early assortment of fashion goods should be in the retail store, available to the customer, two to three months in advance of the peak of a season in order to allow for shopping time and the consumer's decision-making process. New merchandise, normally, begins to filter into the retail outlets in August for the fall season and in February for the spring season. This will vary greatly, depending on the type of store, the normal climate, the weather, and other factors in the region. Economic and social factors have a great impact on the fashion cycle, as we have learned in previous chapters, and, they affect the professional timetable at the retail level as well as at upper levels.

These intricate timing factors control and direct the flow of goods in the fashion industries. The interdependence of marketing activities is apparent at each level. Each operation is dependent on some previous operation, and production decisions at each level must be projections based on anticipated consumer demand. Yet the retailer has the only direct contact with the consumer. In fact, the retailer is actually the purchasing agent for the consumer. This professional timetable has a tremendous influence on the marketing of fashion goods.

THE MARKETING PROCESS FOR FASHION GOODS

It is increasingly evident that the unique nature of fashion evolves around the elements of change, acceptance, prevailing styles, and reflection. Due, in part, to the interaction of these elements, the marketing process for fashion goods is unique, compared with the marketing process for other consumer products.

Basic Marketing Patterns

The four major patterns of distribution for manufacturing goods are depicted in Figure 7.2. Two factors are indicated: the flow of goods from producer to consumer and the effort of sales from producers to consumer.

Although some manufactured goods are sold directly to the consumer and delivered by the manufacturer or picked up by the consumer from the factory, this marketing pattern accounts for only a small percentage of consumer goods. The experience is so rare that most people can remember any item they purchased from the maker (manufacturer, producer). The vegetables a consumer buys directly from a farmer are an example. The macramé belt an individual purchases from a friend is another. These are explicit examples of the first marketing process depicted in Figure 7.2.

Notice the difference in the flow of goods and sales efforts indicated by patterns 2, 3, and 4. A retailer is involved in each of these three marketing processes; however, there is another distribution stage in the last two. The flow of goods most commonly known in the marketing process includes a wholesaler. The producer sells the goods to a wholesaler, or middleman; here an exchange of ownership takes place, along with a change of location, because the wholesaler usually stores goods in his own warehouses. Appliances, hardware, toothpaste, and other staple goods which

the consumer buys in *predictable amounts* on a regular basis are most often distributed through a wholesale-type operation. In some instances, as indicated by pattern 4, the producer sells the goods by direct contact with the retailer, and the goods are moved to distribution centers and transported as requested to the retailer for resale to the consumer.

The marketing process for most manufactured goods follows one of these four patterns, or some variation or modification of one of them. As can readily be seen in Figure 7.3, the process of marketing for fashion goods most nearly follows pattern 2 in Figure 7.2.

The Fashion-Marketing Process

The fashion-marketing process is unique in several aspects. Notice, in Figure 7.3, that the flow of goods begins with the supplier, moves directly to the manufacturer, then to the retailer, and finally to the consumer. Fashion goods are seasonal, and consumer acceptance cannot be predicted accurately enough for merchandise to be processed by a wholesaler or stored at a distribution center over a period of time. Every effort is made by textile suppliers, apparel manufacturers, and retailers to anticipate and estimate in advance the seasonal demands of the consumer. The apparel maker buys fabrics and mass produces fashion goods on the basis of orders and delivery dates specified by the retailer. Fashion merchandise is transported by the *most direct route* from the factory to the retail store. Nationally known multiunit store operations, such

1. Producer ════════════════════════════════ Consumer

2. Producer ═══════════════════════ Retailer ═══════ Consumer

3. Producer ═══════ Wholesaler ═══════ Retailer ═══════ Consumer

4. Producer ═══════════════════════ Retailer ═══════ Consumer
      Distribution
      Center

Sales efforts ─ ─ ─ ─ ─
Flow of goods ──────────

FIGURE 7.2 *Basic marketing patterns.*

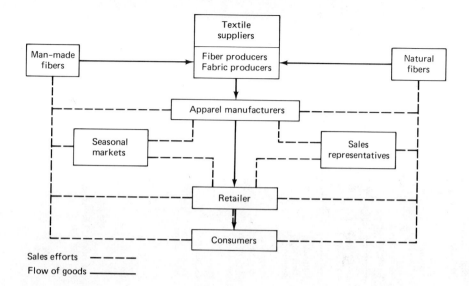

FIGURE 7.3 *Marketing process for fashion goods. The textile industry has strongly influenced this marketing process. Other fashion suppliers tend to follow some variation of this process.*

as Sears' and Penney's, may have regional distribution centers.

Marketing activities begin with the sales efforts of the fiber producers but do not follow the direct flow of goods, as is shown in Figure 7.3. Marketing activities are exerted in the form of sales efforts at each level in the fashion industries; however, these activities at each level also *focus* on the consumer. The sales efforts initiated at the supplier's level are intensified at the apparel-manufacturing level. It is at this level that the fashion industry is unique. A seasonal marketing system has been developed by apparel manufacturers to serve the retailer and to accelerate the flow of goods to the consumer. These seasonal fashion markets are discussed in detail in Chapter 8. As indicated in Figure 7.3, sales efforts of the manufacturer's representatives also contribute to the marketing activities at this level. Most apparel firms have salesmen assigned to regional territories who contact retailers on an individual basis in an effort to maximize the flow of fashion goods to the retailer, who is the purchasing agent for the consumer. At the retail level, the marketing process culminates with the sales efforts of the local merchants, who have direct contact with the

consumer. Thus, the entire fashion marketing process is directed toward stimulating and maintaining the flow of the seasonal fashion goods that will meet the anticipated consumer demand.

MARKETING ROLES IN THE FASHION INDUSTRIES

The fashion industries are alive with marketing activities. According to the concept of fashion marketing as defined in this chapter, marketing activities are sales efforts and other activities that accelerate, stimulate, and maintain the flow of fashion goods to the ultimate consumer. The marketing activities in the fashion industries are presented in Figure 7.4. The suppliers at the upper level of the fashion industries are actively involved in the marketing process, which terminates in the actual satisfaction of the consumer's needs for fashion goods. The marketing activities of both fiber producers and fabric producers focus on accelerating the flow of fashion goods to the customer.

Since the advent of man-made fibers, marketing activities at the supplier's level have focused

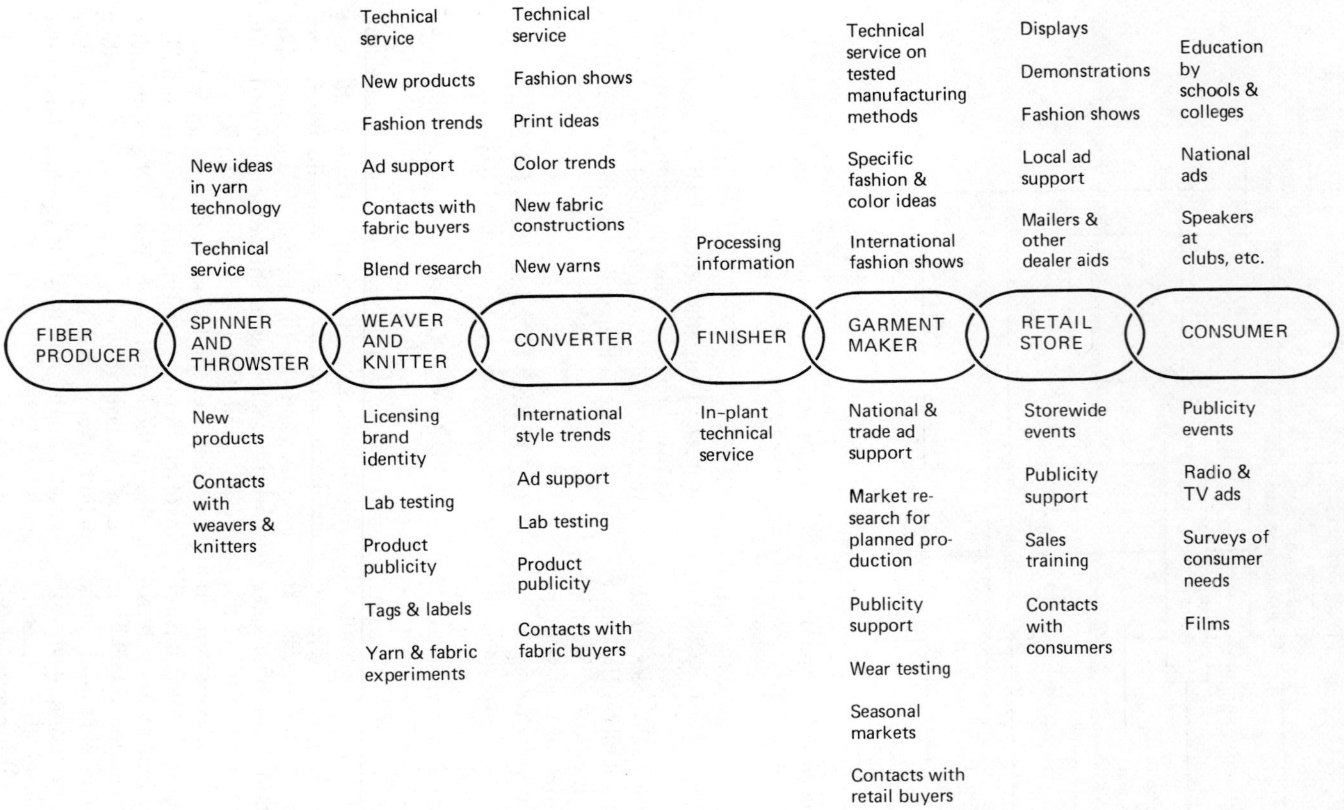

FIBER PRODUCER — SPINNER AND THROWSTER — WEAVER AND KNITTER — CONVERTER — FINISHER — GARMENT MAKER — RETAIL STORE — CONSUMER

SPINNER AND THROWSTER
New ideas in yarn technology
Technical service
New products
Contacts with weavers & knitters

WEAVER AND KNITTER
Technical service
New products
Fashion trends
Ad support
Contacts with fabric buyers
Blend research
Licensing brand identity
Lab testing
Product publicity
Tags & labels
Yarn & fabric experiments

CONVERTER
Technical service
Fashion shows
Print ideas
Color trends
New fabric constructions
New yarns
International style trends
Ad support
Lab testing
Product publicity
Contacts with fabric buyers

FINISHER
Processing information
In-plant technical service

GARMENT MAKER
Technical service on tested manufacturing methods
Specific fashion & color ideas
International fashion shows
National & trade ad support
Market research for planned production
Publicity support
Wear testing
Seasonal markets
Contacts with retail buyers

RETAIL STORE
Displays
Demonstrations
Fashion shows
Local ad support
Mailers & other dealer aids
Storewide events
Publicity support
Sales training
Contacts with consumers

CONSUMER
Education by schools & colleges
National ads
Speakers at clubs, etc.
Publicity events
Radio & TV ads
Surveys of consumer needs
Films

FIGURE 7.4 *Marketing activities in the fashion industries.* (Adapted from "The Modern Marketing Chain," American Fabrics and Fashions 74, Winter/Spring 1967, pp. 52–53.)

on producing fibers, yarns, and fabrics that have the performance characteristics desired by the consumer—easy care, permanent press, stain resistance, for example.

The Marketing Role of the Fiber Producer

At the *fiber production* level in the United States, several fiber producers were leaders in developing marketing activities: DuPont, Celanese, Eastman, and Chemstrand among them. Research and development constituted the first step in the process of providing fashion goods to meet the desires and needs of the consumer. These efforts resulted in many more fibers by the 1960s, some of which had qualities like those of the competitive natural fibers. Acrilan simulated wool and offered easy-care qualities; and Dacron, Fortrel, and Kodel offered wash-and-wear features for blouses, shirts, and slacks.

These new fibers and new performance characteristics came rapidly and abundantly after 1950. The fiber companies, most of them chemical companies originally, realized that marketing products required different activities in the fashion industries. At each level of operation efforts had to be made to ensure the flow of goods to the consumer. By the mid-1960s there had been a revolution in the structure and function of the textile industry. Thus, the role of the fiber producer in marketing influenced the development of the modern marketing chain in the fashion industries, as depicted in Figure 7.4.

RESEARCH AND DEVELOPMENT

Research and development at the fiber-production level were responsible for the invention of new fibers. The fabric mills had to be informed that the new fibers existed, and the spinners and throwsters (those who throw silk or synthetic filaments) had to be taught a new yarn technology. Product ideas, fashion research, laboratory testing, tags and labels, brand identity, and numerous other marketing efforts were sponsored by fiber companies to solve problems in weaving, knitting, converting, and finishing new fibers.

These marketing efforts could not stop at the supplier level if the flow of fashion goods were to continue to the consumer level. It was at this point that the fiber producers introduced "Quid pro quo," or "push money" as it is commonly called in the textile industry.[6] Monies were needed to stimulate and accelerate the use of new fibers by garment makers and to inform the retailer and the consumer about new products.

Fiber companies put millions of dollars into these marketing efforts at the apparel and retail levels through fashion shows, fashion ideas, manufacturing methods, publicity and advertising, displays and exhibits, wear testing, laboratory demonstrations, sales training, and even more market research at the manufacturing level.

ADVERTISING

Finally, the message reached the consumer: the existence of new fibers with unbelievable performance features—wash-and-wear, no-iron, wrinkle-free. Here the fiber companies found a last barrier that had to be removed. The consumer was not always satisfied with the new product. It did not seem to be so easy to care for as the consumer had been led to believe by the advertisements, publicity, and hang tags. Again the fiber companies accepted the challenge, and more intense marketing efforts were exerted at the consumer level.

Publicity events, filmstrips, speakers, and other educational materials were developed for schools, colleges, clubs, and many kinds of organizations. More push money was allocated for radio and television and local and national advertising campaigns to inform and educate the consumer. More research efforts were directed toward the consumer; this time marketing surveys were aimed at defining consumer needs, wants, and satisfaction factors.

Finally, by the late 1960s, the fiber companies had put it all together: a modern marketing chain was developed for the fashion industries. A revolution changed the structure and function of the textile and apparel industrial complex.

The Marketing Role of the Fabric Producer

At the fabric production level the textile mills had become involved with marketing through the prodding and pushing of the fiber producers. By the late 1960s, leading mills—Burlington and J. P. Stevens—entered the marketing arena. Initial efforts were made to coordinate a total fashion look—color, pattern, texture, and construction—at the fabric production level.

COORDINATING

Marketing activities were aimed at eliminating some of the risk in producing fashion goods. Preplanning the fashion directions for fabrics and establishing production commitments by the mills took some of the gamble out of fashion for the textile industry.

Early marketing efforts by fabric companies led to other marketing activities. Workshops, seminars, and audiovisual presentations, and other informative materials were developed to communicate the fashion story in fabrics to the garment maker at the apparel-manufacturing level of the fashion industry. The advance fashion story is told season after season in terms of fashion trends from Europe and the United States—fashion news in colors, patterns, textures, construction, and new directions for fabrics that coordinate with other fashion trends.

Marketing efforts at the textile supplier's level have been successful in partially answering the contemporary needs of these mass producers of the raw materials of fashion. Giantism in both fiber and fabric production tend to make it difficult for firms to maintain a flow of communication with their customers or selling targets—the users of their product become more anonymous. Marketing efforts focus the attention of the *producer* on the needs of the *product user*.

Mass production and mass distribution of fashion goods have multiplied the risks involved in anticipating fashion trends in line, color, and texture in advance of the consumer buying season. Marketing efforts at the supplier's level in the fashion industry have led to the recognition of the need for a continuation of marketing activities at the manufacturing and retailing levels. Anticipation of consumer acceptance and usage of fashion products on a seasonal basis is an essential part of the planning and coordinating of mass production in the fashion industries.

The Marketing Role of the Apparel Manufacturer

Strategically located midway in the fashion marketing process, the apparel manufacturer utilizes the marketing efforts of the fiber and fabric producers and draws on the retailer's knowledge of the consumer. It is at this level in the fashion industries that decisions are finalized to achieve the fashion marketing goals: to move the right goods, in the right assortment, to the retailer at the right time for the consumer to make seasonal purchases.

In the 1960s, some giants and would-be giants in apparel manufacturing—Jonathan Logan and Bobbie Brooks, for example—set the pace for marketing activities at this level in the fashion industries. To some extent, smaller apparel firms have not followed suit in developing a marketing concept. These smaller garment makers continue to lean heavily on the marketing activities of the textile suppliers and of the giants in the apparel industry.

RESEARCH AND DEVELOPMENT

Research and development at the apparel-manufacturing level have concentrated on technological advances and consumer behavior patterns. Considerable progress has been made in the last decade in automation in the computerization of specialized operations involved in garment making. (Mass production of apparel became a reality in the 1970s.) Thousands of garments can be cut in a single process, and there have been improvements in sewing machines and methods that expedite production. As a result of these advances, we not only have mass production of apparel, but we also have exceptionally well-dressed consumers who are reasonably satisfied with the performance qualities of the apparel and other textile products they purchase.

Some research efforts at the apparel manufacture's level have focused on the consumer. Studies have been undertaken to identify the characteristics of various consumer groups, such as buying patterns, shopping habits, and needs and desires in terms of age, sex, and so on. Marketing surveys have been designed for firms specializing in various kinds of apparel—that is, junior wear, sportswear, men's wear. Consumer panels have been initiated to seek out the reactions of the *users* of existing products and to develop ideas for new products.

PROMOTIONS

Apparel manufacturers, either individually or cooperatively, have participated in many other marketing activities of a promotional and publicity nature, such as trade shows, seasonal press showings, fashion shows, and other fashion publicity events. These marketing activities are supported more by the giants in the industry than by the smaller apparel manufacturers.

Thus, fiber and fabric producers start the process of predicting and shaping the trends of fashion several seasons ahead. The apparel manufacturer utilizes this preplanning and coordinating of styles, colors, and fabrics and injects the feedback from the retail buyer. It is the apparel maker who realistically interprets the projections for the season to come. At this point, the consumer-acceptance patterns dominate the scene, because the retail buyer, who is the purchasing agent for the consumer, greatly influences the production decisions of the apparel manufacturer.

Today the apparel industry continues to build on the marketing efforts of the fiber and fabric producers. Preplanning and advanced projections make it possible to eliminate some of the risks at the supplier's level and the manufacturer's level, as well as at the retail level. Mass production and mass distribution have indeed been achieved in the fashion industries. Thus, the fashion marketing goal is being attained.

MARKET ACTIVITIES

It is at the apparel-manufacturing level in the fashion industries that the marketing activities shift to the seasonal fashion markets and to the sales efforts of the manufacturer's representatives, as indicated in Figure 7.3. At this point in the fashion marketing process—the flow of goods to the consumer—we hear a different drummer. Different marketing activities are employed to stimulate and accelerate the flow of fashion goods to the retailer and, thereby, to the consumer. The *flow* does go on: fashion goods go directly to the retailer and to the consumer, but the marketing activities take on the characteristics of "hard" sales efforts, not the "soft" sell of marketing activities at the fiber and fabric production levels. In the trade, the term *soft* sell means to inform, to educate, to encourage, to motivate, and to stimulate by various attractive means—including push money, as has previously been mentioned. Not so with the *hard sell*. This term has come to describe the "arm-twisting" methods used to persuade the retail buyer to "drop paper" (place orders, make signed commitments), not just to "smile" and "promise," or to remark "That looks great, but . . . ."

It is at the manufacturer's seasonal market that the retailer gets down to the nitty gritty of orders and delivery dates. These seasonal fashion markets have become a ritual in the industry. They are the center of fashion excitement—here is the culmination of all marketing activities. It matters little what the performance features of fibers may be, or whether garments are copies of Paris designers. All of this fades into insignificance, for the retail buyer is king here. At this point, the retail buyer is the apparel manufacturer's customer, or selling target—the purchasing agent for the consumer. If the buyer does not place an order at the market or within a short period of time afterward, there is no way to ensure the transfer of fashion goods to the consumer. This is where the flow stops or goes on. At this point the retail buyer, as the purchasing agent for the consumer, makes the decisions, right or wrong. Apparel that is not ordered is not cut, and sample fabrics are not reordered. The converter gets the signal not to finish more greige goods, the mills get the signal not to weave or knit more fabric, and the fiber mills get the "no go" sign for Qiana, or for whatever it was the retail buyer did not order for the consumer. This is the way it works in the fashion industries: all of the preplanning and advanced projections face reality at the *seasonal fashion markets* across the United States. This is the last step in the fashion marketing process—the *sales* link that controls the direct flow of the goods to the retailer who makes them available for purchase during the consumer buying season.

A more detailed discussion of the seasonal fashion markets in the United States is presented in Chapter 8. The role of the retailer is considered in Part Three.

RELATED FASHION-ORIENTED SERVICES

A myriad of professional activities and services augments the marketing efforts carried on by fashion suppliers, manufacturers, and retailers. These fashion-oriented services aid in stimulating and maintaining the flow of seasonal fashion goods and thus contribute to the achievement of the goal of fashion marketing. Analyzing, interpreting, communicating, and enhancing fashion are some of the aspects of these activities and services that are so important at each level of the fashion industries.

Fashion Trade Publications and Associations

The fashion industries are fortunate to have the services of numerous trade papers and trade groups. Vital to the progress of fashion in the United States, the *Women's Wear Daily* has often been called the "bible" for the various segments of the textile and apparel industrial complex, as well as for the retailers of women's fashions. Five days a week the pages of this trade paper vibrate with the happenings in the fashion industries and in the fashion world of the consumer of apparel and textile products.

Founded before the turn of the century, this Fairchild publication has played a prominent role in the fashion communications system for more than three quarters of a century. The *Women's Wear Daily* (WWD) reports facts and events of common interest to fiber and fabric producers and to apparel manufacturers and serves to keep the retailer abreast of day-to-day developments and new directions within the fashion industries.

Under the innovative leadership of a second generation of Fairchilds, this trade paper has increasingly recognized the importance consumer acceptance plays in fashion, fashion making, and fashion selling. Social activities and cultural events are reported in a manner that reflects fashion—that is, the emphasis is on what socialites are wearing when they attend important functions.

The depth and completeness of the coverage of *WWD* are almost beyond imagination. Most of the pages deal with provocative facts, figures, and issues. The reactions of readers can be violent, but few businesses associated with the fashion industries would be without their yearly subscriptions. Because certain weekly issues focus on a specialized segment of the trade, such as lingerie or children's wear, some firms take only the one or two weekly issues that provide relevant business information. This trade paper, as others, serves as an advertising vehicle for the firms, large and small, that comprise the fashion industries. Business notices and employment opportunities are included in the classified information.

Fairchild Publications, located in New York City near the heart of the fashion industries, also publishes the *Daily News Record*, which focuses on the men's wear and textile industries. The circulation of this trade paper is only about one third that of the WWD, which soared near the 100,000 mark in the early 1970s. Numerous other fashion-oriented educational materials are produced by Fairchild Publications.

A variety of trade papers serve the needs of other smaller and highly specialized segments in the fashion industries: *Body Fashions* for the undergarment trade; *Boot and Shoe Recorder* for the shoe trade; *Chain Store Age* and *Stores*, for management-oriented trades; *Modern Textiles*, *Textile World*, and *American Fabrics and Fashions* for the textile as well as the apparel and the retail trade; and *Clothes*, a monthly publication that has gained prominence at the retail level in this decade. These and many other trade publications serve to inform, educate, communicate, and meet various other needs of business firms in the fashion industries. A partial list of other trade publications in the fashion industry includes:

Department Store Management
Fashion Week
Homesewing Trade News

Fabricnews
Housewares Review
Discount Merchandiser
Homefurnishings Daily
Curtain and Drapery Magazine
Linens and Domestics
China, Glass, and Tablewares
Gift and Decorative Accessories
Apparel Manufacturer
California Men's Stylist
Men's Wear
Masculines
Teens and Boys Outfitter
California Stylist
California Apparel News
Femme Line
Style
Variety Department Stores
Western Apparel Industry
Earnshaws (*children's apparel*)
Small World
Juvenile Merchandising

Trade associations contribute to the progress of the fashion industries. The National Retail Merchants Association (NRMA) is probably the giant in this group. Although its purpose is to serve as a focal point for retailers throughout the United States, some of the problems and issues common to the retailer are of concern at other levels of the fashion industry—for instance, consumer protection regulations, FTC rulings involving manufacturers and retailers, and fair trade laws. Other trade associations that serve more specialized groups are the New York Couture Business Council, The American Designers Group, The National Association of Men's Wear, and The Fashion Group, Inc. The latter group is a nonprofit organization whose sole purpose is promoting professionalism among women in the fashion business. The group is recognized throughout the world for its tireless efforts to unite the endeavors of women in the fashion business and to engage their support of local and regional projects of a cultural and humanitarian nature. Noted annually are regional and national projects such as benefit fashion shows and programs, fashion career seminars, and work with the handicapped and other special groups. Without these supplemental fashion-oriented activities and services, the flow of fashion goods would be severely hampered.

Consumer Fashion Publications and Associations

Consumer magazines, fashion sections of newspapers, and consumer groups serve the common interests of fashion consumers and also have a great impact on the fashion industries at various levels. Most fashion magazines appeal to a particular audience and are read by consumers with certain common characteristics. *Vogue* and *Harper's Bazaar* present fashion directions and innovative ideas to consumers who are among the fashion leaders in our nation and abroad. *Mademoiselle*, *Seventeen*, and *Glamour* provide fashion news and trends for a younger consumer group, a group more concerned with moderate fashion than fashion leadership.

Other consumer magazines, not particularly known as fashion magazines, also have some pages devoted to fashions in clothing as well as in home furnishings and handwork. Women's magazines include *McCall's*, *Good Housekeeping*, *Redbook*, *Ladies' Home Journal*, *Family Circle*, and *Woman's Day*.

Another category of consumer magazines of fashion importance includes the men's publications—*Argosy*, *Cavalier*, *Esquire*, *Playboy*, and *True*, for example.

It has been said that fashion is made on the front pages of our newspapers and reported on the society or women's pages. It is not surprising, then, that newspapers in some cities throughout the country are noted particularly for their fashion reporting in those sections, usually a prominent part of the Sunday edition. Among these prominent contributors to the fashion world are the *New York Times*, the *Los Angeles Times*, the *Chicago Tribune*, the *San Francisco Examiner*, and the *Kansas City Star*.

Both consumer magazines and newspapers serve as vehicles for advertising textile and apparel products and, thus, lend a hand in accelerating the flow of fashion goods to the consumer and providing the consumer with information about product use and care.

The printed media services have been a significant source of communication with the consumer for each level of the fashion industries. However, television has challenged the fashion world. Fashion is a visible expression; and fashion news, trends, and information are readily transmitted by means of television. Although the radio has served many retailers as a means of communication with consumers, television has a facility for dramatic presentations—live and in color—that reach millions and millions of consumers. Excitement and newness inherent in fashion can be transmitted quickly and directly across the country. Even though television is a relatively expensive medium, its potential has been recognized in the fashion industries. At both local and national levels, it is definitely a medium that accelerates the flow of fashion goods. Television services and agencies contribute to the progress of fashion industries in the same manner that consumer publications have in the past.

Consumer fashion groups are not prevalent even in today's highly fashion-conscious world; however, some local women's clubs incorporate a fashion show into the yearly program schedule, and some schools and colleges have clubs or organizations that pay homage to fashion in clothing or some other consumer fashion interest area.

Fashion Advertising and Public Relations Organizations

Agencies that provide advertising, publicity, public relations, and other promotional services are a boon to the fashion industries. Small fashion businesses at the retail, manufacturing, and supplier levels do not have the expertise to handle this highly creative aspect of the trade. Most of these kinds of services are handled on a one-to-one, client-by-client basis. Each client's needs are provided for in an individual manner. However, advertising campaigns may be planned for new products; artwork may be prepared for posters, hang tags, and labels; brochures, catalogs, and other promotional pieces may be designed for various uses; and local, regional, or national advertising layouts may be developed for magazines, newspapers, or other publications.

Fashion agencies may provide models or produce complete fashion shows, and fashion photographers may arrange press releases and materials for press kits and cooperative advertising services. Public relations experts can place articles to promote the features of new products, new services, or new ideas. These agencies and organizations provide creative communications to supplement the ongoing marketing activities at each level of the fashion industries.

Fashion Consulting and Marketing Firms

Fashion services may be provided by fashion consultants, fashion coordinators, and fashion stylists. Experts in this area put it all together and come up with the right fashion answers on an individual, firm-by-firm basis. In the highly specialized realm of fashion, both large and small firms often find a need for outside help in evaluating, analyzing, and interpreting the variables involved in the decision-making process. These fashion services are often provided on a freelance basis by professionals or by agencies that offer specialized services to a limited number of clients or to clients at one level of the fashion industries—retail, or manufacturing, or textile producers—because there may be conflicting points of view and interests among these various levels of operation.

Fashion consultants may come and go, but none yet has exceeded the contributions made by Tobe Coller Davis, who established the consulting agency of Tobe Associates in the late 1920s. Prior to her death in 1962, Tobe had successfully charted the fashion direction for many of the major retailers in the United States. She won many honors and awards in recognition of her professional expertise, her fashion leadership, and her achievements in the fashion world for more than three decades.

Through the efforts of Tobe's agency, employers were provided with a variety of fashion services, including a voluminous weekly report of fashion news, interpretations, and predictions complete with sketches and examples relevant to the trade. Consulting services of this type are competitive with Tobe today and offer services of a supplementary nature for some firms; and for others, business expertise is provided that is not available within the organization on a permanent basis.

Consulting agencies keep abreast of the business and social aspects of fashion at each level in the fashion industries and in our commercially oriented society. Based on thorough, up-to-date knowledge, fashion consultants provide reports and educational materials; initiate clinics, seminars, and other programs; and give advice and direction as needed and requested by the paying clients. Although more often these services are designed for the retail level, with the ultimate consumer in mind, fashion-consulting services are available at each level of the fashion industries and are often utilized by the apparel manufacturer and the fiber or fabric producer.

Marketing firms may perform some of the same kinds of activities as consulting agencies; however, some additional expertise may be directed toward management problems in the area of merchandising control services and consumer shopping and purchasing patterns. Small retailers often use the services of marketing firms to assist in analyzing merchandise problems, planning promotional efforts, identifying characteristics of customers and potential consumer groups, and interpreting general fashion trends and future directions.

In the area of promotional media, such as the use of television and radio, these consulting and marketing services may be similar to, or overlapping with, those services provided by advertising and public relations firms. They are all in the same family, however, and such services are available in most of the major fashion centers in the United States—New York City, Chicago, St. Louis, Atlanta, Dallas, Los Angeles, and San Francisco—and in cities where the hum and the drum of fashion are loud enough to demand fashion expertise of some type.

Buying and Merchandising Services

The resident buying office has long played an important role as the representative for retail buyers in the fashion market place—New York City, Los Angeles, and Dallas—wherever the retailer wants to contact apparel or textile firms and place orders for merchandise. Small retailers may belong to resident buying offices for a fee, and large corporate retailers may maintain buying offices in several markets to service a group of stores.

Regardless of the type of buying office, the activities and services are similar: the store receives advance bulletins with comparative information, buying trends, fashion directions, and features of merchandise available from various apparel firms; schedules are arranged for store buyers during market visits; advice is given relative to merchandise assortments and amounts in units and dollars; contacts are initiated with new apparel firms; and reorders are made and fill-in merchandise is purchased and shipped at the request of the retail buyer during the consumer buying season.

Merchandising services of a somewhat similar nature are offered by other firms located in the major fashion market centers. However, these merchandising firms may be more operationally oriented and may function in a data-analysis and advisory capacity at top management level only.

Various kinds of promotional services and activities are provided by most buying offices—mailing inserts, catalogs for seasonal promotions, advertising materials, promotional campaign strategies, and store clinics in specialized aspects of merchandising. Some of these firms may also act as an employment bureau and assist in finding management personnel or in obtaining other kinds of expertise from fashion-oriented professionals.

In addition to these five major classifications of fashion-oriented services, other professional groups may provide some of these same services in a more individualized or creative manner at one or more of the three levels in the fashion industries. Other kinds of fashion services or activities may be in demand on a seasonal basis and may be provided in a free-lance manner at first; later these may develop into full-fledged business ventures. Some of these fashion experts may cater to a highly specialized segment of the fashion industries, such as the leather industry, the shoe industry, the children's wear industry, or to jewelry or fashion accessories manufacturers.

Regardless of the needs in the fashion industries, some firm or some individual with expertise can be depended on to take up the slack, to keep the flow of seasonal fashion goods moving to the consumer and to keep the consumer informed about fashion today and tomorrow.

END OF CHAPTER GUIDE

Review, Discussion, and Evaluation

Study of this chapter should enable students to:
A. Develop and give evidence of the following kinds of competencies:
   1. Ability to identify the unique aspects of the fashion marketing process, as compared to the marketing process for other manufactured goods
   2. Ability to project advanced time periods and describe selling targets associated with each level of the fashion industries: fiber production level, fabric production level, apparel manufacturing level, and retail level
   3. Awareness of the various kinds of marketing activities and efforts utilized to stimulate and maintain the flow of fashion goods at each level in the textile and apparel industries
   4. Awareness of the importance of the seasonal fashion market system to the textile industry, the apparel industry, and the retailer
   5. Knowledge of the various fashion-oriented services that contribute to the achievement of the fashion marketing goal: direct flow of goods from producer to consumer
B. Develop and/or clarify concepts related to the following key words and phrases:
   1. marketing activities   2. fashion marketing   3. professional timetable   4. selling target or customer   5. fashion-marketing process   6. quid pro quo   7. push money   8. fashion-marketing goals   9. seasonal fashion markets   10. fashion-oriented services

Extended Classroom Learning Experiences

A. Trace the profession timetable for some current fashion item made from a raw material produced in the textile industry, for example, a polyester blouse.

1. Designate the months included in the current consumer selling season.
2. Estimate:
   a. The month when the product was received by the retailer
   b. The month when the retailer purchased the product from the manufacturer through a sales representative or at a seasonal market
   c. The months when the apparel manufacturer was actually designing and deciding on the line to be presented in market's seasonal samples
   d. The months when the apparel manufacturer was actually cutting and sewing the garment
   e. The months when the fabric producers actually wove the yard goods
   f. The months when the fiber producers actually spun the yarn to be used in constructing the fabric's distinctive seasonal characteristics (for example, color, design, and texture)
   g. The months when the fiber was actually developed or when the distinctive characteristics of the fiber were improved
3. Write up this project and illustrate these various stages in an interesting manner.
B. Marketing activities in the fashion industries are somewhat independent at each level and yet overlap and interlace in terms of the ultimate goal, satisfying consumer demand.
   1. Collect illustrations that you feel are representative of one or more of the sales activities or efforts associated with the role of the fiber producer, the fabric producer, and the apparel manufacturer. For example, clip advertisements from consumer magazines stating names of (a) *fiber manufacturers*, such as Dupont or Celanese, (b) *fabric mills*, such as Springs Mills, Burlington Mills, and (c) *apparel manufacturers*, such as Bobbie Brooks, Jonathan Logan, and others you recognize as brands carried by your local retailer.
   2. Collect the hang tags from some apparel items you purchase in the next few months (or ones you have from previously purchased garments). What reference, if any, is made to the fiber, fabric produer, or apparel manufacturer. Do you know if these names refer to textile suppliers or if they are brand names used to identify the product?
   Your retailer or one of the employees in a clothing department of a store in your community may be able to provide additional informa-

tion in order to help you identify names associated with firms operating at various levels in the fashion industry.

3. Note television advertisements by indicating the station, the program interrupted, and the time and give a brief description of what was shown and said.

C. Write a brief summary describing the major sales efforts involved in the fashion marketing process and give examples of the major types of fashion-oriented services.

D. Review the career area of fashion promotion and media in Appendix 6, p. 279:

1. Compare the responsibilities and duties of two or more of the following jobs:
graphic artists, art director, copywriter, script writer, fashion editor, editorial assistant, creative director, account executive, fashion director, publicity coordinator, educational director, audiovisual coordinator, fashion representative, fashion photographer.

2. Describe the differences in responsibility and duties of each of the jobs you studied.

3. Consider the employment opportunities for each of the preceding jobs, and write a brief report of your findings pertaining to this career area of fashion promotion and media.

E. Read two or more of the articles listed here or research current periodicals or trade journals and select two or more articles related to one of the concepts suggested in the Review, Discussion, and Evaluation.

1. Prepare note cards while reading each article.

2. Using your note cards, write a brief summary indicating the relationship of each article to the concepts in this chapter.

3. Using your note cards, give an oral report to your class and point out the important facts included in the articles.

Suggested Articles

"Address Unknown, or What's Happening in Our Industry," *Clothes*, Nov. 15, 1974.

"The Garment Trade Learns Sophisticated Selling." *Business Week*; Sept. 22, 1973.

"Hot Potatoes." *Forbes*, July 1, 1975.

FRASIER, KENNEDY, "On and Off the Avenue—Paris Shows and Fashion Reporters." *The New Yorker*, April 28, 1975.

NOTES

[1] "Textile Marketing," *American Fabrics and Fashions*, Summer, 1966. New York: Doric Publishing Co., 1966, p. 79.

[2] Ibid.

[3] Richard R. Sill and Edward W. Cundiff, *Essentials in Marketing*. Englewood Cliffs, N.J.: Prentice-Hall, 1972, p. 3.

[4] Harry A. Lipson and John R. Darling, *Marketing Fundamentals*. New York: Wiley, 1974, p. 5.

[5] *American Fabrics and Fashions*, loc. cit.

[6] "The Role of the Fiber Producer." *Clothes*, January 1, 1971, pp. 20–26.

8

Fashion Market Centers

Fashion market centers throughout the United States serve as the communication system between apparel manufacturers and retailers. It is in these market centers that fashion trends and predictions are confirmed or buried. Here the apparel manufacturers and textile producers get the reactions (orders) of retailers to the samples of garments designed to be mass-produced for the coming season. Here the manufacturer eliminates some of the risk involved in cutting and sewing garments. Here the manufacturer decreases some of the gamble inherent in making fashion production decisions in advance of the consumer selling season.

It is at this point that the apparel manufacturer forces the retailer to step into the fashion arena—to join in the preplanning and in the advanced production decisions—to become a partner in the two-handed game of change which fashion suppliers and apparel manufacturers have been playing alone up to this point. The stakes are high in the fashion markets each season; the decisions, the actions, and the reactions resulting from the seasonal markets throughout the country can make or break firms at each level in the giant fashion industries: (1) retailers lose if the consumer does not buy the merchandise offered for the next season; (2) apparel manufacturers lose if the retailer does not buy the styles designed for the approaching seasons; and (3) textile producers and other suppliers lose if the apparel maker does not buy the raw materials produced

for the coming seasons. The fashion industries may suffer a devastating blow, because, for the most part, success or failure depends on the season-to-season activities in fashion markets throughout the United States.

In this chapter, we will examine the manner in which the apparel manufacturer uses seasonal fashion markets to bridge the gap between the *planned* output of the fashion industries and the *actual* mass production of consumer fashion goods. We will ascertain how the fashion market system operates, how the sales representative fits into the market system, and what kinds of activities take place at seasonal markets and between seasonal markets. We also will compare three major fashion markets and note the contributions of other regional markets in the United States.

THE FASHION MARKET SYSTEM IN THE UNITED STATES

Fashion is seasonal, and each new season means change. Season after season the flame of fashion is ignited and the fashion world becomes a blaze of colors, fabrics, and styles conceived and expressed in anticipation of the consumers' demand for innovation. These fashion fires are fanned and fed with fuel by the seasonal fashion markets throughout the country. These fashion markets have developed in centers where there is a concentration of apparel manufacturing.

Usually some suppliers of raw products for fashion goods are located in these areas as well.

Growth and Development

The fashion market system in the United States has grown up as a counterpart of the women's apparel industry. Production and distribution have had an interlocking relationship because of the nature of fashion and the fashion-marketing process.

The First Fashion Market Center

During the early part of the twentieth century, garment making—ready-to-wear—was highly concentrated in the garment district, Seventh Avenue in New York City. Most of the textile producers and other fashion suppliers had sales offices located in the area.

Retailers in the vicinity, as well as from other major cities, bought fashion goods *directly* from the manufacturers, and found it advantageous to visit the garment district from time to time to make new contacts and to purchase fashion goods. Manufacturers usually had sales representatives hired on a *regional* basis to call on retailers throughout the country. Retailers, particularly those who perceived their stores as fashion leaders in the community, made at least one or two buying trips a year to the New York fashion market center. Each apparel firm had showrooms in the garment district to display seasonal samples of styles and fabrics that could be ordered by retailers. As more retailers found it advantageous to buy from the apparel firms in the garment district, more fashion goods were produced and sold in that vicinity. Thus, New York City became known as the first fashion market center in the United States.

Other Fashion Market Centers

During the two decades between 1930 and 1950, important fashion markets developed in other parts of the country. The establishment of other markets was partially attributed to the growth of the apparel industry in *several regional areas*; and these markets, no doubt, were aided somewhat by the difficulties involved in traveling to New York City and obtaining delivery of fashion goods at the right time in distant towns and cities. Regardless of the reasons, manufacturers in other cities first set up showrooms in nearby factories or in hotels where space was designated for exhibits and displays of fashion goods. Manufacturers' sales representatives came in off the road during the market season and usually sold many more retail buyers than they could during day-by-day road contacts.

By 1950, *focal market centers* were found in major cities throughout the United States. Chicago was the second largest apparel market, known as a misses' dress market. Los Angeles and San Francisco formed the California market, the third largest, known for colorful sportswear, sophisticated town clothes, and the "movie star" influence; Boston and Philadelphia flanked the New York market center and were known for coats, suits, skirts, blouses, dresses, and some children's wear. St. Louis, a midwestern market, was known for men's wear, women's skirts, blouses, junior miss clothes, and for shoes; Cleveland was known for coats and suits; and Kansas City was known for women's wash dresses. Dallas was known for sportswear and play clothes; Miami was known for swimwear and sportswear; Atlanta was known for women's and children's wear; and Denver was known for Western wear. [1]

Present Status

The fashion market system in the United States today is a highly sophisticated structure. Influenced by the seasonal nature of fashion and the competitive spirit of change innate in fashion goods, a network of fashion markets is held across the country. As we answer some of the questions often asked by persons outside the fashion industries, we will discover some fundamental information about seasonal fashion markets.

1. *What is a seasonal fashion market?* It is primarily a center where textile and apparel man-

ufacturers can *exhibit* and *sell* seasonal fashion goods to the retailer. It is a merchandise center for men's, women's, and children's apparel and accessories and other related soft goods such as linens, domestics, and associated products.

In the women's apparel industry, manufacturers prepare a sample line of garments for each fashion season. Most apparel firms present sample lines in seasonal market showrooms six to eight months prior to each consumer buying season. Retail buyers view the advanced fashions in one or more of the seasonal fashion markets. Thus, as indicated by the professional timetable discussed in Chapter 7, the fashion industries revolve around a network of seasonal fashion markets.

2. *When are these seasonal fashion markets held?* The fashion spotlight usually falls first on the seasonal fashion market in the New York garment district, Seventh Avenue, and then moves to other fashion market centers across the country. Seasonal fashion markets are not necessarily scheduled in a progressive order, but they tend to concentrate in seasonal patterns. In the seasonal fashion markets across the country, apparel firms show *summer* fashions in January–February; *transitional* (late summer and early fall) fashion in March–April; *fall and winter* fashions in May–June; *holiday and late winter* fashions in August–September; and *spring and summer* fashions in October–November. The market dates and schedules are usually established by a board of directors for the market center. The period of time scheduled for seasonal fashion markets may vary from season to season and from market to market; however, it usually ranges from three days to two weeks. Actually, most fashion market

centers are open to retail buyers five days a week on a yearly basis. Some are used more than others between seasons on a day-to-day basis by retail buyers within close proximity of the market center. This tends to be the case particularly in the New York area where there is a significant number of mass retailers and in the Los Angeles area where there is less climatic differentiation from season to season. Seasonal schedules for several major fashion markets are presented in Table 8-1.

3. *Where are seasonal fashion markets held?* Today, in major market centers across the country, seasonal fashion markets are housed in enormous market complexes—a far cry from the hotel rooms of yesterday. Sometimes these market centers are a cluster of huge buildings that house not only the seasonal fashion markets, but markets for other industries, such as home furnishings, gifts, and other products.

Usually, one or more of the buildings is designated as an apparel mart and has space for hundreds of manufacturers' showrooms and for the thousands of retailers who throng to the seasonal markets on buying trips. Although some space is allotted each season to temporary showrooms for members of the apparel trade who do not show merchandise on a regular basis or for new firms that have not been able to make permanent arrangements for space, a large percentage of the apparel market space is committed on a long-term basis as permanent showrooms for apparel firms.

In some market centers there is space for numerous kinds of services, such as fashion shows, exhibits, and banquet and other food facilities; offices for buying and merchandising firms; ad-

TABLE 8.1 Seasonal Markets

Seasonal Showings	New York	Los Angeles	Dallas
Summer	First week in January	Third week in January	Fourth week in January
Early fall	Second week in March	Third week in March	Second week in April
Fall	Second week in May	Third week in May	Fourth week in May
Holiday	Second week in August	Fourth week in August	Third week in August
Spring	First week in October	Second week in October	Fourth week in October

vertising agencies; attorneys; travel agencies; barber shops and beauty salons; printing facilities; answering services; and parking for cars.

4. *How do the seasonal fashion markets operate?* Nothing this side of the circus can match the excitement of a seasonal fashion market. The atmosphere is charged with tension, anticipation of good buys and fears of mistakes. Billions of dollars are at stake for the retailer, for the apparel trade, for the textile producers, the other suppliers, and for the consumer.

Most national apparel firms and many smaller regional manufacturers are represented in the market showrooms. The expensive decors are aglow with fashion goods, flanked by tables filled with order pads and pencils; anterooms are afloat in coffee and food; and catering services are prepared to walk in special orders to tempt *important* buyers. The apparel firms' top management is usually present or represented, and the key road sales representatives are in their places. All are ready to pounce on the retail buyers—the apparel firm's selling target, or customer.

The primary purpose of the manufacturer's showroom in the seasonal market is to obtain "paper," signed orders, definite commitments from the retailer for *x* number of dollars, for *x* number of styles, in *x* number of sizes, in *x* number of colors, in *x* number of fabrics, and with specific delivery dates for the coming season. At the close of a major seasonal market the *signed orders* from the retailers become the manufacturers' most valuable estimate of consumer demand, indicating fashion acceptance for the coming season. The retailer serves as the pulse of the consumer for the manufacturers' purposes. Decisions are made based on orders received by the manufacturer as to which fabrics to cut for certain styles and which styles to cut into certain sizes; thus, production starts. Delivery dates must be met so that the retailer can be billed for the order.

5. *What are the buying activities at seasonal fashion markets?* The seasonal fashion market is where the real work starts for the retailer. The number of buyers descending on a market area at a given season depends on the day of the week and the regional reputation of the market. Regardless of when the buyers arrive, there is never enough time to go to the showrooms on the store's "must" list—apparel firms that the retailer relies on for the bulk of the fashion goods that meet the needs of the store's customer. There is never time to eat; hence, the food in the showrooms. Most important of all, there is never enough time to make buying decisions with confidence, to total the cost of merchandise ordered, or to figure out how much the buyer has left to spend.

Nevertheless, the minutes run into midnight, which may find the buyer socializing, being wined and dined by the apparel maker, or working on the totals of orders already signed or to be signed before market days are over for the season. From time to time, depending on the location of the seasonal market, the buyer sneaks an hour or so to see what is happening on the retail scene in the vicinity—departmental decor, merchandise assortments, displays, fixtures, and local newspaper advertisements.

6. *What are some of the services at seasonal fashion markets?* The primary purpose of each seasonal market is for the manufacturers of apparel and associated products to meet to show and sell the newest seasonal merchandise to retail buyers. Each apparel firm provides a full sample line of garments with an assortment of colors, fabrics, and prices. The retail buyer may view the groupings of styles on hangers; however, in some instances, the merchandise is modeled to show the fashion features of the season and to help the retail buyer envision the end use of the product by the consumer. Manufacturers' representatives assist the buyer in making comparisons of styles and in making decisions as to the right assortment of colors, fabrics, prices, and sizes.

Many apparel firms offer additional inducements to buyers in order to gain an advantage over competitors. Some have advertising campaigns, publicity materials, and promotional plans for the retail store's local use with monies allowed on a matching basis. Other services offered may include departmental decor plans, ideas for merchandise arrangements, displays, fixtures, and various merchandising record forms and materials.

Some seasonal fashion markets provide merchandising and promotional seminars; fashion shows that feature and summarize the fashion trends and new directions in styles, fabrics, and colors; programs with panels of retail experts and fashion professionals who give advice to novice buyers and new store owners and discuss new procedures, policies, and controversial issues of interest to retailers.

7. *Where does the merchandise come from at seasonal fashion markets?* Much of the merchandise in the fashion markets is offered by major national apparel firms. The smaller manufacturer may have showrooms only in the seasonal fashion markets in nearby regional areas. A recent study of apparel manufacturers indicated that the larger the number of sales representatives the firm has, the more likely it will have permanent showrooms in several fashion markets in addition to the New York fashion market.[2] Apparel firms showing merchandise in Los Angeles and Dallas also tended to show merchandise in the New York market. In other words, if a small apparel maker has a sample line of fashion goods to sell, he may utilize the facilities of only one seasonal fashion market. As the manufacturer is successful and grows larger, he may take his sample line to other markets throughout the United States, perhaps even abroad. Some seasonal fashion markets in this country will have merchandise from Europe, the Near East, the Far East, South America, Central America, Mexico, and Canada.

8. *How is the seasonal fashion market organized?* Most apparel markets are owned and operated as private enterprises, often by corporate development groups. There is usually a board of directors with representatives from the various groups involved in the market—for example, the apparel firms, the sales representative organization, and the retail store groups using the market. Some executive management personnel may be responsible for various aspects of the operations—for instance, showroom rentals, promotional activities, food services, and maintenance. Each manufacturer and his sales representatives operate the showrooms. This is not a wholesale operation per se. There is no transfer of ownership. The seasonal markets are, in fact, simply a sales promotion (marketing) activity through which the manufacturer sells fashion goods to retail buyers.

The sales representative encourages the retailers he contacts on the road to attend the next seasonal fashion market in the regional area and to see the manufacturer's complete sample line in the showroom. "The salesmen make the markets on the road," in the opinion of numerous apparel makers.

9. *Who attends the seasonal fashion markets?* Most notably, those who attend are the retailers, owners, buyers, assistant buyers, store managers, department managers, merchandise managers, and other store employees. Most fashion markets restrict attendance to the retail trade only and require admission badges obtainable only if a person can meet the specified admissions requirements. Most fashion markets have rigid security policies not only to prevent unqualified attendance, but also to protect the tons of merchandise and the expensive facilities.

Retail stores, both small and large, are represented in every market. In the research referred to previously, it was found that apparel firms using fashion markets other than New York tend to serve small stores, such as boutiques, specialty shops, and junior department stores. Most of the major seasonal fashion markets boast the attendance of buyers from all types of stores, including multiunit department stores, chain stores, and mail-order houses. Buyers from large, multiunit stores probably attend the New York fashion markets regularly and place a larger proportion of total orders season by season. However, these buyers for large stores will visit other seasonal fashion markets and perhaps go abroad once or twice annually, depending on the fashion orientation and competitiveness of the store merchandising policies. Discount outlets, variety stores, mail-order houses, and some mass chain stores may find it more advantageous to deal directly with manufacturers outside of the seasonal market setting because they usually make commitments for huge quantities of merchandise and do their buying further in advance of the consumer season.

SEASONAL FASHION MARKETS

A network of seasonal markets, unique to the distribution process in the fashion industries, has developed in the United States. These seasonal markets for fashion goods are perceived as vital both by manufacturers and retailers. Seasonal fashion markets scheduled in regional centers across the country provide the manufacturer an opportunity to obtain the retail buyers' reactions to the sample lines of apparel before final production decisions are made. Retailers also have an advantage in the seasonal fashion market because they are exposed in advance to the total fashion picture presented in the various showrooms. They can shop numerous manufacturers' lines and can compare differences in quality, price, and styling before placing orders for specific quantities and items of merchandise.

Fashion markets are also scheduled on a seasonal basis in regional centers across the country. A number of cities serve as regional marketing centers for fashion goods in the United States. For example: (1) New York City traditionally has been a dominant fashion market center in the Northeastern region, as well as for the entire nation; (2) Chicago has served the Midwestern region over a long period of time; (3) Atlanta more recently has functioned as a fashion center for the Southeastern region; (4) Dallas has developed to an important status as a market center in the Southwestern region; and (5) Los Angeles has become the focal point of market fashions for the Western region. Other regional markets of importance in the fashion industries are located in San Francisco, Denver, Kansas City, St. Louis, and Miami. Numerous other small fashion markets are scheduled in various other cities throughout the country on a local basis.

A recent study of women's apparel manufacturers in the United States indicated that most of these firms have permanent showrooms in three market centers: New York, Los Angeles, and Dallas, as shown in Table 8.2 New York City has long been known as a national and international fashion market; Dallas and Los Angeles have earned acclaim as regional markets because of the volume of apparel trade and the wide geographic representation of retailers using these two facilities. However, the latter two markets have a long way to go to actually compete with the New York market, as shown by the comparative statistics in Table 8.3. The following description of each of the three seasonal fashion markets fur-

TABLE 8.2 Apparel Manufacturers' Permanent Showroom Locations

Market city	Number of responses	% of total
New York	29	63.0
Los Angeles	19	41.3
Dallas	18	39.1
Other permanent showrooms*	20	43.4

* Atlanta, Chicago, Miami, Charlotte (N.C.), San Francisco, Kansas City, St. Louis, Seattle, Portland (Ore.), Cleveland, Boston, Baltimore, Philadelphia, Honolulu, Indianapolis, Denver, Weathersfield (Conn.).
Source: Edith Ann Scott, "Survey of 46 Apparel Manufacturers in Representative Regions of the U.S." (Master's thesis, Oklahoma State University, 1975).

nishes information on the location and physical facilities, the size and use of markets, seasonal market schedules, significance of the market, and future trends of the market.

New York City

Probably no one fashion market compares with New York City, the mecca of fashion markets. Very little equals the excitement of being where the fashion industry was born in the early 1900s, where it grew up in the twenties and thirties, and where it came of age in the forties and fifties. In New York City, fashion manufacturers, retailers, and experts from all over the world congregate to exchange fashion ideas, fashion wares, and billions of dollars.

At the beginning of each retail buying season the press, American couture designers, and manufacturers of higher-priced clothes take the fashion stage. They are followed by retailers from across the United States and from abroad. These buyers from small, medium, and large stores descend on the Seventh Avenue manufacturers. On the basis of anticipated consumer acceptances of fashion, orders and delivery dates are specified. What happens in a New York seasonal market is of major importance to every fashion manufacturer in the United States—and in the world, for that matter.

TABLE 8.3 Size of New York, Los Angeles, and Dallas Apparel Markets

Type of merchandise	New York City		Los Angeles		Dallas	
	No. of firms	Volume (in $)	No. of firms	Volume (in $)	No. of firms	Volume (in $)
Women's coats and suits	346	750 M	31	53 M	1	600 T
Women's blouses, dresses, and sportswear	1,354	3,300 M	167	325 M	51	220 M
Women's intimate apparel	399	1,200 M	224	40 M	None	None
Men's apparel	768	1,500 M	107	500 M	13	94 M
Totals	2,867	6,750 M	529	918 M	65	315 M

Source: National Credit Office, Marketing and Management Services Division, Specialized Division of Dun & Bradstreet, Inc., New York, 1974. (M = million, T = Thousand)

LOCATION AND PHYSICAL FACILITIES

The New York fashion market is concentrated in the garment district, Seventh Avenue. Modern skyscrapers with manufacturer's offices and showrooms are mixed with old loft-type garment operations. Streets between 33rd and 42nd Street, in the Broadway area, are crowded with retailers from all over the United States and from many foreign countries. A map of the garment center district is shown in Figure 8.1.

The New York City fashion market is still segmented, despite efforts to provide skyscraper buildings for manufacturers' showrooms. Some buildings are well known for a particular type of merchandise. The higher-priced couture trade is concentrated on Seventh Avenue. The buildings numbered 498, 512, 530, and 550 house some of the American greats—Norman Norell, Pauline Trigère, Donald Brooks and Bill Blass. Sportswear, recently king of the mass-production trade, is concentrated in the Broadway area in buildings numbered 1400, 1407, and 1411. The children's wear houses are mostly to the west on Eighth Avenue, though several are located to the east on lower Broadway. The undergarment trade is south and east, on Fifth and Madison Avenues between 29th and 34th Streets. At the peak of the fashion market season, hotels accommodate temporary showrooms for manufacturers. One hotel near the garment district has been used to show boutique-type merchandise of small manufacturers as well as foreign imports.

The seasonal fashion market in New York City is very large. It is segmented both in specialized merchandise and in physical location. Therefore, the market facilities are not visually unified. There is little effort by the market organizations to provide general services for large groups of buyers; however, prominent textile and apparel manufacturers do their own fashion shows, usually on a very elaborate scale—DuPont, Milliken, Jonathan Logan, and Bobbie Brooks, for example. Some of the buildings afford other services, such as advertising agencies, fashion consultants, and eating places, including smart clubs.

THE SIZE AND USE OF THE MARKET

Some indication of the size of the colossal New York fashion market can be drawn from the statistics in Table 8.3. In 1974 more than 60 per cent of the apparel produced in the United States was designed and marketed in New York City. More than $5,000 million in volume was sold annually by the women's wear firms alone. Including men's wear, the figure was close to $7,000 million, from nearly 3,000 firms. Women's blouses, dresses, and sportswear were the largest segment, $3,300 million, from nearly 1,400 firms.

There is no question that the New York fashion market is utilized by most of the stores in the United States, stores of every type—specialty shops, small department stores, chain stores, dis-

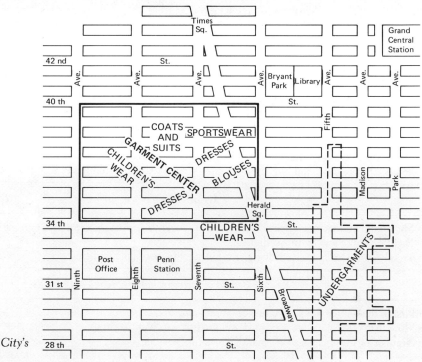

FIGURE 8.1 *New York City's garment center.*

count outlets, and variety stores—and by many stores located abroad. Either through visits by buyers or contacts through resident buying offices, practically every kind and price of fashion goods can be bought in New York. The range and variety of merchandise is considered greater here than any place in the world. You name it— they have it or can get it made for you whenever you want it.

SEASONAL MARKET SCHEDULES

The New York fashion market is open five days a week on a year-round basis and is used heavily on a daily basis by buyers from the New York City stores, such as Lord & Taylor, Bloomingdale's, B. Altman, and Saks Fifth Avenue. The scheduled seasonal markets draw buyers from many stores across the country and from abroad. Some major stores send apparel buyers to the New York market as often as once or twice a month. The seasonal market schedules for the New York fashion market are listed in Table 8.1.

SIGNIFICANCE OF THE MARKET

The New York fashion market is where the garment trades originated and where they grew up. They presently dominate the world fashion trade. In Table 8.4 a summary of factual information about the New York Women's Apparel Market is presented.

FUTURE TRENDS OF THE MARKET

The New York fashion market has a long heritage and it has a justified reputation for having any merchandise a retailer wants. The apparel trade is not as concentrated in this area as formerly, and there has been increasing competition from seasonal fashion markets in other regions of the country. Nevertheless, there is little doubt that the New York fashion market will continue to enjoy its position as the fashion capital of the ready-to-wear world. In the future, the importance of New York City as an international fashion market may be enhanced.

TABLE 8.4 New York Women's Apparel Market

Significance of market

- Historically considered the fashion capital of the United States.
- Considered the world capital for women's ready-to-wear in terms of variety, sales volume, and production.
- Produces all types of women's apparel including coats, suits, day and evening dresses, sportswear, and accessories of all kinds.
- Maintains supremacy in abundance of production knowhow and design talent.
- Remains the nation's largest center for marketing, merchandising, and promoting ladies' ready-to-wear.
- Manufacturing largely done in multi-plant operations (jobber-contractor system).
- Serves retailers small and large from all over the United States and many countries abroad.

Location of physical facilities

- Showroom and factory space concentrated on Seventh Avenue between 35th and 40th Streets and bounded by Eighth Avenue and Sixth Avenue.
- Trend to locating manufacturing plants outside the metropolitan area.

Size of industry in immediate market area

- First in the United States in terms of production.
- More than 60% of apparel designed and produced in New York.
- Number of firms engaged in manufacturing of women's coats, suits, blouses, dresses, and sportswear: about 2,000.
- Annual dollar volume of these firms: $4,050 million (approx).

Source: Scott, op. cit., 1975.

Los Angeles

A giant fashion market for the California area rises in the midst of downtown Los Angeles. The casual color of the West is captured in this California fashion market. Not unlike the New York City garment district in some ways, older buildings in this urban district continue to house apparel firms. Arpege, Patty Woodward, Ernest Straus, and numerous other apparel firms operate showrooms in the buildings where the factories are located. Some maintain an additional showroom in the California Apparel Mart. Throughout the sprawling city of Los Angeles and in outlying areas many of the sportswear and swim wear companies maintain factories and showrooms as they did before the California Mart opened in 1966. Many of the apparel makers on the West Coast now consider the Los Angeles fashion market center as the main outlet for fashion goods. However, San Francisco is still a stronghold of fashion manufacturers and the giant Levi firm maintains a smaller but important fashion market in the vicinity.

This West Coast area is the second most important fashion market in America, and the focal point is the California Mart in Los Angeles. The uniqueness of California fashions is obvious in the excitement of the displays and exhibits in the showrooms. Bright, sharp combinations of colors are found in the groupings of apparel, in the designs of the fabrics, and in the lively wall decor and showroom displays that accent the long corridors in the California Apparel Mart.

The California Mart is a dream come true for the two enterprising brothers who conceived the one market place idea for Los Angeles, a dream come true for the New York retail buyers in search of something different for their customers on Fifth Avenue, and a dream come true for today's consumers, who can find exciting, colorful California sportswear in local retail stores across the country.

LOCATION AND PHYSICAL FACILITIES

The California Mart is in the heart of the central city area of Los Angeles. Prior to the completion of the first two buildings in 1966, retailers usually visited showrooms from factory to factory, covering a large number of miles along the coastal area in one buying trip. The new California Mart building, located at 110 East Ninth Street, eliminates the distance factor for the retail buyer. This fashion market facility was designed to house all types of wearing apparel, accessories, and related goods under one roof—more than 4,000 lines. Many major United States apparel manufacturers maintain showrooms for sales representatives here. Fashions from Europe are displayed, along with those from the Near East, Far East, Mexico, and South America. Retail buyers move about rapidly via the high-speed escalator system or the sixteen elevators. As many as 7,000 individual buyers may come and go to the showrooms during a single day.

This working community comprises twenty floors, including the sublevels used primarily for parking. Displays and showrooms for women's, men's and children's wear and accessories are concentrated on designated floors; linens and domestics are also included. In addition, the Mart provides such services as buying offices and travel agents, two restaurants, a barber shop, a beauty shop, a printing firm, attorneys' offices, and an answering service.

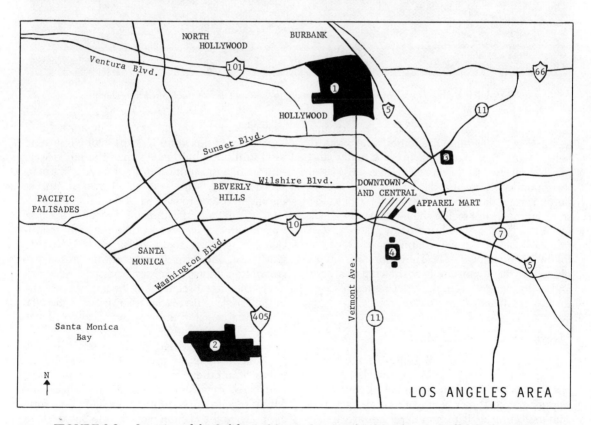

FIGURE 8.2a *Location of the California Mart in Los Angeles. Map key: 1—Griffith Park. 2—Los Angeles International Airport. 3—Dodger Stadium. 4—Coliseum Sports Arena.*

FIGURE 8.2b *The California Mart, Los Angeles. (Courtesy of the California Mart.)*

The main occupants of the Mart are sales representatives, showroom personnel, and clerical help for the manufacturing firm. Usually, the manufacturers' sales representatives use the showroom as home base for their road operations. Several days a week they may travel to the stores in their sales region showing fashion goods to the retail buyers, and one or two days a week they will be in the showroom to analyze and follow up on orders. The showroom personnel often have the responsibility of showing new lines and taking orders while the sales representatives for the manufacturer are on the road.

Size and Use of the Market

The statistics in Table 8.3 indicate the actual size of the fashion market in Los Angeles. It is estimated that this fashion market accounts for approximately 10 per cent of the manufacturing and marketing of all apparel in the country today. However, in women's apparel only, the production amounts to little more than 6 per cent of total sales in the United States. The annual dollar volume of the women's firms alone is around $400 million, which is less than the men's wear volume of $500 million in the Los Angeles market area. The sales volume of manufacturers' shipments soared toward $1,000 million in 1973. Of the total of 529 apparel firms in the Los Angeles area, 422 were women's apparel manufacturers, making coats, suits, blouses, dresses, sportswear, and intimate apparel. In terms of dollar volume, blouses, dresses, and sportswear represent the largest segment of the apparel industry in the Los Angeles market area. In 1974 the total California apparel industry reportedly reached nearly $2,000 million.[3]

The California Mart tends to serve its own regional retailers on a consistent basis and retailers from other areas of the country on a periodic basis. Retail buyers from the Northeast and Midwest go to the California market to get a fresh approach to the fashion picture or to buy the California lines, which often introduce styles, colors, and fabrics not yet shown by manufacturers

View of Central Court Looking North

FIGURE 8.2c *View of Central Court, the California Mart. (Courtesy of the California Mart.)*

on Seventh Avenue. Southeastern and southwestern buyers often visit the California market to buy garments made with lightweight fabrics, which are more appropriate to their climate and attuned to their customers' wants and needs.

The California market area is primarily known for sportswear and swimwear. Some formal wear and elegant "after 5" wear have always been designed in this market, probably stimulated by Hollywood and Beverly Hills social groups. Broad ranges of apparel and accessories at moderate to higher price levels are available in this market.

Seasonal Market Schedules

The California Mart, a super shopping center for retail buyers, operates practically at full speed fifty-two weeks of the year. Retail buyers and resident buyers scan the market lines daily. Although market weeks are scheduled in the California Mart just as in other markets, there seems to be a continual flow of buying activities, rather than the high concentration of buying during the one- or two-week market period characteristic of New York and Dallas. In 1974 five market periods consisted of the summer lines in January, the

transitional lines in March, the fall lines in May, the holiday lines in August, and the spring lines in October. A typical seasonal market schedule for the California Mart is presented in Figure 8.3.

Significance of the Market

The California market area is significant for casual, colorful sportswear, as has been noted previously. However, there is a far more unique element in the focal Los Angeles market center: a combination of experimental design efforts and an unusual variety of consumers, both of which allow for testing innovative fashion ideas. Then, too, climate and an informal life style contribute to the development of the *test-market concept*. The Los Angeles area is considered a test-market for consumer acceptance of styles, colors, fabrics, and other fashion variables.

Table 8.5. contains a summary of factual information relative to the Los Angeles Women's Apparel Market.

Future Trends of the Market

The California Mart has established a reputation for fashions with distinctive features. Some

California Mart Events

APRIL 27-30—WESTERN CHILDREN'S BRAND WAGON FALL OPENING
Sixth Floor

MAY 12-14—HAWAIIAN SHOW
Market Mezzanine

MAY 13—OPENING OF FALL LINES
Fashion Theater

JUNE 15-18—BRIDAL SHOW
Market Mezzanine

JUNE 16-18—WESTERN CHILDREN'S BRAND WAGON OPEN HOUSE
Sixth Floor

AUGUST 12—OPENING OF HOLIDAY LINES
Fashion Theater

AUGUST 24-27—CALIFORNIA BOUTIQUE SHOW
13 Floors– California Mart

AUGUST 24-27—WESTERN CHILDREN'S BRAND WAGON HOLIDAY OPENING
Sixth Floor

AUGUST 25-27—BODY FASHIONS AND INTIMATE APPAREL MARKET
Seventh Floor

FIGURE 8.3 *Typical seasonal market schedule for the California Mart.*

of the California designs acclaimed as "firsts" were truly original: the backless bathing suit of the 1930s shocked America to some extent, but the topless swimsuit created by Gernreich in the 1960s caused reverberations that are still being felt. Other more modest firsts are the topper jacket and pedal pushers. In the future, apparel firms and retailers may use the California test market to great advantage as a barometer for consumer acceptance of styles, colors, and fabrics.

TABLE 8.5 Los Angeles Women's Apparel Market

Significance of market

- Primarily known for sportswear and casual wear, although broader categories and price lines are being produced annually.
- Known as an international merchandise center—products from United States, Canada, the Far East, and Central and South America.
- Presents five major market openings, although Mart is open for business 52 weeks a year.
- Considered a test market for consumer acceptance of styles, colors, and fabrics.
- Size of California Mart recognized as a major factor in marketing of goods—4,000 lines shown annually.

Location of physical facilities

- Showrooms located in California Mart, 110 East Ninth Street, Los Angeles, and other showrooms in nearby factory location.

Size of industry in immediate market area

- Second to New York in terms of production of women's apparel: 6.2% of United States' sales.
- Number of firms manufacturing women's coats, suits, blouses, dresses, and sportswear: 422.
- Annual (1973) dollar volume of these firms: $378 million.

Source: Scott, op. cit., 1975.

It has been noted previously that the California Mart includes merchandise from the Near East and the Far East, as well as from other foreign countries. If world trade and the receptiveness of the consumer continue to increase, the California market area may become a dominant center for fashions from the Orient. Design orientation has turned in this direction from time to time throughout history. However, with the tremendous industrialization in certain regions, such as Japan and China, the import aspects in the California market center have potential mainly because of their strategic geographical location, just as is true with the New York City market center.

Dallas

The size that can only be found in Texas is found in a huge market complex, located in the heart of Texas, not far from downtown Dallas, or "Big D" as it is usually called in the Southwest. The "wide open spaces" and "Don't fence me in" feelings that symbolize Texas are here in the great hall of the Apparel Mart, in the openness of the Home Furnishings Mart, and in the vastness of the new International Trade Hall. This Dallas market complex is considered one of the world's unique merchandising market centers because of the following features:

(1) The world's most unusual wholesale merchandising market; (2) Home Furnishings Mart, Trade Mart, Apparel Mart, Decorative Center, Market Hall, and International Market Hall; (3) furniture, floor coverings, lamps, gifts, decorative accessories, housewares, hardware, jewelry, toys, wearing apparel, shoes, and fashion accessories; (4) more than 10,000 manufacturers and importers show in nineteen markets a year; and (5) in excess of 150,000 retail buyers come annually from thirty-two states and several foreign countries.

One of the focal points of this market complex is the Apparel Mart. This is where the action is during the seasonal fashion markets. Technically called a regional market, the Apparel Mart is the largest building of its kind in the world. More lines are sold here than in any other building in the world, according to spokesmen for the Apparel Mart, who prefer to call it a national marketing center.

LOCATION AND PHYSICAL FACILITIES

The Apparel Mart is part of the Dallas Market Center, a cluster of giant buildings, each a buying center for its own industry. It is located just off the Stemmons Freeway, one of the main traffic arteries into the Dallas area and in close proximity to the innovative facilities of the Dallas/Fort Worth Regional Airport.

The developers of the Dallas Apparel Mart originated the concept of unifying and concentrating the location of showrooms for apparel manufacturers in order to have other coordinating activities. Operating with a board of directors, both manufacturers and retailers are provided with the conveniently organized services so vital to the smooth flow of fashion goods to the retailer.

Permanent showrooms are maintained in the Dallas Mart by apparel firms in the southwestern area, as well as by major manufacturers across the country. According to a recent study, by Edith Ann Scott, apparel firms with permanent showrooms in the New York and Los Angeles markets also have permanent showrooms in the Dallas Apparel Mart.

One of the unique facilities of the Apparel Mart is the Great Hall. The walls scale a height of 57 feet, forming the center core of the Mart, and balconies open onto the Great Hall at each floor level. Used for fashion extravaganzas and various other purposes, this facility accommodates 4,000 auditorium style and 2,400 banquet style—excluding the standing and seating room on the balconies. Outstanding among the many services offered by the Dallas Apparel Mart are those of the fashion director and assistants who have generated the activities that accelerated and maximized the impact of the Dallas Apparel Mart on the fashion world.

The original Apparel Mart building opened in 1963 and has been expanded three times. It now provides concentrated areas for couture manufacturers (Group III), for men's wear, and for other merchandise classifications. The newest feature is "The Territory," including frontier style

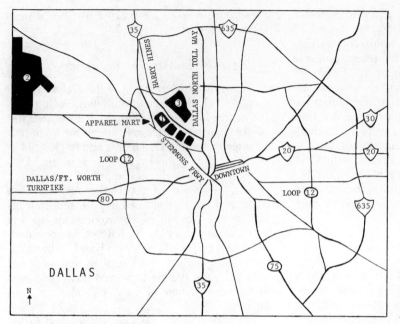

FIGURE 8.4 *Location of the Dallas Apparel Mart. Map Key: 1–Apparel Mart. 2–Dallas/Fort Worth Regional Airport. 3–Love Field Airport.*

showrooms for the western wear manufacturers. Naturally, the Southwest is where the action has been and still is when it comes to western wear, and now the Dallas Apparel Mart has another claim to fame—first with The Territory per se.

Following is a summary of the features of the Dallas market center:

1. It has over $1½ billion in soft goods sales alone (not including furniture, gifts, etc.).
2. It is the largest building of its kind in the world.
3. It is the new capital of soft goods buying.
4. Some 150,000 retail buyers visit it each year.
5. Apparel manufacturers fill the 1,200 to 1,500 permanent showrooms and the 350 to 500 temporary showrooms.
6. The original four-floor building now has a five-floor annex.
7. The Great Hall is used for food and fashion shows as well as other market activities.

SIZE AND USE OF MARKET

The Dallas Apparel Mart competes in many ways with the California Mart in Los Angeles for the place of second in size to the New York market. However, the statistics in Table 8.3 tell a dif-

ferent story. The Dallas Apparel Mart is also small compared with New York. It is estimated that only about 3 per cent of the apparel manufacturing and marketing in the country is contributed by the Dallas market region. Women's apparel accounts for only 1.4 per cent of the total sales volume in the United States. There are only sixty-five firms represented, with sales slightly more than $300 million in volume. Almost $100 million of this volume is contributed by the thirteen men's apparel firms. The apparel produced in the women's categories is primarily blouses, dresses, and sportswear, and there are no firms reported in the intimate apparel group.

The Dallas market area serves two distinctive types of retailers. The seasonal markets are attended mainly by buyers from the smaller department stores and specialty shops in the central and southwestern regions of the country. The large, multiunit department stores in major cities still concentrate buying activities in the New York area and abroad with only a few trips to the California market each year. However, many of the apparel firms in the Dallas area serve the giant international chains through contracts and commitments arranged outside the seasonal market setting; Sears and Penney are examples.

The apparel manufacturers in the Dallas market have been noted for copying or knocking off garments that are best sellers in other markets. The market is known for serving the middle-of-the-road retailer with moderately priced copies of apparel the consumer has already accepted and wants. The Dallas market has also been called a polyester jungle, because the apparel firms replaced cotton with synthetics early in the modern textile era. Polyester is appropriate for the climatic conditions in that regional area and has the advantage of wash-and-wear for the consumer. There has been little attempt in the Dallas market to compete on a national scale with the couture firms. One or two apparel firms, however, do serve retailers in the higher-priced and more fashion-oriented stores.

SEASONAL MARKET SCHEDULES

The Apparel Mart is just one of the many markets attracting retailers to the Dallas area. Although most of the showrooms are open several days a week, the Dallas Apparel Mart is predominantly a seasonal operation. However, because some of the other markets in the complex draw retailers at different times, there is some trade in the Apparel Mart between the scheduled seasonal fashion markets as noted in Table 8.1.

SIGNIFICANCE OF THE MARKET

The Dallas market is midway between the east and west coasts and serves uniquely in the production and distribution of fashion goods. Known for a moderate-priced merchandise, the Apparel Mart serves the retailer who is the purchasing agent for America's great middle class. Apparel manufacturers that contribute to this market are adept at mass-producing styles that are particularly aimed at volume retailing. A summary of factual information pertaining to the Dallas Women's Apparel Market is presented in Table 8.6.

TABLE 8.6 Typical Seasonal Schedule for the Dallas Apparel Mart.

Jan. 3–5	Tennis Show at Dallas	July 2–8	Christmas Gift, Jewelry & Housewares Show
Jan. 9–11	Southwestern Men's & Boys' Western Wear Apparel Market	July 10–15	Summer Homefurnishings Market
Jan. 16–21	Winter Homefurnishings Market	July 31–Aug. 2	Tennis Show at Dallas
Jan. 19–21	CONDES IV—Dallas Contract/Design Show	Aug. 14–17	Southwestern Men's & Boys' Spring & Summer Clothing & Early Spring Sportswear Market
Jan. 29–Feb. 3	Women's & Children's Midsummer Apparel Market	Aug. 21–23	Southwestern Shoe Travelers Spring Shoe Show
Feb. 13–16	Southwestern Men's & Boys' Fall Clothing & Summer Sportswear Apparel Market	Aug. 27–Sept. 1	Women's & Children's Midwinter Apparel Market
Feb. 20–25	Spring Gift, Jewelry & Housewares Show	Sept. 4–9	Fall Gift, Jewelry & Housewares Show
Mar. 13–15	Southwestern Shoe Travelers Fall Shoe Show	Sept. 4–8	Cosmesis Club of Texas, Cosmetic Show
Mar. 20–24	Dallas Toy Show	TBA	September Toy Show
Mar. 26–31	Women's & Children's Early Fall Apparel Market	Oct. 2–5	Southwestern Men's & Boys' Spring & Holiday Apparel Market
Apr. 17–20	Southwestern Men's & Boys' Fall & Back-to-School Apparel Market	Oct. 29–Nov. 3	Women's & Children's Spring Apparel Market
Apr. 24–25	Homefurnishings, Contract, Gift & Accessories Market Days	Oct. 30–31	Homefurnishings, Contract, Gift & Accessories Market Days
May 21–26	Women's & Children's Fall Apparel Market		

TABLE 8.7 Dallas Women's Apparel Market

Significance of market

• Noted primarily for production of medium and popular priced sportswear and dresses.
• Designs largely adaptations of couture designs to meet consumer demand.
• Manufacturing done largely by the inside shop method.
• Promotes apparel made in Southwest.
• Serves primarily retailers from central and southern parts of the United States, although exhibitors and buyers come from all states and a few foreign countries.
• Five women's and children's markets are held annually.
• Apparel Mart structure noted for its size—1,300,000 square feet of permanent and temporary showroom space—and for its convenience—over 4,000 lines shown under one roof.
• Area of Apparel Mart designated exclusively for showing of Western wear.

Location of physical facilities

• Part of Dallas Market Center complex.
• Showrooms located in Apparel Mart, 2300 Stemmons Freeway.

Size of industry in immediate market area

• Produces significant amount of women's wear: at least 1.4% of United States' sales.
• Number of firms producing women's coats, suits, blouses, dresses, and sportswear: 52.
• Annual (1973) volume of these firms: $220,600 (approx).

Source: Scott, op. cit., 1975.

FUTURE TRENDS

Though technically classified as a regional market, the Dallas market has astronomic growth potential in terms of dollars and cents. With its central location and its reputation for serving the moderate-price retailer in both small stores and large chain stores, the Dallas Apparel Mart may serve an increasing number of retailers from coast to coast in the future. The Apparel Mart also is in a strategic location to provide an international marketing facility for Mexico and Central and South America. If the future of retailing is written in dollar volume and best sellers, then the future for the Apparel Mart may well exceed speculations made by the Dallas developers who generated the market complex concept and brought it to fruition.

Other Important Regional Market Centers

The fashion industries are not dependent on the three major markets alone, although it is es-timated that approximately 75 per cent of the fashion goods sold by retailers in the United States are marketed through them. They dominate the fashion industries, and they are strategic in terms of location. Nevertheless, numerous other regional markets provide contact for retailers with the apparel industry.

ATLANTA

The *Atlanta Merchandise Mart* is a major part of Atlanta's Peachtree Center complex. The Apparel Market showroom facilities and services provided in the Mart are similar to those of the three major markets previously discussed. Apparel categories represented at thie market include couture, women's, men's, boys', children's, and accessory lines. The market schedules five seasonal openings annually and is partially open on a daily basis between market seasons. The Atlanta apparel market is one of the fastest-growing market centers in the country.

MIAMI

The Miami Merchandise Mart serves the apparel industry in the Florida area. The showrooms provide space for apparel, gifts, and decorative accessories; however, swimwear and resort wear are the primary classifications of merchandise marketed at these seasonal markets. It is estimated that the apparel industry in the state accounts for 8 per cent of the production of women's, misses', juniors', and children's wear in the country.[4]

CHICAGO

The Chicago Merchandise Mart houses more than 800 apparel firms. A new Apparel Center complex opened in 1976, and the facilities were planned to serve the better ready-to-wear firms, including the fashion creators of New York. The Chicago market area has long been an important link in the fashion-marketing process in the United States and continues to serve an established group of major retailers.

KANSAS CITY

The Kansas City Trade Mart houses the showrooms for the women's and children's apparel firms in the region and for other manufacturers throughout the country. This market has traditionally been known for medium- to low-priced dresses, work clothes, and boys' wear. Approximately 1 per cent of women's and children's fashion goods are manufactured in the general vicinity.

OTHER MARKETS

Several other market centers have made special contributions to the distribution process in the fashion industries. Some examples are St. Louis, junior wear and shoes; Philadelphia, millinery; Boston, rainwear; and Denver, Western wear. In addition to these fashion markets, there is a network of local markets that are scheduled by organizations and usually sponsored by manufacturers' sales representatives. These road salesmen congregate in designated cities on scheduled dates, usually following the major seasonal markets, and set up temporary minishowrooms in hotels, motels, and exhibit halls.

With numerous other marketing activities, these various fashion markets accelerate, stimulate, and maintain the flow of fashion goods to the retailer. Thus, the fashion-marketing process reaches down to the retailer, the purchasing agent for the consumer, who is the focus of Part Three of this book.

END OF CHAPTER GUIDE

Review, Discussion and Evaluation Guide

Study of this chapter should enable the student to
A. Develop and give evidence of the following kinds of competencies:
  1. Awareness of the unique operation of the seasonal fashion market systems in terms of the direct flow of fashion goods to the consumer in the United States
  2. Understanding of the growth and development of the regional fashion markets in the United States
  3. Knowledge of the present status of the fashion market system in the United States in terms of the nature of services provided for apparel manufacturers and retail buyers
  4. Ability to describe three of the major regional fashion markets in terms of location, physical facilities, size, use, significance, and future trends
  5. Awareness of other fashion markets in the United States and some of the contributions of each to the fashion marketing process
B. Develop and/or clarify concepts related to the following key words or phrases:
  1. fashion market centers 2. regional fashion markets 3. seasonal fashion market schedule 4. manufacturer's showroom 5. significance of markets 6. market facilities 7. retail buyer 8. market size 9. paper (signed orders) 10. buying activities 11. market services 12. New York fashion market 13. Dallas fashion market 14. Los Angeles fashion market 15. seasonal merchandise 16. New York garment center

Extended Classroom Learning Experiences:

A. Make a survey of five or more merchants and/or retail buyers in your community or nearby shopping center. Determine where seasonal fashion merchandise is purchased.

1. Ask about the following methods of purchasing merchandise:
   a. from a catalog b. from a manufacturer's sales representative c. from a regional market center d. from a resident buying office e. other methods (list)
2. Ask about the location of regional markets used by the store buyer:
   a. Which major market centers are used—New York City, Los Angeles, Dallas, or others?
   b. What type of merchandise is purchased at each?
   c. How often does the store buyer go to various regional market centers?
   d. Why does the buyer prefer to go to certain regional market centers rather than others?
3. Write a brief summary of the information you collected from the five or more merchants or retail buyers in your community or nearby shopping center.

B. Interview one or more retail buyers who goes regularly to one of the three major market centers.
   1. Obtain their reactions and comments to the five or more of the nine specific questions about seasonal markets listed in this chapter.
   2. Report orally to your class or write a report summarizing the information you gained related to the questions you asked during your interview.

C. Interview one retail buyer at a store that uses a resident buying office.
   1. Ask for some of the following information:
      a. The location of the resident buying office.
      b. The kind of merchandise sent to the store.
      c. Services provided by the resident buying office.
      d. Kinds of forms and procedures used in communicating the stores' needs to the resident buying office.
      e. Advantages and disadvantages of resident buying offices.
      f. Other reasons for using resident buying offices.
   2. Report orally to your class or write a summary of the information you gained related to the questions you asked during your interview.

D. Arrange for a manager of a chain store in your community to talk to the class about the method used in obtaining merchandise through a central buying office. Examples: Penney's, Sears, Montgomery Ward, or other regional chain stores.

E. Read two or more of the articles listed here, or research current periodicals or trade journals and select two or more articles related to one of the concepts suggested in the "Review, Discussion, and Evaluation."
   1. Prepare note cards while reading each article.
   2. Using your note cards, write a brief summary indicating the relationship of each article to concepts presented in this chapter.
   3. Using your note cards, give an oral report in your class and point out the important facts in the articles.

Suggested Articles

CHAPMEN, HEDLEY. "The Early California Market, Los Angeles." *The California Apparel News*, 1971.

"Dallas With a New Viewpoint." *Clothes*, October 15, 1974.

GRAHAM, JANE. "I Remember, I Remember." *American Fashion Magazine*, Spring Market Issue, October 1973.

GRAHAM, JANE. "The Dallas Dress.' NOW: *The Magazine for North Texas*, November 1971.

"New York: Fashion Capital of What?" *Clothes*, October 15, 1974.

NOTES

[1] Jessie Stuart, *The American Fashion Industry*. Boston: Simmons College, 1956, pp. 20–38.

[2] Edith Ann Scott, "Exploratory Study of Selected Fashion Markets in the United States and Their Use by Apparel Manufacturers" (Master's thesis, Oklahoma State University, 1975).

[3] United California Bank, Research and Planning Division, *California Apparel Industry*, revised. Los Angeles, 1974, p. 6.

[4] Jeanette Jarnow and Beatrice Judelle, *Inside the Fashion Business*. New York: Wiley, 1974, p. 112.

PART Three

Fashion Retailers

*M*OST FASHION merchandise is shipped directly from the production line in the factory to retail stores across the nation. Local, regional, and national retailers purchase fashion goods in the seasonal fashion markets or from manufacturers' representatives and provide an assortment of fashion goods and services in stores conveniently located for consumers. Thus is the fashion-marketing process completed.

Local fashion merchants search the apparel and accessory markets in advance of each season in order to keep a continuous array of fashions for the various consumer groups in the community. A few fashion merchants have received national acclaim for creative marketing: Stanley Marcus provided fashion leadership for Neiman Marcus, Dallas's world-famous specialty store; Hector Escobosa shaped the fashion image of I. Magnin, the San Francisco-based specialty store; Marshall Field not only molded the fashion image of the great department store in Chicago that bears his name, but also developed many basic retail concepts; Geraldine Stutz introduced the boutique, which rejuvenated the sedate specialty store known as Henri Bendel in New York City; Dorothy Shaver stirred the spark of fashion that continues to burn at Lord & Taylor, one of Fifth Avenue's leading specialty stores in New York City; and certainly J. C. Penney should be recognized for the important role he played in bringing soft goods to consumers in towns and cities throughout the United States.

The ingenious and tireless efforts of these and other fashion merchants have created all sizes and kinds of stores and have developed buying and selling techniques uniquely appropriate to the fashion industries. Part Three provides information about the retail stores that distribute fashion goods; the merchandising activities involved in retailing fashion goods; and the concepts used in buying and selling various kinds of fashion goods.

Chapter 9, "Fashion Stores," discusses the fashion image of contemporary retailers in the United States and the impact of fashion on mass retailing in specialty stores, department stores, small shops, and giant multiunit retail organizations. Emphasis is on how these stores operate and gear their merchandising policies particularly to retailing fashion goods.

Chapter 10, "Fashion Merchandising," describes fashion's buying-selling cycle, the fashion-merchandising concept, and the major responsibilities of buying and selling fashion goods, along with the impact of the fashion concept on buying and selling. The fashion cycle is interpreted in terms of the buying cycle, the selling-use cycle, promotional message goals, fashion market segments, and some characteristics of various consumer groups.

9
Fashion Stores

Fashion is big business at the retail level in the United States. There are nearly two million retail firms throughout the country. Retail sales have already passed the trillion dollar mark annually. Most significantly, the retail segment of our American economy contributes approximately 40 per cent of the total Gross National Product (GNP). Today, retailing *is* fashion—the right merchandise, at the right price, in the right place, for today's fashion-oriented consumer.

Fashion merchandise, as we learned in previous chapters, is shipped directly from the production line in the factory to retail stores across the nation. Local, regional, and national retailers provide consumers with an assortment of fashion goods and services in a myriad of stores conveniently located throughout the country.

In the past, the term *fashion merchandise* has been more often associated with women's apparel and accessories. Today, however, fashion is important to all age groups and to various socioeconomic, cultural, and ethnic groups. Children and teenagers have their own fashion ideas and frequently make the final decisions in purchasing fashion goods. Young boys and girls know what is new on the fashion scene. Interestingly enough, many men are just as interested in fashion forecasts as are women. Fashion is important in almost every category of retail goods—in food, furnishings, housing materials, and other consumer products. Changes in the fashion profiles of

American consumers are reflected in the retail stores.

In this chapter we will examine the concepts of leading fashion stores in the various regions of our country, consider the operation and merchandise policies of major types of fashion stores, review pertinent facts about retailing in the United States, and note some problems and trends in retailing fashion goods.

THE FASHION IMAGE

The fashion looks of the season can be bought at many price levels in towns and cities across our nation. Numerous women in each community could probably vie for the best-dressed title anywhere in the country. They wear great fashion looks for various social occasions, and they wear equally fashionable clothes for other occasions—at home, to the grocery store, to the golf course, to the laundry, and for other daily activities. These women may shop around or just pick up the current fashions in local stores. On the other hand, some women may maintain their fashionable wardrobes by indulging in periodic fashion safaris to regional shopping centers or to nationally known fashion centers—perhaps in Los Angeles, Dallas, St. Louis, Chicago, New York City, Atlanta, Denver, or even abroad.

FIGURE 9.1 *Leading fashion stores in the United States.*

Within the map:

Portland
Bon Marche

Chicago
Marshall Field
Carson Pirie Scott
Charles A. Stevens
Saks Fifth Avenue

Boston
Filenes
Lord and Taylor

Denver
Denver Dry Goods
May and Company
Neusteders
Joslins

Kansas City
Halls
Swansons
Hartzfelds

St. Louis
Stix Baer and Fuller
Famous Barr
Neiman-Marcus
Saks Fifth Avenue
Bonwit Teller

New York
Bloomingdales
Saks Fifth Avenue
Lord and Taylor
Bonwit Teller
Bergdorf Goodman
Henri Bendel

San Francisco
I. Magnin
Bullocks

Atlanta
Richs
Davidsons
Saks
Lord and Taylor
Neiman-Marcus

Los Angeles
Bullocks Wilshire
I. Magnin
Robinson
Gucci

Dallas
Neiman Marcus
Titche-Goettinger
Sanger Harris
Lord and Taylor

Houston
Foleys
Sakowitz
Joskes
Neiman-Marcus

Miami
Burdines

Fashion Stores

First, we will look at the fashion image of some of the leading retail stores in the United States. The location of some of these stores is indicated on the map, Figure 9-1. Numerous other stores do a significant fashion business in these cities and in others but are well known only in their region. There are also thousands of small fashion shops and boutiques whose fashion image is known only to the comparatively small clientele they serve.

Today, in the United States, the fashion store image is associated with two major types of retail groups: limited-line stores, a specialty-type operation; and general merchandise stores, a departmental-type operation.

Many leading fashion stores are known for their unique specialty-type operations. These stores carry a limited line of related fashion merchandise that appeals to a select consumer group—the budget-minded woman, couture- or designer-minded women, businessmen, teenage girls or boys, and children.

Some of the leading fashion stores are large department stores that carry not only fashions for women, men, and children, but also have a wide range of consumer goods for other family needs—furniture, appliances, hardware, and garden supplies.

Following is a discussion of the distinctive fashion image of several of these major types of retail stores in various regions: the East Coast, middle America, and the West Coast.

The East Coast

New York City is not only the major fashion center in the East Coast region, but it also ranks first as a national and international fashion center, as discussed in Part Two. There are a number of leading fashion stores in the area. Fifth Avenue has traditionally been known for its fashion stores as well as for the Easter Parade. Six of these leading retail stores—Bergdorf Goodman, Bonwit Teller, Henri Bendel, Saks Fifth Avenue, Lord & Taylor, and Bloomingdales—have developed a unique fashion image.

At the upper end of Fifth Avenue, near Central Park, stands *Bergdorf Goodman*, the epitome of fashion among retail specialty stores. Bergdorf's was founded in 1901 to cater to the carriage trade, the elite of the era whose fashion needs were met with the finest made-to-order clothes money could buy. Bergdorf's veered from that course briefly, when the confusion of the late sixties pushed it into high-quality ready-to-wear with a custom-fitting touch where needed or wanted. But in the mid-1970s, Bergdorf Goodman returned to high fashion custom clothing, featuring Dior, Givenchy, and St. Laurent.

Bonwit Teller, also located in the Central Park area of Fifth Avenue, has enjoyed the reputation of a fine specialty store since its fashion image was defined in the 1930s by one of the first women presidents of a major retail firm, Hortense Odlam. Bonwit's has consistently recognized and promoted creative design in the fashion world, both in the United States and abroad. Its Fifth Avenue window displays have been designed even by Salvador Dali, the surrealist artist. The focus on contemporary fashion environment is carried out in the several Bonwit stores in the eastern part of the country and in the newer Beverly Hills store.

Just off Fifth Avenue, in the Central Park vicinity, *Henri Bendel's* Geraldine Stutz has reigned as the queen of the boutique concept since she became president in the early 1960s and rejuvenated Bendel's fashion image using innovative merchandising. A specialty store with a boutique atmosphere, created through emphasis on decor, lighting, displays, and a special kind of fashion savvy, Bendel's image is attributed to management expertise.

Midway down Fifth Avenue, near St. Patrick's Cathedral and Rockefeller Center, stands *Saks Fifth Avenue*. Saks is more of a fashion institution than a specialty store, although it is classified as such in the annals of retailing. It maintains a reputation for exclusive fashions selected from markets all over the world. Fashion leadership in men's, women's, and children's wear was the unmistakable goal of the founder, Adam Gimbel. This fashion image has been maintained in the more than thirty Saks stores located across the country, even though some of the stores are much smaller and more specialized in merchandising groupings for resort areas such as Florida.

FIGURE 9.2 *Bergdorf Goodman, women's specialty store in New York City. (Courtesy of Bergdorf Goodman.)*

FIGURE 9.3 *Lord & Taylor, Fifth Avenue. New York City. View of the street floor.* (*Courtesy of Lord & Taylor.*)

Although there are several other fashion stores along Fifth Avenue, only one other retail firm has made an indelible imprint with its fashion image, *Lord & Taylor*. Here, too, the work of a woman set a fashion course in retailing— Dorothy Shaver in the 1930s. The dazzle and flair of fashion are apparent in the store's decor, displays, and windows. The management concept that guides the several Lord & Taylor stores places few restrictions on promotional efforts, which are fashion-oriented. This specialty store was a leader in developing a youthful fashion concept consistent with the cultural changes and the contemporary life styles in the United States.

Not numbered among the Fifth Avenue specialty stores, *Bloomingdale's*, on the upper east side of New York City, has an unquestioned fashion reputation as a department store. The fashion concept has been expanded into almost every line of merchandise the consumer could ask for. From the leading designer boutiques to the shopping area for customers who are looking for markdowns and sample merchandise, the focus of Bloomingdale's is on fashion. From the de-

signer furniture displays to the "paint it yourself" department, it is fashion all the way. Bloomingdale's, too, has captured the youthful spirit of contemporary life styles in every type of merchandise and in a wide range of prices.

In this group of fashion stores selected from the New York City area, we have recognized *fashion images and concepts* of several types of retailers. Large or small, these fashion stores are revered by many as an integral part of the fashion industries in the United States and in the world.

Other fashion stores have achieved similar acclaim. A few from among these many great fashion stores across the country will suffice as illustrations: Neiman-Marcus, Dallas; Marshall Field, Chicago; Halls, Kansas City; I. Magnin, San Francisco; Bullocks Wilshire and Gucci, Los Angeles. These six stores have been selected in order to underline several fashion concepts important to today's retail setting.

MIDDLE AMERICA

Neiman-Marcus is a name synonymous with fashion all over the world. Stanley Marcus's fashion concept matched the bigness of Texas and the untamed spirit of the West. Where else in the retail world would a Chinese junk or "his and hers" jet airplanes be considered *fashion?* Neiman-Marcus has led Texas and the world to think *big* when they think of fashion. The fall fortnight extravaganzas initiated by Stanley Marcus have been matched by few other retailers. The feature of these annual fortnights is the presentation of the Neiman Marcus Fashion Designer Award, which is coveted in the fashion design world. A fresh yellow rose of Texas may appear on top of the ice cream flower pot you ordered for dessert under a French name in the famed Zodiac Room. The specialty store is the subject of Stanley Marcus' book, *Who's Minding the Store?* (Boston, Little Brown, 1974).

Marshall Field, the store renowned for the slogan "Give the lady what she wants," has done just that in terms of fashion for three quarters of a century. One of the original group of retailers who served the carriage trade, this huge department store stands today as a fashion monument in Chicago, a tribute to its founder. Old World atmosphere still exudes from the walnut-paneled walls of the tea room on one of the upper floors. The merchandise on each floor represents the latest in fashion from each corner of the world. The same fashion image exists in the elegant Chicago designer salon and in the home furnish-

FIGURE 9.4a *Neiman-Marcus. The main store, located in downtown Dallas. (Courtesy of Neiman-Marcus.)*

FIGURE 9.4b *Neiman-Marcus, Bal Harbour, Florida. (Courtesy of Neiman-Marcus.)*

ings and in the men's and children's departments—quality and innovation—fashion at its best.

Halls is a fashion showcase that was an original concept at its birth early in the 1960s. The Hallmark Card Corporation of Kansas City took a contemporary approach to retailing, in some ways giving the effect of a museum of modern art, and implanted it in a 1920s Spanish-style shopping center. The Plaza was one of the first attempts to move retailing to the consumer—the elite of Kansas City, in this instance. The fashion image at Halls is one of classic elegance—the new, the unusual, the one-of-a-kind—displayed in dramatic settings designed to express the fashion tempo of the merchandise and the concept of this specialty shop. Traditionally, fashion has been shown in a salon atmosphere with the merchandise out of sight, except for several exquisite interior displays of the latest designs. This different approach to fashion at Halls has had an impact on retailing in the last decade.

THE WEST COAST

I. Magnin, with several major fashion stores in the California area, has kept pace with the great women's specialty stores in New York City and throughout the world. Theirs is a chronicle of fashion, every step of the way. The ruling concept in the original San Francisco store ensured that women need look no further to find the latest fashion creations from American designers and European couture. The I. Magnin clientele, cosmopolitan in nature due to the cultural milieu of the city of San Francisco, lends an air of sophistication to the fashion image. As a fashion store, I. Magnin has been equaled by few retailers in the country.

Bullocks Wilshire is the pride of Los Angeles and of Southern California. It is a 1930s architectural tribute to fashion and the major retail contribution to the movie star clientele in the Beverly Hills area. It is a specialty store with an atmosphere more like that of an elegant hotel, an atmosphere created by a palm-laden veranda, regal doormen, a canopy for chauffeur-driven limousines, and the marble walls of the interiors. Although some of the exterior palms had to give way to parking lots for the sports cars of its customers, the store's fashion image has been maintained on the inside, much to the delight of the sedately inclined mature clientele and somewhat to the indignation of the youth cult so prominent in Los Angeles. Nevertheless, Bullocks Wilshire

FIGURE 9.5 *Halls' Plaza, Kansas City, Missouri. (Courtesy of Halls' Plaza.)*

still spells fashion in Los Angeles. It is a fashion entity separate from the other Bullocks stores.

Like a few of Hollywood's leading ladies, *Gucci's* went straight to top billing after its Los Angeles opening in the Beverly Hills area. Famous for being a fashion merchant from Italy, Dr. Gucci is an economist and a businessman of note in the leather industry in his native land. Gucci's retail concept is elegance for the connoisseur of fashion. The fashion image is individual attire for which the total effect is of a completely coordinated fashion look. Fashion is conceived and designed with a specific clientele in mind—one that wants to be distinctively dressed, one who wants to create a personal fashion image. Exquisite merchandise, once available only to movie queens, now can be found at Gucci's and in other fashion boutiques along Rodeo Street in Beverly Hills.

In describing each of these twelve fashion stores we have made a distinction between the fashion image of four small specialty stores that carry a limited line of women's, men's, and/or children's merchandise (Gucci, Henri Bendel, Bergdorf Goodman, and Halls) and six large specialty stores (Bonwit Teller, Saks Fifth Avenue, Lord & Taylor, Neiman-Marcus, I. Magnin, and Bullocks Wilshire). The other two retail firms included are large department stores (Marshall Field and Bloomingdale's) that carry a wide general line of merchandise—apparel, home furnishings, and other items. Most of these fashion stores operate in a central city location with one or more stores located in suburban areas and/or in other cities across the country.

Mass Retailers of Fashion

It is not possible to conclude a discussion of the fashion store image in the United States without mentioning another aspect of the fashion concept in retailing. Fashion for the masses *is* Macy's Herald Square, one of the largest stores in the world for more than half a century. An unusual fashion image has been merged with the promotional cry of "You can buy it cheaper at Macy's." It was perhaps at Macy's that the designer dress first came face to face with its knock-off. Some say that the concept "fashion, at every price, all together under one roof" was born at Macy's. Macy's reportedly has everything else under the sun in their many stores from East to West in several major regional divisions.

Perhaps we should use the phrase *retailers of fashion* when we speak of Macy's rather than the term *fashion store*. If we do this, then we can quickly add other stores such as Abraham & Strauss, Bamberger's, Alexander's, Korvette's, Gimbel's, and Ohrbach's in the New York City area; Rich's of Atlanta; Stix Baer and Fuller and Famous Barr of St. Louis; Foley's of Houston; Joske's and Frost Bros. of San Antonio; and Titche-Goettinger and Sanger Harris of Dallas. The list could include J. C. Penney, Sears, and other retail and mail-order organizations. These and numerous other stores could be considered retailers of fashion. Fashion for the masses is the concept that permeates today's competitive retail scene.

Fashion Image

Our purpose in this chapter is not to list all the prominent fashion stores, but rather to identify some of the retail concepts related to the unique fashion image of a representative group of retail organizations. These concepts are concerned with customer approach, merchandise assortments, store environment, and fashion obligations.

Customer Approach. Fashion retailers are concerned with developing an individualized approach to the customers they serve by (1) establishing a personal relationship with the customer, (2) really caring about the customer, (3) desiring to help meet the customer's needs, (4) taking pride in serving the customer, (5) trying to give the customer what he or she wants, (6) building the customer's confidence in the store, and (7) seeking to know the customer's life style.

Merchandise Assortments. Fashion retailers strive to make available an assortment of current fashions to match the life styles of the customers they serve with (1) seasonal fashions in a range to satisfy personal fashion desires and needs, (2) distinctive fashions that reflect trends in the fashion world, (3) quality fashions in keeping with the customer's price level, and (4) exclusive fashions that will give the customer an opportunity to express individuality.

Store Environment. Fashion retailers attempt to create a store environment that reflects the tempo of fashion for the customers they serve by (1) attuning the interior decor to the customers' life style, (2) creating a fashion personality for the store in the mind of the customer, (3) generating excitement and expectation in the mind of the customer, and (4) providing an inviting atmosphere to motivate the customer to return.

Fashion Obligation. Fashion retailers seek to fulfill the roles of fashion leader and fashion educator in their communities. As *fashion leaders* they (1) provide news of trends in the fashion world in the United States and abroad, (2) direct the customers along the fashion pathway from season to season, (3) generate customer anticipation for each fashion innovation, (4) work with apparel manufacturers to create fashions for the customers the store serves, (5) search for fashion goods that will develop the customer's fashion awareness, and (6) experiment to identify the range of the customer's fashion acceptance.

As *fashion educators* they serve (1) to provide fashion information for the customer—what's happening in the fashion world, the textile industry, the apparel trade, and the world fashion centers; (2) to develop an experimental attitude and fashion judgment in customers; (3) to help the customer learn to analyze fashion trends; (4) to assume the responsibility for improving fashion understanding in the community; and (5) to build the confidence of the customer and the community in the fashion leadership of the store.

Each store may have its own fashion image—in keeping with its size, the customers it serves, the retailing goals of its management—within the limitations of its facilities and resources. However, these underlying concepts of a fashion image tends to reflect the nature of fashion at the retail level.

To understand fully the total setting of the fashion store in the retail world, consider the various types of stores that distribute fashion along with other consumer goods. We will focus on the limited-line, or specialty, store and the general merchandise or department store; however, some attention is given to other types of retail outlets, which are presented in the flow chart in Figure 9.6.

RETAILING IN THE UNITED STATES

Fashion merchandise may be purchased in many kinds of retail stores—small or large stores, specialty stores or department stores, variety stores or discount stores, and independently owned firms or group-owned corporations. Some fashion goods may be distributed by mail-order and catalog showroom outlets, and a small amount of fashion goods is sold through the efforts of house-to-house salespeople. Many stores are small, independently owned and operated, and have only one unit with few employees. Other retailers may be large corporations that have many stores—multiunits—and each store with many employees may operate somewhat autonomously. Some stores are located in the heart of downtown areas in large cities or in small towns, and other stores are situated in suburban or regional shopping centers. Detailed in Figure

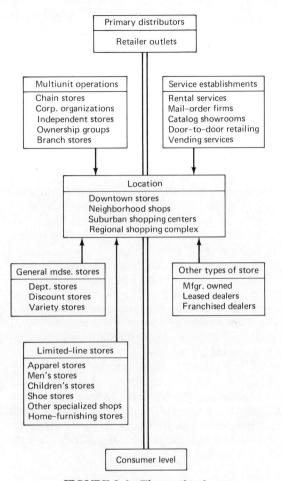

FIGURE 9.6 *The retail industry.*

9.6 are some group characteristics of retail outlets that distribute merchandise to the ultimate consumer.

Although fashion is big business at the retail level, small specialty stores throughout the country account for a significant proportion of the sales of fashion goods. The existence of these small retail stores makes our mass-distribution system work and makes fashion goods available to the various consumer markets.

Limited-line, or Specialty-type, Stores

Small shops that carry limited lines of fashion merchandise are commonly known as specialty shops, apparel shops, or boutiques. Small retail stores such as the traditional specialty shop have consistently accounted for a large portion of total retail sales. Boutique operations have contributed significantly to retail sales in recent years.[1] Many of these small stores specialize in a particular type of merchandise and related accessory items that the customer may want to put together for a total fashion look. Such stores may carry fashion goods for both men and women, or for only one sex. Specialty stores often seek a distinctive age group to serve—for example, children, or, as was the trend in the 1960s, the teenage or junior customer. Thus, specialty retailers may deal with a single line of merchandise, such as shoes, jewelry, hosiery, and shirts; or they may sell several related lines of merchandise, women's apparel and accessories or children's clothes and toys. Some specialty stores deal in other specific kinds of consumer products: books, flowers, and records. Therefore, the term *limited-line store* is somewhat more appropriate than the traditional term *specialty shop*, which continues to be used in the retail trade.

These specialty stores may be *single units*— one store only, usually operated by the owner and manager; or *multiunits*—two or more stores operated under one management group, each with separate store managers. These two types affect the organizational and merchandising policies of the specialty store.

Single-unit Specialty Stores

ORGANIZATION

The owner-manager operation is common among small specialty shops. The shop may be owned by one person or one or more people in a partnership agreement. Owners are usually compelled to function in a variety of ways—as manager, buyer, salesperson, stockperson, janitor, and bookkeeper. In a partnership these responsibilities may be shared or organized according to the individual abilities of the partners.

Often in a partnership, each person assumes the responsibility for those things he or she is most capable of doing, has had experience in doing, or simply likes to do. Thus, small specialty shops are operated in a highly individual

manner, often reflecting the whims of the owners. Many of these small single-unit operations continue to operate on a trial-and-error basis even in today's age of professional retail management. "Experience is the best teacher" seems to be the motto of many specialty shop retailers. Thus, some specialty shops are efficiently managed and others, obviously, are run poorly.

Retailers of these small specialty stores go into and out of business frequently. In 1974 women's apparel stores were reported to have 250 failures and more than 1,200 new stores were started with an average of little more than $10,000 to 12,000 in capital.[2] Approximately 95 per cent of women's apparel shops have annual sales of less than $500,000.[3]

MERCHANDISE POLICIES

The owner or owners of the small specialty shop attempt to purchase merchandise to meet the *individual needs* of the customers served. *Merchandise assortments* are purchased on a seasonal basis at nearby fashion market centers, and/or from traveling salesmen who represent apparel manufacturers in the regional areas.

Customer Approach. An individualized approach is used by the owners or managers of these small specialty shops. They can cater to individual customers simply by developing personal relationships with them and by keeping the customers' merchandise preferences in mind when making buying decisions.

The small specialty shop owner or manager can capitalize on the distinctive nature of the single-unit retail operation, for example:

1. They do their own buying in small quantities, which minimizes not only the financial investment but the risk involved in buying large assortments of fashion items.
2. They provide personally selected fashions for customers, which may minimize the possibility of the customer running into another person in the same outfit.
3. They provide personal services for the customer, such as advanced fashion information, wardrobe advice, social etiquette (what to

wear where), treatment of figure problems and alterations, and special orders.

4. They can adjust their merchandise assortments and control buying, pricing, and selling practices to meet the desired changes in their retail objectives or goals, to suit their customers' changing needs, and to reflect economic conditions from day to day, season to season, and year to year.

Merchandise Assortments. The merchandise assortments of small specialty shops are often difficult to maintain without losing buying efficiency. Some manufacturers will not sell a line of merchandise in small or selective assortments. Some small specialty shop owners may gain the advantage of larger competitive stores by utilizing the services of buying offices. As discussed in Part Two, resident buying offices located in major fashion market centers serve as purchasing agents for small stores as well as large stores. These services not only make it possible to obtain appropriate merchandise assortments, but they also may mean financial savings for the small store owner by reducing the number of trips to market.

A buying office can also provide the small specialty shop owner with comparative sales information from other similar stores, fashion trend information relative to best-selling merchandise in other stores, and new items of merchandise available from apparel manufacturers in various parts of the country. Small retailers may achieve some price concessions from apparel firms when large quantities are ordered in pooled purchases through the buying office. Buying offices may assist small stores with other retail problems, such as inventory control or operational and promotional policies.

Fashion Image. The fashion image of the small specialty shop may be expressed in terms of exclusive merchandise, or medium-price lines, or low-price lines. Most specialty shops cater to the needs of a specific customer type who buys merchandise within a certain price range. The customer types may vary from teenagers, to matrons, to infants; from budget-minded customers to affluent ones; and from the fashion leaders to the "just so it's wash-and-wear" crowd. Most specialty stores make it a point to know their customer types, but also to know the kind of fashion merchandise their customers like as individuals rather than as members of a group. Most specialty store owners buy fashion goods for Mrs. Jones, Mrs. Smith, or for Sara and Mary Jane. This buying and selling is almost on a special-order basis—a one-to-one relationship with the customer. Only the specialty shop can provide this highly personalized service. Specialty shops serve the needs of small consumer groups that the large competitive store cannot afford to serve. They can change directions quickly. They can buy more or less, find new resources, offer more or fewer services, and adjust to local business conditions and changes in consumer demand in these and many other ways.

General Merchandise or Department Stores

Stores that sell all kinds of merchandise for the individual and for the home are commonly known as department stores. General apparel, accessories, and piece goods for the family are sold in most department stores, along with household linens, home-furnishing items, appliances, radios, television sets, and garden supplies. One-stop shopping for the entire family and "all under one roof" slogans originated with these stores; they are traditionally known by retailers as full-line department stores. Bloomingdale's and Marshall Field are examples of these retail institutions, which are more a part of the retail scene in the United States than abroad.

The term *junior department store* is used by retailers to classify stores that follow the same general merchandise pattern but carry a more limited line of home furnishings, appliances, and other consumer goods. Many stores recognized by consumers as department stores technically are junior department stores.

Single-Unit Department Stores

ORGANIZATION

The department store is the place where retail store organization originated. In the 1930s, a functional division of retail operational responsibilities was developed with the aid of the federal government and several prominent business advisors. There may be a board of directors and/or a store president, depending on the ownership. Several vice-presidents or top-level executives will usually be in charge of the various functional responsibilities, such as merchandising and buying, sales promotion and advertising, personnel, operation, and financial control. These divisions of responsibilities are depicted in the organizational chart in Figure 9.7. These functional divisions may be combined or expanded, depending on the size of the store, the talents of the management and key personnel, and the nature of the fashion image the store wants to present in the community. Responsibilities, duties, and authority may overlap; for example, a salesperson may be supervised by a buyer and report to the personnel director or the store manager. Retail expertise and coordinated efforts at the top executive level are vital to the consistency of the department store's image.

The retail department store has had a very successful history in this country. Failures are not as frequent as in specialty stores, since more professional procedures are used in the management efforts of top executives. In the last decade, the department store share of the fashion goods sales has increased noticeably. Although there are a few giants in the country, the department store is usually represented by the one or more general merchandise stores in most communities.

MERCHANDISE POLICIES

It is the department store that has glorified and emphasized the position of the retail buyer in America. Traditionally, each department or group of departments has a buyer who is considered an independent merchant, fully responsible for the buying and the profits of the department. In actual practice, the store manager or merchandise manager is responsible for supervising the activities and the decisions of the buyers.

Merchandise Divisions. In large department stores, merchandise is grouped into divisions according to either the nature of the product or the organization of the selling space on each floor. An example of these divisions is shown in Figure 9.8. Most department stores have a fashion division that includes women's apparel and accessory items; a men's wear division; and one or more other divisions that may include home furnishings, bedding and linens, piece goods, notions, and perhaps some of the convenience or impulse items that are usually called first-floor, main-entrance merchandise, including cosmetics, costume jewelry, and greeting cards.

The fashion merchandise division is actually a specialty shop inside a department store, although it may be more highly organized and the merchandise may be grouped according to the assignment of responsibility for the buying.

Regardless of the number of merchandise divi-

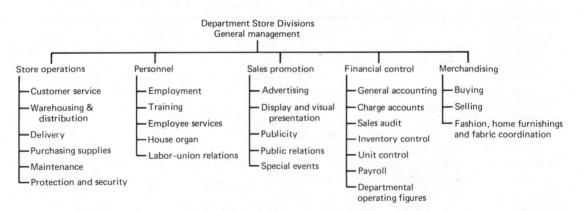

FIGURE 9.7 *Department store, single-unit organization.*

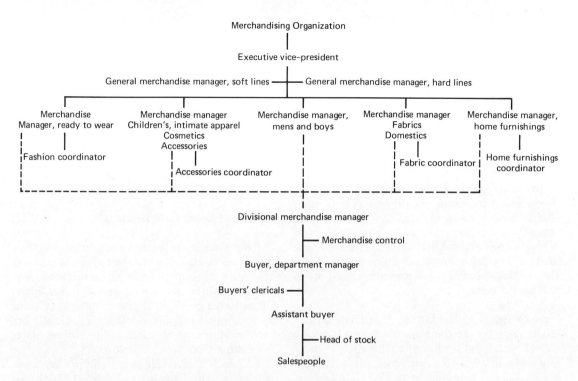

FIGURE 9.8 *Department store, merchandising division.*

sions or the manner in which the merchandise is grouped, the several buyers will have almost total responsibility for designated groups of merchandise. The fashion buyer may be responsible for apparel categories such as better sportswear, junior sportswear, misses dresses, junior dresses, misses coats and suits, and accessory lines such as handbags, hosiery, and costume jewelry.

The Buyer. Traditionally, in a single-unit department store, the buyer has the supervisory responsibility for the total operation of an assigned department or an area with several departments—that is, for buying, receiving, arranging, and selling the merchandise associated with that area. However, a department manager or an assistant buyer may be delegated some of the responsibility. The nature of these duties and their assignment are considered in detail in Appendix 5. Nevertheless, the store management expects the buyer to keep in close contact with the department operation—the appearance of the de-

partment, the salespeople within the department, and the customers.

The Customer Approach. The individualized approach in small single-unit department stores can be much the same as that discussed for the specialty shop. The departmental buyer and sales personnel attempt to satisfy the customer and to build customer loyalty by offering: (1) personalized services, (2) adjustments and returns on an individual, "the customer is always right" basis, and (3) merchandise assortments that provide an opportunity for customers to pick and choose on a personal basis to meet individual needs and desires.

Merchandise Assortments. The merchandise assortments are achieved by the department buyer in much the same manner as by the specialty shop owner. Merchandise is purchased in advance of the consumer selling season at major fashion markets or from time to time through the manufacturer's sales representative who calls on the buyers in a regional area. Many department stores are affiliated with buying offices in one or more fashion market centers, and the buyers use these services just as the specialty store does.

The fashion buyer knows his or her department customer by certain group characteristics identified with the store's clientele and by personal contacts within the selling department. Most fashion departments carry an assortment of merchandise that meets the needs of the customer as perceived by the management of the store. The merchandise assortments may be limited to a price range in keeping with the store's image and the income level of the store's customers. The fashion buyer is fully responsible for making decisions on a season-by-season basis concerning the styles, fabrics, colors, and other selling features.

Fashion Image. The fashion image in a department store may be the responsibility of the divisional merchandise manager, the general merchandise manager for the store, or a fashion coordinator. There may be one or more fashion coordinators in a department store; however, the responsibility in the fashion division is usually assigned to some executive-level employee, and in a large department store the home furnishings division may also have a fashion coordinator. The primary responsibilities of the fashion coordinator are to: (1) develop and maintain a fashion image of the store consistent with the merchandise and service policies established by top management; (2) create and direct promotional activities that will enhance the fashion image of the store in the minds of the clientele and the potential customers in the community or consumer market area; and (3) provide leadership in the fashion direction of the store from season to season through analysis of fashion trends and communication with store buyers, sales personnel, advertising and display personnel, and others. Fashion coordinators are usually given many other responsibilities in a department store, such as producing fashion shows, advising store personnel and customers regarding matters of appropriate fashion for various social occasions, entertaining visiting designers, and so on endlessly.

In small towns and cities across the country, the single-unit department store and the specialty shop provide fashion goods to meet consumer demand in local communities and shopping centers. Fashion buyers from these single-unit retail stores compete with each other in the local consumer market place and in the seasonal fashion markets. The apparel manufacturer considers the needs and the demands of these retail buyers separately from those of the mass distributors of fashion goods—the large multiunit retail organizations that we will consider next.

Multiunit Retail Organizations

This is an era of giants in retailing. Less than 13 per cent of the stores in the United States have multiunit operations (two or more store locations), however, these mass-concept distributors of consumer goods do approximately 40 per cent of the annual volume in retail sales. Only 5 per cent of all the retail stores in the United States have more than twenty employees.[4]

Although a relatively small group when considered in light of the two million retail establishments in the United States, the multiunit retailer represents the growth pattern in our mass distribution system. The twenty-five largest retailers are listed in Table 9.1, along with some statistics about their size.[5] These multiunit operations have developed the contemporary concept of mass retailing in the United States. Sears, Penney, Federated, Allied, and May are some of the giants, and each has retail stores located throughout the country.

OWNERSHIP

In terms of ownership and organization, the multiunit concept was initiated in the 1920s and 1930s with the chain store idea: to serve stores that were centrally owned, operated, and controlled with a more or less uniform image in terms of merchandise and services for the consumer market in different towns. The contemporary multiunit store may be operated by ownership groups or corporations as well as by a chain-type organization. The retail outlets are identified as department stores, specialty stores, discount stores, variety stores, or by some other

TABLE 9.1 The Twenty-five Largest Retailing Companies Ranked by Sales & Employees.

Rank 75'	74'	Company	Sales ($ 000)	Employees Number	Rank
1	1	Sears, Roebuck	13,639,887	377,000	1
2	2	Safeway Stores	9,716,889	126,964	6
3	3	J. C. Penney	7,678,600	186,000	3
4	5	S. S. Kresge	6,888,613	155,000	4
5	4	Great Atlantic & Pacific Tea	6,537,897	92,900	7
6	6	Kroger	5,339,225	56,969	12
7	7	Marcor	4,822,273	145,926	5
8	8	F. W. Woolworth	4,650,290	202,402	2
9	9	Federated Department Stores	3,712,864	88,500	8
10	15	American Stores	3,207,248	42,044	18
11	10	Lucky Stores	3,109,406	42,000	19
12	13	Winn-Dixie Stores	2,962,165	39,165	20
13	11	Jewel Companies	2,817,754	34,985	24
14	12	Rapid American	2,532,347	55,000	15
15	14	Food Fair Stores	2,482,539	35,000	23
16	16	City Products	2,224,968	47,000	16
17	18	May Department Stores	2,017,366	59,000	11
18	19	Southland	1,787,928	28,600	27
19	20	Allied Stores	1,770,645	55,400	13
20	22	Dayton Hudson	1,692,528	30,000	25
21	21	Grand Union	1,611,195	21,000	35
22	24	Gamble-Skogmo	1,559,043	19,000	37
23	23	Supermarket General	1,550,408	26,000	29
24	25	National Tea	1,472,341	18,600	39
25	26	Associated Dry Goods	1,390,966	55,400	14

Source: *Fortune Magazine*, July 1976.

merchandise terminology. Regardless of the type of ownership, the organization of the operation, or the merchandise assortment, most multiunit retailers have one objective in common: to achieve profitable mass distribution of consumer goods and services in selected retail market areas.

Most large department stores and specialty stores operate more than one store of the same general nature in terms of merchandise and fashion image. Many of these multiunits were first developed in suburban shopping centers, and some have since expanded into the regional shopping arena. Other expanding multiunit organizations have skipped from city to city across the country seeking their share of the competitive retail market. For example, Bonwit Teller operates units in Boston, Chicago, and Los Angeles, among other places. Neiman-Marcus has opened stores in Atlanta, St. Louis, and in other cities. Lord & Taylor opened in shopping centers in several cities, including St. Louis and Dallas. Most of these stores had already saturated their market areas with units near the original store.

CENTRAL BUYING

It is in the area of buying merchandise that these multiunit stores have continued to follow the chain-store centralized operational structure.

Most contemporary multiunit stores continue to maintain the buying organization of the original single-unit operation. In general, the buyers in these organizations buy for all of the store units, although a few firms have explored other methods.

STORE OPERATION

In terms of store operation, there are two trends of thought at management level. One concept is similar to that of the early chain store—one of central operation and control —with numerous stores that have the same general nature in terms of store image; the second concept permits the development of almost autonomous store groups within the large multiunit operation. In the latter concept we cite one dramatic example: Federated, one of the giant corporate groups in retailing, includes among its illustrious retail names Bullocks Wilshire, fashion specialty store par excellence. Also on the Federated list is Foley's, in Houston—mass retailers of fashion from the top-designer floor to the budget operation in the lower level of the original downtown store. (The term *basement* is more commonly used by old hands in the retail trade instead of lower level.)

STORE MANAGEMENT

When it comes to store management policies for the contemporary multiunit operation, the votes are not yet in. The general manager, or store manager, is the only common denominator so far. Some stores have department managers, some have group merchandise managers, some have associate or assistant buyers assigned to the various stores, others have not separated responsibilities and duties nor given a title to the employee in charge. Nevertheless, when the latest statistics were viewed, many of the outlying units had exceeded the sales volume of the original store, some twofold, some threefold, some tenfold, some 100 per cent. Multiunit organizations, especially in the fashion goods area, have presented complicated problems with no simple answers. But over and over, when the verdict comes in, many of these operations spell profit, and that is the name of the game in big business and in retailing in the United States.

Other Types of Retailers

Another group of retailers sells fashion goods; this is a miscellaneous grouping that includes discount stores, variety stores, catalog showrooms, door-to-door sales groups, and vending-type operations. Most of these types of retailers have experimented with selling fashion goods—some to no avail. One example is that of a major fashion store on Fifth Avenue in New York City. This elegant fashion store attempted to use the vending-machine concept to sell women's hosiery on a 24-hour-a-day, seven days a week basis. Although the method eliminated the need for salespeople and was convenient for the customer, it did not prove satisfactory because of security problems.

An increasing amount of soft goods is distributed by discount outlets and variety-type stores. However, mail-order and catalog-showroom type outlets have not been as successful with soft goods lines as with hard goods lines such as furniture, appliances, gifts, jewelry, and electronic and stereo equipment. Some small amounts of fashion goods are sold through efforts of house-to-house salespeople and other such methods.

PRESENT STATUS OF RETAILING

We can now consider the big picture of retailing in the United States. Let us look at some additional aspects of retailing in general: (1) the methods used to sell consumer goods, (2) the size of some stores compared with others, and (3) the many different kinds of stores in the United States.

Methods of Retailing

Consumer products are sold at the retail level through stores, mail-order operations, house-to-house selling, and automatic vending machines. Of these four methods of retailing, the most familiar is the retail store, which accounts for about 97 per cent of all retail sales.[6] No doubt most people purchase fashion items for their wardrobe in their favorite store. However, they may also order some by mail. An increasing number of catalogs with fashion items are distributed under the auspices of retail stores. Some people may purchase merchandise from a salesperson at their door. Actually, mail-order retailing and house-to-house selling account for less than 1 per cent of total retail sales, according to the latest Census of Business data. Vending machines and other methods of retailing also account for less than 1 per cent of all retail sales.[7]

Size of Retail Stores

Retail stores are classified as *single-unit* outlets or *multiunit* operations. In 1972 approximately 85 per cent of retail firms in the United States operated only one store. These single-unit operations accounted for 53 per cent of the total retail sales volume.[8] As indicated in Table 9.2, the number of single-unit establishments has decreased about 5 per cent since 1958, and over 10 per cent in sales produced by these stores. This change is related to the growth in number of multiunit establishments and the increase in percentage of sales volume between 1958 and 1972.

Note that in today's era of giants in business, retail firms operating more than one store of the same general nature have increased from 10 per cent in 1958 to 15 per cent of all stores in 1972 and account for approximately 44 per cent of total retail sales.

Figure 9.9 provides more information about single-unit and multiunit store operations in the United States.[9] As a whole, the multiunits have increased consistently in number since 1948, with the greatest growth (approximately 6 per cent) appearing among those stores with 101 units or more. The distribution of sales by size of firm in 1972 is shown for selected kinds of businesses in Figure 9.10. Nearly 90 per cent of department stores are parts of multiunits with eleven establishments or more; approximately 40 per cent of women's ready-to-wear stores are single-unit operations.[10]

NUMBER OF RETAIL STORE EMPLOYEES

Retail stores can be classified by number of employees. As shown in Table 9.3, stores with fewer than four employees made up nearly 65 per cent of the total number of retail establishments in 1972.[11] Stores with four to nineteen employees made up slightly over one fourth of the total. Only 6.5 per cent of retail stores have twenty or more employees. But note that this 6.5

TABLE 9.2   Retail Firm Size in the United States

No. of Units	1972 Firms (no.)	Establishments (% of total)				Sales (% of total)			
		1972	1967	1963	1958	1972	1967	1963	1958
United States, total	1,664,972		100.0	100.0	100.0		100.0	100.0	100.0
Single units, total	1,621,373	84.8	87.5	87.1	89.8	53.4	60.2	63.4	66.3
Multiunits, total	43,599	15.2	12.5	12.9	10.2	44.0	39.8	36.6	33.7
2 or 3 establishment multiunits	33,562	3.9	3.3	4.5	3.8	5.9	5.8	6.5	6.9
4 or 5 establishment multiunits	4,717	1.1	.9	.9	.7	2.0	2.0	1.9	2.1
6 to 10 establishment multiunits	2,821	1.1	.9	.9	.7	2.4	2.7	2.7	2.4
11 to 25 establishment multiunits	1,455	1.2	1.1	1.0	.8	3.1	3.6	3.1	2.6
26 to 100 establishment multiunits	749	1.8	1.7	1.5	1.4	6.1	7.0	6.7	5.4
101 or more establishment multiunits	295	6.1	4.7	4.1	2.8	24.6	18.6	15.8	14.3

Source: Census of Business, *Retail Trade,* 1972, Dept. of Commerce, "Firm Size in U.S.," Washington, D.C.: U.S. Government Printing Office, 1976.

per cent brought in over half (52.9 per cent) of the retail sales dollar annually in 1972.

SALES VOLUME OF RETAIL STORES

Stores may also be classified by annual sales volume. Referring again to Table 9.3, note that in 1972 large retail organizations selling $1,000,000 or more annually represented about 4 per cent of all stores. However, these few large stores accounted for close to half (42 per cent) of total retail sales.[12] What about the smaller stores? Over one third (36.8 per cent) had an annual sales volume of $50,000 or less, and these small stores did less than 4 per cent of total retail sales in the United States. Medium-sized stores, selling from $50,000 to $500,000 annually, represented more than 45 per cent of all retail outlets

SINGLE UNITS AND MULTIUNITS Retail Trade

Change in Proportion of Sales, by Size of Firm:
1948 to 1972

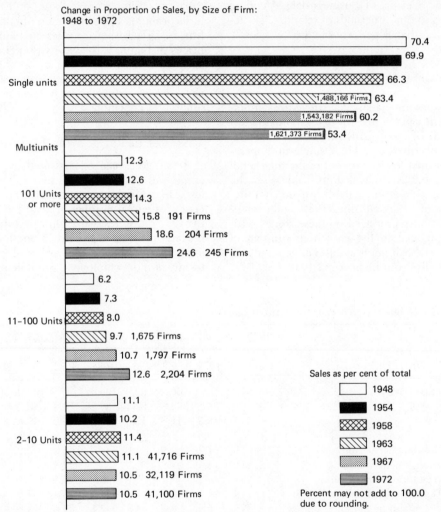

Single units
- 70.4
- 69.9
- 66.3
- 1,488,166 Firms 63.4
- 1,543,182 Firms 60.2
- 1,621,373 Firms 53.4

Multiunits

101 Units or more
- 12.3
- 12.6
- 14.3
- 15.8 191 Firms
- 18.6 204 Firms
- 24.6 245 Firms

11–100 Units
- 6.2
- 7.3
- 8.0
- 9.7 1,675 Firms
- 10.7 1,797 Firms
- 12.6 2,204 Firms

2–10 Units
- 11.1
- 10.2
- 11.4
- 11.1 41,716 Firms
- 10.5 32,119 Firms
- 10.5 41,100 Firms

Sales as per cent of total
- 1948
- 1954
- 1958
- 1963
- 1967
- 1972

Percent may not add to 100.0 due to rounding.

FIGURE 9.9 *Change in proportion of sales, by size of firm: 1948–1972.* (Source: *Census of Business,* Retail Trade, 1972, *Depart. of Commerce, Special Report, "Firm Size in U.S." Washington, D.C.: Government Printing Office, 1976.*)

and did about 30 per cent of the total sales volume annually.

Kinds of Retail Stores in the United States

OWNERSHIP OR LEGAL FORM

Stores may be classified by the type of ownership[13] (see Table 9.3). Although there are no data available for 1967, it is significant to see that *individually owned* stores accounted for 51.6 per cent of the total number of establishments in 1972, and only 15.3 per cent of the sales. However, 29.6 per cent of the stores were corporations and they had nearly 75 per cent of the sales. These data suggest that individual proprietorships were on the decrease and corporations were increasing during the period from 1958 to 1972.

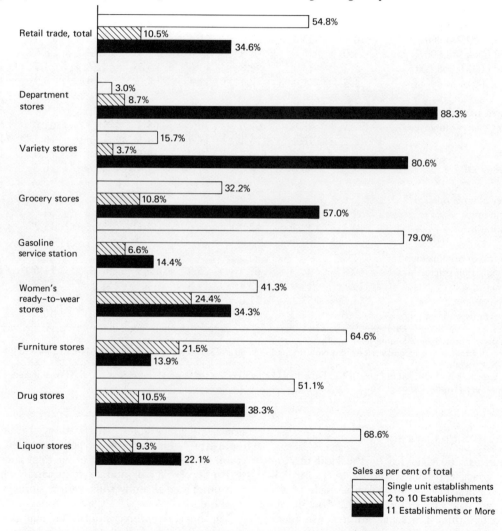

FIGURE 9.10 *Per cent distribution of sales by size of firm, for selected kinds of business: 1972. A firm's sales are based on the total sales of all retail establishments operated by the owning firms in the kind-of-business classification, group, or total for which data are presented.* (Source: *Census of Business*, Retail Trade, 1972, *Depart. of Commerce, Special Report, "Firm Size in U.S." Washington, D.C.: Government Printing Office, 1976.)

TABLE 9.3 Retail Establishments and Sales by Size (% distribution)

Item	1958 Estab- lishments	1958 Sales	1963 Estab- ishments	1963 Sales	1967 Estab- lishments	1967 Sales	1972 Estab- lishments	1972 Sales
Total Retail Trade	100.0	100.0	100.0	100.0	100.0	100.0	100.0	100.0
Sales size[a]								
Less than $30,000	40.5	5.1	33.7	3.2	34.9	2.7	27.0	1.5
$ 30,000– 50,000	17.5	5.9	15.9	4.1	13.6	2.9	9.8	1.6
50,000– 100,000	19.2	11.8	21.5	10.1	19.3	7.6	23.5	4.8
100,000– 300,000	16.1	23.1	20.0	21.8	21.5	20.1	15.9	16.9
300,000– 500,000	3.0	10.0	3.8	9.5	4.4	9.4	5.6	8.8
500,000– 1,000,000	2.2	13.1	2.8	13.0	3.3	12.8	3.7	10.6
1,000,000 or more	1.5	31.1	2.4	38.4	3.0	44.4	3.9	42.4
Employment size[b]								
Fewer than 4 employees	72.1	23.9	69.6	20.7	68.9	18.8	64.6	14.9
4–7	15.2	16.1	16.1	14.9	14.8	12.5	16.5	12.4
8–19	8.9	21.0	9.7	20.7	10.9	20.4	12.4	19.8
20 or more	3.8	39.0	4.6	43.7	5.4	48.2	6.5	52.9
Number of units operated								
Single units	89.8	66.3	87.1	63.4	87.5	60.2	84.8	53.4
Multiunits	10.2	33.7	12.9	36.6	12.5	39.8	15.2	44.0
Legal form or organization								
Individual proprietorships	69.4	31.7	65.9	26.9	n.a.[c]	n.a.	51.6	15.3
Partnerships	14.5	13.9	12.4	9.8	n.a.	n.a.	7.8	5.2
Corporations	15.5	53.1	21.0	61.9	n.a.	n.a.	29.6	74.7
Cooperatives and other	.6	1.2	.8	1.4	n.a.	n.a.	10.9	4.8

[a] Refers only to firms operated entire year
[b] Number of employees as of workweek nearest Nov. 15 for 1958 and 1963, and workweek including March 12 for 1967
[c] n.a.—Not available
Source: Census of Business, *Retail Trade*, 1972, Depart. of Commerce, Special Report, "Firm Size in U.S." (Washington, D.C.: Government Printing Office, 1976).

MERCHANDISE LINES SOLD

Stores can be classified by the kind of consumer goods carried. According to Table 9.4, some $22 billion in retail sales was made by apparel and accessory stores in 1972,[14] while approximately three times that amount was made by general merchandise stores.

Note in Table 9.4 that the general merchandise group accounts for approximately 17 per cent of total retail sales and includes department stores, dry goods stores, variety stores, and mail-order firms. The latter two types of retailers account for less than 3 per cent of the total sales for this group.[15] What kind of merchandise have you purchased recently from variety stores or by mail order?

The apparel group accounts for slightly less than 5 per cent of the total retail sales and includes men's and boys' wear stores, women's apparel stores, family clothing stores, and shoe stores. The women's apparel stores account for a

TABLE 9.4 Patterns of Retail Sales, 1972

| | Retail sales | | | | Retail sales | |
Kind of business	$ Billions	Distribution (in %)		Kind of business	$ Billions	Distribution (in %)
Total Retail Trade	448.4	100.0		Furniture stores	9.3	2.1
				Appliances, TV, radio	7.0	1.6
Food group	95.0	21.2		Appliance dealers	4.6	1.0
Grocery stores	88.3	19.7				
Meat, fish markets	2.6	.6		Lumber, bldg., hardware	26.7	6.0
Bakery products stores	1.3	.3		Lumber, bldg. materials	16.0	3.6
				Hardware stores	4.3	1.0
Eating and drinking places	33.9	7.6				
Eating places	26.8	6.0		Automotive group dealers	88.6	19.8
Restaurants, cafeterias	20.9	4.7		Passenger car, other auto	81.5	18.2
Drinking places	7.1	1.6		Pass. car dealers	74.8	16.7
				Franchised dealers	69.5	15.5
Gen'l. Merchandise Group[a]	74.9	16.7		Tire, battery, accessories	7.1	1.6
Dept. stores, dry goods	56.2	12.5				
Department stores	46.3	10.3		Gasoline service stations	31.0	6.9
Variety stores	7.8	1.7				
Mail-order houses[b]	5.0	1.1		Drug, proprietary stores	14.5	3.2
Apparel group	22.0	4.9		Liquor stores	9.2	2.1
Men's, boys' wear stores	5.2	1.2				
Women's apparel, etc.	8.4	1.9		Other stores	31.2	6.9
Family clothing stores	3.9	.9				
Shoe stores	3.8	.8				
Furniture, appliances	21.3	4.8				
Furniture, hfgs. stores	12.6	2.8				

[a] Includes nonstores
[b] Department store merchandise
Source: Census of Business, *Retail Trade*, 1972, Depart. of Commerce, Special Report. "Firm Size in U.S.," (Washington, D.C.: U.S. Government Printing Office, 1976).

slightly higher percentage of total distribution of retail sales than the men's and boys' wear stores, whereas the other two types of stores, family clothing stores and shoe stores, have about the same percentage of retail sales, less than 1 per cent.

The following conclusions suggest what we need to be aware of in specifically considering the retail distribution of fashion goods:

1. Our system of distribution for consumer goods is still composed of many small single-unit retail stores operated by local merchants. Over 84 per cent of the retail establishments are single-unit stores and do nearly 53 per cent of retail sales.

2. Over two thirds of retail stores have fewer than 20 employees.
3. Nearly two thirds of all the nation's retail stores have a sales volume of less than $100,000.
4. The trend in individual ownership of retail stores has been decreasing, and the trend toward corporate ownership has increased nearly 10 per cent since 1963.
5. There is a trend toward large retail organizations that operate more than 101 stores.
6. Less than a fourth of total retail sales in the United States are made in department stores, variety stores, mail-order houses, men's or boys' wear stores, women's apparel stores, family clothing stores, and shoe stores.

FUTURE DIRECTIONS IN RETAILING

A leading fashion retailer, Robert T. Sakowitz, states that, compared with other nations, we have the greatest system of manufacturer-to-consumer distribution in the world.[16] Now that we have viewed the retail store as the link connecting the system with the consumer, we should consider some of the factors that indicate future directions in retailing.

Factors which are expected to have considerable impact on the retailer of tomorrow include: (1) the shift in location of population, (2) the growth of the consumer movement, and (3) marketing strategy.

Approximately 80 per cent of the population of the United States now resides in urban areas or on the periphery of the existing urban network.[17] The urban services have never been integrated or related to the basic needs of the people living, working, or visiting in these urban centers. Highways, streets, sidewalks, public transportation systems, elevators, escalators, utilities, freight, storage, and waste removal suffer from a "cycle of continuing obsolescence."[18]

Our highways have become traffic arteries carrying the economic lifeblood of America. This system of highways has produced high-speed crossroads and interchanges. Suburban and regional shopping centers are a by-product of the screaming wheels of the "personal transportation vehicle."[19] The shopping and personal service needs of the consumer have been concentrated at the arterial interchanges. Ideally these may become regional centers serving the retail, business, cultural, and recreational needs of the consumer in a manner similar to the central business districts of the small cities in the last half century.[20]

The effects of *consumerism* have been apparent in the last decade. Business and industry have been reminded that they are a part of the community. The retailer will no doubt continue to be expected to provide customers and the community with more than merchandise at a fair price. We may look to merchants to contribute extensively to charity, participate in more civic activities, speak out as citizens as well as businessmen,

and perhaps serve as consultants on how to meet social goals such as equal employment opportunity. Stores may serve as educators by providing instruction in various new crafts, hobbies, or do-it-yourself and aid the consumer in other new and unusual situations. Stores may adopt new marketing strategies; impose stricter standards on manufacturers; pay more attention to the consumer as an individual; use research and planning to develop new markets based on shifts in population, income, age, education, and special needs; and serve more effectively as the intermediary between manufacturer and consumer.

The following directions in retailing may predominate in the future: (1) specialty stores, (2) boutiques, (3) department stores, and (4) discount and variety stores.

Specialty Stores. Specialty stores may have a brighter future than some imagine. Limited-line stores—apparel, furniture, and other products—have an advantage in specialization and have the ability to satisfy the individualized needs of today's consumer. The advent of the enclosed shopping center—a kind of department store for independent merchants—affords many more opportunities for these small retailers.[21]

Individualized boutiques give the customer a greater sense of personal attention and provide a more concentrated array of merchandise. These stores will no doubt increase in the decade ahead, primarily because of their ability to personalize their approach to the customer.[22]

Department Stores. Department stores will fulfill their growth patterns in regional areas. Independents will expand in the same manner that chain and ownership groups have in the past—by acquiring and developing new subsidiaries and adding services, such as catalog showrooms, and mail-order facilities all under one ownership group, which is today the independent department store. The increasing homogeneity of the national market, new enterprises in the area of consumer services, and foreign operations may mean expansion opportunities for the chain that is already national and the catalog department store.[23]

Discount and Variety Stores. Discount and variety stores may move forward with more professional management and financial and merchandising controls. The trial-and-error experiences of the discounter during the last twenty years will begin to pay off. Variety stores will look to broadening their lines into general merchandise, upgrading lines, and competing in foreign operations.[24]

In general, however, lines of difference between retail stores may continue to fade as stores become more alike in seeking the same goals: achieving a better profit margin in the face of constantly rising prices and costs by tapping new consumer markets. Not only must retailers adapt to new socioeconomic profiles developing in our country, they must also be more flexible and more imaginative to successfully survive in the decades ahead.

END OF CHAPTER GUIDE

Review, Discussion and Evaluation

Study of this chapter should enable students to:

A. Develop and give evidence of the following kinds of competencies:
   1. An awareness of the fashion image concept relating to customer approach, merchandise assortments, store environment, and fashion obligations.
   2. An understanding of various types of retail store operations in terms of limited line or specialty stores and general merchandise or department stores.
   3. A knowledge of the organizational differences between single-unit and major multiunit store operations in the United States.
   4. An ability to compare the size of various types of retail operations in the United States in terms of sales volume, number of employees, type of onwership, and merchandise carried.
   5. An awareness of future directions in retailing relative to specialty stores, department stores, discount and variety stores, and other types of distribution.
B. Develop and/or clarify concepts related to the following key words or phrases:
   1. fashion image 2. limited line 3. specialty shops 4. general merchandise 5. department stores 6. single-unit stores 7. multiunit stores 8. single line 9. related lines 10. buying offices 11. discount stores 12. variety stores 13. ownership groups 14. customer approach 15. merchandise assortment 16. store environment 17. fashion obligation 18. hard goods 19. soft goods 20. convenience goods 21. shopping goods 22. fashion goods 23. staple goods 24. service establishments 25. merchandise policies 26. store management

Extended Classroom Learning Experiences

A. Make a list of five or more stores you are familiar with in your community or nearby.
   1. Review the retail terms and definitions in the key words and phrases above and select the terms that best describe each of the five stores.
   2. List any other stores you know that represent one or more of the retail terms.
B. Select one or more of the stores you have listed in A and consider the fashion image in terms of three or more of the concepts discussed in this chapter. Briefly describe the fashion image of one or more of the stores. Include several statements about three or more of the following concepts: (1) customer approach, (2) merchandise assortments, (3) store environment, and (4) fashion obligation.
C. Make a list of several limited-line or specialty stores you are familiar with in your community or nearby where you shop for clothing.
   1. Arrange an interview with the manager or some employee designated by the manager in one or more of the stores. Obtain as much specific information as possible about organizational structure and merchandise policies.
   2. In a written report indicate what you have learned about one or more of the stores where you had an interview. Be sure to include the answers to the following kinds of questions: (a) Is the store single unit or multiunit? (b) What are the names of some of the key employees in the organization? (c) What is the organizational structure in terms of owner, manager, buyer, etc.? (d) What are some of the merchandise policies in terms of merchandise assortments and fashion image?
D. Make a list of several general merchandise or department stores you are familiar with in your community or nearby where you shop for clothing.
   1. Carry out the same instructions as given in steps 1 and 2 in C.
E. Visit two or more stores that you consider fashion

stores in your community or in a regional area shopping center.

   1. Observe the fashion image of the store(s) both from the exterior and interior atmosphere.

   2. Write a brief description in terms of the four fashion image concepts discussed in this chapter: (a) customer approach (b) merchandise assortment (c) store environment (d) fashion obligation

F. Read two or more of the articles mentioned in this chapter or research current periodicals or trade journals and select two or more articles related to one of the concepts suggested in the "Review, Discussion, and Evaluation."

   1. Prepare note cards while reading each article.

   2. Using your note cards, write a brief summary indicating the relationship of each article to concepts presented in this chapter.

   3. Using your note cards, give an oral report to your class and point out the important facts included in the articles.

Suggested Articles

"Boutiques." *Business Week*, January 15, 1972.

"C.B.S. Means Creativity in Buying Services." *Fashion Retailer*, **3**, January 1973.

"Retailing Tomorrow." *Stores Magazine*, February 1973.

"Critique on the Quest for a Common Denominator." *Stores Magazine*, March 1973.

"Total Vended Dollar Volume." *Vend Magazine*, May 1, 1971.

NOTES

[1] "Boutiques," *Business Week*, Jan. 15, 1972, p. 19.

[2] Dun and Bradstreet, Inc., Reports (New York, 1972–73).

[3] "A Guide to Consumer Markets," Report, No. 569, New York: The Conference Board, 1972–73, p. 222.

[4] Department of Commerce, Census of Business, *Retail Trade, 1972 Report*, "Single Unit and Multiunits," Washington, D.C.: U.S. Gov't. Printing Office, 1976, p. 2.

[5] "The Fifty Largest Retailing Companies," *Fortune Magazine*, July 1976, pp. 210–11.

[6] "Total Vended Dollar Volume," Census of Industry, *Vend Magazine*, May 1, 1971, p. 36.

[7] Ibid.

[8] Department of Commerce, Census of Business, *Retail Trade, 1972, Special Report*, "Firm Size in U.S.," Washington, D.C.: U.S. Gov't. Printing Office, 1976), p. xxv.

[9] Ibid., p. 210.

[10] Ibid., p. 223.

[11] Ibid., p. 219.

[12] Ibid., p. 212.

[13] Ibid., p. 220.

[14] Ibid., p. 218.

[15] Ibid., p. 214.

[16] Robert T. Sakowitz, "Critique on the Quest for a Common Denominator," *Stores Magazine*, March 1973, p. 16.

[17] "Retailing Tomorrow," *Stores Magazine*, Feb. 1973, p. 15.

[18] Ibid.

[19] Ibid.

[20] Ibid., p. 16.

[21] "The Future of Retailing," *Stores Magazine*, Jan. 1970, p. 7.

[22] Ibid., p. 8.

[23] Ibid., p. 7.

[24] Ibid., p. 8.

10

Fashion Merchandising

Merchandising activities are vital to the successful operation of a retail store. Since the turn of the century, merchandising has been recognized as an organization function in retailing. The term *fashion merchandising*, however, may conjure up a variety of images: the local downtown department store or specialty shop; little boutiques that have brought new and exciting decors to old houses, small shops, barns, and alleyways; or, on the other hand, a fabulous regional shopping center, architecturally dramatic and functionally complete with food, entertainment, and huge assortments of merchandise arranged in colorful and highly stimulating displays. Fashion merchandising is all of this, but more, too; and those who want to be a part of the scene tomorrow must look beneath and beyond the color and excitement of today's successful merchandising establishments. We must determine what is unique or different about merchandising fashion goods, what kinds of activities are involved, who performs them, and what buying and selling policies are influenced by fashion. The purpose of this chapter is to determine these details by developing the fashion-merchandising concept, by explaining five fashion-merchandising responsibilities, and by considering the influences of the fashion cycle in relation to a number of concepts that determine fashion-merchandising policies in retail stores.

THE FASHION-MERCHANDISING CONCEPT

First, consider the term *fashion merchandising*. In Part One of this book, fashion was presented: what it was yesterday, what it is today, and how to predict fashion for tomorrow. Fashion is what people are doing, saying, wearing, feeling, and thinking at a given time. Fashion is evidenced by consumer acceptance patterns. *Consumer acceptance* is a part of the fashion-merchandising concept.

Traditionally, apparel and other textile products have been referred to as fashion merchandise or "soft goods," which is the term used in the fashion industry. In Part Two we talked about various kinds of fashion merchandise that are produced on a seasonal basis by manufacturers throughout the United States and in many foreign countries. Seasonal change in fashion merchandise is reflected in the styles, fabrics, and colors generally accepted by people at a given period. *Seasonal change* is thus also a part of the fashion-merchandising concept.

Fashion goods move rapidly and directly from the manufacturer's point of production, to the retailer's point of sale, and on to the consumer. This rapid flow of fashion goods from the producer, to the retailer, to the consumer constitutes the marketing process for fashion merchandise and reflects the structure of the fashion industry. The three-stage *marketing process* is a part of the fashion-merchandising concept.

The fashion merchant must make advance commitments to the manufacturer for exact quantities of seasonable merchandise in order to make fashion goods available to the consumer at the right time. Thus, the fashion merchant, as a purchasing agent for the consumer must (1) *anticipate* and *estimate* consumer demand for certain kinds of merchandise, (2) *search* the markets and *select* specific items of merchandise, (3) *present* appropriate merchandise for consumer selection, and (4) *provide* the services needed to complete the sale of available goods to the consumer. The fashion merchant as a *purchasing agent* is a part of the fashion-merchandising concept.

Now that we have developed these four concepts of fashion merchandise, we can summarize the broad fashion-merchandising concept: *Fashion merchandising are the various activities performed at the retail level to effect the purchase and to ensure the profitable sale of appropriate assortments of fashion merchandise in anticipation of seasonal consumer demand.*

These specific responsibilities will now be examined in light of this definition.

FASHION-MERCHANDISING RESPONSIBILITIES

Merchandising was designated in Chapter 9 as one of the several functional divisions in the organization of retail stores. Traditionally, the merchandising division has been responsible for both buying and selling activities.

The Buying-Selling Cycle

Dr. John Wingate, a recognized authority in the field of retail management, has defined the merchandising function in terms of a buying-selling cycle with three distinct phases: (1) estimating customers' requirements, (2) procuring required goods and making them available when and where wanted, and (3) motivating customers to buy the goods made available to them. [1]

The first two phases of this buying-selling cycle are related to buying merchandise; the third phase is concerned with selling merchandise. However, as the term *buying-selling cycle* suggests, these three phases are interrelated and continual by nature. The merchandise requirements of customers cannot be anticipated and estimated unless customer acceptance of available goods is evaluated at the point of sale. On the other hand, an appropriate assortment of merchandise cannot be procured unless the customer's requirements are assessed for specific assortments of merchandise. As a result, the cycle continues with no beginning and no end.

Note that the three phases of the buying-selling cycle defined by Wingate suggest many of the same kinds of activities discussed previously in developing the fashion-merchandising concept.

Responsibilities and Duties

Now you are aware that the fashion merchandising responsibilities are concerned with both the buying and selling of merchandise. Furthermore, these buying and selling responsibilities are interrelated and are considered to be supportive of the fashion-merchandising concept. Five major statements of responsibilities have been formulated to incorporate the various activities involved in the fashion-merchandising concept and the buying-selling cycle. For the purposes of this chapter, the fashion-merchandising responsibilities are:

1. *Planning and evaluating merchandise:* Activities related to anticipating consumer demand and estimating customer requirements.
2. *Procuring merchandise:* Activities related to searching the markets and selecting specific items of merchandise and making them available whenever and wherever wanted.
3. *Promoting merchandise:* Activities related to presenting merchandise to the consumer through advertising and various other media

and motivating consumers to buy goods made available to them.

4. *Merchandising departments:* Activities related to arranging merchandise space for competitive selling and for presenting appropriate assortments of merchandise for consumer selection.

5. *Supervising personnel:* Activities related to providing services needed to complete the sale of available goods to the consumer.

Note that the first two responsibilities represent buying activities. The last three responsibilities are concerned with the selling aspects of merchandising. However, the latter two responsibilities—arranging merchandising departments and supervising personnel—may be separated from the merchandising function in large multiunit operations with centralized buying offices, as explained in Chapter 9.

Numerous duties support these five merchandising responsibilities. The major duties are primarily concerned with the maintenance of records and the maintenance of stock. These two types of duties and a variety of miscellaneous activities contribute to the performance of the fashion merchandising responsibilities.

The owner-manager of a small store or the buyer in a large store may carry out these fashion-merchandising responsibilities. In large department stores, the buyers may delegate certain responsibilities to assistant buyers and sales personnel. Merchandise managers may be assigned the responsibility of working with several buyers in multiunit retail operations. Whatever the size of the store or however the store is organized, some or all of the five kinds of responsibilities will be performed by the buyer, usually with the aid of an assistant buyer and/or sales personnel. (See this job profile in Appendix 5, p. 269.)

MERCHANDISING AND THE FASHION-CYCLE CONCEPT

Successful fashion buying and selling are based on facts, figures, comparisons, and considerable fashion judgment. Several concepts influence fashion judgment greatly and, thereby, have

a tremendous impact on the availability of fashion goods to the consumer. These concepts converge to influence the buying and selling of fashion goods and to bring the retailer and the consumer together. The nature of fashion itself is of primary importance; thus, the fashion cycle (explained in Chapter 2 and illustrated in Figure 2.8, p. 70) is closely related to the buying-selling cycle and to the *communication message goals* that bring the retailer and the consumer together. The fashion cycle is also reflected in some of the market characteristics of the consumer, who is the retailer's selling target. It is one thing to say that a fashion is introduced, moves through the acceptance stages, and declines into obsolescence; we should also understand the relevance of this concept to the actual buying and selling of fashion goods.

Buying and the Fashion Cycle

The fashion buyer must understand the nature of fashion as it relates to the planning, evaluating, and procuring of merchandise. The influence of fashion varies, depending on the nature of the merchandise. Consumer acceptance patterns do not usually rise and fall in one brief season. In fact, it is only possible to view the fashion cycle in retrospect, over one or two, five, or ten years. In Figure 10.1 the cyclical movement of several fashions is traced in order to give an example of the variations in the acceptance patterns in terms of the length of the fashion cycle. This process of analyzing and plotting the fashion cycle, detailed in Appendix 2, offers a means of studying some of today's fashions.

Traditionally women's apparel has reflected the movement of the fashion cycle; however, men's wear and children's wear have become more fashion-oriented in the last two decades. The influence of fashion varies from season to season. Fabrics and colors that were important in the fall usually give way to different textures and color ranges in the spring. The buyer has to make sense out of all this fashion change and put it together in terms of the merchandise in the retail store.

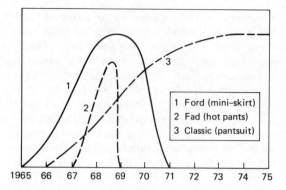

FIGURE 10.1 *Variations of acceptance patterns in fashion cycles.*

Planning and Evaluating Fashion Goods

The buyer must first evaluate what has happened and what is happening in the fashion cycle for each item of merchandise in his or her department. Then future sales can be anticipated and seasonal merchandise plans made. The departmental sales records tell part of the fashion-cycle story. The planning and evaluating take place on a daily, weekly, and seasonal basis. Plans must be made six to eight months in advance of the consumer buying or retail selling season. Estimates are based on *anticipated sales* for the coming season and on the *fashion judgment* of the buyer.

Anticipating Fashion Sales. Much guesswork can be eliminated if planning and evaluating are based on actual sales records. Past and present sales records are translated into anticipated sales for the season ahead or for any designated period of time, as illustrated in Figure 10.2.

The daily record tells the buyer how many of each item of merchandise were in stock at a given time and the number of pieces that were sold. It can be determined immediately how many items have not been sold and so remain in stock. This is the *fashion acceptance* picture for the day, the week, or the month, depending on which time period is being evaluated. These fashion acceptance pictures represent the fashion cycle for the season or for the year.

Usually, the questions in a buyer's mind are

"How did today's sales records compare with yesterday's and with last week's?" And "How do today's sales compare with this same time last year?" This is evaluating merchandise. The daily sales records must be studied by *merchandise classifications*—that is, a group of related items. Merchandise may be grouped by styles, colors, prices, or other important variables in the selling picture, that reflection of consumer acceptance. These sales records must also be broken down and studied item by item on a daily, weekly, and periodic basis. If today's sales of a certain item are more, compared with yesterday's, then the buyer might surmise that sales volume has not yet reached the peak of the fashion cycle. If, however, by comparison with yesterday's, last week's, and that of the period before that, the number of items sold today is less, then the buyer may consider that the peak of the fashion cycle has been reached and sales are starting a downward trend. Of course, there are various other factors that affect sales: for instance, weather and the local economic picture. The buyer evaluates and plans merchandise based on these kinds of sales facts and figures, along with other considerations.

The fashion cycle in the form of sales records for a number of merchandise classifications within one department might appear as depicted in Figure 10.2. This anticipated sales picture is based on the fashion-cycle concept. Note that each of the X positions denotes a buying decision, and each of the O positions represents a buying judgment as to the estimated number of units of merchandise that will be sold at various periods during the current consumer selling season in question. Sales normally are anticipated on a weekly, bimonthly, and monthly basis when projecting the seasonal totals.

Fashion Judgment. A fashion judgment is made in terms of a group of related items, such as shirt-type blouses in a range of colors or prices. This is known as *classification merchandising*. A fashion judgment made in terms of just one item that is selling rapidly is known as *single-item merchandising*. Fashion judgments must be focused on questions that relate to the stages of the fashion cycle. When will certain new fashions begin

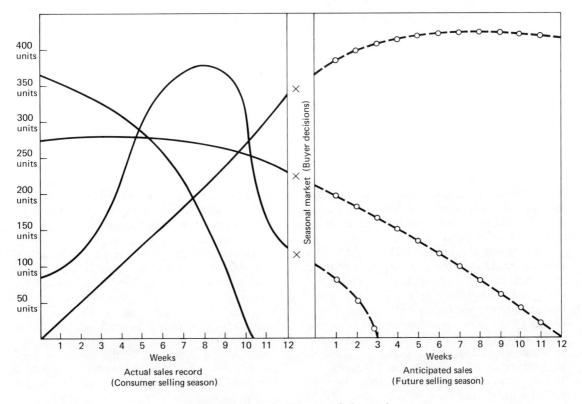

FIGURE 10.2 *Anticipating fashion sales.*

to reach general acceptance? Has a fashion look or an item of merchandise already reached its peak in terms of acceptance by the consumer? Does a small decline in sales of an item mean the regression stage is under way? In Chapter 3 the various awareness factors were discussed in detail along with the measurements and indicators that help the buyer to become more skillful in making fashion judgments.

The fashion buyer uses all the facts and figures available, then applies all the fashion knowledge experience has developed. Fashion judgment is reflected in the planning and evaluating, in the projections of additional assortments of merchandise needed for the coming season, and in the decisions that serve as a guide in the procurement of merchandise. The fashion cycle concept is an inherent part of planning and evaluating fashion goods.

PROCURING FASHION GOODS

The buyer purchases fashion goods on the basis of planning and evaluating activities. In this way the procurement of merchandise is based on the anticipation and projection of sales and fashion judgment—in other words, on the fashion cycle. The merchandise must be procured by the buyer. The fashion cycle concept is related to the *seasonal buying periods* and to the *fashion buying cycle.*

Seasonal Buying Periods. The actual procurement of fashion goods takes place six to eight months in advance of the consumer buying season. Buyers usually go to one or more of the seasonal fashion markets to place orders, in advance of each fashion season. The fashion buyer may go to different market centers, depending on the nature of the merchandise or the season. A sportswear buyer may go to the California or Miami markets from time to time to see the newest fashions in swimwear. These markets are known for their leadership in resort fashions. New fashion ideas are introduced in these markets. For example, the topless swim suit was introduced in the California market. The coat and dress buyer may go to the New York market once or twice a year to be aware of the introductory stages of the fashion cycle. At other times buyers usually go to the regional market nearest their stores. Some merchandise may be bought from the manufacturers' representatives who call on the store and through the resident buying office, if the store enlists such a service.

Each season the buyer procures the fashion goods to meet the anticipated consumer demand. Each time he or she utilizes the facts and figures developed in the planning and evaluating process. The term *open to buy* refers to the amount of money available for procuring fashion goods. These buying plans indicate exact purchases both by number of items and by dollars available for each merchandise classification. Usually, the buying plan is broken down further into the number and dollars for each price line, and for size, color, fabric, and style detail, such as long sleeves or short sleeves. The more detailed the buying plan, the less confusing the buying decisions. This allows the buyer to concentrate on the fashion aspects of the merchandise during the seasonal market.

Fashion Buying Cycle. The buyer evaluates each manufacturer's line on the basis of the fashion cycle as he or she interprets it for a regional area. Fashion judgments must be made on the basis of the styles available for order in each apparel manufacturer's sample line for the season. The buying decisions are made with the anticipated sales picture in mind. The buying cycle presented in Figure 10.3 reflects anticipated sales and is directly related to the fashion cycle. This is the profile of a fashion department—testing fashion trends, maximizing stock, reducing stock, and closing out stock.

The *testing* period gives the buyer an opportunity to let his or her customers see the new fashion trends in design, color, and fabrics, in the in-troductory stage of the fashion cycle. During the *maximum stock* period, there must be complete assortments of merchandise that has general acceptance by the consumer. These assortments include size ranges, colors, styles, and prices to meet the customers' needs and wants.

In the seasonal market, the buyer first selects the fashion items that form the basic stock for maximum coverage in assortments that carry through the season as the inventory is reduced and stock is finally closed out. Usually the buyer will visit the various manufacturers from which she or he regularly buys and will make decisions on basic merchandise. As the decisions are made on the number of sizes, the colors, and the fabrics, *delivery dates* are staggered so that the arrival of new merchandise will correspond with anticipated sales as indicated in Figure 10.2.

Next, the buyer searches for new fashion items both from the store's regular manufacturers and from other manufacturers' lines, if time permits. Fashion judgments will be made relative to the "test styles" indicated in Figure 10.3. Buying decisions will be influenced by the apparel makers' interpretation of fashion trends that have potential for the coming season. Styles will be selected in a limited assortment for the purpose of testing consumer acceptance. This is the introduction stage in the fashion cycle, a very risky time for the apparel manufacturer as well as for the fashion buyer.

Many other factors complicate the buying of fashion goods, but the fashion-cycle concept is basic to planning, evaluating, and procuring fashion goods. Following are some of the aspects of the selling responsibilities influenced by the fashion cycle.

Selling and the Fashion Cycle

The selling of fashion goods includes the responsibilities for promoting sales, merchandising the department and supervising personnel involved in sales and services.

PROMOTING SALES OF FASHION GOODS

The fashion-cycle concept is related directly to the promotional strategy used in selling fashion

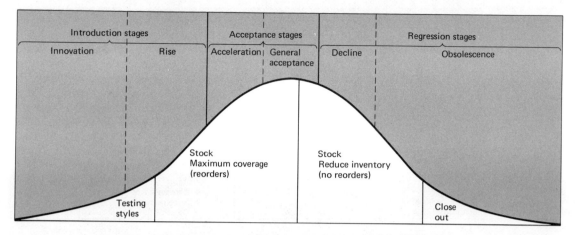

FIGURE 10.3 *Buying cycle for fashion merchandise.*

goods. The fashion message is communicated through promotional events, advertising, display, and so on. New fashions are heralded early, before the actual consumer buying season. Merchandise that has general acceptance is promoted on a day-to-day basis, but little effort is expended in promoting fashion goods that have started down the ladder.

The *promotion cycle* is closely associated with the fashion-cycle concept, as indicated in Figure 10.4. Three promotional goals are to inform, to persuade, and remind.

Informing. This promotional goal coincides with the introduction of new fashions in terms of the fashion cycle. Preseason promotional events may be planned to inform the public about current fashion trends—colors, styles, and fabrics—usually through the efforts of a fashion coordinator and/or buyer, sales promotion director, and/or advertising and display departments. Sometimes this is known as *institutional-type* promotion in the retail field, because the goal is to enhance the store's fashion image in the mind of the consumer community. The promotional message is intended to appeal to the fashion leaders and to inform the fashion consumers that the newest fashions are already available in the store. Fashion designers may be scheduled to make appearances in the store; fashion programs may be presented at charity benefits; fashion shows may serve to educate the store's customers

and the community in terms of fashion news and trends. Newspaper advertisements may acclaim the fashion leadership of the store and invite the public to come. Window displays and departmental displays will pick up the fashion story and repeat the featured fashion trends.

The promotional efforts at this stage are aimed to inform the public—to tell consumers that the store has the latest fashions, the exclusive lines, and the distinctive looks. The store's fashion image is developed by promoting fashions at the introductory stage in the fashion cycle, before general acceptance by the consumer. These efforts are focused on enhancing the prestige of the store as a fashion-leading *institution*. Other promotional efforts may help the store achieve this first goal of *informing* the public—creating a fashion image and building good will in the community, exhibiting at prominent community events, or lending the store's merchandise to local groups. Some of these efforts are rewarded by credit lines in theater programs or recognition in some other form.

Persuading. This next stage in the promotion cycle, as seen in Figure 10.4, stresses the wide variety of fashion merchandise and the range of colors, sizes, and prices. The emphasis now is on *regular price line* merchandise and relates to the general acceptance phase of the fashion cycle. Promotional efforts at this time contribute to the stability of the store's image in the mind of the

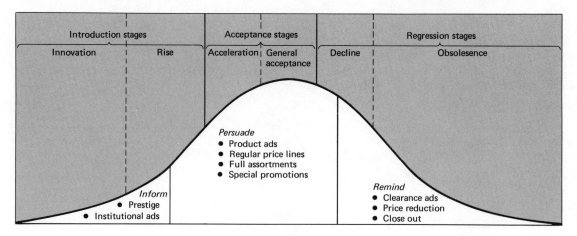

FIGURE 10.4 *Promotion cycle for fashion merchandise.*

consumer. The aim is to persuade the customer to shop at the store and to try to convince the potential consumer that the store can satisfy his or her wants and needs better than some other store. Now the focus is on the merchandise the buyer has in stock in large volume and in complete assortments to meet the customers' demand—The customer must be persuaded that he or she can find what is wanted or needed in the wide assortments of merchandise carried by the store.

Reminding. This stage in the promotion cycle occurs after the peak of the selling season, and it may be near the end of the fashion cycle for some merchandise. The assortments of fashion are broken—an incomplete range of sizes or prices to meet customers' needs. However, remember, the customer is about to stop buying since the season is nearly finished, and the attention of the buyer is already focusing on the fashion trends for the approaching season.

Moderate price reductions come first, and promotional efforts usually remind the customer that the store still has assortments of seasonal merchandise and will give the customer the benefit of the lateness of the season. Markdowns on wanted consumer goods are appropriate in terms of the buyer's concern for reducing stock. Sales at this time will help to reduce the stock at a desired rate for the end of the season. Sometimes special purchases of merchanise are made from manu-

facturers at reduced cost to the retail buyer. Promotion of special-purchase merchandise may bring customers into the store after the selling season has started to decline.

Clearances and closeouts are usually drastic markdowns to clear the stock, to make way for new seasonal fashions, and to release dollars for the buyer's open-to-buy. Little if any promotional effort will be aimed at giving the customer an opportunity to buy end-of-season bargains. This is the decline and obsolescence phase of the fashion cycle. The buyer may not be able even to *give* the merchandise away. The store is already losing money because markdowns at this stage usually mean selling fashion goods at near or below cost.

MERCHANDISING FASHION DEPARTMENTS

The fashion cycle is profiled in the assortment of merchandise purchased by the buyer in the advanced seasonal markets. This same concept is carried into the merchandising of the departments as the consumer buying season approaches. The total fashion feeling for the season should be reflected in the assortments and in the way the merchandise is presented to the customers. The seasonal fashion story is told by the important seasonal styles, colors, and fabrics, both in the new fashions and in the basic fashion goods.

Fashion Image. The fashion image of a department is created by emphasis on those fashions that are in the introduction stage of the fashion cycle. Purchased in small quantities by the buyer, they generate the fashion image of the department in the minds of the customers.

New fashions provide excitement in the department, they stimulate the salespeople, and they inform the customers about what is to come. If these new fashion looks are accepted readily by the consumer, they should be reordered quickly, although caution is needed by the buyer— fashion judgment has to be exercised to make decisions on how many of which fashions to reorder. Sales may be lost if fast-selling items are not reordered—they are on the upward swing of the fashion cycle. Markdowns may have to be taken if too many are reordered; the fashion cycles sometimes move slowly and at other times rapidly.

Although fashion trends are exciting, they do not produce volume in sales, nor do they necessarily increase profits. New fashions that the customer does not accept may even be costly in terms of profit. Markdowns sometimes include the most important fashion looks introduced at the beginning of the season. For some reason, the customer did not accept the new look. Perhaps it does not move on up the fashion cycle; perhaps it moves more slowly than anticipated; or perhaps it will not move into general acceptance until the next season. Remember that time tells the fashion cycle story.

Basic Image. The basic image of the department is expressed in the fashions that have general acceptance by the consumer. The major portion of the merchandise was purchased by the buyer to provide the complete assortments needed to satisfy the largest number of consumers. This is what general acceptance means in terms of the fashion cycle—everyone wants this kind of merchandise—well, almost everyone. The actual percentage of this segment of the fashion market is discussed in detail later in this chapter.

Each season certain styles in each merchandise classification must be purchased and maintained in stock in the right sizes, colors, fabrics, and prices to meet the demand. A close check must be kept on the inventory—the number of items in stock in terms of color, sizes, prices, etc. If the customer cannot find the right size or the right price according to personal need, he or she may go to another store and the sale may be lost. If this happens often, the store may lose the customer, too.

To maintain the basic image of the merchandise in the department, it may be necessary to reorder or make special orders. Reorders should be planned if advance sales indicate sufficient demand. In fashion departments this may be done *only* if it is early in the season before competitive stores have saturated the consumer market with similar fashion goods. Some women's apparel manufacturers do not supply the retailer on a reorder basis, but men's wear and other fashion goods may tend to depend more on the reorder system. Special orders are more prevalent in certain types of fashion goods than others— exclusive lines and special categories of merchandise, such as leather goods and furs, for example.

SUPERVISING PERSONNEL IN FASHION DEPARTMENTS

The buyer, assistant buyer, or department manager usually supervises sales and services in fashion departments. The salespeople need to know what the selling features of the merchandise are and how to sell fashion goods associated with each phase of the fashion cycle. They need to know what fashion is important to the customer and what quality and performance features can be used in selling to the customer.

Sales Meetings. Sales meeting are usually held by the buyer or an assistant on a daily, weekly, or monthly basis. The new merchandise is presented; sometimes new fashions are modeled to produce fashion excitement and to show how to wear a garment. Fashion selling features are pointed out and accessories may be suggested. If there is a *fashion coordinator* in the store, he or she may participate in these sales meetings in fashion departments or schedule seasonal meetings for all store employees or just for salespeople in the fashion departments. Important seasonal fashion information may even be prepared in written form—store news notes or fashion memos—and distributed to salespeople in certain fashion departments. The promotional events and daily advertisements should be brought to the attention of the salespeople. Information of this nature is usually posted in the employee areas or in the departmental stockroom areas.

Customer Contacts. Customer contacts are made by the salespeople, who provide the personal touch in the department. They pass on to the customer the fashion information they have acquired from the buyer, the fashion coordinator, the store owner, trade publications, consumer fashion magazines, and many other sources. Salespeople call the customer's attention to the new and different fashion looks and assist the customer in finding the right fashion item from the basic merchandise assortments. Thus, the salespeople too, are influenced by the fashion-cycle concept.

Salespeople should be aware of the relationship of the fashion *selling-use cycle* to the fashion cycle, as indicated in Figure 10.5. They need to understand why the buyer arranged for fashion goods to be delivered early in the season, usually before the *consumer-use pattern* has

started. Early in the season some customers start shopping at their favorite store; if the right fashions are there, they go no farther; if they are not there, customers may not be back.

The selling pattern and the customer-use pattern move along at the same pace until the peak of the season is reached. The selling begins to slow first. The consumer will continue to wear the fashion goods until the season ends but probably will buy little more. The fashion buyer has already stopped buying, and the promotional efforts are beginning to focus on the next season. Although the selling cycle has peaked, the consumer-use cycle has not started down yet. Sometimes a buyer may have obtained special-purchase fashion goods from a factory; due to lateness in the season the price is lower and the store can give the customer an opportunity to share in the saving and at the same time stimulate sales and customer traffic for a while longer, until the next season gets under way.

Now you should have a better understanding of how very important the fashion cycle is to the buying and selling of fashion goods. You should be aware of the relationship of the fashion cycle to anticipated sales (Figure 10.2), to the buying cycle (Figure 10.3), to the fashion promotion message (Figure 10.4) and to the fashion selling-

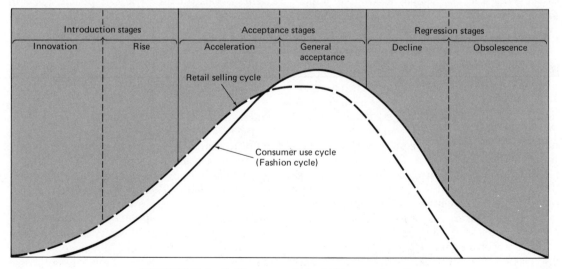

FIGURE 10.5 *Selling-use cycle for fashion merchandise.*

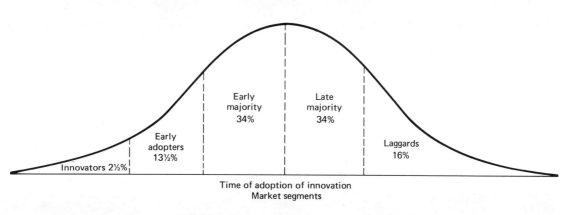

Early majority 34%

Late majority 34%

Early adopters 13½%

Laggards 16%

Innovators 2½%

Time of adoption of innovation
Market segments

FIGURE 10.6 *Consumer market segments.*

use cycle (Figure 10.5). The interlacing of these various concepts takes place in the mind of the fashion buyer, in the office, on the sales floor, in the stockroom, in the seasonal fashion market, in the sales promotion offices—advertising and display—and these concepts are reflected in the consumer's wardrobe. What the consumer buys and uses (wears) becomes the fashion acceptance pattern and will influence the buying and selling of fashion goods. Again and again this buying-selling cycle continues, and on and on the fashion cycle goes, and over and over the buyer takes the risk of anticipating consumer demand for fashion goods six to eight months in advance of the selling season. The buying-selling responsibilities are extremely complicated; each season many fashions are introduced, some are made available in volume assortments on an anticipated basis, and some decline during the season or at the close of the season and give way to the fashion trends of the next season.

Consumers and the Fashion-Cycle Concept

Now we are ready to take the last step—to the consumer market place. There are five distinct groups in the market segments identified by the time of adoption of new products. As seen in Figure 10.6, the consumers in these market segments are designated as innovators, who account for only 2½ per cent of the market; early adopters, who represent 13½ per cent of the market;

early majority and late majority, each of which forms 34 per cent of the market; and laggards, who comprise 16 per cent of the market.[2] The group characteristics in these five market segments are readily associated with the several stages in the fashion cycle and, thereby, relate to the buying and selling of fashion goods. For the purposes of this chapter, we have translated into fashion terms the various characteristics used by several authorities in the consumer behavior area.[3] We have related these market segments to the fashion cycle and have developed the fashion market segments, as indicated in Figure 10.7.

FASHION MARKET SEGMENTS

There are three consumer groups identified with the fashion market segments: The fashion leaders, the fashion followers, and the fashion laggers. Each of these market segments has unique characteristics when viewed in terms of the stages in the fashion cycle—the introduction, acceptance, and decline—and with the other related consumer market characteristics—the innovators, the early adopters, the early majority, the late majority, and the laggards.

Fashion Leaders. These fashion leaders represent the innovators and early adopters and, as such, they comprise approximately 16 per cent of the total fashion market segment, as indicated in Figure 10.7. In relation to the fashion cycle, new

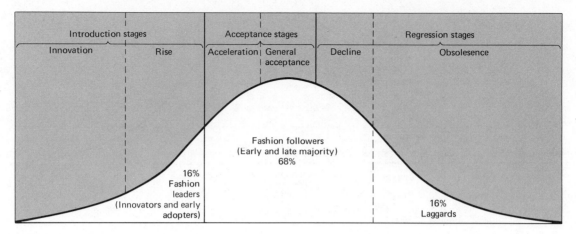

FIGURE 10.7 *Market segments for fashion merchandise.*

styles (innovations) are presented at the introduction stage.

- Fashion leaders are experimental and venturesome. They desire distinctiveness in fashion. They seek new colors, new styles, and new fabrics. They adopt new ideas readily and influence other consumers to do so. They are socially involved people and are usually active in community affairs.
- Fashion leaders have an intense interest in fashion news. They read such magazines as *Vogue*, *Glamour* (depending on the age group) and the fashion sections of newspapers. They may gather fashion news as they travel to fashion centers both at home and abroad.
- Most fashion leaders have developed a cosmopolitan approach to life and search out opportunities to spread the fashion word about seasonal and future trends.
- Fashion leaders often serve as personal fashion consultants for friends, peers, or even professional groups. They judge beauty contests, design contests, etc. They are often called upon to model and sometimes commentate for fashion shows or programs.
- Fashion leaders often seem compelled to deviate from and to show dissatisfaction with traditional ways. The exotic and the dramatic often appeal to them. They are imitated by others because of their social position or status.

- Fashion leaders may be gifted and unusual people. They may have won some distinction in the community, the state, or perhaps with a professional group of national influence.

Fashion leaders are effective *change agents* in the community and in the fashion world. If it were not for this kind of fashion leadership, the fashion industries might come to an abrupt halt. The fashion creators (designers and couture houses) owe their livelihood to this group. The textile and apparel industries count heavily on it to stimulate acceptance of fashion trends. The retailer would find it difficult to develop a consumer market without fashion leaders. Fashion leaders wear distinctive fashion apparel and desire quality in design and fabric. The fashion stores (couture houses, boutiques, specialty stores, and department stores) are especially dependent on customers with these characteristics.

Fashion Followers.   Fashion followers might be referred to as both early and late majority, and in terms of these two market groups they represent approximately 68 per cent of the total fashion market segment, as indicated in Figure 10.7. Within the fashion cycle, the followers are predominantly associated with the acceptance stages.

- Fashion followers are satisfied to emulate others after they become aware of fashion trends.

They may give a great deal of thought to fashion-adoption decisions.

- Fashion followers might be said to follow one of Alexander Pope's dictum, "Be not the first by whom the new are tried, nor yet the last to lay the old aside." They try to stay in the middle of the fashion road.
- Fashion followers approach new fashion ideas cautiously and observe others before they take fashion actions. They are influenced by the opinions of others and respond to the pressure of peers with whom they are involved socially.
- Fashion followers are willingly led by the fashion leadership of their community and by local retailers of fashion, although they may not frequent the fashion stores.
- Fashion followers wait for the majority to adopt a fashion. When they do adopt a fashion they influence their peers to do likewise.
- Fashion followers are the typical mass Americans. They lead a casual way of life and want easy-to-wear, comfortable clothes. They seek out the look of fashion but not the extremes.
- Fashion followers like fashions that are adapted, simplified and homogenized, yet express good taste.
- Fashion followers want the look of affluence within the limits of their life styles and their pocketbooks; they are careful not to offend their friends by outdressing them. The most important factors that influence their selection of fashion are price, color, and material; of less importance are brands, style details, and other features.

Fashion followers are not change agents in the community because they have little influence on their peers. They suffer agonies at looking "out of place," and are likely to consult their friends about what *they* are going to wear at a particular function. However, the fashion industries are completely dependent on these followers of fashion. They make possible mass production in the textile and apparel industries and the retailer could not exist in the small town or the large city without them. Fashion followers buy accepted styles in moderate to low price ranges, usually regular price-line merchandise, but pick bargains when they find them. The entry of the discounter into the retail field was encouraged by the fashion followers.

Fashion laggers. The fashion lagger accounts for approximately 16 per cent of the fashion market, as indicated in Figure 10.7. The lagger is always among the last to accept a fashion. Usually this happens when the fashion is declining in popularity and sometimes when it is at the point of obsolescence.

- Fashion laggers are never anxious to emulate unless it has become economically advantageous or necessary. They adopt fashion ideas last.
- Fashion laggers are traditionally minded. Enjoying past fashions, they are averse to change.
- Fashion laggers, being somewhat isolationist, usually interact with other consumers who share their views. They may feel moral indignation at new styles, finding them immodest, extravagant, and so on.
- Fashion laggers, particularly those of advanced age, may reject fashion completely or may accept it out of necessity, as when midcalf-length skirts were impossible to find. They sometimes influence others—for example, in insisting that boys not be permitted to wear long hair at school or girls not allowed to wear jeans.
- Fashion laggers search for sale-priced fashion goods, discount merchandise, and fashions that are going out of season or are no longer wanted by other consumers.

Fashion laggers definitely do not respond except unfavorably, to change agents. No one in the fashion industries at any level—textile and apparel or retail—actually thinks of them as a preferred selling target. Yet, the laggers are 16 per cent of the fashion market segment (notice that this is the same percentage as the leaders), and absorb a lot of leftovers—mill ends, seconds, retail buyer's mistakes—at markdowns, clearances, and closeouts.

The three fashion market segments—leaders, followers, and laggers—interrelate with the various phases of the fashion cycle and, thus, have a tremendous impact on retailing. These various aspects of the concepts related to the fashion cycle are summarized in Table 10.1. The profile of the three stages of the fashion cycle appears first; then the profiles of four other related concepts: fashion buying cycle, fashion selling-use cycle, fashion promotion cycle, and fashion market segments. Various interrelationships can be studied from the summary of these concepts. The various profiles suggest the interdependence of the fashion industries—suppliers, manufacturers, and retailers—due to the nature of fashion and the concept of the fashion cycle.

Consumer Groups

Fashion market segments are of particular importance to retailers of fashion goods. However, within each segment of the fashion market, there may be several consumer groups of special interest to certain types of retailers—age groups, sex groups, income groups, occupational groups, and special groups. Many fashion stores serve consumer groups with individual clothing needs. Some stores may specialize in clothing for selected age groups or for only one age group. For instance, specialty stores may cater to only one age group—children's wear or young adult's clothes—or to only one sex group—men's wear

or women's apparel. Specialty stores need to know the characteristics of the particular consumer market they serve. These characteristics vary from city to city across the country.

Income groups are of vital importance to retailing in every community. Retailers need to keep up to date on the factors that affect incomes in the consumer market area. Loss of crops for farmers and strikes or lay-offs of factory workers are just two examples of conditions that affect the consumer's income and, thereby, the retailer. Closely related to income is the current state of the economy. For example, inflation and depression plagued the consumer and retailer as well as the manufacturer and supplier in the mid-1970s.

Occupational groups—professionals, executives, skilled workers, day laborers—often are significant at the retail level. Some cities have a high concentration of skilled workers, which greatly affects the retailers' merchandise assortments—price lines might be moderate to low, whereas the opposite would be true in cities where there is a high percentage of professional personnel and executives, such as in headquarters areas for large firms. This occupational factor is readily detected by the multiunit retailers who have stores in several locations in one large city or in different cities across the country. Each

TABLE 10.1 Summary of Concepts Related to Fashion Buying and Selling

Fashion cycle	Fashion buying cycle	Fashion selling-use cycles	Fashion promotion cycles	Fashion market segments
Introduction (innovation and rise)	Testing styles New trends	Retail selling precedes consumer usage.	Information Institutional Prestige	Fashion leaders Innovators Early adopters
Acceptance (acceleration and general acceptance)	Maximum stocks Complete assortments Reorders	Retail selling reaches peak before consumer use.	Persuasion Regular price lines Special promotions	Fashion followers Early majority Late majority
Regression (decline and obsolescence)	Reduced stock No reorders Markdowns Special purchases Closeouts	Consumer use continues as retail selling declines.	Reminders Reduced prices Special promotions Clearances Closeouts	Fashion laggers

store may serve consumer groups with different characteristics due to the occupational factor.

Special groups—the handicapped or ethnic minorities—comprise a small and highly individualized market. In the 1970s more retailers and manufacturers specialized in merchandise for the physically handicapped consumer. The needs and interests of ethnic and subcultural groups also have gained a higher level of concern in the United States in recent decades.

The following ten statements give insight into present and future consumer concerns.[4]

1. By 1980 30 per cent of personal income will be available for discretionary spending; 50 per cent of households will surpass the $15,000 or more income bracket; and 40 per cent of family income will go to families whose head is under age thirty-five.
2. Working wives are a major factor in the increase in family income: 1.66 was the average number of wage earners per family in 1971; 40 per cent of wives (with husbands at home) worked in 1970; and 50 per cent of wives expected to work by 1980.
3. The shift from low- to middle-income brackets will bring accompanying shifts in consumer buying patterns.
4. Personal expenditures during the last twenty years have represented approximately two thirds of the GNP.
5. Consumer expenditures are expected to be up 50 per cent for food and clothing in 1985; textiles, furnishings, and clothing prices are expected to be up an additional 5 to 10 per cent by the late 1970s.
6. There has been an upsurge in home sewing since 1965. More than half (44M) of the 82 million females ages twelve to sixty-five were sewing in 1971. The home-sewing industry is a $2.3 billion market (inclusive of sales of fabrics, patterns, notions, and machines).
7. Influences on consumer choice and decisions to buy affect consumer attitudes and behavior in regard to new products, changing styles, trends, and merchandising methods.
8. To understand the market place is to understand how world supply, demand, policy

control, and monetary values directly affect the consumer market.
9. The American consumer in the 1970s saw evidence of rising prices and an upheaval of consumer spending patterns.
10. Understanding the production-marketing-economic system is vital to intelligent consumer behavior.

THE FASHION MARKET PLACE

Let us take an overview of today's fashion market place, where retailer and consumer meet. Someone has said that the retailer is only eighteen inches from the consumer, but there is still a mighty barrier. The consumer wants the right fashion goods, and the retailer as the purchasing agent wants a reasonable profit.

Role of the Retailer

The role of the retailer in the consumer market place is to make available, on a profit-making basis, the goods and services that correspond with the demand of the various consumer groups served in the *market place*. Two major responsibilities of each retailer are (1) to find out what merchandise the customer wants and (2) to obtain that merchandise from apparel manufacturers. Thus, the retailer functions as the *purchasing agent* for the consumer. As such he or she must stimulate, maintain, and ensure the *profitable* sale of fashion goods. The retailer is responsible for communicating with customers by promoting fashion goods through the various media (newspapers, television, fashion shows, and personal selling).

Role of the Consumer

The *role of the consumer* in the retail market place is to select the fashions he or she wants in the appropriate size and price. These decisions are completely in the hands of the individual consumer. Each consumer has several responsibilities: To find out what fashion looks are appropriate for his or her life style; to find a retail fashion image compatible with the dictates of his or her fashion consciousness and pocketbook; to incorporate the fashion goods purchased into his or her wardrobe and to use them, and enjoy them, expressing a self-concept by manipulating the variables of fashion.

Fashion buying and selling are complicated by many factors, two of which are vital to success in retailing: the nature of the fashion goods offered for sale, and the characteristics of the consumer who is the retailers' selling target.

Fashion reflects the times, people, and culture. Fashion denotes acceptance of change, innovation, interpretations. Analysis of the variables of fashion is a basis for forecasts and predictions.

The giant textile and apparel complex comprises the backbone of the fashion industries. Fashion makers supply fibers and fabrics, produce garments and accessories, and initiate marketing activities. Seasonal fashion markets accelerate the flow of fashion goods to the retailer, the purchasing agent for the consumer. The retail scene is composed of a variety of fashion images. The concept of fashion innovation is evidenced in the marketing process at each level in the fashion industries. Consumer demand is a measure of the acceptance of fashion innovations and of the success of the marketing process. The impact of fashion is apparent throughout the world.

END OF CHAPTER GUIDE

Review, Discussion, and Evaluation

Study of this chapter should enable students to
A. Develop and give evidence of the following kinds of competencies:
1. Awareness of the impact of the buying-selling concept in fashion merchandising.
2. Understanding of the major merchandising functions related to buying-selling responsibilities and duties.
3. Knowledge of the relationship between the fashion-cycle concept and other concepts influencing policy decisions in *buying* fashion goods: anticipating fashion sales, fashion buying cycle, and fashion selling-use cycle.

4. Knowledge of the relationship between the fashion-concept cycle and other concepts influencing policy decisions in *selling* fashion goods: promotional message goals, fashion market segments, and consumer groups.
B. Develop and/or clarify concepts related to the following key words or phrases:
1. fashion merchandising 2. consumer acceptance 3. seasonal change 4. marketing process 5. anticipating fashion sales 6. buying-selling cycle 7. estimating consumer demand 8. seasonal buying periods 9. informing, persuading, and reminding 10. basic versus fashion image 11. selling features 12. customer contacts 13. sales meetings 14. promotion cycle 15. maximum stock coverage 16. fashion-merchandising responsibilities 17. planning and evaluating merchandise 18. procuring merchandise 19. promoting merchandise 20. merchandising departments 21. supervising sales and services 22. fashion judgment 23. merchandise classification 24. single-item merchandising 25. fashion market segments 26. fashion leaders 27. fashion followers 28. fashion laggers 29. consumer groups 30. consumer concerns 31. role of retailer 32. role of consumer 33. fashion market place

Extended Classroom Learning Experiences

A. Study the description of the fashion buyer's job profile in Appendix 5, p. 269.
1. Plan an interview with a retailer who has responsibility for buying merchandise. Review the job profile in Appendix 5, p. 269, and make a list of questions you want to ask about various responsibilities and duties during the interview.
2. After the interview, write a job description for the retailer interviewed. Include the job title, the hierarchy of positions, and a list of responsibilities performed.
3. Compare your job description with the job profiles presented in Appendix 5, p. 269. Briefly summarize the differences in the responsibilities and duties performed by the buyer you interviewed.
B. Fashion decisions are influenced by a knowledge of fashion cycles, which tell the story in retrospect of the life of a fashion. Utilizing the procedures described in "The Process of Quantitative Analysis of Women's Dress Styles," in Appendix 2, p. 258.
1. Trace the stages of two or more styles from their

early introduction as shown by pictures in a selected fashion magazine to the decline or complete obsolescence reflected when pictures of the styles no longer appear in the selected fashion magazine.

2. Prepare a written report. Present the data you collected; compare the various stages of the two or more fashion cycles you traced; and summarize your conclusions drawn from your study of two or more fashion cycles (relate to variations in fashion cycle, Figure 10.1).

C. Select a fashion item that is popular in your community, utilizing the procedure for making a fashion count described in Chapter 3, or note a fashion item that appears most often in two or more current fashion magazines.

1. Arrange an interview with a retail buyer, department manager, or salesperson in a local store where similar items are sold.

2. Find out what the three best-selling fashion items are (according to the store's sales records) in the current consumer buying season.

3. If the fashion item you selected to study is not among the three best sellers, inquire about the retail buyer's reactions in terms of

a. Making a prediction of the anticipated sales of the fashion item you selected in your study (see the anticipated fashion sales model, Figure 10.2, in this chapter.)

b. Make a fashion judgment based on knowledge of the store's customer acceptance or rejection of the fashion item you selected in your study.

D. Arrange an interview with a retail buyer in your community or in a nearby shopping center. Develop a group of three or more questions about seasonal buying periods, such as

1. When and where does the retail buyer go to fashion market centers?

2. How long is the seasonal buying period?

3. Which season is the most important buying period?

4. What other ways does the retail buyer procure fashion goods for the store?

5. Why does the retail buyer go or not go to fashion markets?

E. Collect the fashion advertisements from one or more stores for a month or two. Analyze each ad and group the ads that tend to represent one of the three stages of the promotion cycle. Write a brief report of your findings.

F. Visit a fashion apparel department in two or more stores and make a comparison of the fashion image and the basic image of the departmental merchandise arrangements (such as displays). Write a brief report of your findings.

G. Make a list of the ways in which a store provides fashion information for sales personnel. Arrange an interview with a store manager or department manager and inquire into the extent to which the store utilizes one or more of the ideas suggested here for supervising personnel in fashion departments. Write a brief report of your findings.

H. Review the career area on fashion retailing in the job analysis series in Appendix 6, p. 279.

1. Consider the various job titles in fashion retailing in relation to their responsibilities and duties.

2. Compare the advancement possibilities for a salesperson in a small retail store with those for a salesperson in a large retail operation.

3. Summarize your findings in a brief report on job opportunities in retailing.

I. Read two or more of the articles listed here or research current periodicals or trade journals and select two or more articles related to one of the concepts suggested in the "Review, Discussion, and Evaluation."

1. Prepare note cards while reading each article.

2. Using your note cards, write a brief summary indicating the relation of each article to concepts presented in this chapter.

3. Using your note cards, give an oral report in your class and point out the important facts included in the articles.

Suggested Articles

JUDY COLLINSON, "Your Own Business." *Glamour*, October, 1975.

ANNALEE GOLD, "Buyer Meets Customer on Street Floor." *Stores*, April, 1975.

"Marketing: Last of the Supersalesmen." *Business Week*, September 18, 1974.

TOBI NYBERG, "Fashion Coordinators." *Women's Wear Daily*, July 15, 1975.

"Seven Steps to Increase Sales Productivity." *Stores*, January, 1974.

"Today's Buyer: An Endangered Species?" *Clothes*, Sept. 1, 1973.

NOTES

[1] John W. Wingate and Joseph Friedlander, *Management of Retail Business*. Englewood Cliffs, N.J.: Prentice-Hall, 1963, p. 5.

[2] James Engel, *Consumer Behavior*. New York: Holt, 1968, p. 572.

[3] Stewart H. Britt, *Consumer Behavior and Behaviorial Sciences*. New York: Wiley, 1967, pp. 282–83.

[4] Department of Agriculture, "Focus II, Extension Home Economics," Cooperative Extension Report. Washington, D.C.: U.S. Govt Printing Office, 1974, pp. 7–10.

Appendixes

Appendix 1

Basic Fashion Terms: Names and Style Characteristics

BASIC DRESS SILHOUETTES

Asymmetric Side swept or side closing.

Basic dress A simple, well-designed soft dress generally without front buttons or decoration, made to be worn with a change of accessories.

Draped Fabric arranged in flowing lines or folds from the shoulder; inspired by Greek statues.

Empire High waistline, usually 1 to 3 inches under the bust line, with a low round or square neckline; French influence from the time of Napoleon I.

Kimono The original Japanese kimono is made of one length of cloth with the sleeves, back, and front cut all together. The sash holds it in place. The contemporary kimono is usually seamed at the shoulder.

Middy Follows the details of the sailor uniform. The collar is square in back and the neckline forms a V in front; the blouse is long-waisted, the sleeves are long with a tight cuff.

Peplum A short, flared ruffle at the hipline extending from the waist.

Princess Usually six to eight gores; slim-waisted with a flared skirt.

Sheath Slender and tight fitting dress with no belt, no fullness, no break in the body line; one piece.

Shirtwaist Adapted from the man's shirt; front closing, convertible collar or man's style shirt collar, and yoke; worn with a straight, flared, gored, gathered, or pleated skirt with graceful fullness.

Trumpet Low-placed fullness in godets or pleats in the skirt.

Tunic A long jacket or overblouse over a tight skirt or trousers; tunics may be straight or semi-flared.

BASIC COAT SILHOUETTES

Balmacaan A loose-fitting coat with raglan sleeves.

Battle jacket A hip-length, single-breasted jacket with waistband and patch pockets with flaps (also called lumber jacket or Eisenhower jacket).

Blazer The traditional blazer is a lightweight, collarless jacket, generally single-breasted, sometimes made with contrasting binding and metal buttons. Contemporary blazers have collars and may be double-breasted.

Bolero A short or simulated jacket ending approximately 2½ inches above the waist.

Cape An outer garment with no sleeves falling from the shoulders.

Chanel jacket A classic design made famous by the French designer Coco Chanel; a collarless cardigan-style box jacket with no buttons or fasteners; the center front panels just meet; usually hip length.

Chesterfield A man's formal town, day, or evening coat; solid-color wool, either double- or single-breasted; fitted, semifitted, or box; beltless, with flaps on the pockets. The woman's Chesterfield is similar.

Poncho A rectangle of fabric with a center hole for the head.

Princess A fitted coat, suit, or dress generally single-breasted with six to eight shaped gores extending from the shoulder to a flared hemline.

Redingote A coat of simple lines, generally fitted, made to be worn with a matching or harmonizing dress.

Reefer A single- or double-breasted fitted coat with godets from the shoulder to the hem.

BASIC PANTS SILHOUETTES

Baggies The Oxford baggies of the 1920s; pleats in the front, fly front, unfitted leg from the hip down; cuffs.

Bell bottoms Fitted at the knee and flared at the bottom like a sailor's uniform.

Flared Fitted at the knee, widening toward the hem, but less wide at the hem than bell bottoms.

Harem Gathered at the waist; very full and gathered at the bottom of each leg.

High rise the waist is cut 2 to 3 inches above the natural waistline, usually with straight legs.

Hip hugger The waistline is finished from 2 to 4 inches below the natural waist.

Jeans A Western design, originally made of durable denim with double stitching for work wear. Fashion has cut the jean look in all fabrics.

Jumpsuit One-piece pantsuit cut in a variety of styles.

Slacks Separate men's or women's leisure pants; the name originally used for women's pants before Yves St. Laurent's pantsuit of 1968.

Slim Jims, or capris Tightly fitted pant from the hip down; ankle length.

Stovepipe, or straight leg Fitted at the hips; the pant leg falls straight to the hem.

NECKLINE AND COLLAR STYLES

Bateau A boat-shaped neckline; follows the curve of the collarbone; high in front and back; wide at the sides; ends in the shoulder seams.

Bertha A deep, capelike collar falling softly from a bodice neckline over the shoulders.

Cardigan A high, round, and collarless neckline on a front-buttoning sweater.

Convertible A straight collar; designed and finished to be worn open or closed.

Cowl A soft fold or drape of material at front neckline.

Décolletage An off-the-shoulder, plunging neckline.

Eton A large collar of stiffened white fabric, worn with the Eton jacket; rounded or pointed ends.

Halter A neckline consisting of a strap, rope, or band around the neck, attached to a backless bodice.

Jabot A frill or ruffle; usually lace or lace-trimmed; worn down the front of the bodice and fastened at the neckline.

Mandarin A Chinese collar that stands up all around the neck.

Military A narrow, standing high collar, buttoned in the front.

Peter pan A turned-down collar, from two to three inches in width, having rounded ends in front. Lies flat on the shoulders without much roll.

Surplice A V neckline made by crossing one side over the other; the collar follows the neckline, which sometimes extends from the shoulder to the waistline of the opposite side.

Turtleneck A high, turned-over collar that hugs the throat.

SLEEVE STYLES

Bell A full sleeve that flares at the bottom like a bell.

Bishop A sleeve that is full in the lower part, as in the Anglican bishop's robe, and is either loose or held by a band at the wrist.

Bracelet A sleeve reaching below the elbow about halfway to the wrist.

Cap   A short sleeve just covering the shoulder; not continued under the arm.

Dolman   A sleeve fitted smoothly into an armhole so large it extends almost to the waistline, giving a capelike outline; often held snugly at the wrist.

Leg-of-mutton   A sleeve shaped like a leg of mutton; full, loose, and rounded from the shoulder over the elbow; fitted at the wrist.

Puffed   A sleeve gathered at armscye and bottom.

Raglan   A sleeve that extends to the neckline and has a slanting seamline from the underarm to the neck in front and back.

SKIRT STYLES

Circular   A skirt, often shaped by gores, that hangs in unbroken ripples from waist to hem.

Dirndl   A gathered skirt.

Gores   In skirts, panels of from two to 27 shaped pieces (the number of gores decides the type skirt); usually, the fewer the gores, the narrower the skirt.

Godet   A triangular piece of cloth, set in toward the bottom of a garment to add fullness.

Sheath   A slim, straight skirt, usually with two or three gores, slashed at the side or center of the back hem to allow for walking.

Tiered   A skirt with two or more flounces, or tunics.

Tunic   A skirt with another somewhat shorter overskirt; usually a continuation of blouse.

Wrap   Two free edges of fabric, one of which folds or wraps over the other and usually ties.

Yoke   A piece of material, fitted over the hips, to which the rest of the skirt is gathered, pleated, or gored.

TYPES OF SKIRT PLEATING

Accordion   Fine, even pleating folded like the bellows of an accordion.

Box   Pleats set in pairs of two in opposite directions.

Broomstick   A type of pleating in which wet fabric is tied with a string around a broomstick. When it dries, the material is irregularly pleated.

Cluster   Several kinds of pleats used together, such as box pleats, knife, or inverted pleats.

Knife pleats   Pleats about the width of a knife running all around a skirt in one direction; may be open or closed.

Simulated   Tucks or stitched flaps pressed to resemble pleats.

Sunburst   Pleats graduated from a narrow width at the tip to a wider width at the bottom.

Appendix 2

The Process of Quantitative Analysis
of Women's Dress Styles

To study scientifically stylistic changes in women's dress necessitates the use of quantitative analysis. Data concerning the fashion changes of the twentieth century need to be collected and analyzed to ascertain selected fashion theories in an impartial, statistical manner.

A search of the literature reveals few attempts at such a scientific study. In 1937, Agnes Brooks Young described her work in the area of scientific analysis of changes in women's dress styles.[1] A. E. Kroeber and Jane Richardson recorded their statistical methods in a 1940 publication entitled *Three Centuries of Women's Dress Fashions—A Quantitative Analysis*.[2] The methodology evolving from a combination of the methods used by these researchers contributes uniquely to the following discussion.

The quantitative analysis of styles in women's dress is a process similar to a fashion count, a simple count made of the current fashions observed at a particular place and date. This same principle applies to the more complicated process of quantitative analysis used in the research. Statistical data are obtained by identifying stylistic features in women's dress from year to year over a long period of time. By combining the dominant characteristics of the dresses analyzed in a fashion count, any number of representative dresses may be selected for any designated period of time. The annual representative styles of dress are studied and a measurement is made of specific dimensions that are indicative of stylistic changes

in women's dress, for example, the waistline, the neckline, and the sleeve length. Stylistic changes are thus derived scientifically in a quantitative manner rather than by the more conventional qualitative approach often used in analyzing fashion.

The major steps in the process of quantitative analysis are

1. Securing the resource materials.
   a. Selecting sources.
   b. Sampling sources.
2. Deriving the annual representative women's dress styles, 1900 to the present.
   a. Analyzing the dominant characteristics of dress styles each year.
   b. Selecting annual representative dress styles.
3. Analyzing selected dimensions of the modal components of the annual representative women's dress styles, 1900 to the present.
   a. Measuring certain dimensions of the annual representative dress styles.
   b. Statistical analysis of dimensions and characteristics of dress styles.

A definition of some of the terms used in describing this process enables the reader to work with a higher degree of efficiency. Some of the definitions are in accord with traditional interpretations; others are defined in the manner in which they are used in this process:

Fashion Prevailing style of dress at a given time.

Style Distinctive or characteristic mode of dress.

Stylistic changes Year-to-year variations in design, detail, and decorative treatment of women's dress.

Fashion innovation Introduction of a new style generally accepted by a limited group of customers.

Modal parts of the dress The dominant or most common style observed in the waist, skirt, and sleeve sections of women's dresses; statisticians use "the mode" to represent a kind of average distinguishing or identifying a type within a group that appears the largest number of times.

Dimensions of modal components Measurements in a single line, such as the length, width, or height of the various sections of women's dress.

SECURING RESOURCE MATERIAL

One of the elementary steps in analyzing material of any nature is to make an organized search for available information. It is necessary to know the kind of data desired in order to determine possible sources.

Selecting the Sources. The nature of this study necessitates the use of historical data regarding styles in women's dress, 1900 to the present. The data selected for analysis must be pictorial. The research in this study is limited to the twentieth century because ready-to-wear developed to the point of mass production and distribution during the first half of this century. Research in various fields suggests that a fifty-year period is adequate to analyze significant trends and patterns of change.

Sources of data for this research are fashion periodicals presenting current fashions in the field of women's dress. Public libraries have consecutive issues of publications that present representative styles of women's dress.

Use the following criteria for selecting sources:

1. Publications must present current fashions in women's dress to the public in regular issues yearly.
2. Publications must have had continuous circulation during the period 1900 to the present.
3. Fashions in women's dress must be presented in sketches or photographs; the latter will be used where possible.
4.
5. Fashions must represent a variety of kinds of women's daytime dresses—afternoon dresses, street dresses, and business dresses.

Some magazines that would comply with these criteria are *Vogue, Harper's Bazaar, Town and Country*, and the *Sears-Roebuck Catalog*.

Sampling the Sources. Acceptable standards for adequate samples vary with the nature of the population being investigated; therefore, statistical authorities need to be consulted before the size of a representative sample is determined. The random sampling procedure used in obtaining data for this research requires a 33 per cent sample of the total population and affords access to adequate data for analysis.

Preliminary research supports the theory that the consecutive fall, winter, and spring seasons present a composite fashion picture. During these seasons the integration of style ideas is continual; however, during the summer period, previously accepted styles may be rejected because of desires for physical comfort and changes in seasonal activities. The summer period will not be considered in this research because it would reflect a more abrupt seasonal change in styles referred to by Nystrom as a "broken fashion cycle".[3]

Sources of data used in this study will be sampled in the following manner:

1. The composite fashion picture designated for consideration in this study includes the consecutive fall, winter, and spring seasons.
2. A double-year symbol, such as 1900 to 1901, indicates the fashion picture of each year. (A single year designation, such as 1900, splits or breaks into the normal movement of style pat-

terns from fall through winter and into spring.)

3. The nine-month period analyzed yearly includes the August through April issues of the fashion publication.
4. Three issues during the nine-month period constitute a one-third sample.
5. Rotation of the selected issues equalizes the effect of climatic change in the monthly presentation of fashion; e.g.,

    1900 to 1901: August, November, and February.

    1901 to 1902: September, December, and March.

    1902 to 1903: October, January, and April.

This procedure is repeated in sampling data annually during the entire fifty-year period.

Emphasis is placed on the selection of a source that provides adequate consecutive issues for a systematic sampling procedure. If the desired issues are not available at one location, it is possible to seek the needed material in another. Publishers may give the researcher access to historical files containing yearly issues of magazines, catalogs, and other materials presenting current annual fashions to the public. It may be possible to devise sampling techniques to accommodate an adequate sample from the available sources. Statisticians should be consulted on matters of representative sampling.

COLLECTING THE DATA

The procedure involves the collection of data for a quantative analysis of stylistic changes apparent in particular types of women's dress, 1900 to the present. Exactness in the details of this step assures that the final analysis of dimensions is based on representative styles in women's dress in the twentieth century.

Agnes B. Young states:

The key to studying changes and evolution in the trends of styles was seen to lie in examining the typical, not the exceptional, examples, the representative ones rather than the most pleasing and interesting, and in determining the selection by impartial statistical methods rather than by judgment and preference.[4]

Thus, the main objective is to derive annual representative dress styles for further analysis.

It is first necessary to identify the annual characteristic features of various styles of dress. An accurate tabulation of the features of dress styles indicates clearly the dominant or common characteristics. Selected dresses combining these modal components are, thus, representative of the annual styles.

Tabulating Characteristic Features of Dress Styles, 1900 to the Present. The designated issues for each yearly fashion season will be scrutinized page by page until approximately fifteen to twenty illustrations are tabulated from each issue. A minimum of fifty illustrations for each year provides an adequate sample for this research. Kroeber and Richardson used only ten illustrations for their measurements.[5] Young tabulated fifty illustrations in order to select the one typical style for each year.[6] After preliminary research, a combination of the two techniques, tabulating fifty illustrations and selecting ten representative styles for each year, seems adequate.

The following points have been summarized to serve as a guide in the tabulating procedure:

1. Analyze the characteristic features of a variety of women's daytime dresses.
    a. Include afternoon dresses, street dresses, and business dresses.
    b. Exclude coats, suits, formal wear, active sportswear, and beach wear.
    c. Exclude fashions designed for stout women and young girls. (As Young points out, "In both these groups the normal figure is distorted enough to cause havoc in the averages, if they are inadvertently included in the data.")[7]
2. Identify and tabulate the following types of characteristics for each of the modal parts of dresses:
    a. Skirt styles: Fullness details, yoke details, etc.
    b. Waist styles: Waistline details, neckline details, etc.
    c. Sleeve styles: Armscye details, shoulder details, etc.

3. Tabulate the styles illustrated in the three issues designated for the yearly fashion seasons. Use a page-by-page analysis procedure until fifteen to twenty daytime dresses have been analyzed.
4. Provide a minimum of fifty tabulations for each year as an adequate sample of the data.

The definition of various features will be kept clearly in mind by means of sketching the characteristics of each style on a tally sheet. A new sketch is made each time a new feature is recognized in sampling the data. When completed, the tally sheets will portray the trend of the changes in women's dress styles year by year.

After preliminary research, the tally sheet is designed to serve as a guide in the collection and tabulation of data. During the course of the investigation, these categories will be subject to revision as new data make such revision necessary.

Selecting Annual Representative Styles, 1900 to the Present. From the yearly tabulation, it will be easy to identify the particular characteristics appearing the greatest number of times in the annual styles. The identified *modal* parts will be indicative of the central tendencies of dress styles during the various annual periods.

Following is a guide for this procedure:

1. The most dominant characteristics, or the modals, form the components requisite for selecting the ten representative women's dress styles for each year.
2. It is next necessary to search the sources for each year to find ten dresses that combine, as nearly as possible, the modals for the year.
3. All annual sources will be reviewed in monthly order, page by page, until a minimum of ten representative dresses is identified annually.

Tally Sheet for skirt styles

Years	Sketch: Gored	Pleated	Gathered	Straight
1900-01				
1901-02				
1902-03				
1903-04				
1904-05				
1905-06				
1906-07				

FIGURE A.1 *Sample tally sheet for skirt styles. This form can be adapted to tabulate the characteristic features of other parts of dresses.*

4. It is imperative that these representative dresses be selected from illustrations that meet the following criteria:
   a. Full-front view of the figure and dress.
   b. Full-length view of the figure and dress.
   c. Modal parts of dress in plain view.
   d. Skirt lines and waistline distinctly evident.
   e. Photographs rather than sketches selected where possible.

Deriving representative annual styles is a procedure concerned with the details of collecting raw data. This step is vital to the total process of quantitative analysis. Although it provides observed data of an empirical nature, it assures representative styles for scientific analysis of certain dimensions in women's dress for the period.

NOTES

[1] Agnes B. Young, *Recurring Cycles of Fashion.* New York: Harper, 1937, p. 5.

[2] Jane Richardson and A. L. Kroeber, *Three Centuries of Women's Dress Fashions.* Berkeley: U. of California Press, 1940, p. 112.

[3] Paul Nystrom, *Economics of Fashion.* New York: Ronald, 1928, p. 21.

[4] Young, op. cit., p. 5.

[5] Richardson and Kroeber, op. cit., p. 113.

[6] Young, op. cit., p. 32.

[7] Ibid., p. 160.

Appendix 3

A Brief History of the Women's Apparel Industry in the United States

The women's apparel industry in America is little more than one hundred years old.[1]

PRE-1900

The invention of the sewing machine by Elias Howe in the 1840s and its improvement by Isaac Singer in 1850 made possible the mass production of clothing in America.[2] "The production of ready-to-wear started with men's work clothing, either for slaves in the South or for seamen."[3] These early factories became known as "slop shops" because the sailors stored their clothes in "slop chests" during their expeditions.[4]

The demand for army uniforms during the Civil War hastened the trend to factory production in urban surroundings.[5] The first report on women's ready-to-wear does not appear until the census of 1860, when the primary products noted were hoop skirts, cloaks, and mantillas.[6] After the Civil War, however, the women's and children's industry grew rapidly, as a large portion of the equipment used for making uniforms was converted to produce their clothing.

The nature of the apparel industry before the turn of the century is unique in the history of American industries. "Some large merchants and manufacturers owned outside shops, but many preferred to deal with contractors who operated outside shops and made up the manufacturer's

cut garments."[7] The latter practice, called contracting, spread rapidly; the size of the individual shops decreased when many tried to enter the apparel business through this route. "Fifty dollars was considered adequate capital for embarking on this career in the 1880s."[8] Sewing machines were available at reasonable prices, on installment, or on rental plans.[9]

As more workers crowded into the industry, working conditions became appalling. Tenement buildings housed the worst of the contractor shops. "These were the 'sweatshops,' in which men and women worked excessively long hours in unsanitary surroundings for extremely low wages."[10]

"Public opinion became aroused when epidemics broke out, and women objected to having their clothes made in tenement rooms, where people cooked, ate, and slept."[11] By the turn of the century, factory and tenement laws forced "sweating" to decrease, but working conditions were little better.

"By 1900 the women's clothing industry consisted of 2,701 establishments, turning out $159,000,000 worth of garments."[12] Most garments being produced were cloaks and suits, with a few shirtwaist establishments and some underwear manufacturers. Contracting began to give way to small manufacturing establishments.[13]

In 1900, cloakmakers from Manhattan, Brownsville, Newark, Philadelphia, and Baltimore held a meeting in Manhattan to discuss working conditions. The result was the formation of the International Ladies Garment Workers Union (ILGWU). The new union was not immediately popular, and little progress was seen until 1909, when the union staged a successful strike on the shirtwaist industry, and 1910 when the cloakmakers staged their "Great Revolt." "Louis D. Brandeis, the future Supreme Court justice, made a basis for the settlement of this strike with the 'Protocol of Peace,' providing machinery for the peaceful solution of labor-management disputes in the women's apparel industry."[14]

The garment industry had a great but somewhat delayed reaction to the prosperity of World War I.[15] "Fashion, that strange phenomenon that will lead a woman to discard an otherwise wearable garment simply because it is out of style, became vastly more important in America beginning in the period during and after World War I."[16] American manufacturers began to copy Paris models and mass production moved into full swing.

In the 1920s, American women began to desire rapid style changes. The manufacture of dresses competed with the manufacture of suits.[17] New York City became the nation's center for merchandising the new styles.

The years of the Depression were hard on the apparel industry. But the National Recovery Act (NRA) did bring some improvements. Labeling laws were initiated in the 1930s, and the thirty-five-hour work week became a reality.[18]

As the 1940s neared, there were changes in the industry, particularly in the composition of the labor force. Previously, Jewish laborers had dominated the industry. However, by 1937, more than one half of those employed in the industry were Italian. 32 per cent were Jewish; 5 per cent were Spanish; only 1.5 per cent were listed as native-born American.[19]

The apparel industry in America expanded and diversified during the 1950s and 1960s. The years following World War II were considered the years of sportswear:

> Sportswear, as we think of it today, was not in existence in 1900, but there were manufacturers of separate skirts and blouses who were the foundation of our 1950 sportswear industry. . . . Some active sportswear was being manufactured in 1900, but it bore little resemblance to today's industry.[20]

In sportswear American designers found a field of their own. American sportswear designs had a strong influence on the French couture during these decades.[21]

In the 1960s, financial expansion continued.[22] Firm size became more diversified. E. F. Hayter reflects on this phenomenon:

> Side by side with a few giants like Jonathan Logan and Bobbie Brooks, with annual volumes approaching the hundred million dollar mark, [were] many thriving concerns established on an annual volume of one million dollars and a still greater number flourishing on a volume of less than $50,000 a year.[23]

In addition to the variety in the size of companies, during the 1960s numerous production methods developed within the industry. Some manufacturers operated by the outside shop method. They designed the garments, bought the trimmings and, in most cases, cut the dresses. The garments were then shipped to the contractor for sewing and finishing. Completed garments were returned to the manufacturer for shipment to retail firms. However, some manufacturers still created the entire garment under one roof.[24]

During the 1960s, also, there was a trend toward decentralization in the industry. The jobbers tended to remain in the metropolitan areas, while the contractors moved their sewing plants into suburban and rural areas. This trend became particularly evident in the New York City area.

The status of the ladies' apparel industry in the 1970s has not yet been documented. It has been reported that the entire apparel industry is responsible for a contribution of $50 billion a year to the GNP.[25] The apparel industry employs 1.5 million people nationwide.[26]

MARKETING ACTIVITIES

Marketing has been defined as a business process by which products are matched with markets and through which transfers of ownership are effected.[27] This contemporary marketing concept includes the merchandising of products and the physical distribution of goods and other supporting or related activities.

Although it is one of the largest industries in the nation, the manufacture of apparel is still largely conducted in small operations:

> The apparel industry is unique among major manufacturing industries in that it is still the stronghold of small businesses . . . 70 per cent of those in the industry employ fewer than fifty people.[28]

In the apparel industry, the manufacturer assumes the responsibility for getting his goods directly to the retail outlets. There is virtually no middleman—that is, no traditional wholesaler who distributes the goods, as is the case with many other consumer products. One reason for this development is the seasonal element involved in the handling of fashion goods. Fashion changes are rapid. Direct methods of dealing are usually necessary. Only in some staple items such as hosiery, underwear, and children's wear does the wholesaler distribute appreciable amounts of merchandise. One recent source describes the pattern:

> Over the years, the marketing activities of the fashion industries have established a pattern of direct distribution to the retailer, heavy reliance upon personal contact between manufacturers' representatives and retail buyers, and the use of advertising and publicity to supplement personal selling efforts.[29]

The apparel manufacturer is responsible for the promotion of his own goods. He must advertise and induce the retailer to see his line at the opening of each season.

DEVELOPMENT OF THE NEW YORK CITY APPAREL MARKET

New York City has historically been the center of the fashion industry in America and its main market center. Within a few square miles, buyers have been able to sample a wide representation of lines in each classification.

During the period after World War I, New York became the primary center for the making and selling of mass-produced garments. This superior position remained unquestioned until recent years.

GROWTH OF REGIONAL MARKETS

Over a period of years, as the population spread westward, arrival of goods from the East was slow. Other apparel production and market centers were established and flourished. The presence of raw materials and inexpensive labor aided the growth of other production centers. Griffin has analyzed the westward growth of markets:

> The areas chosen for these apparel markets were not entirely accidental. They developed largely because of their geographical position and the growth of small cities and towns in the surrounding areas which created demand for more and better clothing than that sent them from New York. Demand for different types of garments from those of the East was created by differences in climatic conditions and occupations.[30]

Today, apparel is being manufactured in many places other than New York City and surrounding areas. Over the last ten years, firms from Texas, California, and Florida have become important sources of apparel for stores across the nation.[31] In addition, many retailers in modern America have found that they cannot afford to go to New York more than once a year.

If retailers did not go to New York, then what were Eastern manufacturers to do? Stores across the country must still be served. As a partial solution, the manufacturer sent sales representatives on the road to take his lines to the stores. Somehow he had to induce more retailers to see his lines, so the sales representatives often invited retailers to view the seasonal line in a city hotel for "market."

Slowly these makeshift markets gained in popularity and organization. Groups of salesmen moved from hotel suites to larger buildings, some built specifically for the purpose of showing fashion merchandise. Kay Gomein, President of the American Fashion Association, noted the growing importance of markets such as these:

> Regional markets are invaluable in two ways . . . the small retailers in small towns cannot afford trips to New York or California markets, and the salesmen cannot afford to travel to each small town to service the small store. . . .
>
> Therefore . . . the regional markets are the answer. Stores can cover their needs in from one to four days. Salesmen are able to service stores from all over the territory.
>
> Another fact that is valuable is the ability of the small retailer to observe and be aware of fashion trends . . . which can keep them on a par fashionwise with the city stores.[32]

The term *regional* as applied to the apparel markets is, perhaps, not an entirely correct choice of words, as it may imply to the reader a market with limited distribution. Today, several regional markets are involved in a nationwide distribution of fashion goods. Many have engaged in elaborate promotional activities to attract buyers on this scale. Improved transportation has narrowed time and distance between retailers and markets. In recent years, the production and variety of fashion goods have increased in several regional market areas. Regional, then, could properly be used to differentiate other markets from the original apparel market, New York City.[33]

While the New York market remains in a class by itself for variety and assortment, regional markets are growing rapidly. Besides New York, other markets of national importance are Los Angeles (sportswear and swimwear) and Dallas (sportswear and work and play garments). These have showrooms open year round. Other regional markets have developed specifically for the purpose of showing certain classifications of merchandise. Some of these are Atlanta (medium-priced apparel), Miami (swimwear, dresses, and sportswear), Chicago (medium-priced

women's dresses and children's apparel), and Kansas City (medium- to low-priced dresses, work clothes, and boys' wear).[34]

NOTES

[1] Max Hall, *Made in New York*. Cambridge: Harvard University Press, 1959, p. 47.

[2] Edith F. Hayter, *Behind the Scenes in Fashion Merchandising*. New York: Pageant Press, 1965, p. 1.

[3] Ibid., p. 2.

[4] Hall, loc. cit.

[5] Hayter, op. cit., p. 2.

[6] Hall, loc. cit.

[7] Ibid., p. 48.

[8] Florence S. Richards, *The Ready to Wear Industry, 1900–1950*. New York: Fairchild Publications, 1951, p. 5.

[9] Ibid.

[10] Ibid., p. 6.

[11] Hall, op. cit., p. 50.

[12] Richards, op. cit., p. 8.

[13] Hall, op. cit., p. 51.

[14] Ibid., p. 50.

[15] Ibid., p. 50.

[16] Ibid., p. 52.

[17] Richards, op. cit., p. 18.

[18] Hall, op. cit., p. 54.

[19] Richards, op. cit., p. 18.

[20] Ibid.

[21] Ibid., p. 26.

[22] Ibid.

[23] *Sixty Years of Fashion*. New York: Fairchild Publications, 1963, p. 3.

[24] Ibid.

[25] Richards, op. cit., p. 30.

[26] Hayter, p. 5.

[27] Ibid.

[28] American Home Economics Association, "What Do the Textile-Apparel Industries Expect from Us?" Address by Gene Stone at Proceedings of the Fourth National Conference Association of College Professors of Textiles and Clothing, Charlotte, N.C., Fall, 1971, p. 22.

[29] Ibid., p. 23.

[30] Marshall Doswell, *Architects of Change*. Fort Mill, N.C.: Springs Mills, Inc., 1972.

[31] Richard R. Still and Edward W. Cundiff, *Essentials of Marketing*. Englewood Cliffs, N.J.: Prentice-Hall, 1962, p. 3.

[32] Jeannette Jarnow and Beatrice Judelle, *Inside the Fashion Business*. New York: Wiley, 1974, p. 114.

[33] Ibid.

[34] Ibid.

Appendix 4

The Production Process and Cost Components for an Item of Apparel

The Production Process

1. Design is sketched.
2. Pattern is made.
3. Sample garment is cut out.
4. Sample garment is sewn.
5. Garment is costed for labor.
6. Garment is costed for fabric, trim, cutting, fusing, and freight.
7. Garment is costed for other expenses:
   Markup
   Overhead
   Salesman commission
   Advertising allowance
   Add 8% for $^8/_{10}$ terms.
8. Show sample garment to retail buyers.
9. If sample garment sells:
   Correct the pattern for production.
   Order piece goods.
   Plan production time needed.
   Grade pattern in all sizes.
   Make marker.
10. Mass production process begins.
    Garments are cut and sewn.
    Garments are shipped to retail stores.

The cost of manufacturing a single garment is illustrated in the example.

Example: Cost Components for a Pantsuit

Materials:	3.05 yards of polyester knit @ $1.30 per yard		$4.01
	Fusing		.05
	Elastic		.10
	Buttons		.12
	Lining		.15
	Total cost of materials:		$ 4.43
Labor:	Pants	3.35	
	Top	.70	
	Cutting	.20	
	subtotal	4.25	
	10% surcharge	.43	
	Total cost of labor:		4.68
	Overhead		1.36
Total cost of garment:			10.47
Markup of 16½%			1.73
Manufacturer's selling cost			**12.20**
Possible retail price (about double manufacturer's cost)			25.00

	QUANTITY	CONTRACT #	DATE	SHIP
Style #				
Pattern #				
Material				
Source				
Fibre Contents				

Colors

Sizes	Price
Ratio	
Piece Goods PO #	

Cut # _____ Pcs. _____ Date _____
Cut # _____ Pcs. _____ Date _____
Cut # _____ Pcs. _____ Date _____
Cut # _____ Pcs. _____ Date _____
Cut # _____ Pcs. _____ Date _____
Cut # _____ Pcs. _____ Date _____
Cut # _____ Pcs. _____ Date _____
Cut # _____ Pcs. _____ Date _____
Cut # _____ Pcs. _____ Date _____
Cut # _____ Pcs. _____ Date _____
Cut # _____ Pcs. _____ Date _____

Sketch

Labor   _____
+10%   _____
Cutting   _____
Fabric   _____
@ ____ + _____
                 _____
                 _____
                 _____
Total   _____
Before OH   _____
O.H.   _____
Total cost   _____
of Garment   _____
Selling Cost   _____
MU% _____

YARDAGE	PRICE	FIRM	QUANTITY
Belt			
Button			
Trim			
Special Work			
Remarks			

Marker # _____   Width _____

Yardage Avg. _____

FIGURE A.2 *Sample form for costing garments.*

Appendix 5

The Fashion Buyer's Job

Traditionally, the position of *retail buyer* has been the goal of young people interested in merchandising. As a student pursuing a career in fashion merchandising, you need to acquire accurate job information. A series of job profiles has been compiled based on information obtained from fashion buyers and assistant buyers actually performing the fashion merchandising function in department stores. More than 100 buyers participated in this study, representing ten major department stores in the New York City area and nine major department stores in cities in the central United States, including Chicago, Kansas City, St. Louis, Dallas, Houston, San Antonio, and Denver.[1] These job profiles depict the current roles of the buyer and the assistant buyer in the fashion divisions of contemporary department stores.

This job analysis approach should help you to understand the broad scope of the fashion buyer's responsibilities and to become aware of the specific kinds of activities you might perform as an assistant buyer.

Each of the five job profiles presents one of the following categories of merchandising responsibilities.

1. Planning and evaluating merchandise.
2. Procuring merchandise.
3. Promoting merchandise.
4. Merchandising departments.
5. Supervising personnel.

MAJOR RESPONSIBILITIES

Fashion buyers live in today's world but think and react in terms of tomorrow. They are obsessed with the necessity of beating yesterday's sales figures, last week's figures, last month's figures, last season's figures and, of course, ultimately, the last year's sales figures because it is on this that their salaries and the success of the store depend. However, at the same time, they are absorbed in making buying and merchandising decisions for the next season. Fashion buyers make these decisions according to what they think the customer will want the next season and what the manufacturer has already decided the consumer will want the next season. All of these decisions must be made three months, six months, or a year or more before the actual season in which the consumer makes his or her purchases of fashion goods. The fashion buyer's and assistant buyer's responsibilities related to each job profile are described below.

PLANNING AND EVALUATING MERCHANDISE

The fashion buyer is constantly working in the next season. The process of evaluating what happened today and yesterday in terms of tomorrow is a way of life for those involved in fashion mer-

269

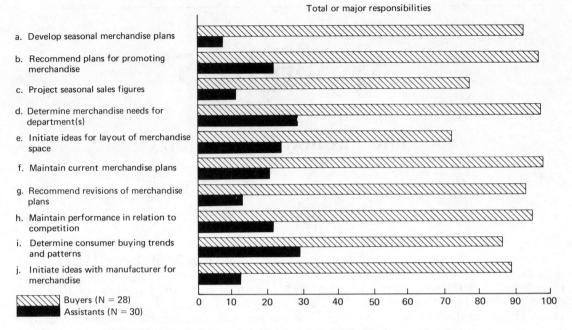

Total or major responsibilities

a. Develop seasonal merchandise plans

b. Recommend plans for promoting merchandise

c. Project seasonal sales figures

d. Determine merchandise needs for department(s)

e. Initiate ideas for layout of merchandise space

f. Maintain current merchandise plans

g. Recommend revisions of merchandise plans

h. Maintain performance in relation to competition

i. Determine consumer buying trends and patterns

j. Initiate ideas with manufacturer for merchandise

Buyers (N = 28)
Assistants (N = 30)

0   10   20   30   40   50   60   70   80   90   100

FIGURE A.3   *Activities related to planning and evaluating merchandise.*

chandising. Some of the responsibilities in planning and evaluating are indicated in Figure A.3.

1. Seasonal merchandise plans for the department must be determined months in advance on the basis of the buyer's anticipation and estimation of the consumer demand for the various items of merchandise carried in the department.

2. Plans for promoting sales must be recommended to correspond with the projected seasonal merchandise plan. Advertising requests must be made in advance by the buyer, along with suggestions for displays, special events, and other types of promotions. These plans must be developed with other persons in the store who are responsible for sales promotion activities.

3. Seasonal sales figures must be projected based on the advance plans made by the buyer. Specific estimates of sales figures must be made for the season or seasons in question. These projected sales figures must be broken down into the exact quantities of merchandise needed to provide an appropriate assortment of items for the consumer.

4. Merchandise needs for the classifications

within the department must be determined by the fashion buyer. These needs will change for fashion items from season to season and sometimes within a season. The merchandise assortment within each classification must be determined in terms of the items that will best fill the needs and wants of the customers the buyer hopes to serve.

5. Ideas for the layout of the merchandise within the department may be initiated by the fashion buyer. The excitement of the next season's merchandise must be visualized by the retail buyer and reflected on the sales floor in the department. Creative ideas for arranging the merchandise space must be presented in advance of the selling season, so that consideration can be given to the buyer's requests by store officials responsible for changes in the physical layout of the departments.

6. Maintaining current merchandise records requires the constant vigilance of the fashion buyer. What has been received from the manufacturer, what has been sold by the sales force, what is on the sales floor, what is in the

stockroom, and what is on order but has not been delivered must all be recorded in exact figures. The fashion buyer must constantly study these records in order to know if planned merchandise assortments are adequate for the current selling season.

7. Revisions of merchandise plans can be made by the buyer as the selling season progresses. Additional merchandise may be obtained if needed and reorders initiated where possible. However, special efforts may be recommended for the sale of overstocked items, and delivery dates may be cancelled on orders if the merchandise plans need to be revised in this direction.

8. Maintaining performance in relation to competition is one of the fashion buyer's greatest challenges. Close observation of other stores where competitive (similar) merchandise is sold is one of the gauges for measuring the fashion buyer's performance. What items are selling at other stores? How much are consumers buying at other stores? The answers to these questions help the fashion buyer to maintain performance in relation to competition.

9. Consumer buying trends and patterns are determined by the fashion buyer on a continuous basis. These trends are reflected in the fashion markets, in the leading fashion stores visited by the buyer, in fashion magazines and trade papers such as the *Women's Wear Daily*, and at social events attended by the buyer. These trends have great influence on the fashion buyer's merchandising decisions.

10. Giving ideas to manufacturers for merchandise the fashion buyer feels the consumer will purchase is also a task of the buyer. To perform the various planning and evaluating activities, the fashion buyer must keep in close contact with the manufacturer. The buyer may work with the manufacturer to develop merchandise to satisfy trends in consumer demand. The fashion buyer's analysis of the customer's wants and desires, as reflected at the point of sale, can provide valuable input for designers and producers of fashion goods.

The trend in recent years to computer analysis of sales data may account, in part, for the buyer having less responsibility for the projection of sales figures.[2] Also, this responsibility may be as-

sumed at the merchandise management level.

The responsibilities for remodeling older facilities and planning departments in new stores are currently considered as the specialized function of a store planner.[3] Arrangement of merchandise space is increasingly designed from a total store layout concept rather than department by department; thus, the buyer's involvement with this responsibility may be decreased.

Few of the assistant buyers tend to have total or major responsibilities for planning and evaluating merchandise classifications in retail stores.

PROCURING MERCHANDISE

Today, fashion buyers may travel all over the United States and to foreign countries. Seasonal markets provide the fashion buyer with opportunities to procure merchandise from a myriad of resources, as discussed in Chapter 8. However, the fashion buyer can keep in contact with manufacturers through regional sales representatives by telephone or store visits. In the trade, the following terms are used interchangably: *manufacturer*, *vendor*, *resource*, and *supplier*. Some of the responsibilities involved in the procurement of merchandise appear in Figure A.4.

1. Buying activities may keep the fashion buyer off the sales floor most of the time. Records of inventory control and open-to-buy require constant vigilance on the part of the buyer; commitments for merchandise, delivery dates, and shipping routes are a few of the responsibilities involved.

2. Fashion buyers establish the retail price of merchandise based on the store's pricing policies and the cost of the merchandise. National brand merchandise may be preticketed, with prices established by the manufacturer. The price established for an item of merchandise must include the cost of the product, the cost of doing business, and a reasonable profit for the store.

3. Proper vendor relations are important to the fashion buyer and to the store represented. Ethical buying practices should be adhered to at all times. The federal government, the associations, and the Chamber of Commerce of the United States are alert to trade abuses. Costly and waste-

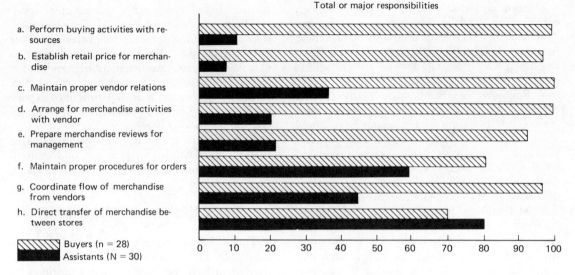

a. Perform buying activities with resources

b. Establish retail price for merchandise

c. Maintain proper vendor relations

d. Arrange for merchandise activities with vendor

e. Prepare merchandise reviews for management

f. Maintain proper procedures for orders

g. Coordinate flow of merchandise from vendors

h. Direct transfer of merchandise between stores

Buyers (n = 28)
Assistants (N = 30)

0 10 20 30 40 50 60 70 80 90 100

FIGURE A.4 *Activities related to procuring merchandise.*

ful controversies can be avoided by fashion buyers with integrity and a spirit of fair play. A vendor's diary, with up-to-date records and background information, will greatly benefit the fashion buyer.

4. Some vendors cooperate in merchandise activities in order to promote their products more vigorously or in order to make a consistent appeal to the consumer. Sharing advertising costs is a common practice of some manufacturers. Fashion buyers may arrange with vendors for such merchandise activities as demonstrations, special promotions, displays, and other events that motivate sales and mutually benefit the vendor and the store.

5. Fashion buyers may be asked to present merchandise reviews for management. These reviews may provide facts, figures, and examples of merchandise required to support promotional events and profit goals. Merchandise reports of this nature include the current year's figures and the preceding year's records.

6. Proper procedures for orders may vary from store to store. The fashion buyer should use the store's order forms and follow the store ordering procedures. Manufacturers' order forms may not contain the information required by the store. A

system for maintaining proper procedures for orders should be established and adhered to by the fashion buyer.

7. The flow of merchandise from the vendor to the store must be coordinated by the fashion buyer. Delivery dates established well in advance of a season should provide the right merchandise at the right time in terms of consumer demand. The flow of merchandise from the vendor may be interrupted due to transportation delays, shipping errors, traffic and receiving mistakes, and other problems.

8. Transferring merchandise between stores may involve some of the same procedures and problems described in number 7. Multiunit operations with numerous branch stores have developed elaborate systems to direct the transfer of merchandise between stores. However, it is the fashion buyer's responsibility to maintain the appropriate assortment of merchandise in each branch store.

The responsibilities associated with the procurement of merchandise are more often than not considered as the one realm where the retail buyer reigns supreme.

The job profiles pertaining to these responsibilities reveal that the buyer tends to assume less responsibility for the proper order procedures, whereas the assistant buyer tends to be given more responsibility than the buyer for the transfer of merchandise between stores. Recent trends in branch store operation suggest that the concept of centralized buying may place more responsibility for coordinating the distribution of merchandise on the assistant buyer or on persons in other merchandising positions. There is a strong movement to incorporate the central buying concept in the operation of multiunit organizations today.[4] Put into effect, this concept removes the buyer from the traditional department setting into a central buying office; it could relieve the buyer of the traditional buying responsibilities. In the latter situation, the buyer would then be free to perform the primary function of managing a department in a multiunit operation.

PROMOTING SALES

The buyer's responsibilities carry over into promotion. It is of utmost importance that advertising and other forms of sales promotion be used to inform the consumer community and to stimulate the maximum sales of fashion goods purchased for the selling season. Most large stores have personnel other than the buyer who are responsible for sales promotion, advertising, display, and the use of such media as special events, radio, and television. In Figure A.5 are some of the buyer's responsibilities pertaining to promoting sales.

1. Scheduling and coordinating advertising is usually a cooperative effort between the buyer and the promotion director. Plans for ads and promotional events are made six to eight months in advance of a selling season because it is at that time that the buyer is actually purchasing the merchandise. However, when the consumer selling season approaches, the plans must be turned to reality—real live advertisements of the fashion goods bought with the customer's wants and needs in mind.

2. Sometimes, in larger cities, there are several choices in the use of media. In these instances, the buyer may have some influence on the decisions as to which newspapers are used for fashion advertising.

3. The buyer has the last word and much of the responsibility for ensuring accuracy in terms of the merchandise information in ads. The buyer is usually the sole source of advanced information about the merchandise: what styles, what colors, what fabrics, what sizes, and especially what prices. These facts must be transmitted to the potential customer, and accuracy in advertising is a constant effort on the part of retailers.

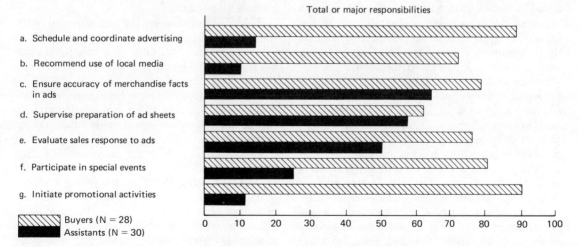

FIGURE A.5 *Activities related to promoting sales.*

4. The supervision of the preparation of advertisements is usually assigned to experts in the layout, copywriting, and art fields. Nevertheless, because it is the buyer who bought the merchandise in the ad, the way the ad appears in the newspaper is of concern to the buyer. In most retail stores, the buyer will have an opportunity to review the advertisement at least once and perhaps twice prior to release for printing in the local newspaper.

5. The evaluation of the sales response to retail advertising is of great importance to the buyer, but this is a difficult task. An advertisement in the local newspaper may have motivated one customer, or many, to come into the store and buy. On the other hand, the customer who made the biggest purchase may not even have seen the ad. That customer may have been satisfying a long-felt need for the merchandise. Although it is a difficult task, most buyers make an effort to keep some record of the response to advertising on a daily, weekly, or monthly basis.

6. Special events supportive of other promotional efforts are usually arranged and supervised by store personnel other than the buyer. The buyer's responsibility here is to be cooperative: merchandise may be loaned, if needed, to stage a fashion show or to present a fashion program. The buyer may be called on also to participate in storewide special events.

7. The buyer may actually initiate promotional activities that will enhance the fashion image of the department and contribute to the reputation of the store in the community. Often, these promotional activities will be keyed to the new season's fashions or to the store's participation in some on-going community charity performance—for example, a designer of note in the fashion world may be invited to an important store or community event, or an annual benefit fashion show may be given by the store in order to raise funds for some worthwhile cause.

As is reflected in the job profile for promoting sales, the buyer does not tend to feel total or major responsibility for most of these activities; retailers usually have advertising and promotional experts who are responsible for this phase of the store operation. It would seem, from the profile in Figure A.5, that the buyer's responsibilities pertain more to the advance planning—the scheduling and coordinating—of advertising and other promotional activities. The assistant buyer has more responsibility for the accurate representation of the merchandise selected for advertising purposes.

MERCHANDISING THE DEPARTMENT

The day-to-day operation of the department and the image the customer perceives about the department are essential to the buyer's purpose. In most stores, the buyer is actively involved in what goes on in the department(s), where the merchandise meets the customer. However, the branch stores have made so many demands on the buyer's time that often it is impossible for the buyer to be physically involved in day-to-day operations. Nevertheless, the responsibilities listed in Figure A.6 indicate the kind of activities that pertain to this vital function of merchandising a department.

1. The impact of the merchandise contributes to the departmental, as well as the total, store image. The presentation of the merchandise within the layout of the department communicates to the customer exactly what the buyer anticipated would satisfy consumer demand for a given selling season.

2. Maximum sales are the constant goal of the salesperson, the department, the buyer, and the store as a whole. No matter how much planning has gone on in advance, the actions and the revision or correction of actions taken on the selling floor contribute to the increase of sales on a day-to-day basis. Revising orders and reorders and adjusting merchandise assortments may ensure maximum sales.

3. Information about the merchandise is vital to promoting and selling what the buyer procured for the customers. What are the selling features? What is the fashion story? How will the merchandise perform when used by the customer? What does the customer need to know to get maximum performance satisfaction from the merchandise? How should the customer use and

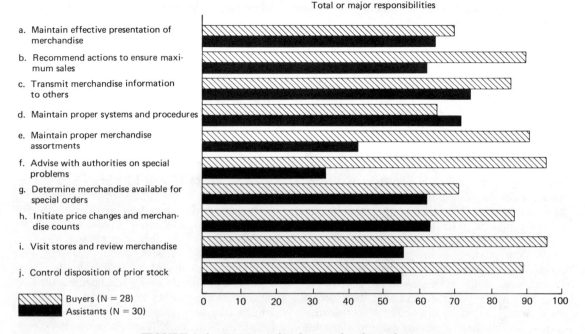

a. Maintain effective presentation of merchandise

b. Recommend actions to ensure maximum sales

c. Transmit merchandise information to others

d. Maintain proper systems and procedures

e. Maintain proper merchandise assortments

f. Advise with authorities on special problems

g. Determine merchandise available for special orders

h. Initiate price changes and merchandise counts

i. Visit stores and review merchandise

j. Control disposition of prior stock

Buyers (N = 28)
Assistants (N = 30)

0   10   20   30   40   50   60   70   80   90   100

FIGURE A.6 *Activities related to merchandising department.*

care for the merchandise? The buyer is the key to unlocking this wealth of information about the merchandise.

4. Maintaining proper systems and procedures is a continual process and involves the cooperation of everyone from the stockroom to the buyer's office. Accuracy of records and information is usually maintained through organized systems and procedures. The "what to do" and the "how it is to be done" are the carrying out of systems and procedures essential to the efficient operation of any department, or store for that matter.

·5. It is of utmost importance to have an assortment of merchandise that corresponds to consumer demand: the right items, in the right size, the right color, the right fabric, and in price ranges that the customer wants or expects. A constant vigil must be kept over the inventory—the number of items in each size, color, and price—in order to provide the factual information the buyer needs to maintain proper merchandise assortments during the selling season.

6. Special problems often arise, and no one

person has all the answers. The organizational structure usually provides for experts in each phase of the retail operation. If the problems have to do with merchandise, then the buyer or merchandise manager is the source of help. If problems pertain to salespeople, usually the personnel department or the store manager needs to be sought out for advice. Other problems need the assistance of other authorities in the store.

7. Special orders may or may not be feasible in certain kinds of merchandise. The buyer usually determines the policy concerning special orders based on the willingness of the manufacturer to provide such services. Seasonal timing greatly affects decisions regarding the possibility of special orders of merchandise.

8. Price changes usually take the form of markdowns, and these play an important role in keeping the assortments of merchandise current and attractive to the customer. The actual counting of items of merchandise is the most accurate way of knowing how many items are presently in stock. Decisions relating to price changes are made on a seasonal basis and usually follow poli-

cies established by the buyer and/or the store merchandise management.

9. The review of merchandise in the department setting has long had an important influence on buying decisions and policies. The image of the department and the type of customer served can be more effectively perceived from the vantage point of the actual physical facilities—the selling floor, as it is referred to in retailing. With the advent of branch stores and multiunit operations, scheduling visits to the various geographic locations of the department have become an essential part of the buyer's responsibilities. Sometimes, the store management has deleted this activity from the buyer's itinerary due to the excessive amount of travel time involved in store visits.

10. Prior stock is a constant problem to the buyer. Merchandise was bought to be resold to the customer. If the stock stays in the department longer than the buyer anticipated, then action must be taken. Usually this action takes the form of markdowns. Sales, clearances, and closeouts are some of the ways of disposing of prior stock.

The tone of the buying is reflected in the merchandising of the department(s). This is the follow-through in the buying-selling cycle. In department stores and larger specialty stores, a divisional merchandise manager traditionally works with the buyer on special problems. The buyer usually has an assistant or there is a department head assigned some of the responsibilities for these detailed follow-up procedures which are involved with merchandising the department.

SUPERVISING PERSONNEL

The day-to-day operation of the department has an aspect in addition to that of merchandising: people. Supervision of personnel involves certain responsibilities for communicating both with management and with subordinates. It is important to provide strong leadership and training for subordinates to maximize the quality of performance and, thereby, the efficiency of the department operation. These supervisory responsibilities are listed in Figure A.7.

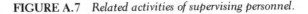

Total or major responsibilities

a. Communicate and cooperate with management
b. Provide strong leadership for subordinates
c. Maintain dialogue with subordinates
d. Direct training of subordinates
e. Assist sales persons on merchandise problems
f. Maintain performance standards of subordinates
g. Recommend recognition for high performance
h. Initiate action for improving performance
i. Provide merchandise training for others
j. Ensure proper physical facilities for others

Buyers (N = 28)
Assistants (N = 30)

0   10   20   30   40   50   60   70   80   90   100

FIGURE A.7 *Related activities of supervising personnel.*

1. Communicating and cooperating with management is a two-way street in retailing as well as in other business organizations. Lack of information often contributes to the growth of misunderstandings, and the failure to cooperate in achieving established goals may result. From the stockroom, to the selling floor, to the buyer's office, and to the offices of top management, the urgency of communicating and cooperating is stressed in retailing.

2. Strong leadership in the retail field is usually characterized by willingness to make decisions and to follow through in helping others to carry out the activities necessary for success. Nowhere in the business world are there as few facts on which to base decisions and greater risks involved in making decisions than in retailing. However, in retailing, responsible leadership is greatly rewarded, both financially and through professional recognition.

3. Maintaining a dialogue with subordinates means keeping those people informed who need to know what you know. Listening, observing, and providing the kind of information necessary to effect good rapport on a long-term basis are the goals of supervisors, managers, and others who work with people and accomplish goals through people.

4. Training people to do certain jobs and to consistently meet high standards in completing the duties associated with the job is the goal of the supervisor. If a person doesn't know what he is doing wrong, he can hardly be expected to correct or mend his ways. The supervisor's task is training people to perform at a level that is acceptable to management and is satisfying to the performer.

5. Salespeople develop a great deal of knowledge about selling from handling merchandise and dealing with customers. However, fashion goods have innate new features, qualities, and uses, and the salesperson needs this kind of information to perform on the job. Also, customers present problems sometimes—personal or merchandise-oriented—and salespeople need assistance and support in solving them.

6. Maintaining the performance standards of subordinates is a constant effort on the part of the supervisor. Checking, rechecking, and detailed, time-consuming review of the work achievements of others are a part of the supervisor's responsibilities. The payoff is efficient operation and good rapport, both essential in retailing.

7. Recognition of performance is vital to the motivation of people. The supervisor is the person most aware of the personal achievements of those persons who perform the essentials of retailing in the line of duty. Policies for recommending promotions and salary increases are usually established by store management, but the supervisor is expected to make and support the recommendations for recognition of high performance.

8. When performance is evaluated it should be recognized in terms of the strengths of the individual and in terms of the areas of weakness. The supervisor is not only responsible for recognizing where the employee falls short of adequate performance of duties, but is also responsible for initiating actions for improving the performance of those duties.

9. Merchandising training in retailing may be of two sorts: concern with employees who maintain the records and information about the merchandise, and concern with training salespeople to sell fashion goods. The supervisor is responsible for both.

10. Physical facilities in retailing are usually thought of in terms of merchandise rather than employees. Buyer's offices are the best example of the lack of emphasis on space other than for selling activities. However, in recent years, through the efforts of personnel executives, many employee benefits have been achieved, along with the improvement of physical facilities other than those on the selling floor. Employee cafeterias, employee lounges, employee medical care centers, rest rooms, and libraries are often supplied by retailers.

The supervision of personnel is of great importance in the merchandising areas related to sales and services. Although salespeople may be responsible to the personnel division in some stores, the buyer's responsibilities may include the supervision of the duties entailed in each departmental area. In many stores, the actual supervision of personnel involved in sales and services may be delegated to an assistant buyer or assigned as a distinct responsibility of management other than the buyer. In the latter instance, the supervisory responsibilities may be organized under a department head or some other such job description.

These five fashion merchandising functions are an integral part of the total store operational system. These responsibilities over-arch a myriad of duties that relate to merchandising—activities related to maintenance of records, maintenance of stock, and a multitude of miscellaneous duties.

Duties pertaining to maintenance of records include

1. Keep sales records
2. Keep stock records
3. Prepare purchase reports
4. Prepare reduction figures
5. Prepare inventory figures
6. Keep credit records
7. Record outstanding orders
8. Record merchandise transfers
9. Record merchandise received
10. Record merchandise on loan

Duties related to maintenance of stock include

1. Arrange and coordinate stock
2. Keep stock area organized
3. Plan and execute stock counts
4. Execute merchandise markdowns
5. Arrange for special orders
6. Handle mail orders
7. Check merchandise for soilage
8. Return merchandise to vendor
9. Check for security of stock
10. Anticipate new stock space needs
11. Supervise stock duties of others
12. Keep stock on sales floor
13. Maintain proper fill-in stock
14. Check marking of merchandise
15. Plan for hold and sold items

Some miscellaneous activities

1. Answer phone and act on calls
2. Handle customer complaints
3. Arrange for relief periods
4. Sell merchandise on floor
5. Transmit reactions to merchandise
6. Follow-up on advertised items
7. Notify salespersons about ads
8. Select merchandise for loan
9. Initiate and secure signs
10. Assist with fashion shows
11. Handle details of inventory
12. Supervise duties of clerical
13. Improve existing procedures
14. Check on delivery dates

These fashion merchandising responsibilities and duties may be organized and assigned in a variety of retail patterns, depending on the size of the store, the nature of the merchandise handled, and the type of store ownership. Regardless of the nature of the store setting, the buyer will be involved to a varying extent with some or all of these five responsibilities that cluster around the buying-selling cycle in retailing.

NOTES

[1] Kathryn Moore Greenwood, "Systematic Approach to the Evaluation of a Fashion Merchandising Program with Guidelines for Student Work Experiences." Doctoral dissertation, Oklahoma State University, *Stillwater*, 1972, pp. 99–120.

[2] Karen R. Gillespie and Joseph Hecht, *Retail Business Management*. New York: Gregg Division, McGraw-Hill, 1970, p. 556.

[3] Ibid., p. 276.

[4] "Today's Buyer: An Endangered Species?" *Clothes* (Jan. 1973), p. 56.

Appendix 6

Careers in the Fashion Industry: Job Analysis Series

FASHION DESIGN.   The coordinated planning and artistic creation of a product according to the specifications of the manufacturer

Job title	Responsibilities and duties	Personal characteristics and background
1. Designer	Generates the idea for a product and develops it by sketching on paper or draping muslin Selects fabric, trims, colors, and accessories Supervises the production of the original model Communicates with production personnel, fabric houses, models, the press, and buyers.	Innate creativity, the ability to visualize and produce an idea; strong fashion sense, good sense of timing; knowledge of principles of art, fit, and fabric; able to sketch, work with people, and communicate Training in the areas of art and construction; apprenticeship includes designing, cutting, and sewing garments
2. Assistant designer	Provides overall assistance to the designer by doing research in the markets, retail stores, textile areas, and fabric libraries for new ideas and resources Assists designer with production personnel Figures amounts of trims, fabrics, and accessories for production May order all fabrics for production Assists designer in model production	Ability to work with people; creativity, fashion sense; organizational abilities Training in construction techniques, fit, and human figure proportions, fibers and fabrics, art principles, manufacturing processes
3. Production coordinator	Coordinates the activities of creation and production Finds the production supplies Determines selling prices and keeps production costs within a budget Decides what items will be produced Analyzes consumer needs and fashion trends	Flexibility, stamina, and fashion flare; a sense of urgency and timing; management ability; ability to communicate with people; action oriented and enthusiastic Training in construction techniques, production methods, management, and fabric performance

279

Employment Opportunities

- Job titles and responsibilities vary with the size and structure of manufacturing organizations (for example, the production coordinator might be the president, vice-president, designer or assistant designer or might hold an individual title).
- Fashion design careers may be available in (1) apparel design, (2) textile design, (3) pattern manufacturing, and (4) design for the theater, movies, and television.
- Apparel designers may design clothing, hats, belts, furs, buttons, fasteners, gloves, scarves, shoes, etc.
- The designer may work with manufacturers of women's, men's, or children's apparel for (1) the mass market, (2) exclusive designer market, (3) custom (one-of-a-kind) market, (4) couture market, or (5) free-lance market.
- Those interested in a fashion design career should locate around manufacturing and market centers.
- Salaries vary. The apprentice may begin at $90 to 125 a week and move up to $10,000 to $50,000 and up, depending on the individual's innate ability and creativity.

FASHION MANUFACTURING. The production of ready-to-wear clothing for distribution to consumers

Job title	Responsibilities and duties	Personal characteristics and background
1. Pattern maker	Converts the designer's sketch or toile into a tag board pattern Evaluates the design Plans with the designer the most feasible means of design relative to construction	Has a mechanical mind that completely understands the concepts of construction techniques and fabric performance; communicates easily; has a feel for translating an idea or a sketch into a reality Training in construction skills, flat pattern design, draping, drafting, fit, fabrics, and mass manufacturing
2. Dressmaker	Constructs the garment for the original model Makes construction suggestions for the best and most economical production methods	Loves sewing; has patience Training in construction skills and in apparel production, fit, and fabrics
3. Production supervisor	Directs workroom production Supervises machine operation Keeps employees working at maximum speed and efficiency Assists in design choices for production	Communicates easily; has knowledge of construction and machine operation Technical school or on-the-job training in mass manufacturing methods
4. Grader	Works from a completed pattern in one size and drafts duplicate designs in other sizes Grades patterns manually or by a computerized grading machine	Understands mathematics; mechanical mind; able to do precision work Technical school training or apprenticeship using graders and computers
5. Spreader	Folds many layers of fabric into a stack of smooth layers in preparation for cutting pattern pieces	Efficiency and speed On-the-job training

Job title	Responsibilities and duties	Personal characteristics and background
6. Marker	Plans efficient layouts in jigsaw puzzle fashion for pattern pieces on large sheets of paper in preparation for cutting Saves the company money by proper layout	Fabric knowledge: understands grain, nap, pile, plaids, prints, and how this relates to construction techniques; efficiency, speed, meticulous attention to detail Technical school or on-the-job training in pattern layout, fabrics, and construction problems
7. Cutter	Transfers a marker's layout to the spread fabric Cuts the pieces for garment production Operates professional cutting tools	Efficiency and speed Technical school or on-the-job training in handling, operation, care, and repair of cutting tools
8. Machine operator	Sews garments quickly and accurately with a high-speed commercial machine Probably will do piece work Follows construction procedures Operates and cares for machines	Ability to do the same thing throughout the day with speed and efficiency Technical school or on-the-job training in power machine operation and repair and garment construction
9. Finisher	Works with a garment at the final stage of production Stitches on buttons, snaps, and labels Presses or packages	Efficiency, speed, and pride in his/her work On-the-job training in garment production techniques

Employment Opportunities

- Careers in apparel manufacturing are available in factories located in market centers such as New York, Los Angeles, and Dallas and in large and small cities throughout the United States.
- Manufacturing jobs are available in men's, women's, and children's clothing and in hats, shoes, notions, trims, belts, gloves, scarves, etc.
- The manufacturing employee may work in the following types of manufacturing plants: (1) Mass market—all jobs available (2) Exclusive market—all jobs available but limited (3) Couture market—pattern maker and dressmaker; other factory jobs are limited and will vary with the firm.
- Many job opportunities are available in factories for people without formal education.
- Salaries will be either an hourly wage or by the piece.
- Piece-work employees must approach their job with speed, efficiency, accuracy, and self-assurance.

FASHION PROMOTION AND MEDIA.   The development and presentation of product information and ideas for promotional purposes

Job title	Responsibilities and duties	Personal characteristics and background
1. Graphic artist	Translates ideas into visual presentations using creative art forms and various media	Aesthetic sense, artistic skills, knowledge of graphic arts, understanding of media

Job title	Responsibilities and duties	Personal characteristics and background
	Develops graphic designs to effectively portray promotional themes Prepares art using various types of media May design advertisements, posters, programs, fashion show settings, displays, and other promotional materials	Training in commercial arts, graphic design, and fashion sketching
2. Art director	Supervises artwork designed to promote products, brand names, and fashion ideas Coordinates photographs, sketches, and layouts for fashion advertisements and other promotional material Develops merchandise ideas used in layouts for fashion advertisements and for other promotional materials Handles problems of reproducing materials in various media May direct artwork for newspapers, magazines, advertising agencies, retail organizations, and other firms in the fashion industry	Design ability, creative talents, thorough knowledge of graphic arts, understanding of how to reproduce materials using various media, and supervisory ability Training in fine arts, design, and media; commercial art work
3. Copywriter	Creates promotional messages and makes fashion impressions with word pictures Presents information about products and fashion ideas Writes copy about merchandise to be featured in advertising and promotion Prepares copy for any printed materials used in promotional activities May work with graphic artist in putting ads together	Clear, concise writing style; fluent; inventive with words; understands fashion and consumer needs and desires Training in journalism, communications fashion writing, or newspaper work
4. Scriptwriter	Creates script that directs and carries out the purposes of various kinds of promotions Translates into words the ideas used for audiovisual materials (filmstrips, slides, cassettes, etc.) Prepares script to direct work of photographers, recording crew, and others producing audiovisual materials Writes scripts for fashion shows and other promotional events Develops themes and fashion stories based on characteristics of audience (age, sex, and life style) and fashion features of merchandise to be presented	Verbal skills; writing skills; understands details involved in producing fashion presentations; knowledge of various ways to appeal to audience groups Training in communications skills; fashion production arts; audio and visual techniques

Job title	Responsibilities and duties	Personal characteristics and background
5. Fashion editor	Decides what will be shown on the pages of fashion publications Establishes the theme for each issue published Selects the fashions, the copy, the artwork, and the layouts to be used in each publication Makes decisions regarding locations for photography Covers the fashion markets and other fashion events Reviews press releases and fashion news from various sources in the fashion industry	Writing talent; fashion sense; fashion analysis ability; managerial abilities; self-sufficient; flexibility and sense of timing; knowledge of production process using various media; understanding of design elements and layout techniques; and knowledge of fashion industry Training in fine arts, journalism; fashion writing and fashion arts; promotional strategy; clothing and textiles; and fashion reporting
6. Editorial assistant	Works with fashion editor to develop materials for publication Collects ideas for promotional themes Obtains clothes, props, and other items to be used in promotions Works with copywriters, artists, and photographers in preparing layouts and materials for publications Obtains editor's approval of final layouts for publications	Patience and persistence in carrying out details of producing fashion publications; familiar with fashion industry and how it operates; understanding of problems with models, photography, artwork, and copy Training in fine arts, journalism, fashion writing, graphic arts and fashion photography, and clothing and textiles
7. Creative director	Conceives and executes layouts and copy for advertising campaigns and promotional materials Supervises the production of artwork, copy, and layouts Develops strategy to achieve promotional goals for advertising campaigns Coordinates visual presentations for advertising agencies or for promotional departments in other companies	Creative ability to work with design elements; understanding of advertising campaign strategy; knowledge of use of media and production process; and managerial skills Training in journalism and advertising arts; promotional strategy
8. Account executive	Serves as liaison between advertising agency and clients Develops ideas for advertising campaigns to meet needs of clients Selects slogans, artwork, photography, and other appropriate materials to promote products and ideas Supervises preparation of promotional materials	Understanding of promotional needs of firms in fashion industry; knowledge of operation of advertising agency; and sales ability in fashion, and advertising writing skills Training in journalism and fashion arts; promotional strategy and advertising work

Job title	Responsibilities and duties	Personal characteristics and background
	Obtains client's approval of final promotional materials Solicits clients who need services of advertising agency	
9. Fashion director (stylist)	Directs efforts toward establishing total fashion programs Translates fashion information into promotional ideas Analyzes fashion directions for seasonal promotions Identifies style features, colors, and fabrics for promotional purposes Selects accessories to complete total fashion story Plans fashion shows and other fashion presentations Selects models and organizes merchandise groupings Supervises production and staging of fashion productions	Fashion knowledge and promotional ability; sense of timing; understanding of design elements; decision-making ability; fashion analysis skills; organizational ability; and knowledge of fashion modeling techniques Training in textiles, clothing, and fashion arts; marketing and promotional strategy; and consumer behavior
10. Publicity coordinator	Develops communication channels to promote fashion trends Generates fashion publicity in newspapers, magazines, and trade journals Prepares press releases, photographs, slides and videotapes to spread fashion news Works with fashion editors of magazines and other fashion publications to inform consumers about fashion products and fashion ideas	Fashion reporting and writing skills; initiative and an inquiring nature Training in journalism, fashion arts, and publicity procedures; fashion writing
11. Educational director	Conceives ideas for educational materials to promote company's products Supervises development of educational materials (audiovisual aids, teaching demonstrations, and literature for students, teachers, and consumers) Coordinates all efforts to provide educational information needed to promote a company and its products	Creative and promotional outlook; knowledge of educational methods; understanding of various media; fashion sense; and management and supervisory ability Training in education, home economics, and communications
12. Audiovisual coordinator	Translates concepts into actual visual materials Develops ideas into sight and sound experiences	Artistic skills; understanding of photographic techniques; and knowledge of types of audiences and consumer needs

Job title	Responsibilities and duties	Personal characteristics and background
	Decides on best approach to express company's ideas to potential viewers Directs staff of scriptwriters, photographers and recording crew in producing audiovisual materials Works with educational director to achieve company's purposes and to meet audience's needs	Training in photography and audiovisual technology
13. Fashion representative	Represents company in promotional activities in various areas of the country Presents information about product use and performance characteristics Gives demonstrations promoting use of products Commentates for demonstrations, fashion shows, and other promotional events Coordinates travel schedule for promotional activities in retail stores and for programs with students and other consumer groups	Dramatic ability; relates to people effectively; sense of timing and flexibility; fashion sense; knowledge of consumer; promotional ability; and commentating ability Training in clothing and textiles, fashion promotion, dramatics and speech, and public relations
14. Fashion photographer	Captures a promotional idea in pictures for newspapers, magazines, filmstrips, television, etc. Decides on best aesthetic setting to project fashion idea to be presented in picture form Works with fashion editor or art director to photograph fashion material in appropriate settings	Artistic sense; flexibility; knowledge of photographic techniques; and understanding of advertising and promotion Training in photography, fashion arts, and newspaper work

Employment Opportunities*

- Job titles and responsibilities will vary with the type and size of firm, the structure of the organization, and with the abilities and skills of the employees in the company.
- Various segments of the fashion industry in which jobs may be available:
  1. *Manufacturing level:* Promotion, advertising, marketing, and educational departments in textile and apparel companies, fashion accessory firms, pattern companies, and other fashion firms located near major fashion centers such as New York City, Dallas, Los Angeles, Chicago, Atlanta, etc.
  2. *Media level:* Editorial and art departments of fashion magazines, newspapers, advertising agencies located in many of the major cities.

* Salaries vary from minimum wages ($85 to $125 per week) for entry-level positions and on-the-job training, to annual wages of $10,000 to $30,000 or more for management and executive level positions.

3. *Retail level:* Sales promotion and advertising departments in large stores throughout the country use copy writers and fashion artists; small stores may have advertising prepared by advertising agencies or by the retail advertising manager of local newspapers.

FASHION RETAILING. The purchase of merchandise from manufacturing resources and the promotion and presentation of appropriate merchandise assortments for sale to the ultimate consumer

Job title	Responsibilities and duties	Personal characteristics and background
1. Sales person	Sells and serves the consumer Determines the customer's merchandise wants and needs Provides merchandise information for customers Arranges and presents merchandise to customers Relates consumer's needs to store buyer	Likes people and merchandise; understands consumer needs and desires; initiative in selling; patience in helping customers make merchandise decisions; familiar with current fashion, fitting problems, and fabric performance Training in salesmanship, clothing, and textiles
2. Stock person	Transfers merchandise from receiving room to department stock area Arranges merchandise in appropriate stock area Keeps accurate count of stock for department records Assists salespeople in maintaining proper assortment of stock on sales floor	Likes to work with merchandise and records; willing to carry out details; and physically able to move quantities of merchandise Training on the job
3. Department manager	Supervises sales activities in department Directs the arrangement of merchandise in department Keeps current records of stock assortments Serves as liaison between salespeople and buyer Arranges for merchandise adjustments and services requested by consumers Works out schedules for salespeople's lunch breaks and days off	Likes selling environment; supervisory skills; handles people and problems effectively; and understands procedures and operation of department Training in selling and supervision
4. Assistant buyer	Assists the buyer with procurement of merchandise Provides the buyer with information about sales and stock Represents buyer in the department operations Writes reorders for basic stock for buyer's approval Checks on pricing and ticketing of merchandise	Initiative and willingness to follow through on details; knowledge of selling techniques and merchandise features; understanding of store systems and operation procedures—ordering, receiving, and marking merchandise Training in fashion merchandising, promotion, marketing, economics, management, consumer behavior, bookkeeping, and retail math; selling experience

Job title	Responsibilities and duties	Personal characteristics and background
	Trains salespeople to maximize sales Direct inventory, stock counts, and flow of merchandise Observes customer's reactions to merchandise Informs salespeople about features of new merchandise Checks on deliveries, special orders, and back orders Supervises preparation of advertisements for buyer's approval Maintains appropriate merchandise assortments in department and in branch stores.	
5. Fashion buyer	Purchases appropriate assortments of merchandise from manufacturer Locates and analyzes resources who have available merchandise Analyzes consumer's needs and demand patterns Plans and budgets merchandise expenditures Controls pricing and inventory to maintain profit goals Trains subordinates to carry out department operations Supervises and coordinates promotional efforts to maximize sales Provides information about merchandise and selling features for salespeople and customers Works with merchandise manager and fashion coordinator to maintain fashion image of store	Flexible, decision-making skills; management ability; knowledge of resources in fashion industry; fashion sense and timing; ability to analyze fashion trends; shrewdness in bargaining skills; sense of urgency Training in fashion merchandising, promotion, marketing, economics, business administration, and consumer behavior
6. Merchandise manager	Supervises activities of several buyers Coordinates efforts of several departments to maximize profits Allocates budgets for expenditures in merchandise and services Directs efforts to achieve desired fashion image of store Reports to top management on merchandising problems Provides merchandising management training for buyers	Management abilities; sense of urgency; knowledge of merchandising; budgeting; and promotion Training in business administration, retailing, fashion merchandising, promotion, and buying experience

Job title	Responsibilities and duties	Personal characteristics and background
7. Fashion coordinator	Promotes the store's fashion image Identifies fashion trends for seasonal merchandise purchases and promotion Interprets fashion trends in terms of store's fashion image Makes recommendations to merchandisers and buyers relative to fashion trends Analyzes advanced fashion information available from various sources in the fashion industry Prepares current fashion information for store personnel Coordinates fashion story told in displays, advertising, and by salespeople	Fashion flare; self-assurance; initiative; knowledge of fashion industry, fashion trends, and modeling; understanding of fashion show production and staging techniques Training in retailing, advertising, selling, fashion writing, and merchandising; promotion experience
8. Display director	Creates window and interior displays to portray fashion image of store Provides visual support for sales efforts and promotional goals Design and prepares props for displays, fashion shows, and other promotional events	Artistic sense, design skills, understanding of merchandising techniques and promotional strategy; lettering ability Training in display, theatre arts, and sign writing
9. Advertising director	Supervises preparation of copy and artwork for ads Design layouts for ads Assists in planning promotional activities to support merchandising goals Controls budget and scheduling of ads with local papers Coordinates advertising schedules with buyer's merchandise plans and delivery dates	Graphic design ability, copywriting skills, and other creative talents Training in journalism, commercial art, printed media and reproduction process layout; copy and sketching experience

Employment Opportunities

- Job titles and responsibilities vary greatly in retailing. Large, multiunit stores have training programs, and jobs are structured with a hierarchy of positions. Advancement follows a promotional ladder. Small stores tend to be less rigid in organizational structure, and job assignment may vary with the abilities and skills of the employees.
- Jobs in retailing are available in towns and cities across the country: boutiques, specialty stores, department stores, chain and other multiunit operations, discount outlets, mail-order and catalog showrooms.
- Other job opportunities may be found in regional fashion centers: central buying offices, buying agencies, retail distribution centers, merchandise service organizations, manufacturer's retail division, apparel markets, and consumer service agencies.
- Salaries vary from minimum wages for persons without experience to $6,000 to $9,500 for executive trainees with college degrees, to

$10,000 to $30,000 and up for management personnel with professional experience in retailing.

REFERENCES

"Careers in the Fashion Industry." A Career Educational Curriculum Package (filmstrip and sound series). Janice Hamilton, educational director. New York: Butterick Fashion Marketing Co., 1973.

CORINTH, KAY. *Fashion Showmanship.* New York: Wiley, 1970.

GILLESPIE, KAREN R., and JOSEPH C. HECHT. *Retail Business Management.* New York: McGraw-Hill, 1970, chap. 43.

GUERIN, POLLY. *Fashion Writing.* New York: ITT Educational Series, Inc., 1972.

JABENIS, ELAINE. *The Fashion Director.* New York: Wiley, Inc., 1972.

JARNOW, JEANETTE, and BEATRICE JUDELLE. *Inside the Fashion Business.* New York: Wiley, 1973, sec. VI.

TROXELL, MARY D., and BEATRICE JUDELLE. *Fashion Merchandising.* New York: McGraw-Hill, 1971, Appendix I.

WILINSKY, HARRIET. *Careers and Opportunities in Retailing.* New York: National Retail Merchants Association, 1970.

Appendix 7

Trade Associations in the Fashion Industries

Amalgamated Clothing Workers of America (ACWA)
15 Union Square, New York, NY 10003
American Apparel Manufacturers' Association, Inc. (AAMA)
1611 North Kent Street, Arlington, VA 22209
American Footwear Manufacturers' Association
342 Madison Avenue, New York, NY 10017
American Textile Manufacturers' Institute, Inc. (ATMI)
1501 Johnston Building, Charlotte, NC 28202
California Fashion Creators (CFC)
110 East Ninth Street, Los Angeles, CA 90015
Cotton, Inc.
370 Avenue of the Americas, New York, NY 10019
Fur Information and Fashion Council
101 West 30th Street, New York, NY 10001
International Ladies Garment Workers Union (ILGWU)
1710 Broadway, New York, NY 10019
International Silk Association, USA (ISA)
299 Madison Avenue, New York, NY 10017

Irish Linen Guild (ILG)
36 West 40th Street, New York, NY 10018
Man-Made Fiber Producers' Association, Inc. (MMFPAI)
1000 Connecticut Avenue, Washington, D.C. 20036
Men's Fashion Association of America (MFA)
1290 Avenue of the Americas, New York, NY 10019
National Association of Glove Manufactuers
Gloversville, NY 12078
National Association of Manufacturers (NAM)
277 Park Avenue, New York, NY 10017
National Retail Merchants' Association (NRMA)
100 West 31st Street, New York, NY 10001
New York Couture Business Council
141 West 41st Street, New York, NY 10036
United Garment Workers of America (UGW)
31 Union Square, New York, NY 10003
Wool Bureau
360 Lexington Avenue, New York, NY 10017

Appendix 8

Fiber Producers
and Trademarks

MEMBERS OF MAN-MADE FIBER PRODUCERS ASSOCIATION, INC.

1. Allied Chemical Corporation
   Fibers Division
   One Times Square
   New York, New York 10036
2. American Cyanamid Company
   Fibers Division
   Berdan Avenue
   Wayne, New Jersey 07470
3. American Enks Company
   A Part of Akzona, Inc.
   Enka, North Carolina 28728
4. Beaunit Corporation
   261 Madison Avenue
   New York, New York 10015
5. Celanese Corporation
   Celanese Fibers Marketing Company
   1211 Avenue of the Americas
   New York, New York 10036
6. Courtaulds North America, Inc.
   104 West 40th Street
   New York, New York 10018
7. Dow Badische Company
   Williamsburg, Virginia 23185
8. E. I. du Pont de Nemours
   & Company, Inc.
   Textile Fibers Department
   Wilmington, Delaware 19898

9. Eastman Kodak Company
   Tennessee Eastman Company Division
   Marketed by Eastman Chemical
   Products, Inc.
   Kingsport, Tennessee 37662
10. FMC Corporation
    Fiber Division
    1185 Avenue of the Americas
    New York, New York 10036
11. Hercules Incorporated
    Fibers Division
    910 Market Street
    Wilmington, Delaware 19899
12. Hoechst Fibers Industries
    1515 Broadway at Astor Plaza
    New York, New York 10036
13. Monsanto Textiles Company
    800 N. Lindbergh Boulevard
    St. Louis, Missouri 63166
14. Phillips Fibers Corporation
    Subsidiary of Phillips
    Petroleum Company
    P.O. Box 66
    Greenville, South Carolina 29602
15. Rohm and Haas Company
    Fibers Division
    Independence Mall West
    Philadelphia, Pennsylvania 19105

FIBER TRADEMAKRS

Number after each TM indicates the producer. See list of Members of Man-made Fiber Producers Association, Inc. (p. 291).

ACETATE
Acete (8)
Ariloft (9)
Avicolor (10)
Celacloud (5)
Celanese (5)
Chromspun (9)
Estron (9)
Estron SLR (9)
FMC (10)
Loftuis (9)
Sayfr (10)

ACRYLIC
A-Acrilan (13)
Acrilan (13)
Bi-Loft (13)
Creslan (2)
Orlon (8)
Zefron (7)

ARAMID
Keviar (8)
Nomex (8)

METALLIC
Lurex (7)

MODACRYLIC
A-Acrilan (13)
Acrilan (13)
Elura (13)
Orlon (8)
Sef (13)
Verel (9)

NOVOLOID
Kynol (produced by Carborundum Company)

NYLON
Actionwear (13)
Anso (1)
Anso-X (1)

Antron (8)
Astroturf (13)
Beaunit Nylon (4)
Blue "C" (13)
Bodyfree (1)
Cadon (13)
Cantreca (8)
Caproian (1)
Captiva (1)
Celanese (5)
Cerax (13)
Cordura (8)
Courtaulds Nyon (6)
Crepsset (3)
Cumuloft (13)
Enka (3)
Enkaloft (3)
Enkalure (3)
Enkalure II (3)
Enkalure III (3)
Enkasheer (3)
Multisheer (3)
Phillips 66 Nylon (14)
Qiana (8)
Random-Set (15)
Random-Tone (15)
Shareen (6)
Stria (3)
Stryton (14)
Super Bulk (3)
Twix (3)
Ultron (13)
Variline (3)
Zefran (7)

OLEFIN
Herculon (11)
Marvess (14)

POLYESTER
Avlin (10)
Blue "C" (13)
Caproian (1)
Dacron (8)
Encron (3)
Encron MCS (3)
Encron 8 (3)
Enka (3)
Esterweld (2)

Fortrel (5)
Fortrel 7 (5)
Golden Touch (3)
Hystron (12)
Kodel (9)
Quintess (14)
Spectrum (13)
Strizline (3)
Texturs (15)
Tievira (12)
Twisioc (13)
Vycron (4)
Zatron (7)

RAYON
Avicolor (10)
Avril (10)
Avril FR (10)
Beau-Grip (4)
Briglo (3)
Coloray (6)
Encal (3)
Englo (3)
Enka (3)
Enkrome (3)
Fiber 700 (3)
Fibro (6)
Fibro DD (6)
Fibro FR (6)
FMC (10)
I.T. (3)
Jetspun (3)

Kolorbon (3)
Skyloft (3)
Softglo (3)
Super White (3)
Supranka (3)
Suprenka Hi Mod (3)
Xona (4)
Zantrel (3)
Zantral 700 (3)

SPANDEX
Lycra (8)

TRIACETATE
Arnel (5)

NOT CURRENTLY PRODUCED IN U.S.
Anidex
Azlon
Lastrile
Nytril
Vinal

SPECIAL FIBERS

BICONSTITUENT FIBER
Source (1)
Monvella (13)

FLUOROCARBON
Teflon (8)

Appendix 9

Major Textile Firms and Types of Operation

I. **Springs Mills, Inc.** (1974 Sales 555.8M.)

Apparel Fabrics Division

The Apparel Fabrics Division produces and markets woven fabrics primarily for manufacturers of men's, women's and children's apparel.

Consumer Products Division

The major products are sheets and pillowcases, quilted bedspreads, towels, and draperies.

Knit Division

These fabrics are sold to the women's, men's and children's markets and are used in the manufacture of dresses, sportswear and shirts.

Retail and Specialty Fabrics Division

Spring Mills' Retail and Specialty Fabrics Division was created in January 1970. It was formed by combining the company's established Springmaid retail fabrics operation with the piece goods businesses bought January 5, 1970 from Indian Head Inc.

International Division

The International Division markets the products of Springs Mills' other operating divisions in more than 50 countries throughout the world. Also operates Springs International (French Subsidiary) and joint ventures in Indonesia and Morocco.

2. **United Merchants and Manufacturers** (1974 Sales 1,015,8M)

Selected Merchandising and Distributing Units

Cohn-Hall-Marz Co.
Comark Plastics
Homestead Draperies
Riverdale Drapery Fabrics
Seneca Textiles
Uniglass Industries

Retailing

Robert Hall Clothes, Inc.

Commercial Factoring and Financing

United Factors
United Factors Retail Service Corporation
U.M. & M. Credit Corporation
U.M. & M. Financial Corporation
U.M. & M. Leasing Corporation

Selling Agents

United Merchants World-Wide Sales
United Merchants Sales

Weaving Mills
Synthetic Yarn Manufacturing Plants
Research and Chemical Units
Finishing Plants

3. **M. Lowenstein & Sons, Inc.** (1974 Sales 551.6M)

Divisions and Subsidiaries

Mills
Printing and Finishing Plants
Carpet Manufacturing
Curtain and Drapery Manufacturing
Sheet and Towel Factories
Fiber Glass Affiliates

Computer and Accounting Division
Cotton Purchasing and Warehousing
Lowenstein Distribution Centers
Research and Development
Trucking
4. **Dan River, Inc.** (1974 Sales 439.7M)
   Manufacturing
   Alabama Division
   Danville Division
     Colored yarn and piece-dyed fabrics
   Dan River Knits
   Floorcoverings Division
   Morgantown Hosiery Mills, Inc.
   Webco Mills
     Synthetic tricot knit fabrics
   Woodside Division
     Print cloths

Research and Development
Finishing
   Danville Division
     Finishing of woven and knit fabrics
   Crystal Springs Textiles, Inc.
     Printing and finishing
Merchandising and Sales
   Dan River Sales
   Dan River International Corporation
   Iselin-Jefferson Company, Inc.
   Webco Mills
   Dan River Carpets
   Wunda Weve Carpets
Factoring

Appendix 10

Twenty Largest Textile Firms

Avondale Mills, Sylacauga, Ala. 35150

Burlington Industrial Fabric Co., 1345 Avenue of the Americas, New York, N.Y. 10019

Cannon Mills, Inc., 1271 Avenue of the Americas, New York, N.Y. 10020

Collins & Aikman Corp., 210 Madison Avenue, New York, N.Y. 10016

Cone Mills Corp., Greensboro, N.C. 27405

Dan River International Corp., 111 W. 40th, New York, N.Y. 10018

DHJ Industries, 1345 Avenue of the Americas, New York, N.Y. 10019

Deering Milliken & Co., Inc., 1045 Avenue of the Americas, New York, N.Y. 10018

Duplan Corp., P.O. Box 2898, Winston-Salem, N.C. 27102

DuPont Co., Fabrics and Finishes Dept., Industrial Product Div., Rm. 8963, Wilmington, Del. 19898

Fieldcrest Mills, Inc., 326 E. Stadium Drive, Eden, N.C. 27288

Graniteville Co., Graniteville, S.C. 29829

J.P. Stevens & Co., Dept. TR, 1185 Avenue of the Americas, New York, N.Y. 10036

M. Lowenstein & Sons, Inc., 1430 Broadway, New York, N.Y. 10018

Pepperell Braiding Co., East Pepperell, Mass. 01437

Reeves Brothers, Inc., 1271 Avenue of the Americas, New York, N.Y. 10020

Riegel Textiles Corp., 260 Madison Avenue, New York, N.Y. 10016

Springs Mills, Inc., Ft. Mills, S.C. 29715

Texfi Industries, Inc., 1400 Battlegrounds Avenue, Greensboro, N.C. 27408

United Merchants & Manufacturers, 1407 Broadway, New York, N.Y. 10018

Appendix 11

Twenty Largest Apparel Companies

Blue Bell, Inc., 335 Church Court, Greensboro, N.C. 27420

Bobbie Brooks, Inc., 3830 Kelley Avenue, Cleveland, Ohio 44114

Cluett, Peabody & Co., Inc., 510 Fifth Avenue, New York, N.Y. 10036

Farah Mfg. Co., 8889 Gateway West, El Paso, Texas 79925

Genesco, Inc., P.O. Box 731, Nashville, Tenn. 37203

Hanes Corp., P.O. Box 5416, Winston-Salem, N.C. 27103

Hart Schaffner & Marx, 36 S. Franklin, Chicago, Ill. 60606

Interco, Inc., 1509 Washington Avenue, St. Louis, Mo. 63103

Jonathan Logan, Inc., 3901 Liberty Avenue, North Bergen, N.J. 07047

Kayser-Roth Corp., 640 Fifth Avenue, New York, N.Y. 10019

Kellwood Co., Murray at Hoerner Streets, Little Rock, Ark. 72209

Koracorp Industries, Inc., 617 Mission St., San Francisco, Cal. 94105

Levi Strauss, 2 Embarcadero Center, San Francisco, Cal. 94106

Manhattan Shirt Co., 1271 Avenue of the Americas, New York, N.Y. 10001

Munsingwear, Inc., 718 Greenwood Avenue, Minneapolis, Minn. 55405

Oxford Industries, 350 Fifth Avenue, New York, N.Y. 10001

Phillips-Van Heusen Corp., 1290 Avenue of the Americas, New York, N.Y. 10019

U.S. Industries, Inc., 250 Park Avenue, New York, N.Y. 10017

VF Corp., 1047 N. Park Road, Wyomissing, Pa. 19610

Warnco, Inc., 350 Lafayette St., Bridgeport, Conn. 06602

Bibliography

"A Guide to Consumer Markets." Report, No. 569. New York: The Conference Board, 1972–73, p. 222.

"American Couture: Toujours Trigère." *Clothes Magazine* (July 1, 1968).

"Apparel in a Billion Dollar Conglomerate." *Clothes Magazine* (Sept. 1, 1970).

"Apparel Mart Extends Fashion Lexicon." *Fashion Retailer*, 3 (Jan. 1973).

ARNOLD, PAULINE, and PERCIVAL WHITE. *Clothes and Cloth.* New York: Holiday House, 1961.

BELL, QUENTIN. *On Human Finery.* New York: A. A. Wyn, 1949.

BENDER, MARYLIN. "Why Your Clothes Cost So Much." *McCall's Magazine* (May 1970).

BERGLER, EDMUND, MD. "A Psychoanalyst Looks at Women's Clothes." *Cosmopolitan* (Feb. 1960).

"Between Market Open-Showroom Days Slated." *Fashion Retailer*, 4 (Jan. 1974).

BEVLIN, MARJORIE ELLIOT. *Design Through Discovery.* New York: Holt, 1970.

BIRREN, FABER. "Color Comes First." *House and Garden* (Sept. 1957).

BOSEWORTH, PATRICIA. "Who Killed High Fashion?" *Esquire* (May 1973).

———. "Halston Looks." *New York Times Magazine* (Feb. 11, 1973).

"Boutiques." *Business Week* (Jan. 15, 1972).

BRITT, STEWART H. *Consumer Behavior and Behavioral Science.* New York: Wiley, 1967.

BRITTON, VIRGINIA. "Clothes and Textiles: Supplies, Prices, and Outlook for 1974." *Family Economic Review.* Consumer and Food Economic Institute, Agricultural Research Service, U.S. Department of Agriculture, Spring 1974.

California Fashion Creators Dictionary. Los Angeles: California Fashion Creators, 1972–73.

"California Mart Host." *Newsletter.* Los Angeles: California Mart Association, 1974.

California Mart News. Los Angeles: California Mart Association, May 1974.

"California Mart Opens New 'Facilities for Retailer'." *The Fashion Showcase.* 9 (Feb. 1974).

"California Shapes the Styles." *Business Week* (Aug. 13, 1966).

"C.B.S. Means Creativity in Buying Services." *Fashion Retailer*, 3 (Jan. 1973).

CHAMBERS, BERNICE G. *Color and Design.* Englewood Cliffs, N.J.: Prentice-Hall, 1955.

———. *Selling Fashion Merchandising.* Ann Arbor: Edwards Brothers, Inc., 1946.

"Chanel No. 1." *Time Magazine* (Jan. 25, 1971).

CHAPMAN, HEDLEY. "The Early California Market." *The California Apparel News.* Los Angeles: The California Apparel Association, 1971.

COLEMAN, ALEX. "Alex Coleman: Homogenized Fashion Sells Everywhere." *Clothes Magazine* (Jan. 15, 1974).

"Color and Textiles." *American Fabrics Magazine*, **96** (Winter 1972).

CORINTH, KAY. *Fashion Showmanship*. New York: Wiley, 1970.

CRAWFORD, M. D. C. *The Ways of Fashion*. New York: Putnam, 1941.

"Dallas Apparel Mart Unveils Max-Wall." *The Fashion Showcase*, 8 (April 1973).

"Dallas Becomes $2 Billion Market." *The Fashion Showcase*, 8 (Jan. 1973).

Dallas Chamber of Commerce. "History of Dallas Apparel Market." Dallas, 1965.

DANIELS, ALFRED H. "Fashion Merchandising." *Harvard Business Review*, **19**, 1951.

DAVES, JESSICA. "Can Fashion Be Immoral?" *Ladies' Home Journal* (Jan. 1965).

DE LONG, MARILYN REVELLE. "Analysis of Costume Visual Form." *Journal of Home Economics*, **60** (Dec. 1968).

DOSWELL, MARSHALL. "Architects of Change." Fort Mill, N.C., Springs Mills, Inc., Feb. 1972.

DRYANSKY, G. Y. "The Couture: Not What It Was, but Still a Power." *Women's Wear Daily* (Jan. 26, 1973).

Dun and Bradstreet, Research Department (various reports).

Editors of American Fabric Magazine. *The Encyclopedia of Textiles*. Englewood Cliffs, N.J.: Prentice-Hall, 1972.

ENGEL, JAMES. *Consumer Behavior*. New York: Holt, 1968.

EVANS, HELEN MARIE. *Man the Designer*. New York: Macmillan, 1973.

"Fibers and Petrochemicals." *American Fabrics and Fashions* (Fall 1974).

Focus. Washington, D.C.: Man Made Fiber Producers Association, Inc., Spring 1976.

"Focus, Economic Profile of the Apparel Industry." Arlington, Va.: American Apparel Manufacturers Association, Inc., 1974.

"Focus II, Extension Home Economics." Cooperative Extension Report, U.S. Department of Agriculture, 1974.

GERNREICH, RUDI. "Fashion for the 70s." *Life Magazine*, **67** (Jan. 9, 1970).

GILLESPIE, KAREN R., and JOSEPH HECHT. *Retail Business Management*. New York: McGraw-Hill, 1970.

GRAHAM, JANE. "I Remember, I Remember." *American Fashion Magazine* (Oct. 1973).

———. "The Dallas Dress." *Now: The Magazine for North Texas*, **1** (Nov. 1971).

GREENWOOD, KATHRYN MOORE. "Systematic Approach to the Evaluation of a Fashion Merchandising Program with Guidelines for Student Work Experiences," Ph.D. dissertation, Oklahoma State University, 1972.

GRIFFIN, TIRA W. "A Survey of Selected Regional Apparel Markets Producing Women's and Misses' Apparel," Master's thesis, Michigan State University, 1949.

GRINDERENG, MARGARET. "Fashion Diffusions." *Journal of Home Economics* (March 1967).

GOLLY, JEANNE. "A Study of the Present Status of the Dallas Women's Apparel Market," Master's thesis, Michigan State University, 1966.

HALL, MAX. *Made in New York*. Cambridge, Mass.: Harvard University Press, 1959.

HARTMAN, GEORGE W. "Clothing: Personal Problems and Social Issues." *Journal of Home Economics* (June 1949).

HAWES, ELIZABETH. *Fashion Is Spinach*. New York: Random, 1938.

HAYTER, EDITH F. *Behind the Scenes in Fashion Merchandising*. New York: Pageant Press, 1965.

HIRSH, B. W., and PETER ELLIS. *An Introduction to Textile Economics*. Manchester, England: The Textile Trade Press, 1972.

HOLTZCLAW, HENRY F. *The Principles of Marketing*. New York: Crowell, 1935.

HORN, MARILYN. *The Second Skin*. Boston: Houghton, 1975.

International Ladies Garment Workers Union, Research Department (various reports).

"Interfacings." *Clothes Magazine* (Dec. 1, 1967).

JARNOW, JEANNETTE A. *Fashion Is Their Business*. New York: Fashion Institute of Technology, 1961.

JARNOW, JEANNETTE, and BEATRICE JUDELLE. *Inside the Fashion Business*. New York: Wiley, 1965, rev. ed., 1974.

JOHNSTON, MOIRA. "What Will Happen to the Gray Flannel Suit?" *Journal of Home Economics* (Nov. 1972).

JOHNSTON, MOIRA, and CHRISTIE HARRIS. *Figleafing Through History: The Dynamics of Dress.* New York: Atheneum, 1971.

"KENZO TAKADO." *Mademoiselle,* (July 1972).

KILBOURNE, JUANITA. "Fashion Talk." *Monthly Newsletter* (Jan. 1974).

KING, CHARLES W. *Reflections on Progress in Marketing.* Chicago: American Marketing Association, 1964.

LANG, KURT, and GLADYS ENGEL LANG. *Collection Dynamics.* New York: Crowell, 1962.

LAVER, JAMES. "Fashion, A Detective Story." *Vogue,* **133** (Jan. 1959).

———. *Taste and Fashion.* New York: Dodd, Mead, 1938.

LEVIN, PHYLLIS LEE. *The Wheels of Fashion.* New York: Doubleday, 1965.

LIPSON, HARRY A., and JOHN R. DARLING. *Marketing Fundamentals.* New York: Wiley, 1974.

LOVING, RUSH. "What the U.S. Textile Industry Really Needs." *Fortune* (Oct. 1970).

MACLEISH, ARCHIBALD. "Rediscovering the Simple Life." *McCall's* (April 1972).

MAUDLIN, WILLIAM L., and MARIANNE S. BEESON. "Reading the Labels on Apparel and Household Textiles." *The 1973 Yearbook of Agriculture Handbook for the Home.* U.S. Department of Agriculture, Washington, D.C.: U.S. Govt. Printing Office, 1973.

McQUODE, WALTER. "High Style Disrupts Men's Wear Industry." *Fortune* (Feb. 1971).

MECKLIN, J. M. "Asia's Great Leap in Textiles." *Fortune* (Oct. 1970).

"Miami Merchandise Mart to Get Professional Face Lift." *Fashion Retailer,* **3** (Jan. 1973).

"New Markets for Knitters." *Clothes* (April 15, 1975).

"New K.C. Trade Mart Opens." *The Fashion Showcase,* **9** (Sept. 1974).

"Non-Wovens." *American Fabrics and Fashions* (Summer 1974).

NYSTROM, PAUL H. *Economics of Fashion.* New York: Ronald, 1928.

———. *Fashion Merchandising.* New York: Ronald, 1932.

"Nylon, The First 25 Years." Philadelphia: E. E. du Pont Publication, 1963.

"Open-End Spinning." *American Fabrics and Fashions* (Summer 1974).

"Out on a Limb with the Midi." *Time Magazine* (Sept. 14, 1970).

Parker, Richard. "The Myth of Middle America." *The Center Magazine,* **3** (March 1970).

PERRY, PATRICIA, ed. *The Vogue Sewing Book.* New York: Vogue Pattern Co., 1970.

PICKEN, MARY BROOKS, and DORA L. MILLER. *Dressmakers of France.* New York: Harper, 1965.

QUANT, MARY. *Quant by Quant.* New York: Putnam, 1966.

Random House Dictionary of the English Language. Unabridged ed. New York: Random, 1967.

"Retailing Tomorrow." *Stores Magazine.* New York: National Retail Merchants Assoc., Feb. 1973.

RICHARDS, FLORENCE S. *The Ready-to-Wear Industry, 1900–1950.* New York: Fairchild Publications, 1951.

RICHARDSON, JANE, and A. L. KROEBER. *Three Centuries of Women's Dress Fashions.* Berkeley: University of California Press, 1940.

RILEY, ROBERT, and WALTER CECCHIO. *The Fashion Makers.* New York: Crown, 1968.

ROBINSON, DWIGHT E. "Economics of Fashion Demand." *Quarterly Journal of Economics,* **85** (Aug. 1961).

———. "Fashion Theory and Product Design." *Harvard Business Review.* **36** (Nov.–Dec. 1958).

ROBINSON, DWIGHT E. "The Rules of Fashion Cycles." *Horizon,* **1** (March 1959).

ROSENCRANZ, MARY LOU. "Social and Psychological Approaches to Clothing Research." *Journal of Home Economics* (Jan. 1965).

RUDOFSKY, BERNARD. "The Fashionable Body." *Horizon,* **13** (Autumn 1971).

SAKOWITZ, ROBERT T. "Critique on the Quest for a Common Denominator." *Stores Magazine* (March 1973).

SCOTT, EDITH ANN. "Exploratory Study of Selected Fashion Markets in the United States and Their Use by Apparel Manufacturers," Master's thesis, Oklahoma State University, 1975.

SHAB, DIANE K. "Haute Couture's High Priest Presents Collection in U.S." *The Sunday Oklahoman* (Nov. 17, 1974).

SHEARER, LLOYD. "Mini–Midi–Maxi—How Ridiculous Can Fashion Get?" *Parade* (March 29, 1970).

Sixty Years of Fashion. New York: Fairchild Publications, 1963.

STUART, JESSIE. *The American Fashion Industry.* Boston: Simmons College, 1956.

SPROLES, G. B., and CHARLES W. KING. "The Consumer Fashion Change Agent: A Theoretical Conceptualization and Empirical Identification," **433** (November 1973). Ohio State University, Columbus, Ohio.

"Total Vended Dollar Volume." *Vend Magazine* (May 1, 1971).

"Textile Marketing." *American Fabrics and Fashions* (Summer 1966).

"The Future of Retailing." *Stores Magazine* (Jan. 1970).

"The Designing Man." *Time Magazine* (Jan. 31, 1969).

"The Fifty Largest Retailing Companies." *Fortune* (July 1973).

"The Garment Trade Learns Sophisticated Selling." *Business Week* (Sept. 22, 1973).

"The Role of the Fiber Producer." *Clothes* (Jan. 1, 1971).

"The Surprising Story of Career Apparel." *American Fabrics and Fashions* (Winter 1971).

"The Territory Opens for Western Wear." *Fashion Retailer,* **4** (1974).

The World Book Encyclopedia. Chicago: Field Enterprises Educational Corporation.

This Fabulous Century. Vols. 1–7. New York, Time-Life Books, 1970.

TOLMAN, RUTH. *Guide to Fashion Merchandise Knowledge.* New York: Milady Publishing Corporation, 1973.

"Towards the Multi-National Textile Company." *American Fabrics and Fashions* (Summer 1972).

"Today's Buyer: An Endangered Species?" *Clothes* (Jan. 1973).

TROXELL, MARY D., and BEATRICE JUDELL. *Fashion Merchandising.* New York: McGraw-Hill, 1971.

"Understated Elegance." *Time Magazine* (July 6, 1962).

United California Bank, Research and Planning Division. "California Apparel Industry, Revised—1974." Los Angeles: United California Bank, 1974.

U.S. Bureau of the Census (various reports).

U.S. Department of Agriculture (various reports).

U.S. Department of Commerce. *U.S. Industrial 1975 Outlook.* Washington, D.C.: U.S. Govt. Printing Office, 1975.

U.S. Fact Book. Department of Commerce. 95th ed. New York: Grosset and Dunlap, October 1974.

Vreeland, Diane. *The 10's, the 20's, the 30's.* New York: The Metropolitan Museum of Art, 1974.

"What Fashion Designer John Weitz Sees Ahead." *Textile World,* **118** (April 1968).

WINGATE, ISABEL, KAREN R. GILLESPIE, and BETTY G. ADDISON. *Know Your Merchandise.* New York: McGraw-Hill, 1964.

WINGATE, JOHN W., and JOSEPH FRIEDLANDER. *Management of Retail Business.* Englewood Cliffs, N.J.: Prentice-Hall, 1963.

Women's Wear Daily. New York: Fairchild Publications (various articles).

YOUNG, AGNES B. *Recurring Cycles of Fashion.* New York: Harper, 1937.

"Yves in New York." *Time Magazine* (Sept. 27, 1968).

Index

Woven greige goods mills, 134
Wright, Frank Lloyd, 24

Y

Yarn-spinning mills, 133
Yarn, definitions, 85

Z

Ziegfeld, Florenz, 22